Lobbyists and the Making of US Tariff Policy, 1816–1861

Studies in Early American Economy and Society from the
Library Company of Philadelphia
Cathy Matson, *Series Editor*

LOBBYISTS
and the MAKING *of*
US TARIFF POLICY,
1816–1861

Daniel Peart

Johns Hopkins University Press | *Baltimore*

© 2018 Johns Hopkins University Press
All rights reserved. Published 2018
Printed in the United States of America on acid-free paper
9 8 7 6 5 4 3 2 1

Johns Hopkins University Press
2715 North Charles Street
Baltimore, Maryland 21218-4363
www.press.jhu.edu

Library of Congress Cataloging-in-Publication Data

Names: Peart, Daniel, 1985– author.
Title: Lobbyists and the making of US tariff policy, 1816–1861 / Daniel Peart.
Description: Baltimore : Johns Hopkins University Press, 2018. | Series: Studies in early
    American economy and society from the Library Company of Philadelphia | Includes
    bibliographical references and index.
Identifiers: LCCN 2017054174 | ISBN 9781421426112 (hardcover : alk. paper) | ISBN
    9781421426129 (electronic) | ISBN 1421426110 (hardcover : alk. paper) | ISBN
    1421426129 (electronic)
Subjects: LCSH: Tariff—United States—History—19th century. | Lobbying—United
    States—History—19th century. | Business and politics—United States—History—19th
    century. | United States—Commercial policy—History—19th century.
Classification: LCC HF1756 .P37 2018 | DDC 382/.7097309034—dc23
LC record available at https://lccn.loc.gov/2017054174

A catalog record for this book is available from the British Library.

*Special discounts are available for bulk purchases of this book. For more information,
please contact Special Sales at 410-516-6936 or specialsales@press.jhu.edu.*

Johns Hopkins University Press uses environmentally friendly book materials,
including recycled text paper that is composed of at least 30 percent post-consumer
waste, whenever possible.

CONTENTS

SERIES EDITOR'S FOREWORD

In this addition to the series Studies in Early American Economy and Society, a collaborative effort between Johns Hopkins University Press and the Library Company of Philadelphia's Program in Early American Economy and Society (PEAES), Daniel Peart recovers the long battles of antebellum North America over tariffs and the manufacturing interests standing behind the debates, as well as their detractors. This volume compellingly demonstrates how duties levied on imports engaged policymakers, manufacturers, distributors, westward expansionists, and consumers of all stripes in a prolonged discourse over the future of the economy, one that was eclipsed only by the debate over slavery during these years.

Tariffs were no small issue in antebellum public preoccupations. They provided the federal government with its most important source of revenue and entrepreneurs with their most significant incentives for investment, largely because tariffs were intended to stifle foreign competition. Consumers, who were by the early nineteenth century well versed in the prices they could expect to pay for manufactured goods, angrily bore the increased costs passed on to them because of rising import duties. Higher tariffs also fueled sectional divisions, as interests in many Northern states demanded a protected home market and Southern interests underscored their need for freer access to foreign markets for their staple crops.

Peart's study is long overdue, and he brings formidable scholarly skills to his analysis of the eleven major tariff laws passed during the antebellum era. One of the most striking things about his findings is the degree to which the tariff issue was neither strictly sectional nor strictly political party driven. Cleavages persisted within regions and parties. And so, among the key actors in the arts of debate and persuasion were a rising coterie of lobbyists, groups of men who were paid to advocate particular points of view. These brokers of policy discourse not only mouthed the points of view of interests who paid them directly; they also carried a great deal of knowledge about the vast thicket of tariff policies and the consequences of this or that bill being proposed in Congress, knowledge that often gave lobbyists sufficient power to influence important outcomes in policymaking.

Just as importantly, Peart helps us understand that the political economy of the antebellum era was not grounded on neat packages of theory, and not shaped by momentous battles and partisan votes in Congress alone. Political economy was a more practical affair, and it was messy. It was in the arena of the day-to-day arts of personally representing economic interests—manufacturers, consumers, exporters, and others—and convincing would-be opponents to change their minds or entertain a compromise over tariffs where, Peart argues, our attention should lodge if we want to understand the great patterns of North American development in this era. And it was the increasingly influential lobbyists, men not afraid to be swayed by large payments or to offer bribes, who worked at these fundamental levels of influence peddling. Lobbyists wielded a great deal of influence over the paths that policymaking took. Moreover, Peart shows us that they did so earlier and far more consequentially in North American history than scholars have allowed until now.

Cathy Matson
Richards Professor of American History, University of Delaware
Director, Program in Early American Economy and Society,
Library Company of Philadelphia

ACKNOWLEDGMENTS

I am pleased to have the opportunity to thank all of the following for the many and varied contributions they made to the research, writing, and production of this book.

A large part of the research was conducted in Philadelphia-area archives thanks to the generosity of a fellowship from the Program in Early American Economy and Society administered by the Library Company of Philadelphia. I would like to thank head librarian Jim Green and all of the staff at the Library Company for their help with my project over the four and a half months I spent in Philadelphia. I am also grateful for the financial assistance provided by an Andrew W. Mellon Foundation fellowship at the Virginia Historical Society, who have always been so welcoming to me, and a Hugh Davis Graham Travel Award from the Institute for Political History, whose Policy History Conference I first attended in Nashville in 2016; I shall certainly return again soon. And I am grateful too for the assistance I received from staff at the following archives: Alabama Department of Archives and History; Albert and Shirley Small Special Collections Library, University of Virginia; American Philosophical Society; Buffalo History Museum; Connecticut Historical Society; David M. Rubenstein Rare Book and Manuscript Library, Duke University; Delaware Historical Society; Francis Harvey Green Library, West Chester University; Hagley Museum and Library; Historical Society of Pennsylvania; Huntington Library; Lawrence Lee Pelletier Library, Allegheny College; Legacy Library, Marietta College; Library of Congress; Luzerne County Historical Society; Maryland Historical Society; Massachusetts Historical Society; New Jersey Historical Society; New-York Historical Society; New York Public Library; Ohio History Connection; Pennsylvania State Archives; Rare Book and Manuscript Library, University of Pennsylvania; Rush Rhees Library, University of Rochester; South Caroliniana Library, University of South Carolina; Virginia State Library; and Western Reserve Historical Society. As an American historian resident in the UK, I am particularly thankful for the cordially efficient remote-research services offered by many of these institutions.

I have also benefited from feedback on papers delivered at the annual conference of the association of British American Nineteenth Century Historians (Cambridge, 2015); the As Others See Us: British Perspectives on Nineteenth-Century American History Conference (Rice University, 2014); the Ireland, America, and the Worlds of Mathew Carey Conference (Trinity College Dublin, 2011); the Policy History Conference (Nashville, 2016); and the Queen Mary University of London–King's College London International Workshop on (Long) Nineteenth-Century US Political Economy (London, 2015). To all those who listened to me present my work, whether they responded with suggestions, criticism, or simple encouragement, I am grateful.

Cathy Matson, editor of the Studies in Early American Economy and Society series at Johns Hopkins University Press, has provided a guiding hand from the earliest stages of the project. The book is all the better for it, as it is from the attention of the entire production team at the press and the expert copyediting of Nicole Wayland. Some material from chapter five has previously appeared in an earlier form in "System, Process, Agency, and Contingency in the Study of Antebellum Policymaking: The Tariff of 1846," *Journal of the Civil War Era* 7 (June 2017): 181–205, and I am grateful for the permission of that journal and of University of North Carolina Press to reuse it here.

It is a pleasure to work with my colleagues in the School of History at Queen Mary University of London, and while some of them seem to have been quite amused by the idea that I was writing an entire book on antebellum tariff policy, they have cheerfully given me the support I needed to complete it. I am also fortunate to be part of the Institute of Historical Research's vibrant North American History seminar, with whose members I have spent many an enjoyable Thursday evening. Among the wider community of American historians, and I firmly believe "community" is just the right word, John Moore (technically an economist, but we can forgive him for that), Don Ratcliffe, and Andy Shankman have all shared their expertise in the field of my research and pointed me toward sources I would have otherwise missed. Jo Cohen, Andrew Heath, Erik Mathisen, Marc-William Palen, Don Ratcliffe (again), Rob Saunders, and David Sim all donated their time to read draft chapters, and their insightful observations have improved the final version immeasurably. Two readers for the press went one step further and read the whole manuscript, and their comments likewise have been of great benefit to me. Adam Smith did not have much to do with the specifics of this project, beyond writing countless references for my funding applications, but it was he who trained me to be a historian in the first place as a graduate student at University College London, so I remain in his debt. My mother, Amanda, and my sisters, Louise and Julia, are always supportive, and the newest addition to our immediate family, my niece Avery, reminds me that while early US political history can certainly be absorbing, there is more to life.

Finally, I redeem a promise made long ago by dedicating this book to Helen, who certainly deserves it. Writing this as I look out from the window of our London flat as the sun shines down on Walthamstow marshes, I am excited to contemplate our future, and many further projects, together.

Lobbyists and the Making of US Tariff Policy, 1816–1861

Introduction

ON 31 OCTOBER 1831, former president John Quincy Adams made a surprise appearance at a convention of the Friends of Domestic Industry in New York City. The delegates had gathered to promote government aid to American producers through tariff barriers that would exclude their foreign rivals from the home market. A generation earlier, Adams's father had been among the most distinguished members of the American Society for the Encouragement of Domestic Manufactures, one of the first such advocates for federal intervention founded amid a burst of energetic nation-building in the aftermath of the War of 1812. During his single term as chief executive, the younger Adams had watched that nation divide between rival parties as his enemies exploited struggles over tariff policy to turn public opinion against his administration, but on this occasion his arrival was "received with loud and continued bursts of applause from the Members, who all rose."[1] It surely did not escape the ex-president's attention, however, that fewer than fifty of the five hundred delegates hailed from the South, a reflection of the growing anti-tariff sentiment in that region that threatened to divide the nation along a different axis. Still, the hall was packed, and while Adams recognized several faces among the crowd, there is no reason to think he paid any heed to a young printer named Horace Greeley, crammed into the spectator's gallery to witness the proceedings. Neither man could then suspect, of course, that three decades later Greeley would make a far more significant contribution to another quasi-national assembly, the Republican Party's nominating convention of 1860, where he helped draft the platform, including a pledge "to encourage the development of the industrial interests of the whole country," that carried Abraham Lincoln to the White House and seven slave states out of the Union.[2]

The tariff is an unbroken thread that runs throughout the antebellum era, connecting disparate individuals and events, and shaping the development of the United States in myriad ways. Duties levied on imports provided the federal government with a major part of its revenue from the ratification of the Constitution to the close of the nineteenth century.[3] More controversially, they also offered protection to domestic producers against foreign competition, at the expense of increased costs for consumers and the risk of retaliation from international trade partners. Tariff policy affected the fortunes of all Americans, fueled conflict between parties, and provoked tensions between Northern states intent on cultivating a home market and Southern states reliant on overseas demand for their staple crops. "Except perhaps for slavery," one historian has recently commented, "it was the most important political issue before the Civil War."[4] Properly understood, this book contends, no issue better illustrates the workings of the antebellum policymaking process, and the critical role that lobbying could play within that process.

Writing in 1824, as Congress and the country again debated a new schedule of duties, the editor of the *Illinois Gazette* mused that "the subject of domestick manufactures—the reasons for their encouragement, and for 'letting them alone'— . . . are themes of great and growing importance, on which, however, our notions appear to be less distinct, than on any other leading question of national concern."[5] Strange to say, the *Gazette*'s assessment remains just as true for our understanding of antebellum tariff policy today. As one of the contributors to a 2014 *Journal of American History* interchange on the history of capitalism observed, the tariff constitutes a key component of that important story, and yet the two standard texts on the topic are now themselves more than a century old, "an eternity in historiographical terms."[6] The content of Edward Stanwood's *American Tariff Controversies in the Nineteenth Century* (1903) and F. W. Taussig's *The Tariff History of the United States* (1888) reflects their age: a focus on the clash of great orators, and grand theories, on the floor of the national legislature, coupled with a determination to prove once and for all whether protection or free trade was the wisest choice for the American economy.[7] A handful of more recent studies do exist, but most examine only an individual act in isolation, rather than the making of tariff policy across this period.[8] Perhaps John Belohlavek had it right when he suggested, two decades ago now, that while "few of us would contest the importance of the issue," still "the confusing maze of rates and duties" have "engendered narcolepsy among generations of American historians."[9]

In the absence of a dedicated literature on the making of tariff policy, the subject has been pressed into service for other purposes. Historians of antebellum politics have portrayed it as a typically partisan dispute. In this telling, citizens who benefited from high duties provided a loyal constituency for Henry Clay and his fellow Whigs, whose activist philosophy embraced state aid to domestic producers, while those who favored low duties flocked to the standard of Andrew Jackson and the Democratic Party, with their mantra of "limited government" and its corollary preference for free trade.[10] Historians more interested in the coming of the Civil War, meanwhile, have interpreted it within a sectional framework. By their account, Northern factory owners in pursuit of greater profits extracted ever-more generous concessions from Washington, while Southern planters fretted over the unequal economic burden forced upon their region and, perhaps more ominously, the other uses to which federal power might ultimately be put.[11] Both perspectives are accurate up to a point, and both are also, at their extremes, irreconcilable: for where would that leave Northern Democrats or Southern Whigs? The problem, as these examples suggest, is that either perspective obscures important divisions within each party or section over the tariff, divisions that help explain why legislation on the issue was so highly charged, and so hotly contested.[12] Indeed, it is remarkable that of eleven major tariff bills considered by Congress between 1816 and 1861, four were decided by a single vote.

Or perhaps not so remarkable. According to Adams, who participated in debates over four of those eleven bills during his long postpresidential career in the House of Representatives, "the progress of the tariff controversy exhibits a signal exemplification of what I have long and often remarked as a law of political gravitation, as uniform in its operation as that other gravitation which governs the system of the universe. It is that of all great systems of policy maintained by antagonist parties and subject to deliberative decision, the opposite practical measures are modified into mutual approximation, till they come to a balance turned by a single vote."[13] Several recent works, equaling Adams in their attentiveness to the intricacies of antebellum policymaking, point toward a similar conclusion. Michael Holt's magisterial study of the Whig Party demonstrates how far decisions arrived at in the national legislature were dependent on innumerable state and local circumstances.[14] Rachel Shelden's account of Washington social life in the decades prior to the Civil War reveals how personal relationships cut across the affiliations and allegiances that define conventional interpretations of the period.[15] And Corey Brooks has shown how abolitionist third parties were able to wield influence beyond their numbers by shrewdly trading off the political capital they held as the balance of power between Democrats and Whigs.[16] Each in its own way draws our attention to the fact that time and again Congress did not divide straightforwardly along partisan or sectional lines. Instead, prolonged negotiation and maneuvering was required to reach an outcome that could command the support of a majority.

It is on these fine margins, where the conversion of a few lawmakers could mean the difference between success and failure, that lobbying becomes so significant. Article 1, Section 1 of the Constitution states: "All legislative Powers herein granted shall be vested in a Congress of the United States, which shall consist of a Senate and House of Representatives." Yet the same Constitution that protects the right of citizens to speak and write freely, to assemble, and to petition the government virtually guarantees that attempts would be made to share in those powers.[17] All such efforts by persons outside of Congress may therefore, in one sense, be said to constitute lobbying. But nineteenth-century Americans would also have been familiar with our more restricted definition of the term today to describe face-to-face persuasion of policymakers by interested persons or agents acting on their behalf. As early as 1819, one New Yorker described "a class of men, whose profession and trade it is to attend at Albany during the sessions of the Legislature, with a view of soliciting or opposing the passing of bills, banks, insurance companies, &c." "They are generally known by the name of Lobby members," he explained.[18] Five years later, an observer of proceedings in the national capital commented that "emissaries, agents and borers [another contemporary term for lobbyists] have haunted the doors of the house [of Representatives], like the ghost of the murdered Banquo; as if determined by the certainty of their appearance to destroy the peace of its occupants, till they granted their request."[19] In 1832, a dispute broke out on the floor of the Senate over "whether their legislation was not influenced by certain lobby members" and "those who acted as their agents within these walls."[20] And by the eve of the Civil War, one newspaper editor could not hide his loathing of the "professional vote-sellers" who "thronged" the "legislative halls." "There is nothing more dangerous to a Republic than the prevalence of such infamy," he warned his readers.[21]

Lobbying is a much-discussed, and much-maligned, feature of modern democratic politics, yet despite its historical importance its incidence in the early United States is, like the making of tariff policy, seriously understudied. Contrary to the plentiful references that may be found in contemporary writings, most scholars treat its emergence as a twentieth-century phenomenon.[22] A few have traced its origins back further, most commonly to the expansion of the American state during and after the Civil War.[23] Very little has been written on lobbying at the federal level prior to that conflict, despite studies that suggest that it was already prevalent in certain states.[24] But in some respects, the antebellum political system offered more scope for lobbyists to contribute to policymaking than its modern counterpart. Legislative sessions were typically shorter, and turnover rates higher, leaving little opportunity for lawmakers, fewer in number than today, to develop expertise on the many issues that demanded their attention. The tariff was a complex subject, and while party affiliation, sectional allegiance, or theoretical treatises on political economy might offer some general guide as to the proper, or popular, course to take, they proved to be of much less assistance when it came to the practical details. A congressman might consider himself for the protection of domestic producers in principle, for example, but that did not help him determine whether the rate of tax on imported wool should be fixed at twenty or thirty percent when textile manufacturers were pressing the former and sheep farmers the latter. All this uncertainty, coupled with the absence of almost any regulation on the subject—the first law against bribing a member of Congress was not passed until 1853—encouraged lobbyists to flock to Washington in a bid to shape the making of tariff policy.[25]

These lobbyists may be divided into two groups: protectionists, who sought to raise tariff barriers, and free traders, who sought to reduce them. Neither was so unified as these labels suggest, however. Protectionists disagreed over what level of duties would serve their purpose, whether state aid should be temporary or permanent, and whether raw materials should receive equal treatment to manufactures. As for the free traders, the sole point upon which almost all concurred was that a complete elimination of customs duties would be impractical, since it would necessitate finding an alternative source of public finance.[26] Instead, most sought the implementation of a "revenue" tariff, which would generate only the minimum necessary to support the federal government. Like their opponents, this often left them at odds over what that proper level should be, as well as whether rates on all articles should be equal or whether some discrimination might still be permitted in order to promote American industry. Over the pages that follow, the protectionists appear earlier and more frequently, most likely because they had more to gain directly from the policies that they advocated and pressed their case accordingly, but it is the interplay between the two groups, and the ebb and flow of their political influence, that provides essential context for the passage of tariff legislation between 1816 and 1861.

The study of lobbying on tariff legislation also directs our attention to neglected aspects of policymaking. The antebellum era is sometimes presented as a "golden age" for deliberative democracy, when "a Clay or Webster or Stevens could give a speech and influence votes by their oratory."[27] Yet as one newspaper correspondent assigned to cover another interminable series of monotonous tariff debates informed his readers, "the truth is, it is an old subject, and every man in the House who is capable of thinking and investigating, had made up his mind for or against the general *principle* of protecting domestic labor, and has read the debates of other years upon the subject."[28] On a typical day, he reported, "the House went into Committee of the Whole on the Tariff Bill—in other words, the whole committee went about their business elsewhere, leaving the speakers to address the chairman and the *House*. [Several congressmen] each made very good and sensible speeches, which will, most likely, be published and read by their constituents, as they were intended to be—They had some listeners, however—a dozen or two, perhaps more."[29] As we shall see, the frequency with which such descriptions recur throughout the period suggests that congressional debates may not be the most useful source for understanding the making of tariff policy. As one editor aptly put it at the time: "to *make a speech* is one thing and to *do a good act* is another. The gentleman whose speeches are listened to with the greatest avidity, does no part of the *business* of legislation, except to give his vote."[30]

This "*business* of legislation" began long before any measure reached the floor of Congress. Prior to the commencement of the session, interested groups in and out of Washington would begin maneuvering to push their particular cause up the agenda and mobilize public sentiment in its favor. Procuring the election of a sympathetic Speaker of the House was also imperative to gain control over the influential committee system. There, bills were drafted and, according to the inclination of those in power, either presented for consideration by the whole or left to languish. Once debate on a measure commenced, parallel negotiations would continue in back rooms of the capitol and at the boardinghouses of the members, as its sponsors sought to navigate the many obstacles that might hinder its progress, while marshaling sufficient support to guarantee success on the decisive roll call. If the bill made it to the Senate, similar efforts would again be needed to secure its passage. And even then, a conference committee might still be required to settle disagreements between the two chambers, or a presidential veto might result in an eleventh-hour derailment. At every one of these stages, lobbyists could, and often did, make an important contribution, and because of the interest it excited outside, as well as inside, the national capital, and its potential to cut across partisan and sectional divisions, tariff policy makes the perfect case study to explore that contribution further.

Incorporating lobbying into the story improves our understanding of the making of tariff policy, and indeed of policymaking more generally during the antebellum period. In particular, it suggests that historians have focused too much on the partisan affiliation and sectional allegiance of legislators, and the abstract principles to which they professed their adherence on the floor, in explaining the outcome of policymaking. Instead, we would be better served by thinking of policymaking not only in terms of outcome but also as a process. Doing so allows for greater appreciation of the importance of rules and timing, of the roles played by elected representatives and lobbyists with their own personal agendas, and of the many contingencies that contributed to the persistent uncertainty that characterizes antebellum politics. Far from sending historians and their readers to sleep as Belohlavek feared, such a narrative should convey the intensity of feeling that contemporaries experienced when they clashed over the tariff question, as well as the messiness inherent in translating neat theories of political economy into practical lawmaking.

This book does not claim that lobbying was the crucial determinant of the success or failure of *every* piece of tariff legislation considered by Congress between 1816 and 1861. It does not—and could not, given the paucity of sources—provide a complete history of all lobbying undertaken in the nation's capital during this period, and nor is it a truly comprehensive history of the making of tariff policy, since certain aspects of that story have already been covered in detail elsewhere. This is especially the case for the clash of ideas that so preoccupied Stanwood and Taussig more than a century ago, but which this book argues were not so determinative as has often been suggested since.[31] As Paul Conkin, in his examination of America's first political economists, has concluded, while "like-minded politicians and economists found each other and freely used each other," it is doubtful whether "arguments drawn from one or another system of political economy had much to do with the basic policy preferences of politicians."[32] And it would take multiple volumes to incorporate a full examination of the economic transformation of the United States, or its fluctuating foreign relations, both fields that overlapped with struggles over the tariff in Washington. Instead, what this book offers is an account of what the study of antebellum tariff policy reveals about the oft-overlooked practice of lobbying, and an argument for what an appreciation of that lobbying adds to our understanding of policymaking during this formative period in American development. While historians rightly recognize that this period was one of both heightened partisanship and mounting sectionalism, recent work has highlighted that congressmen nonetheless often did not vote as their partisan or sectional label would predict. I propose that lobbying, and the attendant negotiation that it entailed, provides an explanation for this conundrum, and that tariff legislation, so important to so many Americans, was only the final outcome of a largely unseen and frequently convoluted process.

The story begins in 1816, when the United States embarked on its first serious experiment with protectionism. The federal government had relied on import duties for revenue since its founding, but Lawrence Peskin has shown that tariff policy remained a relatively unimportant part of efforts to promote American manufacturing prior to the War of 1812.[33] This book picks up where Peskin's left off, with the Tariff of 1816, and chapter one charts the initial efforts of localized clusters of manufacturers to influence lawmaking in Washington. Chapter two follows the escalation of the campaign for increased duties into a nationwide concern, first with the failed Baldwin Bill of 1820, and then passage of the Tariff of 1824. Chapter three sees the interjection of partisan politics into the mix, as conflict between supporters of President John Quincy Adams and his rival Andrew Jackson crucially shapes both the Woollens Bill of 1827 and the Tariff of 1828, or "Tariff of Abominations" to its critics. In chapter four, sectional divisions take center stage, as South Carolina's threat to nullify federal law prompts the passage of the Tariffs of 1832 and 1833, the latter the celebrated "Compromise" that claimed to save the country from the horrors of civil war. Chapter five illustrates the fine margins that often decided antebellum policymaking, through an examination of the Whig-sponsored Tariff of 1842 and its Democratic counterpart in 1846. Finally, chapter six demonstrates how far lobbying had evolved by the eve of the Civil War, with the Tariff of 1857 triggering a full-blown congressional investigation into the subject. It closes with passage of the Tariff of 1861 by a Northern-dominated Congress that seized the opportunity provided by the secession of several Southern states to reaffirm the nation's commitment to high duties, a commitment that would persist without serious challenge well into the twentieth century. Lobbying on the tariff would only intensify in the postwar period, but in the context of a partisan and sectional reconfiguration so complete that this constitutes a natural end point for the present study.[34]

Since the most recent global crisis in democratic capitalism struck in 2008, historians have embraced the challenge of what Jeffrey Sklansky describes as "making tangible the intangible, personal the impersonal, and visible the 'invisible hand' that wields the scepter in market society."[35] This renewed interest in "the politics in political economy" makes it all the more timely to remind ourselves that clashes over free trade and protection were just as controversial in the early United States as they have once again become, and that lobbying, then as now, plays an important, if often overlooked, part in Lincoln's government "of the people, by the people, for the people."[36]

chapter one

"Men of Talents"
The Tariff of 1816

O N THE PROCEEDINGS of the present session of congress, it is expected, will mainly depend the resolution of the momentous question, whether our manufactories shall go on and increase, and be extended to the general wants of the country, or dwindle into nothing," announced *Niles' Weekly Register*, the most widely read newspaper of its day, in January 1816.[1] Seven weeks earlier, in anticipation of the pending contest, a group of Delaware textile producers discreetly dispatched one of their number, Isaac Briggs, on a mission to "communicate with members [of Congress] on the just & reasonable objects of the manufacturers of this District."[2] He was joined in Washington by associates from New Jersey, New York, and Rhode Island— "men of talents," Briggs branded them—and also by a well-connected rival, Massachusetts mill owner Francis Cabot Lowell, set on pursuing his own agenda.[3] This chapter describes the protracted process of lawmaking that these agents encountered and their efforts to shape the outcome, which provide the first documented example of lobbying on the tariff.

Those efforts took place against a backdrop of circumstances arising from the War of 1812, which generated widespread sympathy for an upward revision of rates, though there was little in the way of an organized campaign to that end. Here and there manufacturers cooperated to call for increased duties, but they neglected to coordinate their movements nationally or make sustained efforts to mobilize public sentiment in their favor. Even the dispatch of agents to Washington, though innovative for the time, displayed limited ambition in execution compared to what was to come. Nonetheless, their appearance in the halls of the capitol heralded the significant role that lobbying would henceforth play, as "men of talents" both in and out of Congress collaborated on the "*business* of legislation." The enactment of the

Tariff of 1816 marked the commencement of the United States' experiment with protectionism, and arguments made on this occasion presaged the repeated clashes that would follow over the next half century.

+ + +

In 1776, the United States declared its political independence, but the new nation remained bound within a well-established transatlantic economic network. Two decades of conflict in Europe arising out of the French Revolution temporarily disrupted these ties and encouraged enterprising Americans to provide for their country's wants instead. "A variety of circumstances—the British orders in council and the French decrees—our self-restrictions on trade—and, finally, the late war [of 1812], gave a new direction to wealth and industry in the United States. Manufactories grew up as if by magic," the *Register* recalled with pride.[4] But the return of peace in 1815 reopened domestic markets to foreign producers desperate to divest themselves of stockpiled wares. This dumping was encouraged by British politicians who anticipated the reinstatement of the old commercial relationship between the metropole and its former colonies; "it was well worth while to incur a loss upon the first exportation," one member of Parliament explained, "in order by the glut to stifle in the cradle those rising manufactures in the United States which the war had forced into existence contrary to the usual course of things."[5] Such statements were met with outrage in the American press, and the *Register* was no exception. Our manufacturers, its editor proclaimed, "have made wonderful progress towards perfection; but they have not yet arrived at a degree of strength competent to meet, on equal grounds, the more wealthy and older institutions of Europe. They must be protected and assisted for a while by the government."[6]

Who were these manufacturers that the *Register* deemed worthy of protection? Lawrence Peskin has shown that the meaning of the term "manufacturing" underwent a redefinition in the decades following the Revolution. Where once it had encompassed a wide range of activities including craft and household production, it increasingly came to be identified specifically with large-scale works such as factories, foundries, and mills. Other categories of producer continued to exist, and their support would be enlisted in the campaign for protection, as would that of grain, hemp, and wool farmers oriented toward the home market. But it was the owners of those large-scale works who possessed the wealth, leisure, and connections necessary to lead that campaign, and it was they who captured the attention of editors, politicians, and their fellow citizens.[7] This entrepreneurial class included Francis Cabot Lowell and his fellow proprietors of the Boston Manufacturing Company in Massachusetts, which pioneered the factory system for production of cotton cloth using plans Lowell had personally smuggled out of Britain.[8] It included the Du Pont clan, father Pierre Samuel du Pont de Nemours and his two sons, Victor Marie du Pont and Éleuthère Irénée (known as E. I.) du Pont, who fled the excesses of the French Revolution to Delaware, where they engaged in gunpowder and textile manufacturing and were early advocates of state aid for American industry.[9] And it included others like them in New York, New Jersey, Pennsylvania, and Rhode Island, early centers of industrial capitalism, more of whom we shall encounter in due course.

These manufacturers wanted protection from foreign competition in the form of increased duties on imported goods to raise their price relative to those produced domestically. The first federal tariff, enacted in 1789, had listed the "encouragement and protection of manufactures" as one of its objects, but the rates imposed were actually lower than in much of the state legislation it superseded.[10] Subsequent revisions, chiefly for revenue purposes, had little impact on the level of protection, which remained insignificant until Congress doubled the existing duties when war broke out with Britain in 1812.[11] That was strictly a wartime measure, however, timed to expire one year after the return of peace, a prospect that filled factory owners with dismay. Writing to the Secretary of the Treasury following the cessation of hostilities, James Ronaldson, whose Philadelphia type foundry was the largest in the country, warned that "already the great importations glut the market, lower the price, and extend the credit, and I am certain in two years will lay in ruin, eighty percent of the present existing manufacturers, which if protected at the end of the war would in the same time have advance[d] to double what they now are."[12] This pessimistic assessment was shared by Thomas Leiper, proprietor of several Pennsylvania tobacco mills. "The Double duties you must continue," he urged his congressman. "Our own manufacturers require the Double duties and above all you ought to take into view we never can say we are independent when we are obliged to send to England for our Coat and to Ireland for Shirt."[13]

As Leiper's letter suggests, there were additional motives for a modification of the tariff besides protecting certain economic interests. A second, underscored by recent experience, was the danger of reliance on foreign rivals. "Every nation should anxiously endeavour to establish its absolute independence, and, consequently, to feed and clothe and defend itself," declared one prominent statesman in the period following the War of 1812, and until the United States could fulfil this ambition, "we are a sort of independent colonies of England—politically free, commercially slaves."[14] The most notable, and noted, convert to this argument was Thomas Jefferson. The former president, long associated with the promotion of agricultural pursuits, now urged his fellow citizens to "place the *manufacturer by the side of the agriculturalist.*" "To be *independent for the comforts of life we must fabricate them ourselves,*" he explained in a widely reprinted letter of January 1816. "He, therefore, who is now against domestic manufactures, must be for reducing us to a *dependence upon foreign nations.—*I AM NOT ONE OF THESE."[15]

The third motive was money. Despite the wartime rise in rates, conflict with Britain had added considerably to the national debt, which politicians from across the partisan spectrum were committed to repaying. Increased duties, at least relative to previous peacetime levels, were therefore necessary to meet demands on the public treasury.[16] With these considerations in mind, the House of Representatives was quick to act once the Senate ratified the Treaty of Ghent on 15 February 1815, setting in motion the countdown to repeal of the double duties. Just eight days later, with the Thirteenth Congress approaching its close, John W. Eppes, chair of the Committee of Ways and Means, offered a motion "that the Secretary of the Treasury be directed to report at the next session a general tariff of duties proposed to be imposed upon imported goods, wares, and merchandise."[17] In this, the legislature followed a precedent set by the First Congress, which had ceded leadership in financial affairs to Secretary of the Treasury Alexander Hamilton.[18] The motion was adopted without dissent, a reflection of the degree of unanimity that prevailed at this time on the need for a revision of the tariff to reflect the nation's changed postwar circumstances.

The man charged with preparing the report was Alexander J. Dallas.[19] The secretary approached his task systematically, issuing a circular letter soliciting commercial intelligence and suggestions as to suitable rates, which he ordered customs collectors the length of the Atlantic seaboard to distribute among the leading men of business in their communities. Many recipients did take this opportunity to offer their advice, although, as one observed to a friend: "[T]he information he will obtain, no doubt, will vary according to the interest or bias of persons giving it."[20] How far Dallas was influenced by the responses he received is unclear, but the secretary admitted in his report that the attempt "to obtain detailed and accurate information upon the subject has only been successful in a very limited degree; and, consequently, the result must be presented to the view of Congress rather as an outline and an estimate than as a complete and demonstrative statement of facts."[21] Nonetheless, his efforts in this regard illustrate the willingness of policymakers to be guided by testimony from sources outside the capital and provided precedent for more substantial information-gathering exercises for future tariff legislation.

Dallas's report proposed that American manufactures be divided into three classes:

First class. Manufactures which are firmly and permanently established, and which wholly, or almost wholly, supply the demand for domestic use and consumption.

Second class. Manufactures which, being recently or partially established, do not at present supply the demand for domestic use and consumption, but which, with proper cultivation, are capable of being matured to the whole extent of the demand.

Third class. Manufactures which are so slightly cultivated as to leave the demand of the country wholly, or almost wholly, dependent upon foreign sources for a supply.[22]

Duties on the first and third classes could be set primarily with regard to revenue; the former would flourish even under low rates, while the latter were not sufficiently developed to take advantage of high rates. The second class, however, was "the most interesting," and Dallas believed it "to be in the power of the Legislature, by a well-timed and well-directed patronage, to place them, within a very limited period, upon the footing on which the manufactures included in the first class have been so happily placed."[23] This would be effected through a combination of ad valorem duties, meaning a tax equal to a percentage of the value of an article, and specific duties, meaning a tax measured by weight or quantity rather than value. So, for example, Dallas proposed that iron bars be subject to a specific duty of seventy-five cents per hundredweight, while articles manufactured from iron would be assessed at an ad valorem rate of twenty-two percent of their value.[24]

The secretary's report also set out the fundamentals of protectionism as he understood it. These are important, for the doctrine would become the subject of much controversy over the decades that followed. For Dallas, there was no question that protection was a legitimate function of the federal government. "There are few, if any, governments which do not regard the establishment of domestic manufactures as a chief object of public policy. The United States have always so regarded it," he declared, pointing as evidence to the preamble to the Tariff of 1789.[25] However, there were limits on what government should, or could, do. First, Dallas asserted, "[T]he amount of the duties should be such as will enable the manufacturer to meet the importer in the American market upon equal terms of profit and loss."[26] The purpose of the tariff was not to shield domestic producers from all foreign competition but merely to allow them to meet that competition in fair combat. Second, "the present policy of the Government is directed to protect and not to create manufactures."[27] This was no doubt intended to reassure those who considered government regulation of the economy an artificial restraint on the liberty of men to labor as they pleased. Finally, as suggested by the secretary's comments on the second class of manufactures, protection would be a temporary policy; its very success would soon render it redundant. These principles would be embraced by Congress and would shape the design of the Tariff of 1816.

The Fourteenth Congress opened on 4 December 1815. One of its first actions was to receive the annual message of the president, in which James Madison drew attention to "the influence of the tariff on manufactures" and recommended "a protection not more than is due to the enterprising citizens whose interests are now at stake."[28] It would be another three months, however, before Dallas was ready to present his report. The delay did not sit well with some. "If a foreign government were to pay a man for doing its business, and undoing our manufacturers, that foreign government could not be *better served*," grumbled William Duane, editor of the Philadelphia *Aurora*, an influential advocate of the protective policy.[29] To mollify such concerns, Congress passed an act on 5 February to temporarily continue the wartime double duties until the end of June. The following week, on 13 February, the secretary finally laid his plan for the tariff before the legislature.[30] It was immediately reprinted throughout the nation's newspapers, and widely praised. Even Duane admitted that its author "has done much better than could have been expected."[31]

Tariff bills, because of their revenue-raising function, were constitutionally required to originate in the House of Representatives. There, Dallas's report was referred to the Committee of Ways and Means.[32] Beginning with the First Congress, both chambers had sought to ease the burden on their members by referring some business to committees that could examine a subject in detail and draft suitable legislation for consideration on the floor. Some were select committees, created for a specific purpose and disbanded when their work was done; others were standing committees, continuing from one session to the next. Ways and Means was the most important standing committee in the House, charged with supervising all federal taxing and spending.[33] Its newly appointed chair was William Lowndes, a representative from South Carolina and, according to his biographer, "widely regarded as one of the most able political economists in Congress." Lowndes and the other six members, chosen according to parliamentary convention to represent a spectrum of partisan and geographical interests, immediately set about putting the secretary's recommendations in proper shape to present to the House.[34] In completing this task, they would soon encounter some of America's earliest lobbyists.

+ + +

"Are there in congress, men able to weigh and perceive the various and complex particulars which enter into a mercantile tariff?" enquired the *Aurora*, one month into the session. "There may be some, but it must be very few, from the very nature of its composition. How then is information to be had?"[35] The answer, Duane hoped, was from sources out-of-doors. The founders may have expected the Constitution to provide for "the total exclusion of the people in their collective capacity" from any share in governance, but as the *Aurora* editorial suggested, few elected representatives could be considered experts on political economy, or any other topic; indeed, with a turnover rate of approximately one-third from one Congress to the next, a significant proportion lacked any national lawmaking experience whatsoever.[36] Consultation with their constituents, therefore, whether informally in correspondence and conversation or through the receipt of petitions and other formal communications, was invaluable for legislators seeking both a general gauge of popular sentiment and specific recommendations that would assist them in crafting appropriate solutions to the country's problems.[37]

The Fourteenth Congress entertained petitions for higher tariff rates from several groups who would benefit directly, such as the cotton manufacturers of Providence, Rhode Island, and the sugar planters of Louisiana.[38] By advocating their cause in this manner, the authors followed well-established precedent; indeed, the first memorial ever presented to the House had carried the signatures of "tradesmen, manufacturers, and others, of the town of Baltimore," who prayed for "an imposition of such duties on all foreign articles which can be made in America."[39] The right to petition was enshrined in the First Amendment and provided an important practical expression of the meaning of republican government. According to historians Richard John and Christopher Young, "large numbers of Americans had found it an effective instrument for participating in the work of nation" long before the adoption of universal white male suffrage and the advent of mass political parties.[40]

Yet the manufacturers' petitioning also illustrates how limited their ambitions were at the outset of this period. Richard Newman's description of the "deferential" mode employed by Pennsylvania's Quaker abolitionists, characterized by respectfully couched appeals for political favor and stressing the respectable character of the signatories, applies equally to these early pleas for protection, each confined to its particular branch of industry.[41] Even so, their infrequent interventions were not always well judged: "the manufacturers, particularly of cotton, are very earnest in their demand for protection, and are perhaps, a little extravagant in their suggestions," reported Pennsylvania congressman John Sergeant, who was otherwise sympathetic to their cause.[42] Nor was any substantial effort made by these memorialists to promote a broader public campaign for enhanced tariff barriers. Instead, they relied on friendly newspaper editors such as Duane and also Hezekiah Niles, the proprietor of *Niles' Weekly Register*, to convince their readers that reform would benefit the nation as a whole.[43] "The battle for protection after the War of 1812 would have seemed quite familiar to an eighteenth-century Englishman," concludes Peskin, relying as it did on "the time-honored procedure of forming ad hoc committees to write and sign petitions requesting assistance from heads of state."[44]

Yet in one important respect, the manufacturers did depart from "time-honored procedure" in 1816, by dispatching agents to lobby the federal government in person. The presence of such agents in the national capital has been recorded as far back as the First Congress, but this occasion offers the earliest documented cases with respect to tariff legislation.[45] Foremost among these lobbyists was Isaac Briggs of Delaware. The superintendent of a Wilmington textile factory, Briggs was a man of many talents. Born in Haverford, Pennsylvania, in 1763, he had studied mathematics, engineering, astronomy, and surveying at what was then the College (now University) of Pennsylvania. After graduating in 1786, he worked in a number of capacities, including secretary to the Georgia state constitutional ratifying convention, surveyor of the boundaries of Washington, DC, teacher, printer, and inventor. He was elected a member of the elite American Philosophical Society in 1796 and went on to form the American Board of Agriculture in 1803, with fellow founders including James Madison. He was also on good terms with Thomas Jefferson, who appointed him as surveyor general of the Mississippi Territory following the Louisiana Purchase that same year. When that post ended, Briggs moved into cotton textile manufacturing, founding the mill town of Triadelphia, Maryland, in 1809. It was the failure of that venture in 1814 that prompted his move to Delaware, where he took on the management of the Wilmington factory of Thomas Little and Company.[46]

Briggs was deputed by a meeting of local manufacturers, including E. I. du Pont, Louis McLane, and William Young, to deliver their petition for protection to Congress. The process by which this petition was drawn up was typical of the period. A meeting was held, and "after a free discussion of the various subjects relating to the manufacturing interests of this District it was resolved that a Committee of Five be appointed to draft a memorial to be presented to the Congress of the U. States adverting the Claims of the manufacturers & claiming a reasonable protection"; Briggs was a member of this committee.[47] Two weeks later, the draft memorial was read, considered, and adopted by a second meeting, and Briggs was instructed to accompany it to Washington and "communicate with members [of Congress] on the just & reasonable objects of the manufacturers of this District."[48] This instruction was less typical, as most petitions were simply entrusted to the care of a well-disposed congressman for presentation, but it was not without precedent. Still, it would incur additional expenses, and to meet these another committee was appointed to raise two hundred dollars by "levy[ing] a Tax on each and every Manufacturer (and those immediately concerned therewith) within a circuit of twenty miles of Wilmington."[49] This was duly collected, after some delay, with individual subscriptions ranging in amount from five to twenty-five dollars; even the former would have been far beyond the purse of a mill worker, so this was evidently an undertaking of a small circle of proprietors.[50]

Briggs reached Washington on 19 December 1815 and would remain there for another three months. His regular letters home provide invaluable insight into his activities on behalf of the manufacturers. The day after his arrival, he met with the Secretary of the Treasury, and the following day he dined with the president. He also made an early visit to the capitol, where he "saw several of my former acquaintances and friends, members of Congress, all very friendly and respectful."[51] One of the Delaware senators, William H. Wells, had actually been a pupil of Briggs's during his time as a teacher, and to the latter's evident delight this familiarity earned him an invitation "into the Senate chamber on the same floor with the members, where none are admitted but privileged characters—so says a writing on the door."[52] Access to policymakers has always been a vital asset to any lobbyist, and no doubt the emissary from Delaware had been chosen in part for his personal connections.

Briggs also sought the acquaintance of other protectionist agents, or as he referred to them, "my colleagues, the delegates who have charge of the manufacturing interests before Congress."[53] These were James Burrill Jr., representing Rhode Island; Matthew L. Davis, of New York; and Charles Kinsey, for New Jersey. Burrill was a lawyer of some repute, recently appointed chief justice of his state's supreme court and sent to Washington by the textile mill owners of Providence and its vicinity.[54] Davis was a journalist and printer, and Kinsey a paper manufacturer. Both Burrill and Kinsey had legislative experience at the state level, and while Davis held no public office he was a practiced political operative, having received his education at the hands of Aaron Burr.[55] "They are all men of talents" was Briggs's verdict after their first meeting, "and in the selection of them the manufacturers have given a proof of wisdom."[56]

Briggs was determined that the small protectionist lobby act in concert. To this end, on 13 January, following the arrival of two more New Yorkers, Thomas Morris and Seth Jenkins, the six men met in a committee room within the capitol to discuss strategy. "I made to them a little speech; on the importance of our speaking the same language, as we had in view the same object—if we should be found some pressing one point, and some another, incompatible, one using this mode of reasoning, and another that, irreconcilable with each other, we should not succeed," Briggs recorded. He then proposed "that we form ourselves into a Society, under a proper organization, have regular and stated meetings, and each one should communicate his ideas to the Society previously to publication elsewhere." "This motion was unanimously approved," he noted happily, "and accordingly James Burrill was appointed President and Matthew L. Davis Secretary." Thus was founded Washington's first ever lobbying agency.[57]

Briggs and his new associates were certainly kept busy. Attending congressional debates, conversing with members, and writing in favor of protection, all these were "engagements laborious and incessant," he complained to his wife, adding: "I have seldom gone to bed before midnight."[58] Several times they were invited to address the House Committee on Commerce and Manufactures, to which the petitions of the manufacturers had been referred, and these occasions were attended by "a very crowded audience, mostly of members of Congress," who listened "with great attention and respect" to their arguments on the need for increased duties.[59] Briggs was gratified to hear his own speech complimented by lawmakers "who had been rather opposed to us, but who frankly confessed that their views were changed and that I had placed the subject in a point of light to them quite new."[60] His industry in the cause did not go unnoticed. "I have often the pleasure to see our friend and your delegate Briggs," one Senator informed Victor du Pont. "[H]e is very zealous and active in [illegible] with the Members and I have no doubt is an excellent choice—I think so far as I can collect that the Manufacturing Interest stands well in the minds of a considerable majority of Congress."[61]

One member upon whom the man from Delaware made a particular impression was Thomas Newton, chair of Commerce and Manufactures. The Virginian was one of several legislators to share a boardinghouse with Briggs, and after a few weeks the latter's familiarity with his messmates was such that, as he recounted with much amusement, a new lodger mistakenly "believed me to be a member of Congress and put to me several questions concerning the business before the House."[62] Of Newton, Briggs wrote that he "has shown a growing esteem for me which is extraordinary . . . we often spend an hour together, separate from other company." The chairman offered his new companion full use of the committee room, with "plenty of books, pens, ink, papers, wafer and wax," and "a good fire."[63] He also offered some advice on persuading his colleagues: "you must not appear to teach men what to think, but dextrously place the subject before them, at proper times, and in proper quantities too, in such a manner that they may flatter themselves, the ideas are their own."[64]

Newton's advice was timely, for Briggs worried that "there is a danger of much importunity amongst us, I am afraid it is more calculated to injure than to promote our cause."[65] He was particularly concerned by the arrival of William Young, another of the Wilmington manufacturers who joined him in Washington late in January.[66] "I dare say he expected (in which expectation, I have no doubt some wise heads at home, concurred) that he would find a good deal to do in correcting my mistakes and supplying my deficiencies," Briggs grumbled to his wife, and he was gratified when Newton publicly upbraided Young for his impatience, telling him: "Mr. Briggs has done every thing that he ought to have done, and exactly as he ought, and when he ought—he has done neither too little, nor too much."[67] Young's appearance was not welcomed by others among the original lobby either. "His earnestness and zeal in the cause does in my opinion much more hurt than good[;] were he away our efforts might from our union of action in all cases be much more beneficially exerted for by his unceasing importunity he rather disjoins than convinces," complained Kinsey. "He is not calculated for a diplomatist for to direct the proud mind the effect must be felt unseen we must be all things to all men thereby to gain some."[68] It was not the last time that protectionists would fall out among themselves over the correct tactics to employ in pursuit of their common goal.

Briggs's friendship with the chair of Commerce and Manufactures facilitated his efforts to shape that committee's report in favor of the factory owners' petitions. "A part of every evening he has me with him in his room—reads to me what he has written—requests me to be entirely candid in my remarks—and alters and amends as I advise," the delegate from Delaware informed his wife. "He says no one, not even the members of his own committee shall see it, until it has undergone my corrections."[69] When completed, the report declared "the situation of manufacturing establishments to be perilous" and predicted that "a liberal encouragement will put them again into operation with increased powers; but should it be withheld they will be prostrated."[70] It was received by the House on 13 February, the same day that Dallas submitted his own tariff report for consideration. If Briggs is to be believed, he had a hand in the latter too. One week earlier, he recorded: "I received an application from the Secretary of the Treasury to assist him in completing his Tariff—I went to his room—as soon as I entered and sat down, he said 'I am glad to see you, Mr. Briggs, I have been sometime employed on the Tariff, I have not finished it, but I wish your opinion of what I have done, and your assistance in filling some blanks.'" Dallas then "read what he had written, frequently stopping, to ask me if I approved." The degree of accord with Briggs's own views on the subject was, the latter recalled, "beyond my most sanguine anticipations."[71]

Unfortunately for the high-tariff men, however, it was the Committee of Ways and Means, not Newton or Dallas, that would write the bill for consideration by the House. Lowndes and his colleagues accepted the guiding principles set out in the Secretary of Treasury's report, but when it came to the particular rates he recommended they were more discriminating, judging that in many cases domestic producers could meet their foreign counterparts in fair competition under a lower duty. On imported cotton and woolen textiles, for example, Dallas had suggested a tax of 33⅓ percent and 28 percent, respectively, but Ways and Means reduced this to 25 percent on each, a mere continuation of the wartime double duty, much to Briggs's chagrin. In all, the secretary's report enumerated 139 articles that would be subject to duty, and critics charged that the committee had revised these downward in nearly one-third of cases.[72]

One manufacturer who was satisfied with the Ways and Means bill was Francis Cabot Lowell, who had also traveled to Washington to have his say on the subject. Lowell's Boston Manufacturing Company built its first mill in 1814 and initially proved very profitable, but the return of peace, and with it renewed competition from abroad, saw production of cotton cloth fall by two-thirds across New England, where the industry was concentrated.[73] While some of his fellow producers had responded by petitioning Congress for a prohibition on the importation of certain types of fabric and high duties on the remainder, Lowell was confident that the technological advantages enjoyed by his factory would enable it, under only moderate protection, to outsell its foreign rivals on all but the cheapest, or "coarse," fabrics.[74] For these, Lowell advocated an innovative alternative to prohibition: the "minimum valuation."

As written into Dallas's report, minimum valuation provided that for cotton textiles, "the original cost of which, at the place whence imported, shall be less than twenty-five cents per square yard, shall be taken and deemed to have cost twenty-five cents per square yard, and shall be charged with duty accordingly."[75] This meant that a piece of imported cloth valued at 9 cents a yard would be assessed as if its value was actually 25 cents, and under Dallas's proposed tax of 33⅓ percent would therefore pay a duty of 8⅓ cents rather than 3 cents. The effective rate of tax in such a case would be almost 100 percent (much higher than the nominal rate of 33⅓ percent), the amount of protection offered to domestic producers would be correspondingly greater, and it would also remove the incentive for importers to deliberately undervalue their goods in order to avoid paying the correct duty.

Lowell's precise contribution to the adoption of the minimum valuation is unclear. Edward Stanwood states that the scheme "was devised and urged upon Congress by Mr. Francis C. Lowell," and this claim has since been widely accepted.[76] Yet the minimum appears in Dallas's report, so if the Massachusetts manufacturer truly devised it, then he must have first urged it upon the Secretary of the Treasury. Accounts of Lowell's role rely on the memoir of his friend Nathan Appleton, who writes that "the Rhode Island manufacturers were clamorous for a very high specific duty. Mr. Lowell was at Washington, for a considerable time, during the session of Congress. His views on the tariff were much more moderate, and he finally brought Mr. Lowndes and Mr. Calhoun, to support the minimum of 6¼ cents the square yard, which was carried."[77] There is no evidence either for or against Lowell's original authorship in this source, but it does suggest that he was instrumental in securing congressional approval. The endorsement of the chair of Ways and Means was particularly critical. Where many of the Secretary of the Treasury's other recommendations were modified or discarded, the minimum section of his report was left unchanged in the committee's bill, which Lowndes reported on their behalf on 12 March 1816.[78]

The experiences of Briggs and Lowell illustrate the influence of lobbying on the making of tariff policy even at this early date. Certainly, their efforts were unsophisticated compared to what would follow. There was little coordination between different groups of manufacturers across the country, leaving Briggs to arrange some means of concert with his fellow delegates once they arrived in Washington. Lowell, meanwhile, pursued his own agenda; he was deputed by no one and succeeded by pushing the minimum scheme as a moderate alternative to the exaggerated claims of the same interests that Burrill, Davis & Co. were trying to promote. Yet when Newton assured his new friend that "you and I, Mr. Briggs, could manage the matter better than all of them together," he not only expressed his displeasure at the methods of some of the latter's associates but also hinted at the sort of close relationship between legislators and lobbyists that would become commonplace over the following half century.[79]

+ + +

The tariff bill was taken up for consideration in the House on 20 March, and out-of-doors pressure would continue as it was discussed on the floor.[80] Even before the measure had been reported out of committee, the Wilmington manufacturers received notice, presumably from their agent in Washington, that Lowndes and his colleagues intended to scale back the duties proposed by Dallas. "We have been informed that the Committee of ways & means has reduced the tarif [sic] to 20 on Cloth & 25 on Cotton if it passes so, these two branches of industry are *ipso facto* destroyed never to rise again at least for 50 years," complained Victor du Pont to Henry Clay, Speaker of the House. Clay had entered the lower chamber in 1811 and immediately been appointed Speaker, a sign of the confidence that his colleagues placed in his extraordinary political abilities. He was a fervent nationalist, a firm believer in the capacity of government to do good, and like many of his Kentucky constituents had a financial stake in the manufacture of hemp. He would become the foremost champion of protectionism in Congress over the following decades, making it a core component of his "American System," a program of federally sponsored development that promised to unite all sections and interests in the enjoyment of increased national prosperity. Knowing Clay's sentiments on this issue, du Pont sought his intercession to reverse the changes made by Ways and Means. "In the name of all the manufacturers on the Brandywine I protest against any extension of the old duty which is so evidently insuficient [sic]," he wrote.[81]

As debate on the bill began, Clay immediately moved to restore the original duty of 33⅓ percent on cotton textiles proposed by Dallas. He made this motion, he explained, "to try the sense of the House as to the extent to which it was willing to go in protecting domestic manufactures—assuming that there was no difference of opinion on the propriety of such protection, but only on the degree to which encouragement should be carried."[82] Briggs had prepared the way for Clay's proposition by seeking Lowndes's approval, addressing both him and another member of his committee, John W. Taylor, with arguments in support of the higher rate.[83] Despite these efforts, however, the chair of Ways and Means spoke against the motion, offering "an ample and particular defence of the system reported on the subject by the committee," and it was defeated, but only narrowly. Sensing the mood of the House was favorable, Clay then proposed a duty of 30 percent, and this was carried over Lowndes's continued opposition.[84]

Clay's victory was welcome news for Briggs and his employers, but less so for the Boston Manufacturing Company. Lowell and fellow proprietors were confident they could flourish under the moderate rate proposed by Ways and Means, and feared that a higher rate would only encourage other American firms to encroach on their market. To forestall this, the Bay State entrepreneur was active among the New England delegations. One congressman he befriended, with whom the manufacturers would enjoy a fruitful relationship over the following decades, was Daniel Webster. Like Clay, Webster was a young, energetic advocate of active government, although as a Federalist he had no partisan incentive to support a measure sponsored by the Republican administration, and the commercial interests of his constituency made him wary of increasing duties to a degree that would seriously diminish trade.[85] "In the session of 1815 & 1816 I also made the acquaintance of Mr. Francis C. Lowell," Webster recalled in his autobiography. "He passed some weeks at Washington. I was much with him, & found him full of exact practical knowledge, on many subjects."[86]

Three days after Clay's proposal had been adopted, Webster made his own motion: that the 30 percent rate be reduced after two years to 25 percent, and then reduced again after another two years to 20 percent.[87] Speaking in its support, he assured his colleagues that "he had conversed with those well informed on the subject, and had understood that the manufacturers would be satisfied" with this decremental duty.[88] The identity and motive of Webster's source were no secret; one opponent explained to the House that "the individual consulted by the gentleman, though intelligent and honorable, was a manufacturer of large capital, and could better stand under the operation of the amendment than many others whose means were limited, and who had not got well established."[89] Nonetheless the decremental scale was favored by Lowndes, who called it "a proposition which would, in prospect, produce a return of correct principles."[90] This was a reference to the conviction, expressed in Dallas's report and endorsed by Ways and Means, that protection would be only be needed until domestic producers were sufficiently established to compete on fair terms with their foreign counterparts. These arguments evidently proved effective, because the motion passed by "a large majority."[91] Following further debate, this decremental scale was then reduced again to three years at 25 percent, the level at which it had originally been fixed in committee, and twenty percent thereafter, reversing the earlier gains made by the Wilmington group with Clay's assistance.[92]

The Speaker's claim that there was no disagreement over the propriety of protection was not entirely accurate; opposition to the bill as a whole was led by the eccentric Virginia congressman John Randolph. A former floor leader for the Republicans, Randolph had broken with Jefferson and his successor in the White House over what he saw as their departure from the constitutional principles of limited government. The notion of using the tariff to reward factory owners, rather than to raise revenue, he considered nothing more than "public robbery."[93] "I am making a desperate, tho feeble stand against the new system which out-Hamiltons Alexander Hamilton," he told a friend, referring to the support of the first Secretary of the Treasury, and founder of the Federalist Party, for state aid to manufactures.[94] The Virginian went about this task in his usual erratic fashion, publicly declaring that he would "never wear, nor allow any of his people [i.e., slaves] to wear, a single article of American Manufacture" and challenging Webster to a duel after arguing with him over the duty on sugar, a challenge that Webster declined.[95] "John Randolph has, in his speeches in the House, bestowed on those who are attending as Agents for manufactures, almost every epithet expressive of dislike and contempt and poured upon them a torrent of invective," Briggs wrote to his wife.[96] In particular, the Virginian concentrated his fire on the cotton minimum, arguing that it levied "an immense tax on one portion of the community," the planters who bought coarse fabrics to clothe their slaves and the merchants who shipped them, "to put money into the pockets of another," the textile manufacturers.[97]

Randolph's attack on the minimum brought out John C. Calhoun in its defense. Calhoun, from South Carolina, was elected at the same time as Clay, and like the Kentuckian he entered the House as a rising star in the nationalist wing of the Republican Party. Over the following four decades, however, he would undergo a profound transformation, becoming his section's most prominent spokesman against protectionism. Yet Calhoun's opponents, particularly Clay, would never let him forget the contribution he made to the passage of the Tariff of 1816, a contribution that Appleton ascribed to the persuasive skills of Lowell.[98] Challenged on the subject two decades later, Calhoun denied that he "took the lead in its support"; "it was in the charge of my colleague and friend, Mr. Lowndes," he maintained. "I took no other part whatever but to deliver an off-hand speech, at the request of a friend."[99] Yet in that speech, which was prompted by Randolph's motion to strike the minimum section from the bill, Calhoun proclaimed his desire to provide "adequate encouragement" to the cotton manufacturers and described the threatened provision as being of "vital importance" to that end.[100] Time would change his opinion. The Tariff of 1816 "contained a principle, which experience has shown to be decidedly pernicious," he wrote sixteen years later, "I mean the minimum."[101] His intervention in its favor was decisive, however, as Randolph withdrew his motion, convinced that it could not succeed.[102]

Randolph's vocal opposition notwithstanding, most members of Congress agreed with Clay that it was only the degree of protection, not the principle itself, that was in dispute. This sentiment was encapsulated by Senator Rufus King, who wrote his son that "a strong interest has been raised up in favor of manufactures" and "moderate encouragement would be politic and prudent," although "too high protecting Duties may impair the customs [i.e., reduce revenue], diminish foreign trade, and impose too high Duties upon the consumers."[103] The details of the bill were discussed at some length; John Ross of Pennsylvania spoke for those who found the proposed rates too high when he "wished that the ambassadors from the cotton factories had at once made a treaty with the Committee of Ways and Means which the House might have swallowed, and have left the other manufactories to themselves, and not be burdening the people in every possible way under the plea of protection."[104] However, most motions to amend particular duties were defeated, with Lowndes leading the fight to preserve the measure's original form.[105] A proposition made by one member to bar any congressman "being a proprietor, or having any share in any factory of cotton or cotton yarn," from voting on the tax to be placed on cotton goods was also greeted with derision.[106] "This miserable principle would exclude merchants from legislation on commerce, and farmers from legislating on objects connected with agriculture," charged one critic.[107] With debate at an end, the tariff bill passed the House comfortably on 8 April by eighty-eight votes to fifty-four. The Senate considered it for less than a week before passing it without division on 20 April; the vote held the previous day to proceed to a third reading, the stage immediately prior to passage, showed twenty-five in favor and seven against. The Senate amendments, "none of great importance," as one contemporary noted, were concurred in by the House on 25 April, and the bill was signed into law by President Madison on 27 April 1816.[108]

The margin by which the Tariff of 1816 passed both chambers reflects the general support, both in and out of Congress, for its modest brand of protectionism. This was not, at this time, a partisan question. Hamilton may have been an early advocate for state aid to manufactures, but as Federalism retreated into its New England stronghold it inherited that region's mercantile sympathies for free trade, while many Republicans came to appreciate the policy of encouraging domestic industry, as the public endorsements of Jefferson and Madison indicate.[109] "As respects Taxes, Army, Navy, and some other points, the practice of the Republicans now seems to be the same as that of the Federalists formerly," observed Senator King, himself of the latter persuasion, "but I am not inclined to oppose measures proposed or done by Republicans, which Federalists proposed and did in former times."[110] This was reflected in roll calls on the tariff. Taking House and Senate together, the Republicans provided eighty-one votes in support and thirty-five against, while the Federalists split more evenly with thirty-two for and twenty-six opposed. "As to *party*, we see little of it," Webster reported to a friend. "On the *Tariff* Federalists as well as Democrats [i.e., Republicans] were much divided." Interestingly, Webster added that "the manufacturing interest has become a *strong distinct political party*," suggesting even at this early date the capacity of organized protectionism to manifest as an independent force shaping national legislation.[111]

Nor was the tariff a strongly sectional issue in 1816, although some regional preferences were evident. The free states, where almost all of America's nascent manufacturing sector was concentrated, voted seventy-seven to seventeen in favor of the bill. Twelve of those negative votes were cast by New England Federalists, who feared the impact it would have on the seagoing and shipbuilding trades upon which their constituents depended. Still, while New Englanders, including Webster, sought to have the duties proposed by Ways and Means reduced on several articles while the bill was on the floor, they largely endorsed the retention of the cotton minimum, an indication of the growing importance of that manufacture to the region, and they also supported final passage of the measure by a ratio of nearly two to one.[112] The South was even more divided. Its economy was dominated by staple-crop growers whose produce would receive little benefit from protection, indeed might even face retaliatory duties in foreign markets, but who would surely pay higher prices for the imported goods they consumed. Yet leading Southern politicians, most notably Lowndes and Calhoun, endorsed the view that increased duties were a temporary necessity in order to repay the war debt and render infant industries, so vital to national defense, on a more secure footing. The decremental duty on cotton goods, sponsored by Webster with the backing of Lowell, confirmed to their satisfaction the impression that manufacturers would consent to protection being scaled back over time. Like their New England counterparts then, legislators from the slave states generally backed motions to reduce particular duties, but when the fate of the bill as a whole was to be determined, thirty-six lined up behind it, while forty-four arrayed themselves in opposition.[113]

+ + +

The protection offered by the Tariff of 1816 fell short of that desired by many manufacturers but was nonetheless an improvement upon prewar levels. Buoyed by this success, and hopeful of obtaining still more from government, local groups immediately began to put their organization on a more official footing by forming societies with written constitutions and regular meetings. In some cases, plans had been laid even before passage of the tariff; in Delaware, for example, the same men that sent Briggs to lobby Congress also appointed a committee "whose duty it shall be to devise means to connect the manufacturers within Twenty miles of Wilmington into One Body for mutual benefit."[114] But the new legislation provided an obvious stimulus, and one year after its passage an approving observer was able to report that "numerous societies have cotemporaneously [sic], and in rapid succession, arisen throughout the Union," including in Connecticut, Delaware, New York, Maryland, and Pennsylvania, and it was expected that Ohio, Kentucky, New Jersey, and Mississippi "will soon add their strength and weight to the common stock."[115] By these actions, the manufacturers conformed to the tendency, famously celebrated by Alexis de Tocqueville, of "Americans of all ages, all conditions, and all dispositions [to] constantly form associations" in order to achieve objects that they were incapable of as mere individuals in a democratic society.[116] More recent historians have supplemented Tocqueville's analysis by suggesting additional contributing factors that help explain the explosion of associational activity witnessed in the decades that followed the War of 1812: visions of human progress associated with the Enlightenment, a burst of evangelical fervor in the shape of the Second Great Awakening, improvements to the national infrastructure, and a burgeoning newspaper press.[117]

In fact, associations of members with an interest in promoting manufacturing were nothing new, as Lawrence Peskin has shown.[118] Like their predecessors, the first wave of these postwar creations was largely the province of wealthy "gentleman" proprietors. The most imposing was the American Society for the Encouragement of Domestic Manufactures. This association, despite its all-encompassing name, drew its leadership almost exclusively from New York where it was based, though it did count former presidents Jefferson, Madison, and John Adams among its members.[119] Whereas earlier groups had largely confined their efforts to securing government support for specific ventures in the form of grants, loans, and other legal privileges, however, the new ones sought general tariff protection. The American Society joined with its lesser counterparts elsewhere in petitioning Congress to extend the higher rate of duty on cotton and woolen textiles, which was due to be reduced shortly under Webster's decremental scale.[120] The Philadelphia Society for the Promotion of American Manufactures collected funds for a "Washington expedition" and promoted the circulation of protectionist literature.[121] And a "General meeting of the Iron Masters," also in Philadelphia, appointed a committee to solicit signatures from "those immediately interested in Iron Works, and . . . Citizens of all denominations friendly to these establishments" to memorials calling for increased protection for their industry; "it is in contemplation to sent [sic] competent persons to Washington to superintend the prosecution of our claims," one supporter recorded.[122] These efforts, the details of which are sparse, met with success early in 1818 when the Fifteenth Congress passed separate bills to continue the existing rates on textiles until 1826 and to increase the rates on several raw and finished articles of iron.[123]

The Tariff of 1816 marked the first serious effort by the federal government to encourage domestic industry by imposing substantial duties on imported goods, and also the first serious effort by protectionists out-of-doors to shape that legislation. That the latter was extremely limited in comparison to what would come later reflected both the widespread acceptance that some increase in rates was required, rendering further campaigning on the subject unnecessary, and more importantly the lack of organization among the factory owners and their allies across the country. The Tariff of 1816 owed most to Secretary of the Treasury Alexander J. Dallas, who established the guiding principles for its design, and to the House Committee of Ways and Means under its chair Congressman William Lowndes, who drafted the bill and defended it on the floor. Nonetheless, the part played by Isaac Briggs, Francis Cabot Lowell, and other representatives of the manufacturing interest in Washington should not be overlooked; their presence signaled the commencement of a new era of collaboration between lobbyists and legislators, with the latter including the triumvirate of Henry Clay, Daniel Webster, and John C. Calhoun, who would each in their own way exert a substantial influence over antebellum tariff policy. Party and sectional identities as yet held little significance for the issue, in the patriotic afterglow of the War of 1812. Over time, however, the wisdom of Dallas's brand of moderate, temporary protectionism, and of Lowell's particular contribution to the measure, the minimum valuation, would provide fuel for both partisan and sectional controversy. A burst of activity followed the passage of the bill, but with the enactment of supplementary legislation two years later, calls for further protection were quieted, and the societies that had been established fell into abeyance. The economy prospered, and businessmen returned to counting their profits, little suspecting the disaster that was about to befall them.

chapter two

"More Than a Mere Manufacturing Question"

The Baldwin Bill of 1820 and the Tariff of 1824

S O FAR AS PROPERTY was concerned, the devastation caused by an invad-
ing army could not exceed the destruction that was exhibited in various
parts of the United States," recorded Philadelphia essayist Mathew Carey of
the economic crisis that hit the young republic in 1819.[1] Commodity prices
plummeted, bankruptcies multiplied, and tens of thousands found themselves without work. "This distress pervades every part of the Union, every
class of society," proclaimed Henry Clay, Speaker of the House. "It is like the
atmosphere which surrounds us—all must inhale it, and none can escape it."[2]
Clay, a Southerner, and Carey, a Northerner, were among a growing number
of Americans who believed that only through the general imposition of protective tariff barriers could prosperity be restored. "When, in the years 1816,
1817, and 1818, the subject of a modification of the tariff, and an increase
of duties, was pressed with earnestness on the public, it was little more than
a mere manufacturing question. . . . How grievous and lamentable soever
the case of the sufferers was, it did not very materially affect the nation at
large," Carey acknowledged. But following the financial crash, he argued,
even "if every manufacture and manufacturer in the United States were
prosperous, a change of system is imperiously necessary. For the question at
present assumes a totally different aspect—it is altogether a national one."[3]

Carey and Clay would be the most able, and most active, protectionists
of their generation, acknowledged by friends and enemies alike as giants in
their respective fields. For with the Panic of 1819, the making of tariff policy
had indeed entered a new phase, one that would be characterized by expanded efforts to bring popular pressure to bear on lawmakers and sustained
lobbying in the capital itself. Outside Washington, Carey urged greater cooperation between advocates of increased duties across the country, in pursuit

of a far more ambitious agenda than their counterparts had envisaged just a few years earlier. Working in tandem within Congress, Clay made effective use of the committee system to bring suitable legislation to the floor and marshaled the votes required to see it enacted. To succeed, they would have to overcome the bitterness generated by the efforts of free state congressmen to block Missouri's admission to the Union as a slave state and acrimony arising out of a four-way race for the White House. Their combined efforts were initially thwarted in 1820, as the Senate narrowly resolved against an upward revision in rates, but would eventually triumph with the passage of the Tariff of 1824. Still, the legacy of partisan and sectional divisions during this period would exert an influence over the making of tariff policy for decades to come.

+ + +

The change in the character of the protectionist campaign post-Panic was most notably manifested in the meeting of a Convention of the Friends of National Industry in New York City on 29 November 1819, one week before the opening of the Sixteenth Congress. Whereas efforts to promote the Tariff of 1816, such as there were, had been independently conducted by local groups of manufacturers, this gathering brought together thirty-seven delegates from nine states to pursue their common goal. Of the slave states, only Delaware and Maryland were represented, a portent of things to come, but nonetheless given the logistical obstacles of the period this was no mean feat; it would be another decade before any political party held its own national convention.[4] William Few, who had served in the Constitutional Convention of 1787, was elected president, and Carey acted as secretary. Several of those present are familiar from their exertions four years earlier, including E. I. du Pont of Delaware, Matthew L. Davis and Thomas Morris of New York, and William Young, here representing Pennsylvania. The participants adopted a resolution recommending to their fellow citizens the formation of "societies for the encouragement of domestic industry" and a memorial recommending to Congress the enactment of three legislative measures: the abolition of credit on payment of import duties, the imposition of a tax on sales at auction, and an increase in tariff rates. The first and second of these were designed specifically to curb the dumping of cut-price foreign goods on the American market; the third promised broader protection for domestic producers. The memorial of the Friends of National Industry was received by the House of Representatives on 20 December, and its recommendations provided the text for debates over tariff policy for the remainder of the session.[5]

The Convention of the Friends of National Industry was the culmination of an organizational impetus that dated back to the early days of the Panic in the spring of 1819. At the center of this impetus was Philadelphia's Mathew Carey, an Irish-born immigrant to the United States, a successful bookseller and publisher, and a whirlwind of energy. Carey had sympathized with the manufacturers' plight in 1816, but it was the subsequent financial crash that made their cause his own. "Struck with the calamitous state of the Country," he later recalled, "the result, as I was and am persuaded, of its unsound policy in withholding its support and protection from that important branch of human industry employed in converting the rude produce of the earth into elaborated articles suited to the necessities and the comfort of mankind, I commenced writing on political economy."[6] And once Carey had commenced, there was no stopping him; by his own estimate, he would produce fifty-seven pamphlets on the subject over the next fourteen years, alongside countless newspaper articles, petitions, and circular letters.[7]

The vision of American development that Carey promoted, with a home market for domestic producers at its heart, was one that acknowledged regional differences yet undertook to cultivate all interests within an integrated national economy. The first principle of his creed, he later wrote in his autobiography, was that "the prosperity of this country in all its departments of industry, agriculture, trade and commerce, as well as manufactures, depended on the protection of manufactures, and that therefore this was not a sectional or manufacturing, but a great national question."[8] Here Carey's thinking aligned him with Clay, whose "genuine American system" would "afford a gradual but adequate protection to American industry, and lessen our dependence on foreign nations, by securing a certain, and, ultimately, a cheaper and better supply of our own wants from our own abundant resources."[9] No doubt such eloquence was, in part, a shelter for selfish motives. Carey was an Anglophobe who longed to see his adopted country challenge Britain's economic preeminence on the global stage, and Clay firmly believed the American System would provide his ticket to the White House, just as many of the most vocal advocates of increased duties were the same manufacturers who would reap the profits of such a policy. Yet together, these men crafted a version of political economy to which any patriotic American could subscribe, and in so doing brought new legitimacy to the protectionist cause.

But writing was not the sum of Carey's exertions, for the Philadelphian also took the lead in the formation of two protectionist associations in his hometown during the course of 1819. The first of these, the Philadelphia Society for the Promotion of National Industry, is comparable to a modern think tank. Composed of its founding father and nine other local business-men, each of whom pledged one hundred dollars to promote its objectives, the Philadelphia Society churned out essay after essay in favor of increased duties, almost all written by Carey, and distributed them free of charge across the Union. The second, the similarly named Pennsylvania Society for the Encouragement of Domestic Manufactures, operated a very different strategy. With a subscription fee of just fifty cents, and more than one hun-dred agents employed to solicit signatures to its constitution across the state, the Pennsylvania Society positioned itself as a grassroots pressure group. Members promised to "give a preference to American manufactures" in their private consumption and to "vote for no man who is known to be unfriendly to the support and protection of domestic manufactures."[10] Eight of the ten Philadelphia Society members, including Carey, also sat on the Board of the Pennsylvania Society, and it was the latter that first issued the call for a national convention.[11] The alacrity with which this call was an-swered is evidence that enthusiasm for increased protection was no longer confined to a narrow circle of interested manufacturers. Across New England and the mid-Atlantic region, new organizations were being inaugurated and old ones reinvigorated, and by the opening of the Sixteenth Congress state-wide associations mirroring the Pennsylvania Society were at work in nine states, alongside many smaller ones at the local level.[12]

The Panic of 1819 provided the catalyst for the nationalization of the protectionist campaign, but it was men like Carey and the network they created who were the agents of that nationalization. In key respects, this process mirrored the contemporaneous spread of evangelical bible and tract societies; just as ministers taught their congregations new "organizational repertoires" for shaping public affairs, so Carey and his allies, the partici-pants of the first-ever Convention of the Friends of National Industry, per-formed the same function for the citizens they converted to their cause, by publishing the constitutions and proceedings of their associations accom-panied by exhortations for readers to replicate them in their own localities.[13] Their efforts helped reframe tariff revision as "more than a mere manufac-turing question" and gave it both an urgency and a popular character that had been lacking in 1816.

+ + +

As they first took their seats on 6 December 1819, members of the Sixteenth Congress could hardly have been unaware that tariff policy had been pushed to the forefront of their legislative agenda. The shape of that agenda, how-ever, would be determined not on the floor before them but behind the closed door of the committee room. For this reason, it was of especial significance when Peter Little of Maryland rose the following day to propose "that a distinct Committee of Manufactures be appointed, as an additional standing committee." Thomas Newton, who remained chair of the existing Committee on Commerce and Manufactures, spoke against the proposal, asserting that these two interests "were intimately connected" and "would be best promoted by being both before the same committee." Little's counterargument that commerce and manufactures were "frequently at variance" and that the latter was "of sufficient magnitude to occupy, of itself, the undivided attention of one committee" evidently won out, however, for the amendment carried by eighty-eight votes to sixty.[14] "I am much pleased at the success that attended the motion of my friend Little for separate committees on commerce & manufactures," remarked protectionist editor Hezekiah Niles to his friend, New Jersey congressman William Darlington. "It assures us a good prospect."[15]

The creation of a separate Committee on Manufactures did indeed assure a good prospect for the high tariff men because it provided them with a secure headquarters from which to plot their legislative operation. The Committee of Ways and Means was controlled by members who believed that retrenchment offered the only sure route back from Panic to prosperity and would recommend no change to the rates during this session. Anticipating this, Clay, who made all committee appointments in his capacity as Speaker of the House, packed the Committee on Manufactures with advocates of the protective policy.[16] The committee comprised "all warm manufacturing men," complained one dissatisfied congressman, who found it "a little strange" that not one member was appointed "of opposite sentiments, although the house was nearly divided on this great question." This was no small matter either, he explained, "as every body knows how much the success of [a] measure depends on the committee which introduces it."[17] Protectionists in the House also declined to follow the precedent of 1816 by seeking direction from the Treasury Department, which was likewise firmly in the hands of the retrenchers. The selection of an effective chairman for the new committee was therefore of particular importance, and for this role Clay chose Henry Baldwin. Representative for the industrial town of Pittsburgh, the so-called Birmingham of America, Baldwin had been elected by a bipartisan coalition whose chief object was tariff revision and was himself financially interested in a number of factories.[18] "On the manufacturing question Baldwin will bear down all opposition," reported William Lee, a Treasury official and one of Carey's numerous contacts in the capital. "[H]e has studied the subject—is master of it and will inevitably create a strong interest."[19]

Protectionists out-of-doors would not put their trust in the Committee on Manufactures alone, however. Three months before Congress even met, Carey received a proposal from John Harrison, a chemist and fellow member of the Pennsylvania Society, that their allies across the country "be requested to send in delegates to Washington, as nearly as may be about the same time, competent to answer at the Bar of the House if required such questions in relation to the subject as may be put to them." Like Isaac Briggs four years earlier, Harrison was keen that "there shall be an uniformity of sentiment (in particular) carried to Congress from all parts," though he also recommended that this uniformity "shall not appear to be the result of any pre-concert."[20] From New York came word of a similar scheme. "We hope to get enough [subscriptions] to defray the expences of a Delegate to Washington," wrote Peter H. Schenck, textile manufacturer and member of the recently revived American Society for the Encouragement of Domestic Manufactures. "I think a suitable person ought to be sent from all the Principal towns North of Virginia." These grand plans were not realized, at least not on this occasion, but both the Pennsylvania Society and the American Society did send agents to represent them at the Sixteenth Congress, and one in particular would play a central role in the struggle over tariff policy.[21]

The first to make the journey was Condy Raguet, a lawyer, merchant, and Pennsylvania state legislator, who agreed to spend one week in Washington late in December 1819. Raguet was a member of the Pennsylvania Society but did not undertake his assignment on the strength of goodwill alone; "as my finances at this time would not warrant me in bearing my expenses myself, I should be obliged (however reluctantly) to calculate upon their reimbursement," he insisted on receiving his instructions. Raguet appears to have viewed his mission as a fact-finding one, informing Carey that "I could be more useful in promoting the views of the Society, by presenting myself there as a mere spectator of passing events, in my situation as a member of the State Legislature would enable me, to have a more free communication, particularly with members of Congress from Pennsylvania, than I should be likely to have, as an individual deputed to effect a particular object."[22] In the event, he was able to report that "I have spent a good deal of time with Mr. Baldwin, Chairman of the committee on manufactures, and as far as I have been able have endeavoured to give him the views of the friends to the manufacturing cause, resident in Pennsylvania." Raguet concluded his short stay with the recommendation "that a confidential well informed individual should be deputed here to continue for some weeks to whom application might be made by the Chairman of the committee for information as to details &c., and who could be ready to procure some such particularly respecting the various branches of manufacture, as might be required on the draft of a bill."[23]

Heeding this advice, the Pennsylvania Society next turned to Harrison, who reached Washington one week after Raguet's departure. The good doctor was probably selected for the task because, like his predecessor, he was on cordial terms with several members of the Pennsylvania delegation, including Thomas Forrest, who sat on the Committee on Manufactures. "Our old friend Col. Forrest . . . seemed very much rejoiced," Harrison wrote to his wife on arrival, "& having sat with him in his chamber for some time, he invited me into the drawing room, where I met a very agreeable association of members from our City, & from New York . . . & spent the Evening in a cheerful, & I may say interesting manner as it relates to the object of my mission." He much regretted that "as economy is the order of the day" he could not accept "the pressing invitations given me" to room with Forrest and his companions. Another set of lodgings, likewise occupied by several Pennsylvania congressmen, was also deemed unsuitable because "I should not have had a private place for reading or writing." Eventually, Harrison settled on a boardinghouse that offered him not only a place to lay his head but also "entire controul of the dining room with a good fire, closets &c. except at meal times, where I can see without interruptions & in a reputable way such persons as the nature of my business may require me to consult with."[24]

Like Raguet before him, Harrison spent much of his time mingling with lawmakers. "I have already had several private conferences with members who are friendly to our views, & I find it is the best policy to feel my way, before I make my appeal to those who are either doubtful or notoriously opposed," he explained in a letter home.[25] His situation also allowed him to monitor the activities of persons hostile to the protectionist agenda. "I was much surprised, this morning by the appearance of [two Philadelphia auctioneers] at my lodging, & I believe they were equally surprised to see me," he reported to Carey, two weeks into his stay. Perceiving that they were "convened for the purpose of being introduced" to the Pennsylvania congressmen with whom he messed, and conscious "that my presence might occasion embarrassment," Harrison "withdrew confident that I should be made acquainted with the purpose of their visit in due time." He subsequently learned that his unexpected callers were traversing the city "assailing the Penna. & N. York delegations" against the pending auctions bill.[26] Nonetheless, Harrison remained confident of success, writing that "our prospects are better than I had reason to hope for." His chief concern seems to have been a lack of direction from Philadelphia, a lacuna that highlights the still ad hoc character of these early lobbying expeditions. "I have not received one line from the Board of Manufactures," he grumbled shortly after his arrival, "not even my Instructions, or answers to enquiries on particular points, or the letter of introduction to a Gentleman from New York who is here on the same subjects to enable me to consult with him upon the cause that ought to be pursued;—so that I stand as perfectly insulated as if there was no one who felt an interest in the affair but myself."[27]

The "Gentleman from New York" was Eleazar Lord, agent of Schenck's American Society, and it was he who would represent the protectionist cause in the nation's capital after Harrison's mission was prematurely curtailed by the death of his child.[28] Born in 1788 in Franklin, Connecticut, Lord originally planned to devote his life to the church, obtaining his license as a Presbyterian preacher in 1812. But a recurrent eye complaint forced him to abandon his spiritual calling and reenter the secular world, prompting a move to New York City and the commencement of a successful career in finance. He remained active in religious causes, though, most notably as a founding member of the New York Sunday School Union Society, and retained a rather pious attitude toward Washington society. "I can give but a poor account of the levees, for I have not been to one," he informed Carey two months into his stay, "nor to any balls, events, or other places of idleness, dissipation, folly, iniquity, & nonsense. Were I disposed to attend such assemblages any where it should not be here. With the views & feelings I have of the solemn responsibility of the representatives, especially at a period like this, & of the manner in which 4 months of their time was whiled away I should feel humbled & ashamed to meet one of them at such a place."[29] Lord took his own responsibilities seriously, however, remaining in the capital until the close of the session, a residence of over four months, in spite of frequent carping that he was "sick of staying here," "worn out & dispirited to the last degree," and unable to conceive "what would tempt me to place myself in so unpleasant a situation again."[30]

The letters of Raguet, Harrison, and Lord reveal the uncertain place occupied by lobbyists in the young republic. Legislators were expected to act for the good of the whole, and the potential for corruption when they were exposed to the solicitations of particular interests was manifest; yet few Americans would deny what Isaac Briggs in 1816 had claimed was his right "as a republican citizen" of "addressing, with respect and decorum, orally & in writing, any man either in or out of congress."[31] Raguet was adamant, therefore, that any envoy dispatched by the Pennsylvania Society should be "a private and not a publickly declared agent," for "if there is room for the exercise of individual persuasion, that can only be effectual where the instructing party appears as a voluntary <u>amateur</u>." The notion of a professional lobbyist, able to make a living from the practice, was not completely unknown at the time; one New York politician wrote in 1819 of "a class of men, whose profession and trade it is to attend at Albany during the sessions of the Legislature, with a view of soliciting or opposing the passing of bills, banks, insurance companies, &c."[32] But such behavior was not yet tolerated in the nation's capital. "A committee of several members openly deputed for the purpose [of advocating protection] would I apprehend (and that apprehension is founded on the best authority) be productive of harm rather than good," Raguet assured Carey. "Nobody except Mr. Baldwin is acquainted with the object of my mission and I am satisfied that I should be able to meet a combatant in argument upon infinitely more commanding ground, than if all his suspicions were awakened by a knowledge of the fact that I came here for a special purpose."[33]

The same concern for maintaining "amateur" status is evident in Harrison's selection of housing arrangements. Like several recent historians, he was well aware that policymaking did not take place solely on the floor of Congress. Social occasions could provide the perfect cover for political interchange, or what Raguet had termed "the exercise of individual persuasion." With no formal standing, and no office to work from, Harrison could still, by securing access to the dining room of his boardinghouse, meet with lawmakers discreetly, "in a reputable way," without accosting them in the halls of the capitol. In a period when lobbying lacked respectability, or even legitimacy, for many contemporaries the blurring of lines between public and private spheres was even more important than it is today.[34] As another emissary of the manufacturing interests subsequently noted, "the truth is members should be brought together and there is no other way so proper or so pleasant as a dinner party."[35] The reluctance of Lord, who also declared himself "satisfied of the policy of not being known here as an agent," to engage with the Washington social scene marks him out as unusual in this regard.[36] But the minister-turned-businessman also stands out for another reason, as the close relationship he formed with Baldwin over the course of his mission provided him with unprecedented opportunity to shape federal tariff policy.

+ + +

The tariff that was debated by the Sixteenth Congress would take Baldwin's name, but Lord's share in the measure was hardly less substantial. As head of the Committee on Manufactures, the congressman from Pittsburgh boldly elected to draft three separate bills to effect the recommendations of the

Friends of National Industry: the abolition of credit on import duties, the imposition of a tax on sales at auction, and a general increase in tariff rates. The newly appointed chair swiftly found, however, that the tariff in particular was "a work of labor to write," observing that "it is impossible for one mind to view a subject in all its possible scope." In a bid to ease the burden, he corresponded frequently with allies outside Congress, sending Carey early versions of the various proposals he was working on accompanied by a request to "suggest any amendments or alterations which strike you or your friends."[37] The appearance of Lord was clearly a blessing: "I did not arrive here a moment too soon," the New Yorker reported on 11 January. "I am set at work drafting a schedule of a new tariff. Material alternations & additions can be made if adequate information & statements can be furnished. Please give me such hints, & observations as will be of use in this view."[38] "Mr. Lord is here and is very useful," Baldwin reiterated to Carey on 6 February, as he warned that "preparing a bill on the Tariff . . . will be a work of some time."[39] Unlike Briggs and his associates in 1816, the agent from New York preferred to collaborate with the chairman in private, rather than appear publicly before the Committee on Manufactures, and by the end of the month the two men were laboring on Sundays and dining together in the committee room as they struggled to complete their mammoth task.[40]

Lord's influence was felt in both the design of the bill and the strategy by which the protectionists sought to have it passed; indeed, the two were very much connected. "I had insisted from the moment of my arrival, on the Tariff being modelled on great general principles, . . . & disregarding all mere local & present effects," he subsequently explained to Carey.[41] This approach was embraced by Baldwin, and the product of their joint endeavors reflected it. The petition of the New York convention had specified the duties that its members wished to see imposed on important articles such as cotton and woolen textiles and various forms of iron, and then recommended a further thirty articles to the consideration of Congress.[42] Baldwin's bill did not raise duties as high as the Friends of National Industry had requested in every instance, but it did encompass a far wider range of products than had received protection from the Tariff of 1816.[43] In lieu of seeking guidance from the current Secretary of the Treasury, Baldwin also relied heavily on the report prepared by his predecessor and adopted many of the rates that had been originally proposed by Alexander J. Dallas before his measure was modified by the Committee of Ways and Means.

The "great general principle" that Lord referred to as underpinning the design of the tariff bill was pure unabashed protection. Where William Lowndes and his coadjutors had considered the revenue-raising function of a tax on imports as an equal, if not a primary, concern four years earlier, the situation in 1820 was very different; as Baldwin reminded Carey, Ways and Means had abdicated responsibility for the measure, and "the authority of our committee to write it is only with a view to the protection of our manufactures."[44] And where the previous tariff had been presented by its supporters as necessary merely to ensure parity for America's infant industries with their foreign competition, Baldwin's bill would be pressed as the means by which the home market was to be exclusively secured for domestic producers, as per Carey's and Clay's nationalizing brand of political economy.

For this nationalizing project to succeed, however, it would first have to overcome a sectional obstacle: the Missouri Controversy. The efforts of free-state congressmen to prevent the admission of Missouri to the Union as a slave state occupied the attention of legislators throughout the winter and into the spring of 1820 without any sign of a resolution. Baldwin became increasingly agitated: "[T]he Missouri Question this is our devil and it must be got rid of," he wrote to Carey in February. "We cannot succeed without aid from the South. This is not the time to provoke them."[45] In his eagerness to break the impasse, the Pittsburgher would ultimately desert his section by joining with several other pro-tariff Northern representatives to provide the crucial votes for a slave Missouri, an act that cost him much popular support in the free states and earned him little from the South beyond the unflattering nickname of "doughface," bestowed by John Randolph.[46] Baldwin "grossly mistook" in "siding with the Southern interest," Lord reported to Carey. "He is in a very uncomfortable state of mind; and I fear nothing can be done to calm or conciliate him." Yet while their chief spokesman in Congress remained convinced that "the petitioners for protection of manufactures, have themselves to answer for the defeat of such protection, by their zeal against slavery," the agent from New York was confident "that very little indeed will be really lost to us by that means; & that nothing is wanting to us (as has been the case heretofore) but union among numbers."[47] Tariff men out-of-doors were likewise at odds on this point. "That infernal Missouri Question will defeat us. Our Northern & Eastern Members ought the most of them to have their ears boxed," Schenck complained.[48] But another letter writer agreed with Lord that advocates of high duties would gain nothing by bidding for Southern support, commenting bitterly that "the northern & middle states, who do not breed <u>Black</u> <u>Cattle</u> (two leged ones) for market, may breed <u>four</u> leged black Cattle, Horses, Sheep &c. but they must not expect to be indulged in any thing that may in the least curtail the sale of Virginia Stock—or in any way enhance the expence of the Southern

Planter, in <u>raising his Stock of Cattle</u>, or curtailing a market for them when raised."[49]

One point on which protectionists could agree was that delay endangered their cause. The Missouri Compromise did not pass until 5 March. Another two and a half weeks went by before Baldwin reported his bill to the House on 22 March, and it was mid-April before legislators were persuaded to give it their attention.[50] Lord much regretted the inactivity. "I have proposed to Baldwin to have a meeting of the decided friends of manufactures & National industry, with a view to have them agree on some plan of supporting the measures. But I have little hope of his doing any thing about it," he lamented to Carey one week after the bill was first reported.[51] Three weeks later, his message was blunter still: "Another day & nothing done!"[52] Carey shared Lord's dissatisfaction and was rebuked by Baldwin for his impatience. Justifying his refusal to call the tariff up for early consideration, the chairman wrote: "[Y]ou must recollect that being in the [illegible] & mixing freely with the members it is easier for us here to judge of the best mode of bringing our measures forward. You are not aware of half of the difficulties in our way or of the plotting and counter-plotting to defeat us."[53] Carey, who described his own temper as "inflammable," was not a man to accept such admonishment in good humor, and before a vote on the tariff was even taken he set pen to paper on a new pamphlet that labeled the current Congress "a deep stain on the annals of the United States" for its "indefensible and shameful waste of time." Copies were put in press, but in a more reflective moment the Philadelphian wisely decided to suppress its circulation.[54]

The "plotting and counter-plotting" to which Baldwin referred revealed itself on 15 April, and it came from an unexpected quarter. Lowndes, champion of the Tariff of 1816, rose in the House to call on the Committee on Manufactures for "such estimates or evidence as it may be in their power to present" to justify the rates enumerated in the pending bill.[55] Debate on this resolution, which took place on 17 April, was only briefly reported, but it appears that those in favor argued that since "encouragement was demanded for our manufacturers by increased duties, on the ground that they were now oppressed and ruined," "it was necessary to have these facts to know how far these allegations were true or otherwise." Those who spoke in opposition, including Baldwin, retorted that "the revision of the tariff had been proposed by the Committee on Manufactures from considerations of national policy, and not from a minute investigation of details," and that Lowndes's motive was only to delay consideration of the bill itself. The resolution was then defeated by ninety votes to seventy-two, but this preliminary skirmish foretold the strategy that each side would adopt when debate on the bill began in earnest on 21 April.[56]

+ + +

Baldwin opened proceedings for the protectionists with a lengthy speech in which he urged that the proposed tariff be judged as a statement of national political economy, in conjunction with the two other measures sponsored by his committee, rather than discussed section by section in relation to its effect on specific industries, as had happened four years previously. Reminding his fellow congressmen that the level of protection offered "exceeds but in a small degree that recommended, in 1816, from the Treasury," Baldwin effectively accused Lowndes of abandoning American industry on that occasion, noting that "the report of Mr. Dallas was strongly in favor of domestic manufactures; yet, in that of the Committee of Ways and Means, it is remarkable that the word manufactures is not mentioned." Referring back to the discussion over the South Carolinian's earlier resolution, he declared that "the committee have not [as its critics charged] considered themselves a private committee, acting on the private petitions of individuals who sought support and encouragement from Government, at the expense of the nation." He and his colleagues "have not acted, and would not act, on the statement, or even the affidavits, of interested persons," Baldwin insisted, a statement that somewhat fudged Lord's involvement in drafting the legislation. "If this bill, either in its general principles or its details, cannot be supported on national principles, we are willing that it should fall," he concluded.[57] Lord pronounced himself pleased with the chairman's effort, noting that the latter had followed his advice on presenting the measure and reporting that several members had since stated that though they disliked aspects of the bill, they were now persuaded to vote for it in service to the doctrine of protection.[58]

Those seeking to defeat the bill, in contrast, concentrated their fire on particular details in a bid to strip away supporters until there was an insufficient number remaining to secure its passage, a kind of reverse logrolling. To effect this, motion after motion was made to lower the rate on one item or another, accompanied by charges of collusion between members and manufacturers. Lowndes reminded his colleagues that "the rates of duty proposed in the report of 1816 were founded on evidence of the degree of encouragement which would enable 'the manufacturer to meet the importer.'" The pending bill, he suggested, went far beyond what Dallas and the Fourteenth Congress had ever intended.[59] Baldwin was forced to defend his relationship with factory owners in his own constituency: "[T]his has been called a Pittsburg, a cut-glass bill, local, partial in its operations; and I have been charged with framing it from interested motives," he acknowledged, reiterating that "if you are not convinced that the interests of that place are identified with the nation; that cut glass can be defended on national grounds, then I agree that Pittsburg, its Representative, its favorite manufacture, and the tariff, may go together."[60] Clay also stepped down from the Speaker's chair to warn that "if the friends of the general features of [the bill] listened to every application which should be made to change this or that particular item, the effect would be, that they would lose the whole."[61] This strategy was approved by protectionists outside of Congress. "I think it wants some amendment," wrote Niles to Darlington, "but should have considered, if your house had broke in upon it, that the whole system would have gone to pot, at this stage of the session. If its general principles are maintained, by the passage of the bill into a law—you will, indeed, deserve well of your country."[62]

"What means of information any of this body may have I know not; but if the proposed measures fail, it will be with them. What can be done to escape this issue?" Lord had enquired of Carey after taking his first view of the national legislature.[63] In fact, efforts by campaigners outside of Washington to secure the votes they needed had commenced even before the session began. One of the main weapons in the protectionist arsenal was their publishing arm. Carey was a prodigious writer, and backed by the financial largesse of wealthy manufacturers a sustained effort was made to distribute his work, and that of his literary collaborators, where it would do most good. These efforts prompted one critic to complain on the floor of the House, of "an association in Philadelphia, calling itself a Society for the Promotion of National Industry, [which] has its branches in every part of the Union, with which it corresponds, and which it directs, and instigates, and sets in motion, by the means of pamphlets and newspaper essays. Its inflammatory and unfounded statements have pervaded every part of the Union. Each member of the present Congress has been favored with enough to make two large volumes at least."[64] Lord also consulted with Forrest from the Committee on Manufactures to identify wavering lawmakers and hand-deliver them protectionist literature, while Lee, from his vantage in the Treasury Department, provided Carey with his own list of twelve members that he deemed particularly susceptible to persuasion; ten of those named would subsequently vote in favor of the Baldwin Bill.[65]

The reach of Carey's writings is testified to by the frequency with which they were recycled in congressional debate. Reviewing a speech by Clay on 26 April, Lord wrote that "he showed a good deal of practical knowledge;

and a familiar acquaintance with the addresses [of the Philadelphia Society] & N.[ew] O.[live] Branch [another of Carey's pamphlets]; from which many of his arguments & facts &c. were evidently drawn."[66] Many years later, Lord would claim that it was in fact he who "furnished [Clay] with the plan of speech which would be safe to him politically looking ahead, whether these bills passed or not," and thereby helped earn him the title of "Father of the American System."[67] Other legislators were explicit about their debt to collaborators out-of-doors. Louis McLane, one of the Delaware factory proprietors who had sponsored Briggs's mission in 1816 and now represented that state in the House, praised "the book from Philadelphia, as it has been called, in which the zeal and ability of its author have imbodied a mass of the most useful and important information."[68] Even opponents found a use for Carey on occasion. Philip P. Barbour of Virginia, for example, cited "an estimate made of the immense productiveness of manufactures, in the Address of the Philadelphia Society," as evidence that no further protection was needed.[69]

Advocates for increased duties also maintained pressure on their elected representatives by directing a stream of petitions their way. "The intense distress of the country, and the ruin of so many manufacturers and large manufacturing establishments, has produced a greater number of memorials to congress for a modification of the tariff, than has ever been addressed to that body on any former occasion," Carey recorded before the session had even closed.[70] Protectionist societies and meetings facilitated this process by circulating templates and appointing agents to solicit subscribers, experimenting with methods that would be employed to greater effect by a subsequent generation of abolitionists. These efforts were rewarded by frequent displays of public support for new legislation, a far cry from the few manufacturers' petitions that were dispatched in 1816. By one calculation, more than thirty thousand signatures were collected in support of the cause, a similar number to those amassed sixteen years later during the American Anti-Slavery Society's drive to abolish slavery in the District of Columbia, which resulted in the adoption of the Gag Rule.[71] In contrast, remonstrances against the proposed changes were comparatively few, though drafted by men of some distinction. A protest from the merchants of Salem, who feared the impact on commerce, was authored by Associate Justice of the Supreme Court Joseph Story, while members of Virginia's United Agricultural Societies, convinced that farmers would bear the brunt of augmented rates, articulated their grievances through the pen of Edmund Ruffin, who would go on to greater fame for firing the first shot of the Civil War.[72]

In late April, with debate on the tariff finally under way in the House,

Lord wrote to Carey that "every new memorial does as much good as ten at the early part of the session."[73] Petitions, like pamphlets, could furnish important information to buttress the case for protection. The Pennsylvania Society in particular took considerable care to engage with the arguments put forward by the remonstrances of their adversaries, and to refute their conclusions point by point.[74] A simple count of the number of petitions received, and of the signatures affixed thereon, also provided politicians with a rough guide to public opinion. That congressmen paid attention to these indicators is suggested by the case of Maryland representative Samuel Smith, who as chair of the Committee of Ways and Means had reported against any revision of the tariff, but who ultimately voted in favor of Baldwin's bill in the House. Another member subsequently recounted that Smith "told me, that he should vote for the bill, bad as it was," because "a great portion of his constituents had petitioned congress on the subject of manufactures— that the bill had been published in the Baltimore papers—that no remonstrance . . . had been sent to him or his colleague; nor had he received a single letter, *disapproving*—he must, therefore, conclude that it was agreeable to the wishes of his constituents."[75] No wonder, then, that opponents of increased duties feared the impact of the well-organized protectionist campaign and the connection that the campaign's agents in the capital were able to make between their efforts on behalf of their employers and the demands of a much wider constituency. "I am certain that a majority of the Senate are convinced in their [illegible] judgement and consciences, that it is an unwise and inexpedient measure," observed Alabama senator John Williams Walker. "But such a clamor has been raised out of doors that the nerves of some may be too delicate to resist the shock."[76]

Nor were Senator Walker and his colleagues the only intended audience for this "clamor." Citizens across the country monitored events in Washington closely, a fact that their elected representatives sought to take every advantage of; indeed, this same session of Congress gave the English language a new phrase, "speaking bunkum," which originated in one North Carolina representative's avowed intention to give a speech not for the benefit of those few who were present to hear it but for his constituents in Buncombe County.[77] By inserting their pamphlets and memorials into the congressional record, or even debate on the floor itself, advocates of increased duties could therefore be assured that their arguments would soon be recycled in the columns of sympathetic newspapers such as *Niles' Weekly Register* and in the letters that legislators circulated among friends and neighbors back home. This two-way communication between congressmen and their constituents allowed tariff activists not only to influence the outcome of the legislative process but also to define the very terms of public debate on the topic. As one consumer of protectionist literature subsequently recorded: "Mr. Carey wrote volumes in support of his doctrines, and created at one time a great sensation. I confess myself to have been one of those who believed almost implicitly in the soundness of his mode of thinking."[78]

+ + +

It would be nearly five months from the beginning of the session until a vote was taken on Baldwin's tariff bill. Lord had labored tirelessly throughout, filing near-daily reports to Carey of proceedings both on and off the floor, but as the session dragged on even the New Yorker's relations with friendly legislators became strained: "[T]here is not a member of Congress of my acquaintance, of whom I can ask a favour, without having my feelings injured by some appearance of hesitation, reluctance, hurry, impertinence, or the like; indicating that they don't wish to be troubled," he complained on one occasion.[79] As early as mid-April, Lee informed Carey that "I am very apprehensive that nothing will be done about the tariff—the members begin to be uneasy and wish to get home."[80] Yet few legislators were willing to risk the wrath of their constituents by leaving while the fate of the bill remained in doubt. "I really consider the interests of Boston and indeed of Commerce jeoparded by this bill, and my vote and exertions may be very much wanted," explained Massachusetts senator Harrison Gray Otis, in refusing his wife's entreaties to return home.[81] Any member who did dare depart would also require formal permission from his colleagues, a decision complicated by its likely impact on the relative strength of the two sides in the decisive roll call, though this was not always possible to predict. "Yesterday Mr. Meech of Vermont asked leave of absence [and] it was easily granted by the Southern gentlemen thinking he was in favor of the tariff," Lee reported to Carey on 19 April. "[B]ut after they found out he was not & that he was on their side they were sorry he was permitted to go."[82]

On 29 April, after eight days of debate during which its supporters repeatedly united to block amendments to the bill, the tariff finally passed the House with ninety-one yeas to seventy-eight nays. Five days later, following only a brief discussion, the Senate voted to table the bill by twenty-two yeas to twenty-one nays. "The Gig is up—the Tariff is gone! The Senate have postponed the consideration by a majority of <u>one</u> vote to the next Session," Lord wrote Carey. "The chief pretence is <u>want of time</u>. Several of the pretended friends of it were not quite ready to decide so <u>suddenly</u>. <u>Delay has killed it</u>."[83] Niles was equally disappointed. "Your bill has indeed been butchered [in] the great slaughter house of good things," he lamented to Darlington.[84]

This result also signaled the demise of Baldwin's two other measures. The bill abolishing credit on import duties failed in the House, but the bill imposing a tax on sales at auction actually passed that body by a narrow margin on the same day that the Senate postponed consideration of the tariff. A federal tax on auctions would hurt states that already collected a tax on the same, such as New York and Pennsylvania, but their congressional delegations were willing to accept this if it formed part of a comprehensive system to encourage domestic industry. Once these representatives learned of the loss of the tariff in the Senate, however, motion was made to reconsider the House vote on the auction bill, and it shared the fate of its two associated measures. "Such is the mode in which we are compelled to legislate," Darlington recorded bitterly in his diary.[85]

The margin of defeat for the tariff bill was a narrow one, and the reasons that explain it are complex. The most obvious division on the crucial roll calls was sectional rather than partisan. Taking both chambers together, members of the Republican Party, which now held a huge majority of seats, were to be found in almost equal numbers on either side, with ninety-one in favor and eighty-eight opposed, while the few remaining Federalists split twenty-one in favor and twelve opposed. Just as had been true four years earlier, partisan affiliation gave little indication as to how a particular legislator would vote. Where 1820 differs from 1816, however, is in the growing division between, rather than within, sections, as first witnessed in the register of attendees at the Convention of the Friends of National Industry. While the free states provided ninety-six votes for protection and twenty-four votes against, roughly a similar proportion to four years previously, the slave states provided only sixteen votes for protection, less than half the number in 1816, and seventy-six against. For the first time in 1820, it was possible to speak, as Lee did to Carey, of "the Southern gentlemen" as a reliably anti-tariff bloc.

Some historians have endorsed Baldwin's analysis that "the manufacturers might have depended on support from the Southern quarter, if they had not destroyed it by their zeal on the Slave subject."[86] No doubt the proximity of the tariff debate to the Missouri Controversy was unfortunate for the protectionists, for there were certainly some Southerners who viewed encouragement of manufactures as "the undisputed progeny of the policy that seeks to promote the interest of one portion of the Union at the expense of another."[87] Yet there is reason to conclude, as Lord did, that the slave states possessed sufficient motive to oppose any increase in import duties, even without the unwelcome discussion of their peculiar institution.[88] In 1816, many Southerners had been willing to shoulder the burden it would impose on their section, accepting that the revision was necessary to raise revenue and to offer temporary protection to infant industries that might prove vital to national defense. Four years later, however, the need for revenue was reduced and the prospect for renewed war had receded, yet Baldwin's bill now seemed to promise permanent, and more generous, protection to a manufacturing sector situated almost exclusively in the North. It was the economic inexpediency of the measure, the reframing of protection as a preferred policy rather than simply a temporary practicality, that was the chief complaint of the South in 1820.[89] Hence the news that Thomas Newton had furnished one of the few Southern votes in favor of the tariff was greeted in his native Virginia with a pointed 4 July toast: "*The Hon. Messrs. Newton and Baldwin, chairmen of the committees of Commerce and Manufactures. . . .* May they have the benefit of a new course of political economy, with a teacher more sane than Mathew Cary [*sic*]."[90]

Still, the South provided only sixty of seventy-eight negative votes in the House and sixteen of the twenty-two votes to postpone in the Senate; crucial opposition also came from the North. The main source of this opposition, as it had been in 1816, was the mercantile community. "The principles avowed by some of the supporters of the measure have alarmed the navigation interest & we have thus lost a part of the support we might have justly expected from New England," noted Rhode Island senator James Burrill Jr., who, like McLane, had made the transition from lobbyist to legislator.[91] This assessment was echoed by New York Senator Rufus King, who believed that "the cotton & woollen manufacturers, disconnected with their associates, would have received the protection asked for; but the bearing of the Bill on ship building & navigation was insufferable," singling out, in particular, "the articles of Iron, Hemp, Duck, and Copper."[92] Otis had cited the impact upon commerce as motive for his vote against the bill, which provided the decisive margin in the Senate, and New England as a whole furnished twenty-one of the twenty-four free state votes for rejection.[93] Lee had foreseen this result early: "[T]he Commercial interest being opposed to us and the slave holding states almost unanimously so," he wrote in January. "[T]he combination of the two will defeat us & finally ruin this Country."[94] With the increasingly solid South and a deeply divided New England together holding two-thirds of the seats in the House and nearly three-quarters in the Senate, the challenge facing the protectionists was always a formidable one.

But there was also a third constituency whose support for Baldwin's bill was, perhaps surprisingly, lukewarm at best. This was the large cotton textile manufacturers, such as the Boston Manufacturing Company, who had benefited most from the Tariff of 1816 and whose small number belied their considerable political influence, particularly in Massachusetts. "The truth is the Yankee capitalists are doing remarkably well in their fabrics & they will unite to prevent others of less heavy metal from engaging in them," Lee had warned Carey before the session even began.[95] This was confirmed by Christopher Gore, a confidant of the Bay State entrepreneurs, who wrote to King that "our Manufacturing People, I mean those of Waltham, would be more satisfied with the Prospect of the present Duty being permanent than to see it increased. Under the latter Plan, should it take place, they would greatly fear a Reaction in Public Sentiment, that might deprive them of the advantage now enjoyed."[96] While protectionist spokesmen publicly urged the preservation of the American market for American industry, some factory owners were privately calculating that they could compete more favorably against a few foreign producers than a potentially limitless number of domestic ones. Dissent within their own ranks would be a persistent problem for advocates of increased duties throughout the antebellum period.

The margin of defeat was so narrow that errors by the bill's staunchest supporters must also be accounted for. Carey, for one, believed that "the mismanagement of its friends was at least as fatal to the measure as the deadly hostility of its enemies."[97] "The business was managed by its leading advocate [i.e., Baldwin] in the house of representatives, in a manner that displayed but slender tact or energy," he subsequently claimed, and the failure of the Committee on Manufactures to press the subject on Congress until "above four months of the session had passed over, and when the members, worn out by the everlasting debates on the Missouri question, were yearning after home . . . was fatal to the bill, and destroyed whatever chance it might otherwise have had."[98] In this, the Philadelphian reiterated what Lord had reported to him at the time. "The bad planning & obstinacy of B[aldwin] has been abundantly apparent," the latter had written on 3 May, adding the following day, when the tariff's defeat in the Senate was confirmed: "I hope it will not fall into the same hands here next year."[99] Baldwin's personal stake in manufacturing, which looked to be an asset when he was appointed chair of the Committee on Manufactures, may also have hampered his efforts to secure passage of the bill once it reached the floor. "Congress all knew he was deeply concerned in the Steubenville factory," one observer later recorded, "and therefore when he was no doubt bona fide advocating a great national measure, many members may have conceived he was merely grovelling among the petty interests of individual manufacturers."[100]

Lord too, and even Carey, must take some share of the responsibility, however, for it was the design of the bill, and the strategy that underpinned that design, that was most frequently blamed by members of Congress for its rejection. Sympathetic legislators had voiced their concern the moment it was reported out of committee. "It contemplates an entire change of the whole system of impost on which account, I very much fear, the whole project will fail. It is too much to attempt at one time, more especially at the close of a Session," commented McLane.[101] Others were even more blunt. Jonathan Roberts, who as senator for Carey's home state had been counted on by the protectionists for his support, declared that the proposed legislation was "most wild & extravagant without any admitted object or ascertained effect. . . . There were some articles I should have been glad to have raised but to touch the whole impost system was the act of Madmen."[102] Otis too, after converting to protectionism in later life, would explain away his opposition to Baldwin's bill on the grounds of "not so much the amount of duties proposed on certain articles, as the *sweeping universality of the system, and the avowed principles of its friends*," which "went not merely to protect such manufactures as were adapted to the condition and faculty of the country, but was predicated on the *principle of forcing manufactures in general*."[103] Viewed in this light, it is difficult to escape the conclusion voiced by King: "Had not the friends of the Tariff embraced a system too comprehensive and complicated, they would have succeeded."[104]

+ + +

"Do not be discouraged," Lord urged Carey on the day the Baldwin tariff was tabled. "A great deal has been gained although the Bill is not yet a law."[105] In particular, and despite this temporary setback, the value of close cooperation between lobbyists and legislators had been established to the satisfaction of many protectionists, both in and out of Congress. As Jeremiah H. Pierson, iron manufacturer and representative for New York, assured Carey the following year: "I think the great Cause, of Protecting the Manufacturing Industry of the Nation, is on the whole gaining Ground here, a thing you must be sensable [sic] is to be effected by gaining the Candid attention of Members to the subject, at their Lodging, & not by Sparring on the Floore [sic] of the Hall."[106] Lord was rewarded for his efforts with the editorship of a new protectionist newspaper established in New York and the presentation of a silver pitcher from the "friends of National Industry in Philadelphia," in approbation of "the Zeal, talents, and intelligence he displayed at Washington, in support of American Manufacturers, during the first session of the sixteenth Congress."[107] Already plans were in motion for another national convention, scheduled for June 1820, and for the creation of a permanent coordinating body under the imposing title of the National

Institution for the Promotion of Industry.[108] In this the protectionists followed the lead of the American Bible Society, whose headquarters in New York, established in 1816, supervised an extensive network of state and local auxiliaries. This federal model of organization, mirroring the structure of the American political system and allowing for the same balance between grass-roots participation and centralized decision-making, would become the preferred template for the major antebellum reform movements.[109] "The advocates of the manufacturers are foiled, but are not defeated," concluded the *Richmond Enquirer*. "They will be busily engaged during this summer in recruiting their troops to take to the field next winter."[110]

In this context, the next few years proved a serious disappointment. Baldwin's bill was not resurrected during the short second session of the Sixteenth Congress, which was dominated by the revival of the Missouri Controversy.[111] The National Institution was also short-lived, with Carey falling out with other leading members over the tactics it should employ, even to the point of refusing to put his name to their productions; this would become something of a recurring pattern for the irascible Philadelphian over the next two decades.[112] Clay then declined reelection to the Seventeenth Congress, distracted by the deranged state of his private finances, and the new Speaker was Philip P. Barbour, a determined opponent of protection. The Virginian's tenure underscores the importance of the Speakership, as he reconstituted the Committee on Manufactures to reflect his personal convictions. Baldwin, who remained as chair, was compelled to report to the House during the first session that a majority of his colleagues deemed it inexpedient to proceed with a revision of the existing rates. "Mr. Baldwin seems to have relinquished his visionary schemes of 'national wealth' & 'national prosperity' by means of tariffs; he being outvoted . . . in his own committee," gloated one opponent of increased duties.[113] A tariff bill did make it to the floor late in the second session, but after desultory debate it was quietly laid aside and quickly forgotten.

The Eighteenth Congress, which opened on 1 December 1823, presented a much-improved prospect, however. Clay's return to the Speaker's chair guaranteed a sympathetic Committee of Manufactures, and the Kentuckian retaliated for Barbour's meddling by stacking the Committee on Agriculture, which Southern planters expected to use as a vehicle for their free trade views, with a protectionist majority. It was the passage of Baldwin's bill by the House in 1820 that had prompted North Carolina congressman Lewis Williams to urge, that same day, the creation of such a body, arguing that, unlike commerce and manufactures, "the agricultural, the great leading and substantial interest in this country, has no committee—no organized tribunal in this House to hear and determine on their grievances."[114] Clay's intervention was therefore poorly received south of the Potomac. "If it were any advantage at all to have a committee, it was one which the agriculturalists were deprived of," complained one of the minority members, but the Speaker was unrepentant.[115] "Believing as I most sincerely do that the prosperity of our Country mainly depends upon the naturalization of the [manufacturing] arts among us, my best and most zealous exertions will be faithfully employed to that great end," he assured Carey.[116] The decennial reapportionment of the lower chamber also seemed likely to benefit advocates of increased duties. Twenty-six seats were added, eighteen of which went to New York, Ohio, and Pennsylvania, whose delegations had voted almost unanimously in favor of Baldwin's bill. Surveying the results of the congressional elections, Niles confidently predicted that "there will be a positive majority of at least forty-five of the representatives of the people in favor of the protection of domestic industry, and the subject will not be talked to death as it has been."[117]

Ill-health had forced Baldwin's retirement midway through the Seventeenth Congress, but his replacement as chair of the Committee on Manufactures was another staunch Pennsylvania protectionist: John Tod.[118] Like his predecessor, Tod chose to consult not with the Treasury Department but with the manufacturers directly, particularly those engaged in the iron industry of his home state, although there is no indication that he collaborated as closely with any one person as Baldwin had with Lord. Instead, Tod took the bill debated during the previous session as a starting text and circulated copies along with a request for suggested improvements. As always, the manufacturers were happy to oblige. Mark Richards, for example, a principal mover in the Philadelphia iron meeting of 1817, urged an increase in the rates imposed on several articles and the introduction of specific duties for various others not enumerated in the original version; while these recommendations were not followed to the letter, many were subsequently incorporated into the committee's bill.[119] Tod was also the recipient of Carey's largesse, receiving from him copies of various protectionist literature.[120] These attentions did not go unnoticed. Some years later, South Carolina nullifier Thomas Cooper would claim that Tod had been "sent [to Congress] by the iron masters of Bedford, Somerset and Alleghany counties, himself not having an idea on the subject [of the tariff] but what was supplied by the persons whose cause he was sent there to advocate." "It is a fact well known to the members of 1823 and 1824," Cooper claimed, "that the committee on which Mr. Todd [sic] was made chairman, because he was a fit person to do as he was bid, received all their information, and all their instruction from the manufacturers within the house, and their lobby friends without."[121]

The tariff bill that Tod reported to the House on 9 January 1824 reveals how the protectionist strategy had evolved over the past eight years. Tod's bill, as had Baldwin's before it, did away with the limited doctrine of protectionism devised by Dallas in 1816; there are but two classes of articles, the chairman declared, those that "do not much interfere with any home production," on which duties may be laid "for the purpose of revenue chiefly," and those that do so interfere, comprising "the important duties proposed in the bill," laid explicitly "for the purposes of protection." The intent of the proposed legislation, he explained, was "to extend and equalize a system which experience had shown to be most beneficial."[122] As one critic observed, "the protection of th[o]se establishments, which originated in the war [of 1812], is not the object of the present bill. It does not even assume the modesty of pretension. Doctrines are now advanced, which never entered into the conception of those who advocated the tariff of 1816."[123] Whereas Dallas had envisaged, and the Fourteenth Congress had enacted, a set of rates that would be both selective and temporary, this new measure would, ostensibly at least, be neither.

Yet Tod also differed from Baldwin in his willingness to compromise on the abstract principle of protection in order to secure practical advantage. Warned by allies outside of Congress not to repeat the mistakes of "H. Baldwin's mammoth tariff," Tod's bill was, in fact, more selective than his predecessor's.[124] A study by economist Jonathan Pincus has found that industries that made their presence felt through petitions and lobbying had their rates set at the higher levels proposed, but not adopted, in 1820, whereas those that remained silent were left to languish at the lower levels of 1816. This process of "coalition formation" aimed to win over influential constituencies to the bill while sacrificing those that had not demonstrated their capability to mobilize support in an attempt to deflect the same charges of extravagance that Baldwin had faced. The most cynical manifestation of this strategy was the inclusion for the first time of duties on a range of agricultural products of interest to Northern and Western farmers, including beef, pork, potatoes, grain, and raw wool, and an increase in the duty on raw cotton, aimed at Southern planters. These duties are described by Pincus as a "cheap bribe for support," since in most cases the United States exported more than it imported, but together with Clay's well-judged appointments they were sufficient to secure endorsement of the bill from the Committee of Agriculture.[125] "I expected no good from the tariff mongers," sniffed one of Daniel Webster's correspondents. "I suppose this bill is the result of some bargain between different interests, & that the owners of a few merino flocks are let in for a share."[126]

Finally, the promptness of Tod's report suggests that the protectionists had learned the danger of delay. The bill's managers pressed hard for its consideration and succeeded in having the subject brought up for debate on 10 February, a full ten weeks earlier than had been the case in 1820. This was crucial if progress was to be made, for opponents of the measure were determined to stall at every opportunity. "If we can obtain time we will exert all our energies to defeat Mr. Speaker Clay and his Magnus Apollo Mathew Carey," explained South Carolina congressman Joel R. Poinsett. "I have some hopes that we shall not have time to get through this bill. We . . . will discuss fully every item."[127] Tariff men in the House were alert to this tactic but struggled to combat it. Tod's bill "can be successful only by the utmost forbearance on the part of its friends. If they persevere in the debate, the bill will be lost for the want of time," cautioned McLane.[128] This judgment was concurred in by John C. Wright, Ohio congressman and member of the Committee on Manufactures, who wrote that "debate on the part of the majority ought to have been given up, and the other side left to speak against time."[129] However, if the blows of its adversaries were not met and matched, support for the measure might slowly be whittled away as article after article was stripped from its provisions. As Niles observed in his *Weekly Register*, "there is a handsome majority in favor of the general principles of the bill, but they differ about its details; and its opponents in principle, who always act against it, thus obtain majorities on many questions."[130] "Your enemies did not play fair they should have fought the grand battle first on the principle of the bill and then have compromised the details," complained one distant observer to Tod, "but this skirmishing on every item will destroy your forces—for you must have a man killed every now and then."[131] The tariff had reached the floor, but even with the recent reapportionment in favor of the protectionists its passage was far from assured.

+ + +

"The debate upon the [1824 tariff] bill was one of the ablest and most thorough and profound in the history of Congress." This was the verdict of Edward Stanwood, and it has been oft-repeated since.[132] The implication is that arguments on the floor made a real impact on the success or failure of legislation. As Richard Edwards, in a comparison of tariff speeches from 1824 and 1894, states: "[T]he earlier Congress convened for honest debate and discovery of knowledge through mutual interchange of ideas. The later Congress debated the issue only as a formality to be endured before the final and entirely predictable vote."[133] This was not a view shared by many contemporaries, however. Samuel Breck, a Pennsylvania congressman whose diaries mark him out as one legislator who was open to persuasion, recorded that "we have heavy debates daily upon Political Economy. Old maxims revived—old truisms repeated, and interminable, long-winded speeches full of old ideas and old speculations."[134] The debate "is in reality not an able one, comparatively, & most of the speeches have been tedious in the extreme," agreed McLane. "The House was completely tired out with the subject, and the speaker, often spoke to a less number of auditors than the hours he occupied in his delivery."[135] This latter comment is hardly suggestive of mass conversions achieved through sheer oratorical prowess. Even Poinsett, who had reason to welcome any delay, groused that "the debate begins to flag and is becoming a dull and tedious repetition of what has before been said, nothing can be so stultifying as that I am now compelled to hear."[136] Such complaints would remain a perennial feature of congressional tariff debates in the decades to follow and should give pause to scholars who seek to explain antebellum policymaking by citing extensively from exchanges on the floor.[137]

All the supporters of the bill could do was bring pressure on the House to hasten its proceedings. In this respect, 1824 represents a refinement of the protectionist campaign that had been conducted since the Panic of 1819, rather than introducing any significant innovations. Pro-tariff newspapers demanded action from the people's representatives. "As the bill has been much discussed, item by item, so much at large, and no *new* matter, in illustration of its principles, can be expected," wrote Niles in early April. "[I]t is important to the nation, that it should be disposed of, one way or another; if it is passed, that the senate may have time to act upon it."[138] Petitions also continued to pour in to Congress. Rebutting the charge that "there existed some general conspiracy against the interests of agriculture," Clay observed that "if all who had petitioned for the tariff were to be considered as conspirators, the conspiracy was extensive indeed," and proceeded to list seventeen states, out of twenty-four in the Union, from which memorials endorsing Tod's bill had been received.[139] Carey too continued to write, and proudly counted among his converts Rollin C. Mallary, a Vermont representative who had opposed Baldwin's bill in 1820 but would vote in favor of protection on this occasion and go on to play an even more prominent role in tariff battles to come.[140] Even their detractors admitted a grudging respect for the campaign waged by protectionists out-of-doors. "Nothing could exceed the zeal and activity with which they had promoted their objects," acknowledged Virginia representative Robert Selden Garnett. "It was almost incredible."[141]

That is not to say that relations between friends of the tariff in and out of Congress always ran smoothly. Early in the debate, E. I. du Pont submitted to Clay "some remarks on the part of the tariff connected with the woolen interest," most probably focusing on the balance to be struck between duties on raw wool and finished textiles, and enclosed a letter from James Wolcott Jr., a Massachusetts mill owner.[142] Clay's reply was unremarkable; he promised to give du Pont's suggestions "a consideration corresponding with my high opinion of the intelligent source whence they have emanated," mentioned the challenge he and his colleagues faced "to reconcile jarring interests, and especially to accommodate the protection proposed for the Manufacturing Industry of the Country to the National Agriculture," and closed by stating that "whatever may be the final result, I am sure we shall find in you a liberal and considerate judge of our perplexing labors."[143] An unsent draft version of this letter in Clay's papers, however, reveals some of the frustration that he experienced when dealing with distant allies. In it, Clay wrote: "I wish you were a member of Congress; you would then practically feel all the difficulties of our actual situation." "You must recollect," he instructed du Pont, "that in the H. of R. there are 213 persons to satisfy & 1000 interests to conciliate. And you complain of a miserable affair of quills and rifles and muskets!" "We must aim at great results. Perfection in matters of detail, if ever attainable, must be left to the future," Clay explained, a remark that reflected Tod's strategy in the design of the bill. And then, for good measure, the Speaker concluded with a stinging rebuke for du Pont's friend: "With respect to your correspondent Mr. Wolcott, he is a sour grumbling unmannerly fellow. And I will thank you to tell him that Congress is not legislating only for the Wolcott Woolen Manufacturing Company but for a great nation & a great national interest."[144]

Still, despite the inevitable friction generated, evidence for a close working relationship between the two groups is provided by the complaints of their opponents. On the floor of the House, Churchill C. Cambreleng of New York charged that "the Committee on Manufactures have adopted, in every instance, the rates proposed by the manufacturers themselves." This was echoed by James Hamilton Jr. of South Carolina, who "believed there had been more outdoor than indoor legislation in regard to the measure. . . . If he had understood correctly, all sorts of pilgrims had travelled to the room of the Committee on Manufactures, from the sturdy iron master down to the poor manufacturer of whetstones, all equally clamorous for the protection 'of a *parental*, of an *American* policy.' " Tod rose to rebut these allegations, declaring that "as to the persons who have attended the Committee of Manufactures, on the invitation of the committee, or without invitation, it is due to them and to us to say, that they have all been citizens of our country, and gentlemen of good appearance and good credit. And it may be further said, that among the few of them who had any particular interest and manufactures of their own to promote, there has been scarcely one who has not gone away disappointed."[145] Yet his critics remained unconvinced. "The more manufacturers have been assisted, the more assistance have they required," wrote one correspondent to the Philadelphia *Aurora*. "Memorials, petitions, addresses, remonstrances, have met the eyes of the committees at every session; & emissaries, agents and borers [a contemporary term for lobbyists] have haunted the doors of the house, like the ghost of the murdered Banquo; as if determined by the certainty of their appearance to destroy the peace of its occupants, till they granted their request."[146]

Advocates of increased duties were not the only ones to make an appearance in Washington, however; their opponents were also beginning to engage in lobbying of their own. Webster, now representing Massachusetts in the House and seeking to balance his obligations to friends engaged in both manufacturing and mercantile pursuits, was one legislator who actively solicited their guidance. Throughout his career, Webster was a frequent recipient of what he referred to as "subscriptions," "gifts," and "sweeteners" from a group of entrepreneurs that historians have dubbed the Boston Associates.[147] In return, Webster promoted the interests of the associates in Congress, and in 1824 those interests were largely still concentrated in commerce, which would suffer under Tod's bill. Webster stayed out of the debate initially, preferring that the measure "should die a natural death, by postponement or other easy violence," but he also transmitted copies to his Boston benefactors, acknowledging: "I am aware that something is expected from me."[148] By way of reply, one of the associates informed Webster that arrangements were being made to "send a deputation to Washington, of some of their practical men."[149] Nathan Appleton, the chronicler of Francis Cabot Lowell's contribution to the Tariff of 1816 and, by his own account, "the largest holder of cotton manufacturing stock in the U.S.," was selected for the mission, and he arrived in the capital at the end of March.[150] There he spent "8 or 10 days … very pleasantly," listening to congressional debates and dining with Webster, whose stance on the tariff, he was able to report, "meets my own views."[151] It was during Appleton's stay that Webster made his most significant intervention in the debate, a speech of two days' duration that directly challenged Clay's attempt to denominate protection for manufactures as an "American policy," although the author admitted that "there may be good reasons for favoring some of the provisions of the bill."[152]

Webster's speech was well received by critics of the bill; "a beautiful and enduring monument" to free trade, one commentator later called it.[153] For these compliments, the speaker was indebted to his collaborators out-of-doors. As New Hampshire representative William Plumer Jr., a close friend of Webster, later recalled: "[T]he knowledge displayed in this speech surprised those who did not know his practice of levying contributions on all occasions, and making other minds subservient to his purposes. He told me that immediately after that bill was reported to the House, he obtained from the printers 50 copies of it. These he sent to the best informed merchants, manufacturers, agriculturalists, and speculative men requesting their opinions and remarks, in detail, on the bill. In due time he received from his correspondents a mass of facts, calculations and reasonings, which furnished abundant materials for debate."[154] This was common practice among members of Congress during this period, who frequently wrote to prominent men to seek their advice on pending legislation.[155] Not everyone was impressed by Webster's contribution, however. "His speech is a plea for his Boston Constituents," remarked one of Clay's correspondents. "[H]e is against it because of them, but he is for those parts which favour their present interests."[156]

Webster's pleading for his constituents reflects an important reality about policymaking during the decade following the War of 1812: the predominance of local over national considerations in elections. With the Federalist-Republican system disintegrating, lawmakers had been free to follow the sentiments of their own districts without regard for party consistency. The situation in 1824 was more complicated, however, because with four contenders for the presidency all running under the Republican banner, attempts to distinguish between them turned on the stance of each candidate, and their supporters in Congress, on the political issues of the day. Clay made his "American System" the centerpiece of his campaign for the White House, but the other three aspirants, Secretary of State John Quincy Adams, Secretary of the Treasury William H. Crawford, and the "Hero of New Orleans" General Andrew Jackson, all equivocated on the subject of protection to avoid alienating potential supporters on the other side of the question. When Jackson publicly declared himself a proponent of a "judicious" tariff, New York senator Martin Van Buren later recalled: "Mr. Clay attempted to scandalize it, for its ambiguity, by a characteristic shrug of his shoulders, a toss of his head and the counter-declaration—'well, by—, I am in favor of an *in*judicious tariff!'"[157] Pennsylvania had no favorite son of her own in the field, and many observers expected the beneficiary of her substantial electoral vote to be determined by the fate of the tariff bill in Congress. Thus, one commentator suggested, "we may imagine the genius of this great state, in the sober guise of a Dutch or Quaker manufacturer, standing before the candidates for the Presidency, and offering to them Mr. Baldwin's bill, in one hand, and a blank ticket in the other."[158]

+ + +

The tariff was before the House for more than two months. It was much amended during that time; whereas in 1820 the bill's managers had sought to preserve the rates reported from committee intact, on this occasion Tod himself proposed several reductions to the original levels in order to conciliate wavering legislators.[159] Of the version that was ultimately passed, Niles reported: "[I]n its present shape, it is far short of what the friends of the measure desired to have—but on that account, perhaps, it may be more agreeable to its opponents, and so stand as a sort of *compromise* between the two great parties."[160] Yet, still, the margin of victory was small. One senator later recalled that on 16 April, the day of the crucial roll call, "several members were brought in upon their sick couches," and only two were absent, which the Washington *National Intelligencer* pronounced to be a record attendance.[161] The result was 107 votes for passage and 102 votes against. Clay was in high spirits, despite several eleventh-hour defections, including Samuel A. Foot of Connecticut and Charles A. Foote of New York. Congratulated by one congressman on the result, the Speaker joked that "we made a good *stand*, considering we lost both our *Feet*."[162]

The Senate received the bill on 19 April and proceeded to pore over it for another three weeks. Southern planters and Northern merchants were proportionally better represented in the upper chamber, and the protectionists were forced to make further concessions to save the measure from defeat. "I inform you that the Senate are cutting up the <u>dear</u> Tariff to your heart's <u>discontent</u>," wrote Congressman Breck, who had fought the bill on behalf of Philadelphia's commercial community, to a friend of opposing sentiments. "Iron & Hemp are gone, and the only encouragement Hemp can now receive, is in the advance that will take place, when the Tariff men buy halters to hang themselves."[163] As it had in 1820, the bill's fate hung in the balance. When Massachusetts senator Elijah H. Mills revealed his intention to depart from Washington early, he found himself "waited upon by our whole delegation, who expressed to me their undivided opinion that I could not go without an inexcusable dereliction of duty." "According to the best calculations that can be made in the Senate, there will not be a single vote to spare,"

Mills explained to his wife, "and if, under these circumstances, I should be gone, and the bill should pass for want of my vote, I should never forgive myself, nor should I ever be forgiven."[164] Though divisions on several amendments to the bill were decided by a single vote, the final roll call was not quite as close as Mills predicted, as it passed the Senate on 13 May by twenty-five yeas to twenty-one nays. A Committee of Conference, consisting of members from both chambers, was required to resolve the differences between the House- and Senate-approved versions, but a compromise was reached with little difficulty and concurred in by both chambers without further dispute.[165] "Its opponents, modified as it has been, now appear to regard it as a *revenue* bill," noted Niles, though he too urged the acceptance of the changes made by the Senate, rather than risk losing the bill entirely by fighting to restore the rates set by the House.[166]

The Tariff of 1824 would not have passed without the aid of Andrew Jackson. The General was placed in a bind by Tod's bill. His hopes of obtaining the White House rested on the backing of both strongly protectionist Pennsylvania and several anti-tariff slave states, hence his equivocal endorsement of a "judicious" solution.[167] But as senator of Tennessee, Jackson was the only candidate who would actually have to vote on the tariff, and in so doing he risked alienating a substantial section of his supporters whatever his course.[168] Congressman Wright, of the Committee on Manufactures, suspected that Jackson's friends in the House were trying to kill the bill there, to relieve their leader of this responsibility, but these efforts failed.[169] Compelled to act, Jackson and his fellow Tennessee senator John H. Eaton, who was also effectively the General's campaign manager, backed several amendments reducing the rates on particular articles but ultimately provided the crucial votes that secured the bill's passage.[170] This decision, one of Wright's correspondents suggested, was directly attributable to the coming presidential election: "Had not Penn: played the fool and nominated him for President he would not have voted for the tariff, neither would his colleague Eaton—We may thank the double folly of Penn: and of Jackson for the tariff."[171]

This episode highlights Jackson's ability to straddle the tariff issue and still retain the backing of both protectionists and free traders, a characteristic that would define his political career. Taking House and Senate together, his supporters provided forty-seven votes for Tod's tariff bill and thirty votes against. Six months later, the General secured electoral votes from twelve states, five of which had favored increased duties in Congress and seven of which had fought them. Clay, who secured electoral votes from only four states, all protectionist, was bitterly disappointed. "It is a little remarkable that my support of the Tariff has excited against me in the South, a degree of opposition, which is by no means counter-balanced by any espousal of my cause in Pennsa. and other quarters, where the Tariff was so much desired," he lamented.[172] Nonetheless, since no candidate achieved a majority in the Electoral College, the contest was thrown into the House of Representatives, where Clay's endorsement of Adams proved sufficient to secure victory for the latter. The new chief executive promptly appointed the Kentuckian as his secretary of state, while the Hero of New Orleans vowed to take his revenge in the next presidential campaign. The old party lines were dissolving, and the new alignments that emerged out of this election would shape the making of tariff policy for decades to come.

Despite all this, regional differences remained more discernible from congressional roll calls on Tod's bill than political affiliations. Southerners in and out of the national legislature were now beginning to adopt the position that federal encouragement to manufactures was not only inexpedient, it was also unconstitutional. Advocates of protection located the necessary authority in Article I, Section 8, which granted Congress the power "to lay and collect Taxes, Duties, Imposts and Excises" and "to regulate Commerce with foreign Nations." Critics retorted that duties should only be laid to raise revenue, not to encourage industry, and the power to regulate commerce did not extend to prohibiting it in order to benefit some other sector of the economy.[173] Behind at least some of these arguments, no doubt, was a fear of what other powers Congress might assume in the future. As John Randolph wrote to a friend, in his customarily colorful style: "[I]t is very plain to me, that if 'Count Tariffe' carries his project, we should be better off as English colonies than nominal allies (like those of Rome) to his Countship: I speak of the slave states."[174] In this context, it must have been of particular concern to strict constructionists like Randolph that certain among those slave states seemed willing to put profit ahead of principle. Across both chambers, the South cast eighty-seven votes against the tariff but also twenty-five votes for it. The latter, from Delaware, Kentucky, Maryland, Missouri, Tennessee, and Virginia, reflected the interest that parts of these states felt in the production of hemp, grain, wool, textiles, and other articles covered by Tod's bill.[175]

As on previous occasions, the North generally backed the bill, providing 107 votes in its favor. Resistance once again came chiefly from districts dependent upon commerce. Of thirty-two free state votes against the bill when it first passed the House, twenty-three were cast by New Englanders, including virtually the entire Massachusetts delegation, along with eight New Yorkers and Samuel Breck alone among Pennsylvania's Representatives. "Our duty, as we thought, was to uphold the shipping interest of our constituencies, which we believed to be in danger of losing its carrying trade, by the passage of a protecting law," the latter subsequently recalled.[176] Unlike in 1820, however, Tod's bill was sufficiently amended in the Senate to preserve it from defeat at the hands of this interest. Only four Northern senators opposed its passage: three from New England and Rufus King of New York. "I suppose it will pass in its modified shape. There is nothing very objectionable about it," Appleton reported.[177] Sure enough, Webster was one of several Massachusetts representatives to switch sides and give the bill his support when it returned to the House for concurrence.[178]

+ + +

The Tariff of 1824 represents the culmination of a campaign for protection that commenced with the cessation of the War of 1812 and was galvanized by the Panic of 1819. It was a success that had been by no means assured. Pro-tariff states may have gained in the decennial reapportionment of the Eighteenth Congress, yet the margin by which John Tod's bill passed the House was smaller than that of Henry Baldwin's bill four years previously.[179] For some contemporaries, the result was more directly attributable to lobbying by its supporters out-of-doors. "I believe the subject never before was so fully discussed in congress nor were the friends of domestic industry ever so well organized before," wrote one Ohio textile manufacturer to a member of the Du Pont clan.[180] Daniel Webster concurred; the measure would never have passed, he judged, "if there were not so many members who would vote on the judgement of their constituents, not on their own."[181] Reflecting three years later, Thomas Cooper assured his fellow Southerners: "I do not therefore consider that tariff as having been passed by our national representatives in congress at Washington, but by the manufacturers and the representatives of the manufacturers." The first of those groups he denominated "a combining, club-meeting, planning, schemeing, petitioning, memorializing, complaining, statement-making, worrying, teasing, boring [i.e., lobbying], persevereing class of men," a description that stands as testament to the indelible impression that the protectionist organization, with Mathew Carey in its vanguard, had made upon their opponents.[182]

The Tariff of 1824 demonstrated that lobbyists for increased duties, and their allies in the legislature, had learned from their previous mistakes. The new bill offered enhanced, and more extensive, barriers against foreign competition than the Tariff of 1816, which it replaced, but at the same time it departed more readily from the abstract principle of protection that Baldwin had clung to in 1820, sacrificing some industries that needed encouragement, and rewarding others that did not, in order to win over crucial votes on the floor. Under the leadership of Henry Clay, the friends of the tariff also proved increasingly adept at using the committee system, which during this period reached maturation with the establishment of separate bodies for manufactures and agriculture alongside commerce. Indeed, Clay's role highlights the particular value now attached to the Speakership. As one spectator of the contest to elect a successor to the Kentuckian commented: "[T]he election of a Speaker is a matter of great importance and produces no little excitement; more so now than formerly. The power vested in him of appointing all the committees is a very formidable one; because as the management of business is almost entirely in the hands of those committees, the power which appoints them may be said to control the proceedings of the House." One implication of this development, the same observer noted in passing, was that "if Speaker be so disposed, he may cause a great deal of trouble and embarrassment to the administration, by appointing committees hostile to its measures."[183] The accuracy of this forecast would be attested to during the presidency of John Quincy Adams, with important implications for the making of tariff policy.

Prophetic too was Eleazar Lord's explanation of regional voting patterns on the tariff as reflecting more than what Baldwin attributed merely to ill-feeling over the Missouri Controversy. "Why have not the representatives from the middle and northern states been more <u>united</u> in questions relative to the manufactures and industry of their states? And why have the representatives from the Southern states been uniformly opposed to the others on these questions?" he pressed Carey. The answer, he suggested, is that "in the Southern states there is but one great and general interest. This interest is liable to no fluctuations or changes—the labor is done by slaves who can neither remove, nor apply their industry to new objects. The representatives therefore are always united as to their great interest and have taken ample care to protect it by law." In the North, by contrast, "there are several leading interests; agriculture, trade, manufactures, commerce. Every man goes and comes as he pleases, changes the object of pursuit whenever he is so disposed. Representatives are chosen who are partisans to their several interests, and, being assured that they cannot consist together, their representatives are never united on questions that concern any one of them," a flaw that proved fatal to the Baldwin Bill of 1820 and came close to defeating its successor in 1824.[184] In this analysis, sectional divisions over protection were rooted in a fundamental difference in the economic organization of the slave and free states.

For both Carey and Clay, this realization only prompted them to redouble their efforts to convert Southerners to the benefits of a secure home market, an obsession that would ultimately lure the Kentuckian into his greatest misstep in the Compromise of 1833.[185] And yet there was an alternative logic in Lord's conclusion that "nothing is wanting to our object . . . but union among those who ought to be united."[186] Disgusted by the South's intransigence in the Sixteenth Congress, William Lee had warned that "the great object now is to create a number of new slave states so as to give that interest the preponderance in our country. A direct tax or a discriminating duty to protect your rising fabrics will then be opposed with success. . . . [D]o you think the Southern nabob will permit you to tax him? No he will enjoy his thousands a year and make you pay the piper."[187] If the economic differences caused by slavery really were too great to be overcome, then only a struggle for political dominance between the sections could decide the fate of the tariff; or, as another Carey correspondent advised, "the sooner the line is drawn & union established between the non Slaveholders, the better."[188] Such views still remained a distinct minority among protectionists at this juncture, but within them were seeds that would eventually reach fruition with the rise of the Republican Party in the 1850s.[189]

For the present, though, individuals on both sides of the tariff question professed to be satisfied with the outcome. North Carolina representative Willie P. Mangum had voted nay on both its original passage and when it was returned to the House for concurrence but afterward wrote that "the Bill as passed is not so exceedingly objectionable, instead of being a law for the *protection* of Domestic Manufactures, it is a revenue bill—[i]t was gutted in the Senate."[190] Clay, meanwhile, admitted that "the measure of protection which it extends to Domestic industry is short of what it should have been." "But we have succeeded in establishing the principle," he continued, "and hereafter I apprehend less difficulty will be encountered in giving to it a more comprehensive & vigorous application."[191] If opponents of high duties hoped that the Tariff of 1824 would be the final word on the matter, they would soon be disappointed. Yet at the same time, the consolidation of previously inchoate partisan and sectional alignments would only further complicate the task of lobbyists for a protective tariff.

chapter three

"An Engine of *Party* Purposes"
The Woollens Bill of 1827 and the Tariff of 1828

O N 30 JULY 1827, a "General Convention, of Agriculturalists and Manufacturers, and others friendly to the Encouragement and Support of
the Domestic Industry of the United States," opened to much fanfare in
Harrisburg, Pennsylvania.[1] It was by far the most ambitious protectionist
gathering to date, with nearly one hundred delegates arriving from across
the Union, including such luminaries as Mathew Carey, Hezekiah Niles, and
Eleazar Lord. "We may venture to assert, with little fear of contradiction,
that [the convention] embraced men of the greatest talent, ever assembled
in our legislative hall, or indeed perhaps, in any deliberative national assembly, since the congress of '76," boasted one local newspaper.[2] And yet there
were some notable absences from the protectionist roster. Louis McLane,
part of the circle of manufacturers who had deputed Isaac Briggs to represent their interests in Washington in 1816, and subsequently himself elected
to Congress, where he gave his votes in favor of the tariff bills of 1820 and
1824, was one who declined a nomination to attend by his Delaware constituents. McLane assigned as his reason the appearance of impropriety if
"I should, by participating in the deliberations of the Harrisburg convention,
commit myself in relation to particular measures, on which I may hereafter
be called to act in my public representative capacity." Yet he also concluded
his letter with a cryptic warning: "any administration of the general government" must acknowledge protectionism as "essentially connected with the
national prosperity," unless "its friends, consenting to use it as an engine of
party purposes, involve it in the fate of *party* struggles."[3]

Unfortunately for supporters of a higher tariff, this was precisely the fate
that would befall their favorite measure in the run-up to the presidential
election of 1828. The contest was first renewed by Massachusetts mill own-

ers who initiated a campaign for federal intervention on their behalf, hoping to forge an alliance with wool growers in other states who depended upon the manufacturers for their own market. Still, this focus on just one branch of industry represented a shift in strategy, and one that caused divisions within the protectionist ranks. And these divisions were exacerbated by the escalating struggle between supporters of John Quincy Adams, who aspired to build a nationwide majority coalition around the American System program of his secretary of state Henry Clay, and their opponents, who backed his rival Andrew Jackson and sought to tar the administration as preoccupied with facilitating the pet project of a regional minority from the president's native New England. Despite significant lobbying, the wool manufacturers proved unable to enact their Woollens Bill in the waning days of the Nineteenth Congress. But this failure only prompted a redoubling of their efforts, culminating in the convention at Harrisburg, which set the agenda for the next meeting of the national legislature. In response, the Twentieth Congress did eventually approve a substantial revision of the rates, but the product of their deliberations was profoundly shaped by the approaching presidential election, leaving both friends and opponents of protection dissatisfied with what has gone down in history as the Tariff of Abominations.

+ + +

"It appears to me that all the principal interests which [the Tariff of 1824] was passed to protect have been protected," declared Rhode Island representative Dutee Pearce in January 1827, "except that of the woollen manufacturer—an interest as important as any in this country."[4] The Tariff of 1824 had indeed proved a disappointment to that sector. The ad valorem duty on woolen textiles had been raised from 25 percent to 33⅓ percent, but the duty on raw wool was also increased as part of its sponsors' bid to conciliate the agricultural interest, rising from 15 percent to 30 percent by the middle of 1826. Manufacturers could now sell at a higher price, but they would pay a higher price for their materials too. Furthermore, a clause in the bill reported by John Tod that would have imposed a minimum valuation on woolens, like that which already existed for cotton textiles, was purged in the Senate. This left producers exposed at the lower end of the market and did nothing to prohibit the widespread practice of merchants fraudulently undervaluing their cargoes in order to pay a reduced tax. Finally, Britain responded by slashing its own duty on imported wool, with the express purpose of allowing its manufacturers to continue to undersell their American competitors.[5]

Pearce was also correct in his emphasis on the economic importance of the woolens industry, particularly to New England. The monied-men of that region, already attracted by the profits realized by the Boston Manufacturing Company under lower rates, responded to the Tariff of 1824 by transferring their capital from commerce into textile manufacturing. Factories mushroomed almost overnight, only to be swamped by a glut of goods from across the Atlantic. By the beginning of 1827, Niles was reporting that "there is not at this day a single woollen establishment in N. England in full operation."[6] Daniel Webster, who had been permitted by his canny manufacturing friends to purchase thousands of dollars' worth of shares in their projects on credit, was now pressed by them to intervene.[7] "Our woolen manufacturers are meeting with great difficulties, from the low prices of the imported articles, & the high price of wool," he wrote to Ohio representative John C. Wright, who served on the Committee on Manufactures in 1824, before the opening of the second session of the Nineteenth Congress. "It is supposed that several of the establishments, this way, will stop unless relieved by a further interposition of the Govt., either to reduce the tax on wool, or enhance that on cloth," Webster reported. "I suppose your neighbours, engaged in that line of business, have heard, or will hear from their friends in this quarter; and I mention the subject to you now, by request, in order that you may confer with them on the subject, prepatory to the meeting of Congress."[8]

As promised, Webster's manufacturing associates were indeed active. Meetings of woolens producers were held in Boston in September, October, and November 1826, and it was agreed to petition Congress for further protection. A circular letter was also prepared for distribution throughout the country, urging "that meetings be held of manufacturers of wool, and that memorials be prepared and sent to the national legislature, praying for an increase of duties."[9] The five signatures affixed to this missive tell us something about the men at the forefront of this new push for increased duties. All five were proprietors of, or heavily invested in, woolen factories. They included James Wolcott Jr., the "sour grumbling unmannerly fellow" who had provoked Clay in 1824, and Lewis Tappan, a cloth merchant–turned-manufacturer more famous today for bankrolling the abolitionist movement.[10] Chief among them was Jonas B. Brown, "the *working-man* of the whole concern," according to one Boston newspaper editor.[11] Even Carey, who carped on about the lack of support he received from other quarters, considered Brown "one of the few men to have displayed a proper spirit on this subject."[12]

The Boston meetings resolved to focus on securing increased protection for woolen textiles only, rather than demanding another general increase in rates. This reflected their frustration with the Tariff of 1824. "[I]t is abominable on the woollens," Victor du Pont had complained while that measure was still under consideration, adding that "the only way to go to work, was to pass one or two short bills every year, go on gradually and separately, begin by iron, woollen, paper, hemp, cotton, never mind which is taken first, but take them one after another; any member can vote at once, without all this battle array & systematic opposition to a mammoth tariff."[13] "If the Woollen Manufacturers had memorialized Congress unconnected with any other interests or Manufacturers, I think they would have succeeded better," agreed another observer.[14] Yet the mill owners were also conscious that they could not accomplish their object if they antagonized the wool growers, who formed an influential constituency in several states. For this reason, the Boston memorial did not request a reduction in the duty on wool, or even an increase in the duty on textiles, only the imposition of a system of minimum valuation. "Such a measure may protect the manufacturer. It can injure no one," the authors claimed, pointing out that more demand for their product would benefit domestic suppliers of their chief raw material.[15]

The second session of the Nineteenth Congress opened on 4 December 1826 and soon received numerous petitions on the subject of the tariff from both wool manufacturers and growers, which, as had become customary, were referred to the Committee on Manufactures. Tod had retired from the House after his success in 1824 and was replaced as chair of the committee by Rollin C. Mallary, the Vermont representative who Carey claimed credit for converting to protectionism.[16] To assist Mallary in crafting a suitable bill, the Boston manufacturers dispatched Brown to Washington along with two others from among their ranks: Isaac C. Bates and Aaron Tufts. "The deputation was sent to represent to the Congress of the United States the depressed state of the woollen manufacture, the consequent low price of wool, the great influx of foreign woolen goods, as connected with that subject, and to obtain further protection to the wool-growers and manufacturers of woolens," Tufts subsequently recalled.[17] They spoke before the Committee on Manufactures, as Isaac Briggs and his associates had in 1816, and that body duly prepared a bill that would impose a graduated minimum valuation on woolen textiles, as well as further increase the duty on raw wool to 35 percent in 1828 and 40 percent the year after. At first glance, this package might seem like a defeat for the manufacturers, but, in fact, the minimum was so arranged as to provide them with substantial protection, notwithstanding the anticipated rise in the cost of their materials; a piece of cloth valued at 41 cents, for example, would be assessed as if its value was actually $2.50, and thus pay an effective rate of over 200 percent, much higher than the nominal rate that remained at 33⅓ percent.[18] The Boston manufacturers seemed well pleased with the efforts of their lobby. "[T]he delegates did all in their power, and all that could be done," declared Abbott Lawrence, another contributor to the campaign.[19]

+ + +

Mallary reported the Woollens Bill to the House on 10 January 1827. With Clay serving as secretary of state and Webster preferring to labor behind the scenes, the Vermonter would take chief responsibility for its defense on the floor. Attacks duly arrived from the expected quarters. The minimum provision was merely a "*disguise*," claimed Churchill C. Cambreleng, and "very few members were aware that under it almost the entire mass of woollen manufactures consumed in the country would be prohibited—absolutely prohibited." Furthermore, the New Yorker warned, "it would be impossible to touch this subject without reviving the whole question of our tariff," and legislators would be compelled to "go from one article to another; . . . from woollen manufactures to bar iron; from bar iron to cotton bagging."[20] Yet criticism came too from some professed friends of the tariff, on precisely the grounds that the protection offered was too partial in its operation. Samuel D. Ingham declared the measure "an effort among a powerful class of men, as we now perceive, to persuade Congress to make up to them the loss of a bad season's business."[21] His fellow Pennsylvanian James Buchanan cautioned that whereas "our former tariffs have been a compromise among the various and extended interests of the Union," the pending bill "embraces a single article of manufactures, and seeks to establish a local monopoly in New England." Buchanan moved to recommit the bill to the Committee on Manufactures with instructions to increase duties on a range of additional articles.[22] Its supporters protested that the effect of motion would be "to defeat the bill for the present session, by procrastination," and were just barely able to prevent it from being pushed through by an odd coalition of free traders and disgruntled mid-Atlantic protectionists.[23] Whether the latter, who were mainly Jacksonians, were more disgruntled by the content of the bill or its identification with the Adams administration became the subject of much dispute in the press, with rumors that a secret "caucus" held at the commencement of the session "to concentrate the present scattered members of the opposition" had resolved "*that the law should not pass.*"[24]

Questions were also asked as to why the new minimums would come into effect from 1 August 1827, but the duty on wool would not increase until ten months later. Mallary explained that the reason for the deferral was that "the farmers would not at once be able to supply the demand for the raw material, and would require at least a year to increase their flocks."[25] Critics, however, sought to divest the bill of support among the agricultural community by charging that the manufacturers intended to "supply themselves with a stock of wool by importation, and thus anticipate the farmers market."[26] The Boston lobbyists would subsequently face accusations of "acting in bad faith towards the wool growers." In response, Brown maintained that *"he and his associates had been sent* [to Washington] *by the manufacturers,* and not by wool growers," but that they had nonetheless "truly represented" the interests of both constituencies. In any case, agents of "the wool growers in Virginia and Ohio" had also appeared before the Committee on Manufactures and asked only for incremental increases of 2 percent on their product, not the 5 percent actually written into the bill.[27] Nonetheless, suspicions persisted, and divisions between producers of raw materials and finished goods, just as between larger and small manufacturers, would continue to dog the protectionist coalition in the decades that followed.[28]

The bill's backers responded to these assaults by seeking to rally support outside of New England. Writing from Washington, Brown implored Victor du Pont to "urge the importance of this measure" upon legislators from Pennsylvania and Delaware. "I well know that letters from practical men have an important influence with Members of Congress," he insisted.[29] In a subsequent letter, the Bostonian elaborated on his fears that the Pennsylvania delegation would oppose the bill. "Can you not in some way bring the wishes of their constituents to operate upon them?" he pleaded. "[N]ew memorials from Pennsylvania would be of immense benefit to us, a memorial from your state ought by all means to be prepared immediately if no more than ten or twenty persons sign it, . . . I am convinced you may do much toward carrying the bill though."[30] Du Pont, in turn, sought to enlist Carey's pen for the cause.[31] "I have shewn [your letter] in confidence to our Great General Mathew Carey, who is better acquainted than I am with Pennsylvania Politics & Pennsylvania members of Congress," he informed Brown, adding that he too was in correspondence with various lawmakers.[32]

Securing Carey's cooperation could prove tricky, however, for the Philadelphian was growing increasingly frustrated by what he felt was a lack of appreciation for his efforts from his fellow protectionists. The Philadelphia Society had terminated in acrimony after several members refused to pay for a series of pamphlets that he had written without their sanction. "In a fit of scorn and indignation," the author subsequently recalled, "I withdrew from the society—justly considering that if I had to write, and print, and publish, and pay the expense of paper and printing, I had no need of a society."[33] Carey also resented the timing of New England's sudden conversion to the benefits of high rates, which he berated in a series of circular letters to his erstwhile allies. When they were interested primarily in cotton manufacture, which was adequately protected under the Tariff of 1816, they proved themselves "wholly indifferent about the rest of the industry of the country" by their votes against the Tariff of 1824, he observed. But many of them, having since switched their investments into the woolens industry, "which is now in the same danger of ruin as menaced other branches in 1824," suddenly "their eyes [were] wonderfully opened, to see the necessity of further protection."[34] This situation was exacerbated when one of the Boston meetings failed to give Carey the praise he felt he was due because they feared it would offend Webster and others who had been severely criticized by the Philadelphian for their past opposition to protection.[35] "What a pity he is so irascible and what a pity we do not better acknowledge his indefatigable services in the cause, by compliments which would cost us very little as he really deserves them, and would be to him the best of remuneration for his toils & expenses," du Pont wrote to Brown. "Entre nous he is very sore at your having denied him a vote of thanks in your Massachusetts Convention and you were wrong—he would write no more, and the next day began a new series of numbers on the woollen interest."[36] Carey would indeed publish in support of the Woollens Bill, but he remained skeptical that such partial legislation could pass Congress.[37]

+ + +

Time would prove Carey correct. The Woollens Bill did pass the House on 10 February 1827, with 106 votes in favor and 95 against. But after two weeks before the Senate, and with the end of the session just three days away, a motion to lay the bill on the table, postponing its consideration indefinitely, resulted in a tie with twenty votes on either side. Vice President John C. Calhoun, the South Carolinian who had supported the Tariff of 1816 but since embraced his section's aversion to protection, cast the deciding vote to kill the bill. This outcome had actually been predicted by Clay prior to the election of 1824: "If Mr. Calhoun is elected [vice president] we shall have, in a body already nearly equally divided as to that policy, the presiding officer against us. I *know* that his opinion is that the Tariff of 1816 went far enough, and that he was opposed to that of the last Session. But if he were favorably inclined towards that policy, he would be controled by his Southern position."[38]

Historians have speculated that the tie was engineered as part of a plot to destroy support in the North for Calhoun, who harbored hopes of riding

Jackson's coattails into the presidency, by forcing him to go on record with his opposition to protection.[39] Such concerted action seems unlikely. Eight senators were absent for the crucial roll call, some of whom were considered friendly to the bill; there was little incentive for these men to participate in a scheme that would result in the defeat of a piece of legislation they desired, even if it did serve to embarrass a political opponent.[40] It is possible, however, that at least one of the absentees had an ulterior motive. New York senator Martin Van Buren was seeking to build a national party organization behind Jackson's presidential bid and was therefore a rival of Calhoun for the General's favor. The Woollens Bill placed Van Buren in a difficult position; many of his own constituents were wool growers, but his political ambitions also made it imperative that he retain the support of Southerners who opposed any increase in the cost of the "coarse woollens" in which they clothed their slaves, the very article that would be most affected by the proposed minimum valuation. The senator was logged as present shortly before the final roll call, but his name was notably absent from the yeas and nays on that division.[41] Van Buren subsequently claimed that he had been fulfilling a promise "to accompany a friend on a visit to the Congressional Cemetery," but his critics charged that "finding the friends of the Tariff more powerful than he expected, [he] was compelled to absent himself from the Senate, and by refusing to vote suffered the bill to be lost."[42] It would not be the last time that the Little Magician was suspected of making mischief on the tariff.

Analysis of the key roll calls in Congress confirms the shift in regional preferences on this issue. Taking House and Senate together, the slave states provided ninety-three votes against and only nine votes in favor, the latter scattered among the Kentucky, Maryland, Missouri, and Virginia delegations. Concerned solely with wool and woolens, this bill offered even less benefit to Southerners than previous incarnations, and sectional sentiment hardened accordingly. The free states, meanwhile, provided 117 votes in its favor and 22 votes against, a spread not hugely dissimilar to the Tariff of 1824. But whereas more than two-thirds of Northern opposition on that occasion had come from New England, three years later just five negative votes were cast by the same region. This swing was partially counterbalanced by some dissatisfaction among the mid-Atlantic delegations, with seven Pennsylvanians rejecting the bill, but was still sufficient to see it through the House. Buchanan blamed this result on a "coalition between the East & the West," plus "the votes of 19 Pennsylvanians—who whilst many of them disapproved of the Bill, believe their constituents to be so tariff mad that they were afraid to vote against it."[43] In the Senate, however, where free and slave states were equally balanced, it was the almost unanimous hostility of the latter that left the final decision in the hands of Calhoun.

Partisan alignments also shaped preferences on the bill. Supporters of Adams gave ninety-eight votes for and twenty-one against the bill, while the opposition coalescing around Jackson gave twenty-eight votes in favor and ninety-four against. Of twenty-two Northern votes against the bill, seventeen were cast by Jacksonians, including Cambreleng, Buchanan, and Ingham, all of whom were identified as attending the secretive caucus at the commencement of the session.[44] For Webster, who had thrown in his lot with Adams and Clay, the Woollens Bill, though defeated, was "attended with important political results" that boded well for the administration. "B[uchanan], I[ngham] & others, went over to the *anti protection* party, & made an effort to take their friends with them, but it *did not succeed*," he crowed. "It is supposed Pennsylvania will perceive, ere long, that she must give up, either her favourite *Candidate*, or her favourite *system of politics*."[45] Some among the opposition were reluctantly reaching the same conclusion. Pennsylvania representative Andrew Stewart, who earned the nickname "Tariff Andy" for his wholehearted endorsement of protectionism, wrote to John Tod while the bill was still before the House that "I fear Genl. Jackson's friends are going to make Interl. Impts. & Dom. Manufactures the rallying ground of opposition to the administration[;] in this you know we can't go with them & in Pa. it will have a bad effect. This policy is too important to us to be surrendered for any consideration. We can't give up measures for men, at least, measures of such vital concern."[46] Stewart supported the bill, and soon after switched his allegiance to the administration.

Southern Jacksonians, meanwhile, were resolute in their hostility to protection; eight of the nine slave state votes for the Woollens Bill were provided by Adams supporters. McLane, who had cast Delaware's lone vote in the House for protection in both 1820 and 1824, was a notable defector to the opposition on this occasion. "While the votes of the manufacturers were of importance to him at a popular election—he was their staunchest friend; but those votes being no longer useful to him, he joins in the coalition of the south against the north, because by doing so he may reap some advantage at a future day if that party should prevail," remarked the state's administration senator Thomas Clayton, though he too voted against the bill.[47] Writing to Jackson shortly after Congress adjourned, South Carolina senator Robert Y. Hayne was adamant that "the people of the South (as you know) are opposed to this system in any shape." Still, he assured the General, "they can and always will distinguish, between those who supported the Tariff of

1824 (as modified in the Senate,) and those who advocate such a Bill as that of the last session, between one (who like yourself) looks to the moderate protection of manufactures, without oppressing any branch of Industry, and one (who like Mr. Clay) wishes to form a party, & for purposes *purely self-ish*, convert the whole system of Internal Improvement & the Tariff into a political engine, of management, intrigue and corruption."[48] Hayne's letter illustrates how partisan considerations were beginning to seriously interfere with the making of tariff policy. It was also a profession of faith in his preferred presidential candidate's capacity to redress Southern grievances that the author would live to regret.

+ + +

"During the session of congress, 1826–7, the manufacturers of Boston and its vicinity incurred great expense for agents to attend at Washington, in the capacity of what are vulgarly termed 'borers,'" Carey reflected in his autobiography. "This was doubtless a wise measure—but lost half, or more than half its value, by the want of adequate previous publications, to open the eyes not merely of the members, but of their constituents." Carey appreciated the worth of lobbying, but he believed it must be situated within a wider campaign to convince the American people of the need for protection. "If they were converted," he concluded, "the conversion of their representatives would follow of course."[49] With this object in mind, the Philadelphian was one of the principal movers in a project that emerged from the failure of the Woollens Bill to call a new national protectionist convention.

The Harrisburg Convention was proposed by the Pennsylvania Society for the Promotion of Manufactures and the Mechanic Arts, an organization that Carey had helped establish in 1826 as a successor to the earlier Pennsylvania Society.[50] The members met on 14 May 1827 to discuss "the depressed state of the woollen manufacture, and of the market for wool, together with the injurious effect the depression of those two important branches must have on other departments of industry, and on the general welfare." The result was a resolution calling on the "farmers, manufacturers, and friends of both branches of industry, to hold conventions in their respective states as early as convenient in the month of June next, to appoint at least five delegates from each state, to meet in general convention at Harrisburg, Pennsylvania, on the thirtieth day of July, to deliberate on what measures are proper to be taken, in the present posture of their affairs."[51] The idea for such a convention did not originate with the Pennsylvania Society, however. Instead, it came from Lewis Tappan, one of the Boston manufacturers, who suggested it to Carey in a letter dated 4 May. The Philadelphian, as chair of the Acting Committee of the Society, then presented the scheme for its public endorsement.[52] Presumably, given criticism of the Woollens Bill as a measure designed solely to benefit New England, Tappan deemed it advisable to have the call for such an assembly emanate from outside of the region. If so, the ruse appears to have succeeded—even one month after the convention met. Secretary of the Treasury Richard Rush informed Charles J. Ingersoll, the president of the resurrected Pennsylvania Society, that "the idea of the thing having originated in N. England is new to me—I never heard of it as springing from that quarter."[53]

The project did face allegations of a different sort, however. "The real design of this convention at Harrisburg is not to advance American industry, but to organize a political club under the direction of the Administration of the general government to direct and control public sentiment and particularly to operate upon the election in the state of Pennsylvania," was the message of the Pittsburgh *Mercury*. Henry Baldwin, now firmly in the Jackson camp, provided the editor with a letter from a Kentucky correspondent, who contended that "doubtless there are manufacturers among its members, who think they have an interest in its proceedings; but the greater part of them are unquestionably actuated only by a desire to seduce Pennsylvania from the cause of Jackson, under false pretences that himself and friends are opposed to a tariff, while Mr. Adams is in its favor."[54] How far these claims were simply the invention of Jacksonians from protectionist districts who feared that their electoral prospects would be damaged by a reinvigorated campaign for increased duties is open to debate. Evidence from private correspondence suggests that some politicians at least genuinely believed them. John C. Calhoun wrote to his brother-in-law that since the defeat of the Woollens Bill, "an extensive scheme, originating, as it is thought, with those in power, has been got up to have a general convention of the manufact[ur]ing interest at Harrisburgh [*sic*], avowedly to devise measures for the passage of this Bill."[55] From Connecticut, meanwhile, another Jacksonian reported that in conversation with an administration congressman, the latter had let slip that "the friends of the American System means the friends of Adams and Clay and none are to attend our meeting but such."[56]

Advocates of the convention were quick to deny these charges. "The friends of Domestic Manufactures would have been madmen to break down their strength by mingling the economical plans with political matters," declared the Philadelphia *Democratic Press*.[57] Carey wrote a letter for publication in the *National Intelligencer* in which he admitted to being "myself decidedly in favour of the administration," but nevertheless maintained that he could "never consent to be instrumental in amalgamating the question of the presidency with that of the protection of manufactures." "The former question," he explained, "I consider as comparatively insignificant."[58] Niles, meanwhile, urged "those interested, who apprehend, or *affect* to believe, that the object of this convention is connected with the presidential election, . . . to wait a little—for the meetings will be public, and the whole proceedings shall be proclaimed as 'on the house top.' "[59]

These denials were likely sincere. Carey and Niles were both fiercely proud of their independence, and it would be out of character for either to agree to act as a tool for partisan ends.[60] It is true that Clay had been communicating with sympathetic politicians on the need to unite "friends of D[omestic] M[anufactures] I[nternal] I[improvements] and the Admin." in Pennsylvania for some time, but no suggestion of using a national convention for the purpose appears in his surviving papers.[61] Two letters that the secretary of state exchanged with Carey in May 1827 also contain no hint of collusion.[62] And other prominent members of the administration also appear unaware of any plot. "I am sure that you were the first person from whom I ever heard of the project of the Harrisburg Convention as it finally assembled," Rush assured Ingersoll. "So thinks Mr. Clay also, viz that it was from you he first heard of it, either as mentioned by yourself to him, or by me."[63]

Still, administration supporters were quick to see how the proposed convention could be turned to their advantage. On hearing of the plan from Ingersoll, Rush pronounced it "highly judicious and expedient" and offered to help in any way he could.[64] "We are much excited on the subjects of internal improvement & domestic manufactures.—These will form the turning point of Penna. politics. If we can completely identify the present administration with these favourite measures, all will be well," reported one of Clay's contacts in Pennsylvania.[65] "We shall send a very numerous delegation to the Harrisburg Convention, as well on account of the intrinsic importance of its objects, as because it will afford a favourable opportunity to the friends of the Admn for concerting the means of counteracting the systematic attacks of the opposition," added another from New York.[66] Daniel Webster, who no doubt saw the scheme as a chance to benefit both his political allies and his wealthy benefactors, wrote to friends in other states urging them to make the required arrangements, and even persuaded his brother Ezekiel to attend as part of a contingent from New Hampshire.[67]

Inevitably then partisan considerations thrust themselves into many of the meetings that were called all across the free states, and in some of the slave states too, to choose delegates to Harrisburg. In Albany, New York, Van Buren made an unexpected appearance to defend his course on the Woollens Bill. In a lengthy address, the Little Magician managed to win over his audience without ever actually committing himself to the support of protection; he subsequently recounted in his autobiography a conversation between two friends who agreed that the speech had been "very able" but were unable to answer "on which side of the Tariff question was it?"[68] One point on which Van Buren did make himself clear was his caution against "the feverish attempts of designing partizans, and the artful contrivances [*sic*] of those who seek to pervert a great national question to their own personal and political advantage."[69] In Wilmington, Delaware, E. I. du Pont was determined to have "an american meeting, adopting the purest american measures without any distinction or influence of political party of any kind," but when a slate of five Adams and three Jackson delegates was selected to attend at Harrisburg, the latter, McLane among them, all declined their appointments.[70] And in Pennsylvania, Baldwin and Tod also refused to involve themselves; the former, Niles reported, "is d—— [damned] in his own city," as a result.[71] These interactions remind us of what Reeve Huston has described as the "dialectical relationship" between an emerging national party system and extrapartisan or explicitly nonpartisan movements, as both administration and Jackson camps sought to co-opt the enthusiasm generated by the tariff issue even as the demands of rival protectionist and free trade constituencies shaped what was possible for ambitious politicians.[72]

Preparations in Pennsylvania were also disrupted by discord between Carey and other leading protectionists. "A variety of circumstances concurred to induce me to believe, that in the course of this year, a regular plan was formed to lay me aside, and bring forward '*eleventh hour men*' in my stead," the Philadelphian later recalled in his autobiography.[73] Principal among these "*eleventh hour men*" was Ingersoll, who Carey suspected was behind an attempt to exclude him "by dextrous management" from the delegation to Harrisburg, which was chosen at a state convention. "It was agreed by the members from the city and county [of Philadelphia], that they should nominate Mr. Ingersoll, Mr. Huston and me," he explained. But when the moment arrived, "my name, however, was unexpectedly omitted, to the surprize of those who were not in the secret." Fortunately for Carey, "a member from a distant county, indignant at this manoeuvre, defeated it by nominating me."[74] The situation was then exacerbated when Carey's efforts to amend the address of the state convention, which had been drafted by Ingersoll, were summarily rebuffed. Carey consequently refused to append his signature to the finished article, "even at the expense of a warm personal altercation with the writer," and the presence of both men in Pennsylvania's delegation to the national convention hardly boded well for the harmony of that assembly.[75]

+ + +

"The town at this time is in a complete bustle; every stage that arrives adds to the number of visiters [*sic*], already extremely numerous," reported the editor of the Philadelphia *United States Gazette* who was in Harrisburg to observe the opening of the convention on 30 July.[76] Ninety-eight delegates, representing thirteen of the twenty-four states in the Union, would participate in its deliberations.[77] McLane's opinion on the impropriety of sitting legislators attending did not prevent two senators and four representatives from taking part, including Mallary, who remained chair of the Committee on Manufactures.[78] A further nineteen of the delegates had previously served in Congress, a figure that illustrates both the familiarity that the convention possessed with the legislative process and also the permeable boundary between business and politics in this era of high turnover; of that nineteen, nearly half had served only a single term before returning to their previous occupation.[79] Niles claimed that a majority of the members were "agriculturalists," but there were plenty of representatives for the manufacturing interest too, and some familiar faces among them, in addition to those already mentioned.[80] Massachusetts sent Jonas B. Brown, along with Abbott Lawrence and Bezaleel Taft Jr., who had helped Brown agitate for the Woollens Bill, and from New Jersey came Charles Kinsey, a charter member of Burrill, Davis & Co. in 1816. "There never was an assembly of the same number of individuals in this country, which contained so much practical knowledge," concluded the editor of the *Gazette* proudly.[81]

The most important decision facing the Harrisburg Convention was whether to concentrate on securing passage of legislation resembling the recently defeated Woollens Bill or inaugurate a new campaign for a general revision of rates. The original call of the Pennsylvania Society had suggested the former, but this approach was subsequently challenged. German political economist Friedrich List, residing for a time in Pennsylvania, wrote a series of public letters at the invitation of Ingersoll in which he declared: "I believe it to be a duty of the General Convention at Harrisburg, not only to support the interests of the wool growers and wool manufacturers, but to lay the axe to the root of the tree, by declaring the system of Adam Smith and Co. to be erroneous—by declaring war against it on the part of the American System."[82] In the convention itself, Carey too came out for a broader conception of their object. "He now thought it not only policy, but justice to place in the bill to be offered to Congress, as many interests as possible," the Philadelphian explained. "Gentleman talked of jeopardizing the bill, by crowding it with an enumeration of articles that required protection; the contrary was the fact; . . . the more subjects enumerated, the more would be interested in its passage, the greater would be the extent of territory to be benefitted by granting the petitions for aid, and consequently the greater would be the number of voices to be raised in its behalf."[83] The result was that while one committee was appointed to begin work on a memorial to Congress focusing on wool and woolens, other committees were also appointed to report on the expediency of providing further protection to a host of other articles.[84]

The staffing of these committees provided the occasion for a renewal of divisions within the Pennsylvania ranks. Carey found himself excluded from all the important assignments, subsequently learning from a friend that "*much pains were taken by the Pennsylvania delegation, or most of them, to keep you in the back ground*."[85] Another member allowed the Philadelphian to assume his place on the memorial committee, but this immediately threw Carey into collision with Ingersoll, who chaired that body. The former drafted a petition, but the latter opposed its adoption, claiming that nothing satisfactory could be produced while the convention was sitting, and asking the members to delegate the task to him and a few associates to complete after it had adjourned. Jonathan Roberts, the former Pennsylvania senator who had called Carey a "mad man" in 1820 but now emerged as one of his staunchest supporters, wrote privately that Ingersoll "was present, more for personal than public ends; & from innate crookedness was willing to thwart Carey . . . being desirous of a mission to Washington." The convention refused Ingersoll's request but permitted him to take charge of drafting a memorial to be signed by the members the following day. "The convention clos'd its deliberations in good feeling; & Mr. Ingersoll miss'd his mission to Washington," recalled Roberts, but Carey was less pleased with the outcome and subsequently addressed a fiery letter to all those present, complaining about the way he had been treated. Ingersoll's conduct "threw me off my guard," he wrote ruefully in his autobiography, and "made me display a degree of temper which I ought to have controlled, and of course exhibited me in a very disadvantageous light to a body of respectable men assembled from thirteen different states."[86]

The memorial of the Harrisburg Convention focused primarily on the woolen interest, arguing that "forty millions of manufacturing capital, together with forty millions of farming capital, composing this great national concern, for want of adequate protection, have lost half their value."[87] But it also recommended increased protection for iron, steel, flax, hemp, distilled spirits, and cotton textiles; its vision was not merely a revived version of the Woollens Bill, of which Carey observed that "its best friends now acknowledge was not very judiciously drawn up," but something more wide-ranging, which would reconcile the various interests now clamoring for the attention of Congress.[88] The memorial was accompanied by an address to the American people, produced by a committee chaired by Niles, who was granted more time to collect additional information through contacts made at the convention. "I am at work about eight hours a day, & shall hardly finish in less than 10 days more," the latter reported to Ingersoll three weeks after the adjournment. "It must not be hurried. It is designed to open the eyes of the blind, and I believe that its efforts will be powerful."[89] One month later, the manuscript was finally complete.[90] "The leading object has been to furnish a general *text book* for the use of all parties, friends or opponents," Niles explained in the *Register*, and to this end the address contained twelve pages of closely printed text making the case for protection, supported by an appendix of more than fifty pages providing statistics for different branches of industry.[91] The contrast with the difficulty that Alexander J. Dallas had in collecting detailed information on the subject of tariff just over a decade earlier is a striking testament to the extent to which the protectionists had coordinated their efforts in the interim.

The Harrisburg Convention sat for only five days, but its deliberations captured the public's attention. "This was not a talking body," explained Niles. "It was made up of business-men, who had reflected deeply upon the subjects which had brought them together, and much discussion would only have been a waste of time."[92] Critics attacked the convention in press and pamphlets, and their efforts were matched by the pens of its defenders.[93] Public meetings were held to show their support, and petitions were circulated endorsing its recommendations to Congress; the assembly thus served as a focal point for pro-tariff organizing through the country at large, providing a common agenda on which all could unite.[94] It also provided an opportunity to foster collaboration among protectionists working in different states, of the kind that had not been attempted since the smaller gatherings of 1819–1820. "All who attended the convention will long remember the new and valuable associations which they formed," predicted Niles.[95] Opponents of increased duties likewise recognized the danger inherent in greater coordination among their adversaries. "Now there is not a petty manufacturer in the union from the owner of a spinning factory, to the maker of a hobnail—from the mountains of Vermont to the swamps of the Patapsco, who is not pressing forward to the plunder," noted Thomas Cooper bitterly.[96] Whether Congress would prove receptive to this pressure remained to be seen.

+ + +

"It is quite obvious," wrote a friend to Clay in April 1828, "that the 'American System' has in its turn obtained the assendancy over all other Subjects of conversation and Legislation." "The 'System' and the 'opposition' to it forms the two elementary principles of the two parties," the author continued. "The line was drawn between the parties at the Session of 1824; if not Some years Sooner; . . . It was the Basis of the Harrisburg Convention: It is the leading Subject of debate in Congress: It is alluded to in *every debate* upon *every other* Subject. It is the leading Subject of State resolutions—some for & some against the System. It is a Standing question in the Newspapers and the principle [*sic*] topic of Conversation in all circles of Society public & private throughout the union. . . . The Country is divided—I hope not equally—upon it. The parties for and against it are emboded, and will not be disbanded for many years."[97]

Clay's correspondent was correct that partisan conflict would play a far more important role in shaping the Tariff of 1828 than it ever had previously. Yet at the same time, sectional cross-currents would contrive to blur party lines, as politicians scrambled to reconcile their allegiance to national candidates with the claims of the Harrisburg Convention and the demands of their own constituents. The American System, with its central component of protection for domestic manufactures, was firmly associated with the Adams administration, and more particularly with his secretary of state. For the first time in the nation's history, however, opponents of the administration held a majority in the Twentieth Congress. "If we can proceed with prudence & moderation to dispatch the business of the country & then go home the battle has already been fought & won," observed Buchanan, looking ahead to the presidential election of 1828. "If on the contrary our friends in the South should display much violence in opposition to such measures as may be calculated to promote the policy of domestic manufactures &c. there may be a reaction in Pennsylvania & New York." This was the dilemma that confronted the Jacksonian leadership as the session opened on 3 December 1827. "God only knows what may be the result," concluded Buchanan, "but I am afraid we have got the power too soon."[98]

The Tariff of 1828 was the product of a partisan plot, masterminded by Martin Van Buren, to resolve the dilemma identified by Buchanan. Historians are in agreement that, as Merrill Peterson states, it was a "clever political stratagem rather than a serious piece of economic legislation."[99] Where they disagree is whether the stratagem worked as it was supposed to. The plan called for the Jacksonians, with their newly won control of the committee system, to design a bill that would offer enhanced protection to the mid-Atlantic and Western states, the key battleground of the forthcoming election, while injuring New England, which was considered safe for Adams. The South would undoubtedly oppose any bill that increased import duties, and according to some scholars Van Buren's design called for New England to provide the additional votes necessary to defeat the bill, which would throw responsibility for its failure on the administration and swing those wavering mid-Atlantic states firmly into the opposition camp.[100] Certainly this appears to have been how Northern Jacksonians sold the scheme to their Southern counterparts. Other historians, however, have argued that Van Buren played an even more Machiavellian hand, gambling that he could secure just enough New England votes that the bill would pass, which would please his own constituents, while reasoning that the South would never abandon Jackson's standard when the alternative was an administration so closely identified with the American System.[101] In either case, there was much truth to the declaration of John Randolph, moments after the bill passed the House, that it "referred to manufactures of no sort or kind, but the manufacture of a President of the United States."[102]

Rumors of a ploy to use the tariff for political advantage began to circulate even as the Harrisburg Convention dominated newspaper headlines. A correspondent of Buchanan's informed him ten days before that assembly met of a report that "the Opposition men were going to introduce [a tariff bill] into Congress next winter, in such a form that the Eastern states could not possibly support it and of course it must fail."[103] Clay too was warned that the leaders of the Jackson party "have resolved to support a tariff, such an one as no sensible man can support, and hope to throw the blame of rejecting it on the North."[104] Niles dated this conspiracy back to the defeat of the Woollens Bill, claiming that "an agreement was made in February last, by certain politicians of New York and Pennsylvania, to offer up the protection of domestic industry and furtherance of internal improvement to the 'Virginia school' of politicians on fixed conditions."[105] It was not until the election of a new Speaker, however, that these stories began to gain foundation.

The choice of Speaker was a crucial test of the relative strength of the parties in the House, and it would have important implications for tariff policy too, since the Speaker would appoint the relevant committees. The obvious candidate for the Jacksonians was Philip P. Barbour, who had served as Speaker in the Seventeenth Congress, but protectionists among their ranks could not forget his naming of an anti-tariff majority to the Committee on Manufactures on that occasion.[106] Instead, Van Buren pressed his Southern allies to support Andrew Stevenson, another Virginian and a "devoted friend" of the Little Magician.[107] "We found the plan had been too long & too deeply laid by certain master-workmen, to be broken up," complained one of Barbour's original backers on the day of the election, hence "we have been compelled for the sake of unity of action & in deference to the will of a majority of our party, however procured, to give him up, & go for Stevenson, who will now be the only opposition candidate that will be run."[108] Meanwhile, Northern Jacksonians were wooed with a pledge that Stevenson, though personally hostile to protection, would "appoint a Committee friendly to the Northern manufacturing and agricultural interest."[109] The contest was a close one, but these maneuvers, coupled with Van Buren's efforts to ensure the prompt attendance of distant Jacksonian members, paid off, as his preferred candidate received one vote more than the required majority and was duly elected.[110]

"The treaty between the Sheep and the Wolves of Aesop is a fair illustration of the compact made by the Northern members to elect an anti-Tariff Speaker on condition that he would appoint a Committee on Manufactures friendly to that interest," was the verdict of administration congressman Henry Storrs, whose diary provides a detailed record of the session.[111] "The Committee on Manufactures he may perhaps in order to redeem his pledge arrange with a majority who are <u>normally</u> friendly to the Northern interest," the New Yorker predicted. "But he will doubtless take care that at the same time a majority of them shall be of such plastick Jackson materials that they maybe managed and moulded to any course that the policy of the party may require to be pursued."[112] This forecast would prove accurate. Rollin C. Mallary was retained as chair of the committee, but five of the six other appointments were "Jackson men of the most thorough going character and ready for any scheme that shall defeat the measure as to <u>wool and woollen goods</u> and at the same time keep up the appearance of friendship to the Northern interests."[113] Even the retention of Mallary did not please Storrs: "[I]t has been politic in the opposition to keep him place," he noted, "for while they got by it the credit of giving to Mr. Adams' friends their own Chairman (& <u>ergo Champion!</u>) of that Committee they are sure of it being in inefficient hands."[114] Instead, Storrs believed, the true author of any tariff legislation emanating from that source would be New York congressman Silas Wright, "who is [Van Buren's] confidential manager on that project in the H. of R. & was placed on the Committee of Manufactures at his suggestion for that purpose."[115] This claim is corroborated by Wright's personal correspondence: "[T]he Committee is perfectly safe, and certain it is that there is but one anti-tariff man upon it," he explained to one ally, but "in order to bring our arrangement about, I had to consent to go on it myself."[116]

The first action of the newly constituted committee was a request to "be vested with the power to send for persons and papers."[117] Congressional committees had heard testimony from lobbyists on the tariff previously, but on a voluntary basis; they had never before been authorized to summon witnesses of their own volition and to compel their attendance, a power that could only be delegated by the House.[118] The resolution was presented by Mallary, but he accompanied it with an explanation that "he had opposed it in the committee, and should be equally opposed to its adoption by the House."[119] This only served to confirm what most observers already suspected: the chair had lost control of his own committee. In debate on the resolution, Wright and his colleague James Stevenson both claimed a want of information on the subject.[120] Protectionists dismissed this explanation as ridiculous, particularly in light of the much-discussed deliberations of the Harrisburg Convention, and condemned the request as an attempt "to postpone indefinitely any means for the protection of manufactures."[121] The roll call on this motion presented the unusual spectacle of free traders such as Cambreleng and Randolph voting in favor of granting more power to the Committee on Manufactures, and with their help it was carried.[122] Observing events from Delaware, E. I. du Pont concluded that "supported as it was by the votes of the southern States, [the resolution] is evidently a political trick, either for delay, or with the view of presenting such a mass of incoherent and contradictory testimonies so as to render the case darker than ever and altogether unintelligible so that nothing should be done."[123]

Unfortunately for its authors, however, their plan miscarried. According to administration congressman Elisha Whittlesey, Wright and his collaborators "had understood there were some half dozen of those who were engaged in manufacturing woollens, who were content with the present rate of duty and to stifle inquiry they passed a resolution that each member of the Committee might send for two persons and no more."[124] This would allow the Adams men to call only four witnesses, against ten for the Jacksonians. The latter proceeded to select manufacturers with no prior record of protectionist agitation, to whose testimony they added that of trusted colleagues; six of the seven sitting congressmen interviewed were members of their party. In reply, Mallary called on Aaron Tufts, one of the Boston agents of the previous session, and James Shepherd, a delegate to the national protectionist conventions of 1819 and 1827.[125] But this meager contingent was also bolstered by a host of familiar faces who, ignoring the committee's self-imposed restrictions, elected to visit the capital on their own account. Jonas B. Brown, Joshua Clapp, and James Wolcott Jr., who had managed the campaign for the Woollens Bill, were among those who made an appearance, as were Abraham H. Schenck, brother of Peter, and William W. Young, son of William, both of whom had served alongside Brown at Harrisburg. "The excitement among those interested has been so great by reason of this proceeding that the City is filled with manufacturers who have come on for the purpose of being examined on oath as to the truth of their memorials," recorded Storrs in his diary.[126] Niles, who had also made the trip to Washington, was heartened to find "a considerable number of wool growers, and other friends of the protecting principle, in this city," hailing, by his count, from ten different states.[127]

Initially, the Jacksonian majority on the committee refused to take the testimony of these volunteers, claiming a want of time. As Whittlesey subsequently recounted, however, circumstances forced a reconsideration, and also revealed the agency of Van Buren in the whole affair. "Finding that great dissatisfaction was expressed in Delaware among the manufacturers on account of the course taken by the committee," Louis McLane had invited E. I. du Pont to Washington as a show of good faith. Du Pont arrived in haste, "dripping with mud, water and sweat," and his host accompanied him to the committee room, only to find "the prospect of his being examined not very flattering." McLane was "much discomfited" and pressed Van Buren to intervene on his behalf. The Little Magician duly "called out Mr. Wright and held a conversation with him, after which Mr. W. returned to the room and then proposed to divide the committee into three sections and to examine the Gentlemen in attendance." This same arrangement, to expedite the hearings by holding them concurrently, had earlier been proposed by the Adams men and soundly rejected.[128] Now, by its belated adoption, Storrs observed, "the Committee on Manufactures have got themselves rather unexpectedly into a tedious and bothersome examination of manufacturers that they little expected when they offered their Resolution to the House on the 31st of December."[129]

The committee ultimately heard from twenty-eight witnesses, double the number originally intended, and discovered a general appetite for enhanced protection across a range of industries. In particular, woolen manufacturers were adamant that no increase in duties on raw wool, of great importance to the constituents of Van Buren and Wright, would be acceptable without a corresponding increase in duties on textiles. "The testimony is very different from what was expected by the Opposition," Whittlesey wrote with evident satisfaction.[130] Meanwhile, while the hearings were still in progress, Storrs recorded: "[T]he friends of Genl. Jackson in New York and Pennsylvania have written to the Jackson men here and communicated to them the fact from all quarters that a great reaction against them will take place in consequence of the passage of this resolution unless they finally pass a Tariff that shall protect Wool and <u>Woollen Cloths</u>."[131] One of Van Buren's lieutenants warned of "a manufacturing excitement raging all over the state (except the City of New York) which will, I apprehend, be got up if Jackson's friends from this state do not all that moral men can do for the success of such a measure."[132] Similarly, Buchanan was notified that "if this bill should fail, or its most important features be so modified as to render it of little efficacy, the whole responsibility ... must inevitably fall upon the Jackson party, who claim a majority in the house."[133] The legislatures of New York and Pennsylvania both instructed their delegations in Congress to secure increased protection in line with the recommendations of the Harrisburg Convention, and these two states together possessed 64 electoral votes, nearly half the 131 needed for victory in the 1828 election.[134] No wonder, then, that Storrs found that "some of the leaders here and some of the Committee too are alarmed and many of them begin now to think it will be better for them to do something seriously for their Northern interests, if they expect to elect Jackson."[135] If opponents of the administration had seriously contemplated postponing action on the tariff until after the presidential election, as du Pont suspected, then the pressure exerted by protectionists out-of-doors rendered that strategy impracticable.

+ + +

How, then, could the Jacksonians act on the tariff in a way that would satisfy both Northern and Southern wings of the party? The answer to this question was provided by Van Buren. The Little Magician was repeatedly spotted "lurking" outside the committee room and "calling out the Jackson members of the committee daily, and many times a day, to hold talks with them," so that "nothing important was done or has been reported without his knowledge and consent."[136] "We believe that everything has been arranged under the superintendence of Mr. Van Buren, who, from managing the Albany legislature, has kindly taken upon himself the management of congress, so far as relates to the tariff," reported the *National Journal*, the administration's mouthpiece in the capital.[137]

The tariff bill reported from the Committee on Manufactures on 31 January 1828 contained some of the highest, and most unevenly distributed, duties in the nation's history.[138] States that would prove crucial in the forthcoming election were assiduously courted. Kentucky hemp producers, Pennsylvania and New Jersey ironmasters, New York and Ohio wool growers, and Western grain farmers would all benefit from the projected rates; five of the seven members of the Committee on Manufactures hailed from these regions.[139] For New England, in contrast, the bill was a disaster. Shipbuilding would suffer from the increased cost of raw materials, rum distillers would pay more for their molasses, and in place of the system of minimums recommended by the Harrisburg Convention, woolen textiles would be subjected to a graduated schedule so ill-designed that it offered little compensation for the augmented tax on wool. Taken as a whole, the level of duties was significantly greater than that proposed at Harrisburg, but it neglected the one industry that most needed assistance while offering aid to others that had not even requested it. Its friends immediately hailed it as a "National Tariff."[140] President Adams disagreed, noting in his diary that "the professed object of the bill is the protection of domestic manufacturers, but there is compounded with it taxation peculiarly oppressive upon New England."[141] Storrs was more scathing in his assessment. "Finding from the examination of the manufacturers that they would be compelled to report an increased duty on Woollen Cloths, they have added to it all that was calculated to destroy the Bill altogether and defeat the whole system of protection and endeavor to throw the blame if the Bill should be lost on Mr. Adams' friends," he complained. "Such a system of mere legislative trickery has no example in Congress."[142]

Protectionists in and out of the legislature condemned the bill. "It is the vilest of cheats," stormed Clay. "With the professed purpose of protecting our Woolen manufactories, it demolishes them. With the purpose avowed of encouraging the growth of wool it destroys the Home market."[143] "The people have asked for bread and are to receive a stone," echoed Niles in his *Register*.[144] Writing to Webster, one Boston entrepreneur advised: "[L]et the friends of the Admtn. not be startled one inch, from the Ground of obtaining *substantially* the Harrisburg Platform and have the yeas & nays. If they can only have *substantially* the Bill as Reported originally by the Committee of Manftrs., let them vote, in solid column, ag[ains]t it."[145] This was also the conclusion of repeated meetings between lobbyists and pro-tariff lawmakers in the capital, while Wright was reduced to dodging the attentions of infuriated woolens men from his own state.[146] Across the country, public meetings urged resistance to the measure and again endorsed the recommendations of the Harrisburg Convention as the preferred alternative. Carey, who had resigned from the Pennsylvania Society after his repeated run-ins with Ingersoll, returned to the fray to chair the Philadelphia meeting, leading one congressman to remark that "the bill is condemned by the fast friends of domestic manufactures, and among many others, by those champions of the American System, the veteran Niles and Carey." "Those very manufacturers and their agents, who poured in upon the House petitions beseeching that we should sustain their sinking establishments," he observed, "now come here with remonstrances conjuring us to save them from the tender mercies of this measure."[147]

Administration supporters were well aware of the trap that had been set for them. "It is difficult to resist the conclusion that the bill which has been reported was framed, purposely, to create divisions among the friends of the American System, and thus to defeat the measure," Clay explained to one correspondent. "You must not be surprised if you see those who are, and always have been, opposed to any protection whatever, voting, on this occasion, for the highest amount of it."[148] This prediction was concurred in by New Hampshire congressman David Barker, who suggested that "one means of suppressing it will be, by loading it with unpalatable provisions," such as the high rates on wool and molasses. "These duties you may perceive will not benefit the South, but they will nonetheless urge them strenuously. Their only object is to defeat the measure, and they care not how they do it, provided their purpose be accomplished."[149] If true, this was a dangerous strategy indeed. "The Jackson party is playing a game of brag," Clay mused. "They do not really desire the passage of their own measure; and it may happen, in the sequel, that what is desired by neither party commands the support of both."[150]

Was the South a knowing accomplice in Van Buren's plot? Robert Remini, who has studied this episode more closely than anyone, believes not. Southern congressmen "reasoned that by simply beating off all efforts to amend and improve the bill that would make it more palatable to manufacturers, Northerners would join them on the final vote to kill it," he explains. "No knowledge of a 'plot' was necessary to tell them this. No 'assurances' from Van Buren or anyone else were needed to show them what they must do. They had no choice."[151] There is some merit to this interpretation, for any observer could see that the Jacksonians could only hope to triumph in the forthcoming presidential election if each wing of the party was permitted to forsake national consistency in favor of local sentiment. Or as North Carolina representative Willis Alston wrote to an ally back home: "[W]e at the south will go with any side to defeat [the tariff], [and] in truth we all seem very well to understand each other here, that [it] is due to the south [to] vote as we please about Tariff and internal improvement and so will our friends to the west & in Pennsylvania & New York without offence or harm to the great cause of administration or anti."[152]

Yet there is evidence too of more direct Southern complicity. South Carolina congressman William D. Martin, the only anti-tariff member of the Committee on Manufactures, cooperated in the design of the bill; he was "utterly opposed to a tariff bill of any kind," Wright subsequently recalled, "but if any was to be reported, . . . he preferred the insertion of protecting duties on the raw material."[153] In fact, it appears that the New York leaders, in consultation with Speaker Stevenson, specifically selected Martin for that role.[154] Another member of the committee, most likely James Stevenson, also privately informed a friend that "you will be surprised to find that our Southern friends will give us some support, in opposition to the resistance that New England will make to a duty on Wool, Hemp, Iron, and Spirits." When this letter found its way into the newspapers, Storrs commented that the admission "relating to the support that the South was to give to the Tariff, is too significant not to be plainly understood." "The whole letter fully develops the scheme of the Northern Jackson leaders to defeat the Tariff if possible by the New England votes and then raise a 'hue & cry' against Mr. Adams' friends," he explained. "The votes of the Southern members, to keep all the obnoxious features of the project in the Bill as reported, explains the whole trick." What's more, the date on the letter, 10 January, indicated that such an arrangement had been made even before the Committee on Manufactures had concluded its hearings.[155] Southerners too would later claim that a bargain had indeed been struck. A decade on, Calhoun recalled that only after "assurances were given which placed the representatives of the South at ease" did they consent to block any attempt to reduce the duties on the articles named in Stevenson's letter, which would have rendered the bill more acceptable to their own constituents, but also to New England.[156]

+ + +

Whatever understanding did exist between Northern and Southern Jacksonians manifested itself when the tariff came up for consideration in the House. Mallary, who avowed that he had reported the bill as "a ministerial duty only," opened the debate on 3 March by criticizing its chief provisions, and concluded his speech by proposing that the duties on raw wool and woolen textiles be amended to conform to the recommendations of the Harrisburg Convention.[157] Protectionists lined up to praise that assembly. New York congressman David Woodcock, for example, declared that "they were not speculators, nor wild theorists, but practical men—the farmer, the manufacturer, the merchant, the wool-grower and manufacturer, there met," and "he was in favour of the amendment, not only from his own investigation of the subject, but from the[ir] recommendation."[158] In response, supporters of the committee bill charged that the source of those recommendations automatically rendered them suspect. "No combination of wool growers and woollen manufacturers, should ever attempt to dictate a tariff to the people of the United States," proclaimed Buchanan. "They would be more than men, if self-interest did not prejudice their judgment, and call forth propositions for their own benefit, at the expense of the community."[159] When it came to a vote, Mallary's amendment was defeated, 78 yeas to 102 nays.[160] "Every Jackson man in the House, with [one exception], voted with the South against the proposition," noted one administration congressman, adding: "I sincerely believe the Jacksonians from N. York & Penn. are laboring with the South to get the Bill into such a shape that the real friends of domestic industry cannot vote for it, and in that state of things it will become a very serious question, with those who are the real friends of the American System, what they ought to do."[161]

This pattern was repeated time and again. On 7 April, Wright informed a correspondent that "five weeks have now been spent in debate upon this bill. More than four weeks of that time have been spent in settling the question between the bill as reported by the Committee and the bill reported by the Harrisburgh [sic] Convention."[162] The same day, Storrs recorded in his journal that "no amendment whatever moved by Mr. Adams' friends had been admitted," regardless of whether it would raise or lower the proposed rates. "[T]hey have all been voted down in Committee of the Whole by the united vote of the Southern anti Tariff members and the Northern Jackson party." "The course of debate too has further illustrated the scheme and plan of operations which they have determined to pursue," he continued. "The South have remained silent and the debates have been between the Northern Jackson men (professing to be in favor of the farming interest) & Mr. Adams' friends in the Northern States."[163] These speeches were, of course, intended purely for the benefit of the electorate, to establish the protectionist credentials of the orators, rather than for the edification of those within earshot. Not that there were too many of the latter: "34 seats in front of me have only 5 persons in them, & only one listening, & he is so deaf that the Speaker's voice can't reach him," an administration congressman wrote to his wife in the midst of one lengthy sermon.[164] "Day after day passes without any sensible advance in the public business," echoed another. "One dull prosing speech on the tariff is followed by another & arguments for the fiftieth time repeated are hashed up & dished in new covers."[165] It was left to the protectionist press to point out the "singular coincidence" of a majority of the Pennsylvania and Virginia delegations voting in unison on the tariff.[166] There was nothing, it seemed, that their allies in Congress could do. As Ingham crowed after one more day of tedious debate: "D—n you—you wanted Tariff and we mean to give you Tariff enough."[167]

Behind the scenes, however, some Adams supporters were calculating the circumstances under which they could accept the enhanced protection offered by the bill, even with all its flaws. The crucial moment came on 9 April, when Mallary once again attempted to introduce a version of the minimum valuation that was favored by the woolen manufacturers. Buchanan then offered a substitute for Mallary's amendment, stripping out the minimums but raising the duty on most imported textiles incrementally to 50 percent ad valorem, from its current rate of 33⅓ percent.[168] According to Storrs, Buchanan only made this motion to earn credit with his constituents, fully expecting the administration party to vote it down in preference for Mallary's original wording; he had already laid the foundation for this maneuver in a previous speech that accused protectionists of demanding: "[W]e must have the amendment, in regard to woollens, recommended by the Harrisburg Convention, or we will have nothing."[169] Instead, though, the chair of the Committee on Manufactures called his bluff, accepting the proffered substitute as "decidedly preferable to the bill as reported by the committee, and having little hope that his own amendment would carry."[170] This about-face caused "a ludicrous fluttering in the Jackson ranks," and "several of the leaders of the Jacksonism ran to Mr. B[uchanan]'s feet in a state of consternation and alarm," but the damage was already done.[171] Members of that party who were responsible to protectionist constituencies could not be seen voting against a proposal to increase duties that originated within their own ranks, as was demonstrated when an immediate effort to limit the rise to 40 percent was beaten back, with many Northern Jacksonians, including Wright, voting in the negative.[172]

The best the Jackson leaders could do was put forward a second substitute that restored the graduated rates proposed by the committee bill, but with a higher tax on the coarse textiles upon which the South depended to clothe its slaves and a lower tax on raw wool, both of which would benefit the New England manufacturers. This substitute was carried by a single vote over the resistance of administration supporters, who would have preferred Buchanan's version.[173] Nonetheless, the adoption of the now much-revised amendment on 12 April by 183 votes to 17 suggested that many of the latter still saw this as an important victory.[174] Also promising was the news that Mahlon Dickerson, New Jersey senator and chair of that chamber's Committee on Manufactures, had given "assurances" that his committee would recommend further amendments to place woolens "under a fair protection against the British manufacturer."[175] Dickerson, like Van Buren and Wright, was a Jacksonian susceptible to pressure from pro-tariff constituents; he would decline appointment to a subsequent protectionist convention on the grounds that he "wd. prefer to receive, rather than to give instructions."[176]

Clay, who ten days earlier had written of his hope that the bill would be defeated, now declared that it was "my wish, and my advice," that it should pass.[177] Protectionists out-of-doors thought likewise. "Should the bill pass, those who have originated it will become the dupes of their own political tricks," E. I. du Pont advised one Delaware congressman. "[T]heir friends of the south, with whom they had contracted to have no tariff at all, will be highly offended, and on the other side the friends of the administration will have in their power to shew that they have done every thing they could to obtain a good law, and have passed this objectionable one only because the Jackson politicians forced it and would not permit them to make a better one."[178]

Too late, Southerners were reaching the same conclusion. "Some of the Southern members are very angry with Mr. Buchanan and a few others of the party from the North for inclining to raise the duties on woollen fabrics," Storrs reported. "In their zeal (they are of hot & excitable blood) they very incautiously speak of the existence of an understanding in the party that the Bill is to stand essentially as reported and their hope is that New England members will defeat it."[179] Privately, one North Carolina congressman admitted: "[W]e have not only disclosed our plan, but defeated its success."[180] On 15 April, the bill was engrossed and put to a third reading, the stage prior to passage, by 109 votes to 92, a development that according to Storrs was "contrary to the expectation of the South Jackson party . . . who confidently expected the Bill to be lost by New England votes."[181] In the event, sixteen of the thirty-six Adams representatives from that region swallowed their misgivings and supported the motion, providing the crucial margin of victory in conjunction with their fellow partisans from elsewhere in the country and the bulk of the Northern Jacksonians, who dare not oppose their own creation, however much it would displease their Southern counterparts.[182] The latter, who had previously remained mute, now unleashed a tirade against the bill, and the "manufacturing proprietors and their agents, who patrol the street of the Metropolis, the avenues of the Capitol, and the Halls of Legislation, making attempts to electioneer with members of Congress in favor of the adoption of the proposed system."[183] The administration men were happy to let them rant, since it only drew attention to the hypocrisy of their earlier conduct in voting down amendments that would have reduced the level of duties. "The Jackson Committee were most unmercifully handled by their Southern friends," recounted John C. Wright with evident amusement, and "Stevenson, Buchanan & Co. were much alarmed."[184] Consequently, it took another week before the bill finally passed the House on 22 April by a vote of 105 to 94, with the drama rounded off by one embittered South Carolinian's futile attempt to have it renamed an act "for the purpose of increasing the profits of certain manufacturers."[185]

The tariff bill was read in the Senate on 23 April and the following day referred to the Committee on Manufactures, where Dickerson made good on his promise to render some of its provisions more satisfactory to the protectionists. Any changes made to the bill in committee would still need to be concurred in on the floor, however, and desperate Southerners still clung to their plan for defeating the whole project. "The hated tariff bill—that curse to the whole South—is reported to the Senate with sundry villainous amendments," wrote Virginia senator John Tyler. "Its fate rests on our ability to preserve the bill in its present shape. If we can do so, it will be rejected."[186] As in the House, the stance taken by New England would surely prove decisive, and its senators were still calculating whether the mediocre protection offered to textile producers was sufficient to counterbalance the increased costs of various articles upon which the region's other industries relied. Rumors began to circulate that the Jacksonians intended to arrange the vote in such a way that responsibility for its success or failure would fall on Daniel Webster, who voted toward the end of the alphabetical roll call.[187] The Massachusetts man was in a quandary. "I fear we are getting into trouble here about the *Tariff*," he wrote to Harrisburg delegate Joseph Sprague. "Can we go the *hemp*, iron[,] spirits an[d] molasses for the sake of any woolen bill? [And] can we do it for a poor woolen Bill?"[188]

Also facing a dilemma was Van Buren. "He must now vote (if not <u>absent</u> again as he was last year, or sick) <u>Tariff</u> or <u>No Tariff</u> and either way much commit himself against great political interests hereafter," remarked Storrs with evident satisfaction.[189] The tension took its toll; "the 'great magician' ... seemed tired & jaded," reported one observer.[190] Privately, though, the New Yorker had made his decision: the bill must pass. On 5 May, a series of divisions were taken on amendments made in committee that would finally establish a system of minimums for woolens akin to that which existed for cotton textiles, as the Harrisburg Convention had requested. In each instance, the amendment was agreed to by twenty-four votes to twenty-two, and in each instance Van Buren voted in favor; had he been opposed, the result would have been a tie, and the amendments undoubtedly would have been lost on the casting vote of the presiding officer, Vice President Calhoun.[191] The significance of these amendments was crucial. Abbott Lawrence, who had been dispatched to Washington "to look after the manufacturing interests" earlier in the session, advised Webster that "so far as Woollens are concerned the bill is very much improved and is thought by many to be now good enough."[192] Similarly, protectionist editor Joseph T. Buckingham wrote from Boston that "our friends here, the Manufacturers, after deliberation and consultation among themselves, have come to the conclusion that the Tariff Bill, as reported by the Committee on Manufactures in the Senate, will answer their purpose. It comes so near to the Harrisburgh Platform, that the operation[,] they think[,] will be satisfactory and advantageous."[193] Still, though, Webster hesitated. "How I shall vote, if the final passage depends on me, nobody knows," he wrote to one friend, "& I hardly know myself."[194]

On 13 May, the Tariff of 1828 passed the Senate by twenty-six votes to twenty-one. Webster voted yea, prompting charges that he had done so only on the urging of "his manufacturing friends in Boston."[195] So too did Van Buren, having given a short speech in which he declared that "he was opposed in principle to the Bill but having been instructed by the New York legislature to vote for a Tariff he should for vote this Bill."[196] Cynics suggested that the Little Magician had arranged these instructions in preparation for just such an eventuality; Tyler would later describe his Northern colleague "with instructions in his pocket, liable to be construed after any manner he might please, sheltering himself behind them for his tariff vote."[197] Because the bill had been amended, it now returned to the House for its concurrence, but with a significant bloc of New Englanders brought over to join the mid-Atlantic and Western states in favor, Southerners could do nothing to prevent it, and were reduced to pointing out grammatical errors in a vain bid to delay its progress.[198] A few minor disagreements between the two chambers were easily resolved in a Committee of Conference, and the bill was sent for President Adams's signature. "The Tariff Bill has finally passed the two Houses," reported the *National Journal*. "In the shape in which the bill has been returned from the Senate, many of the objections which originally existed [to] its passage have been removed; and the measure has assumed a character which will make it much more agreeable to those interests which most needed the protecting arm of the Government."[199]

+ + +

"The South are exceedingly angry and disappointed and even rail at their Northern Jackson allies," wrote Henry R. Storrs when it became clear that the tariff would pass the Senate. "They now say openly that they took the course which they did in the H. of R. on the Bill under the full assurances from their Northern friends that it would defeat the Bill—they do not hesitate now to say that the molasses duty & some others were put into the Bill expressly to defeat it—that they followed the advice of their Northern friends who they say have grossly miscalculated throughout on the effect of their plans to defeat the Tariff for the South and to throw the responsibility on Mr. Adams's Northern and Eastern friends."[200] Taking both House and Senate together, the slave states had provided eighty-one votes against the bill and twenty-five votes for it, with seventeen of the latter cast by the entire delegations from Delaware and Kentucky, which both stood to gain directly from its provisions. This was counterbalanced, as expected, by the mid-Atlantic and Western free states, which voted eighty-four to six in favor. As its makers intended, the bill's fate would be determined by New England, and the twenty-two yeas from that region, though still a minority against twenty-eight nays, were sufficient to ensure its success. Storrs's commentary therefore poses two important questions: Was there an understanding between Northern and Southern Jacksonians that the bill would be defeated? And, if so, was its passage the result of mere miscalculation or something more sinister on the part of the former?

The answer to the first question is, surely, yes. Reflecting on the failure of the Woollens Bill, protectionist activists meeting at the Harrisburg Convention reverted to their previous strategy of enlisting a wide-ranging coalition in support of a comprehensive schedule of duties. Northern Jacksonians, having just seen their party gain control of Congress, then came under tremendous pressure to act on the tariff from petitions and public meetings that took their cue from Harrisburg: "[T]here is not, perhaps, an example in all history, so strikingly demonstrative of the influence which clubs and societies are capable of exercising over public opinion," remarked one astonished observer.[201] Determined to avoid following the lead of an assembly they associated with their opponents but convinced by testimony heard by their own Committee on Manufactures that further postponement might cripple their party's presidential prospects, Martin Van Buren, Silas Wright, and their allies designed a bill that would win them votes in the mid-Atlantic and Western states while punishing the East for its loyalty to the administration. Southerners were naturally opposed to any increase in rates, and Robert Remini has argued that they had no choice but to block New England's efforts to remove the most obnoxious features of the bill in the hope that that region would then join them in defeating it. But, in fact, there was another option, one the South had relied on with success in the past. If they, in combination with New Englanders, had mustered majorities against specific provisions that neither section favored, then support for the bill as a whole might have been gradually stripped away. Remini dismisses this as "an idle threat," but Wright repeatedly expressed concern that "the doubts, and ifs, and propositions to alter, and ask more . . . will exasperate the Southrons to join the Yankees and cut out the Iron, Hemp, Flax, Molasses and everything else but the woollens. If this should turn out so, I think Pennsylvania and the west will kill the remainder, and Jackson votes will do the deed."[202] The New York member more than once felt compelled to assure his associates back home that "if our friends are not unjust to themselves it will be lost by Adams, New England votes," and it seems reasonable to assume that Southern Jacksonians would have sought similar assurances before agreeing to join in their plot for partisan gain.[203] Indeed, the frequency of contemporary references to an understanding, in Storrs's diary and elsewhere, testify that this was no retrospective invention of John C. Calhoun.[204]

As to the second question, the weight of evidence suggests that Van Buren and his coconspirators were guilty of a calculated betrayal. Wright would later claim that when he discovered his Southern colleagues "sanguine in the belief that if the bill should be thus framed, the New England members would vote against it, and it would consequently be lost," he "did all he could to undeceive them."[205] This hardly seems plausible, since the letters quoted previously reveal Wright preferred that outcome to anything but passage of the measure in its original form. Furthermore, it was not merely inaction on the part of Northern Jacksonians that allowed the bill to pass; they actively contributed, at critical moments, to its success. James Buchanan's ill-judged proposal to raise the rate on textiles in the House might be excused as merely rash, but Van Buren's support for the woolens minimum in the Senate was a deliberate attempt to make the measure more palatable to New England manufacturers. "Had he acted in good faith, the bill of 1828 never would have become a law," was Calhoun's verdict, and most likely an accurate one.[206] If Remini is right to argue that "at no time did Van Buren intend to defeat this tariff," then he is surely wrong to claim that "there was never any deception; Southerners simply chose to believe that there was."[207]

The passage of the Tariff of 1828 would have momentous political consequences. In the North, the *Albany Argus*, Van Buren's pet newspaper, credited the Jacksonians with "the merit of having given to the country a national tariff, which protects, with a just and natural equality, all the great interests of the nation."[208] With the General's protectionist credentials secured, he went on to sweep the mid-Atlantic and Western states in the presidential election. The South, meanwhile, labeled it a "Tariff of Abominations," but still they backed Jackson for the White House as the lesser of two evils.[209] The partisan alignments growing out of the Adams-Jackson rivalry would subsequently evolve into the Democrat-Whig party system that dominated American politics until its collapse in the decade prior to the Civil War.[210] The Little Magician's plan had succeeded, though at some personal cost. One furious Virginia senator reportedly told him: "Sir, you have deceived me once; that was your fault; but if you deceive me again the fault will be mine."[211] Most Southerners still hoped, though, that the new administration, in which Van Buren would serve as secretary of state, would relieve them of the burdens imposed by the tariff. Some, however, including Calhoun, who stayed on as Jackson's vice president, were beginning to contemplate a more radical solution, one that would push the protectionist policy, and the country, to the brink of ruin.

chapter four

"Calculate the Value of the Union"
The Tariffs of 1832 and 1833

A T A PUBLIC MEETING in Columbia on 2 July 1827, Thomas Cooper, president of South Carolina College and free trade pamphleteer, delivered his famous "calculate the value of the Union" speech, in which he urged his fellow South Carolinians to consider the future of the federal compact. "The avowed object now is, by means of a drilled and managed majority in congress, permanently to force upon us a system, whose effect will be to sacrifice the south to the north, by converting us into colonies and tributaries," he claimed. "To tax *us* for their own emolument—to claim the right of disposing of our honest earnings—to forbid us to buy from our most valuable customers—to irritate into retaliation our foreign purchasers, and thus confine our raw material to the home market—in short, to impoverish the planter, and to stretch the purse of the manufacturer." Historians have cited Cooper's speech as evidence of mounting Southern discontent with federal tariff policy, but they have overlooked his more specific objection to how that policy was made: the role of lobbying. "The manufacturers are a regular organized community—acting in perfect concert," he declared, and "it is easy to conceive what a decided influence must be produced by the daily and constant importunities of agents, who go to Washington charged with calculations and statements artfully prepared, with a view to present the claims of the manufacturers in the most imposing form." Pointing to the "bargaining for votes, the selfish compromises, and partial statements, the *suppressio veri*, the *suggestio falsi*, the promise insinuated, the threats intimated, and [other] various inaccurate and objectionable practices," the firebrand professor condemned the "mongrel kind of *lobby* legislation attending at Washington, that operates from without on the members within."[1]

The Nullification Controversy, which Cooper's remarks presaged, pro-

vides the backdrop for tariff legislation during this period. As tensions in-
tensified between South Carolina, with Vice President John C. Calhoun
leading the way, and the administration of President Andrew Jackson, campaigners on both sides of the tariff question held national conventions in the
hope of influencing the expected legislative compromise. The Tariff of 1832,
negotiated between leading figures from both sides of the partisan divide
and representatives of the business community, briefly seemed to offer that
compromise, by providing a reduction in duties combined with a reaffirmation of the principle of protection that met the approval of majorities of both
parties and both sections, as well as many prominent manufacturers. But the
nullifiers' refusal to accept the revised rates plunged the country back into
crisis, and with the prospect of civil war looming it took a second compromise, engineered by Henry Clay in the dying days of the Twenty-Second
Congress, to avert catastrophe. Peace was preserved, but at what cost for
the American System?

+ + +

Cooper's advocacy of state action against the tariff placed him very much
in a minority at the moment his speech was delivered; as Calhoun assured
one Northern correspondent, "attachment to [the Union] is deep and steady
to the South. The imprudent decleration [sic] of such men as Dr. Cooper,
and others of similar character gives no indication of publick opinion in this
quarter."[2] Yet passage of the Tariff of 1828, combined with a continued fall
in cotton prices and accompanied by British threats of economic retaliation
purposefully calculated "to alarm the Southern States," soon won his views
many converts.[3] Calhoun himself considered the Harrisburg Convention
"the selected instrument to combine with greater facility the great geographical Northern manufacturing interest in order to enforce more effectually the system of monopoly and extortion against the consuming States,"
and became increasingly convinced that "despotism founded on combined
geographical interest, admits of but one effectual remedy, a veto on the part
of the local interest, or under our system, on the part of the States."[4] This
letter, which establishes the principle of nullification, was written even before the Tariff of 1828 became law, illustrating that the author, like Cooper,
was as much concerned with the process of policymaking as the outcome.
As historians have noted, this preoccupation no doubt reflected the fear of
many Southerners that the federal government would one day use its power
for another purpose: to strike at slavery.[5]

At the request of the South Carolina legislature, Calhoun set forth his
doctrine of nullification in a lengthy document titled the "Exposition and

Protest," which declared a tariff for protection to be unconstitutional and defended the right of any state to prevent its enforcement. The vice president's authorship was kept secret, however, and no immediate action was taken when the report was presented in December 1828, while the legislature waited on the incoming Jackson administration to redress its grievances. As Calhoun himself had written to the General prior to the election: "[T]he belief that those now in power will be displaced shortly; and that under an administration formed under your auspices, a better order of things will commence . . . is what mainly consoles this quarter of the Union under existing embarrassment."[6] This faith was to be disappointed. The new president opposed any substantial reduction in duties until the national debt could be paid off, an objective that would not be achieved during his first term in office, and his chances of winning a second term depended on the same protectionist states that his supporters had courted so successfully with the Tariff of 1828. Thus, one South Carolina senator noted ominously: "[T]here is a profound silence observed on the subject of the tariff."[7] Faced with intransigence in Washington, advocates of nullification continued to gain ground, until Calhoun, confronted by the prospect of losing control of his home state, abandoned all hope of following Jackson into the White House as heir apparent by breaking with the administration and publicly endorsing nullification in July 1831.[8]

Outside of South Carolina, other advocates of tariff reform were also pushing the issue to the forefront of the legislative agenda. For too long, lamented the Philadelphia *Free Trade Advocate* following enactment of the Tariff of 1828, their opponents had been allowed to take the lead, with the result that "there has not been established in the United States, a single permanent association, with the object of promulgating and spreading abroad the doctrines of *Free Trade*, or for the purpose of combining together in a common cause, individuals residing in different sections of the union."[9] The editor of this paper was Condy Raguet, whose sentiments on the tariff had undergone a profound conversion in the decade since his lobbying on behalf of Mathew Carey's Pennsylvania Society in 1820.[10] In the spring of 1831, Raguet endorsed the proposal of Massachusetts lawyer Henry D. Sedgwick, outlined in a letter to the New York *Evening Post*, for an assembly that should "herein, as in all things else, be the converse of the Harrisburg Convention. It should consist of men who desire, by undoing what was done by that Convention, to benefit the American community—*and themselves* only as members of the American community."[11] At a private meeting at Raguet's home on 6 June, attended by Sedgwick and nine other men from the states of Massachusetts, Pennsylvania, and South Carolina, plans were laid and a call issued for "a Convention, for the purpose of securing the efficient coop-eration of the friends of Free Trade, throughout the United States, in pro-curing the repeal of the Restrictive System," to be held in Philadelphia three months hence.[12]

The Free Trade Convention of 1831 would later be cited by Alexis de Tocqueville, who was touring the United States when it met, as a prime ex-ample of Americans' liberty of association for political purposes. "A private citizen of Massachusetts proposed, by means of the newspapers, to all the enemies of the tariff to send delegates to Philadelphia in order to consult together upon the best means of restoring freedom of trade," the Frenchman recounted in his *Democracy in America*. "This proposal circulated in a few days, by the power of the press, from Maine to New Orleans. The opponents of the tariff adopted it with enthusiasm; meetings were held in all quarters, and delegates were appointed."[13] In this respect, the organizers followed a tried-and-tested method employed by their adversaries in Harrisburg in 1827 and New York in 1819, and indeed by an earlier, and much smaller, free trade convention held in Philadelphia following the failure of Baldwin's bill in 1820.[14] Protectionist critics raised the usual objections: the selection meetings were sparsely attended, unrepresentative of local sentiment, and delegates were nominated without their consent by patrons "willing to avail themselves of the influence which the use of such names would exercise upon public opinion in other States, where their disapprobation could not be known."[15] Still, the prospects for the convention appeared pleasing to its sponsors. "Mere politicians will have no influence," promised Raguet's new paper, the *Banner of the Constitution*. "Jackson-men, Clay-men, Calhoun-men, Van Buren-men, will all lay aside their prejudice for and against partic-ular *men*, and meet upon the honorable and truly patriotic ground of *mea-sures*. Farmers, planters, manufacturers, mechanics, merchants, ship-owners, lawyers, physicians, and retired citizens, will all be fairly represented."[16]

The convention opened on 30 September and sat until 7 October, its proceedings presided over by Philip P. Barbour, the Speaker who had shut the protectionists out of the Committee on Manufactures during the Seven-teenth Congress.[17] Seven free states were represented by 78 delegates, while eight slave states were represented by 134 delegates, including 41 from South Carolina alone.[18] The Southern majority were in general agreement that protection was unconstitutional but differed greatly over whether nullifica-tion was the proper remedy. The Northern minority, meanwhile, mostly pre-ferred to make the case for the inexpediency, rather than illegitimacy, of high duties, though Raguet and Henry Lee of Boston, renowned as the author of a scathing review of the Harrisburg Convention, were notable exceptions.[19]

In consequence, many observers anticipated a contentious debate: "[T]hey will disagree as much in principle & degree as they differ from the friends of the Amn. System," predicted one of Clay's Philadelphia correspondents.[20] Calhoun watched on warily from his plantation, expressing to a Northern friend his hope that "something [may] grow out of it to harmonize our differences," while cautioning another ally from his own section that "unless its movements should be judicious [it] will do much more harm, than good."[21]

Discord was avoided through the mediation of Albert Gallatin, the septuagenarian former Secretary of the Treasury and leader of the New York delegation. Gallatin had been appointed to chair the committee tasked with preparing an address to the people of the United States, a selection that did not please the nullifiers present: "[H]e is a cunning, subtle old fox and hopes to stave off the constitution question," grumbled one.[22] This was indeed Gallatin's aim, and he achieved it by working closely with John M. Berrien, a Georgia member who had recently lost his seat in Jackson's cabinet due in part to his friendship with Calhoun but who nonetheless was not an avowed nullifier. Berrien drafted an address that, rather than directly asserting the constitutionality or otherwise of the protective system, simply stated as fact that a significant portion of the American people considered it unconstitutional, and detailed the standard arguments for this position. On the floor of the convention, Gallatin then moved to strike out this section of the text, explaining that his intent was to allow those present who, like him, accepted the constitutionality of protection to place their opposition to that specific passage on record, so that their subsequent vote on the question of adopting the address as a whole could not be misconstrued. Gallatin clearly expected his motion to be defeated, as it was by 159 to 35, but it served its purpose by preventing extended discussion of the constitutional question, and the address was then adopted by an even wider margin.[23]

On the final day of the convention, a second committee was appointed, again with Gallatin at its head, to prepare a memorial to Congress "setting forth the evils of the existing Tariff of duties, and asking such a modification of the same, as shall be consistent with the purposes of revenue, and equal in its operation on the different parts of the United States, and on the various interests of the same." The committee were also instructed "to attend personally, or by sub-committee, at Washington, for the purpose of promoting the same."[24] One member from South Carolina objected to this clause, declaring that he was "averse to lobby members." "He did not doubt it was very efficient" to employ such agents, he explained. Indeed, "much of the very evil this Convention is assembled to consider the means of removing, is to be attributed to this kind of agency." Nonetheless, "the Constitution had pointed out the true mode of proceeding. Every individual had his agent in his representative." Gallatin replied that he "could see nothing improper in agents attending Congress to promote any business, either public or private. If men would disgrace themselves by improper conduct, that could be no objection to sending honorable men there on honorable business," and he volunteered to go himself. The motion to strike the lobby clause was then defeated, and shortly thereafter the convention adjourned, its members having signaled their willingness to "meet the enemy . . . with their own weapons."[25]

The free traders' organizational endeavor was matched by their opponents. Loose plans for a protectionist convention had been laid at a gathering of wool manufacturers in New York in May, with Peter H. Schenck part of a three-man arrangements committee, but these were given renewed impetus by events in Philadelphia. On 15 August, an address was issued to "Farmers, Mechanics, and Manufacturers," calling on them to meet and appoint delegates "three times the number of the state delegation in congress."[26] Despite complaints about the short notice, the assembly that opened in New York on 26 October was an imposing one, with more than five hundred attendees from thirteen states, although Delaware, Maryland, and Virginia were the only slave states represented.[27] Those present included E. I. du Pont, Hezekiah Niles, and virtually all of the prominent Boston manufacturers, while Mathew Carey and Charles J. Ingersoll were both named as part of the hundred-strong contingent from Pennsylvania. Samuel Breck, a recent convert to protectionism after casting his state's lone vote against the Tariff of 1824, recalled that traveling up in the company of "70 or 80 of our colleagues," one wag dubbed the group "Mathew Carey's chickens."[28] Nonetheless, there was a serious point to these large delegations. In the past, newspapers had made much of the presence of former presidents as members of the American Society in 1816, or a founding father presiding over the Friends of National Industry convention in 1819, as testament to the respectability of the cause. But in America's increasingly democratic political culture, sheer numbers held more weight than celebrated names as an index to public opinion, and protectionist editors considered it a positive omen that their convention was twice the size of their opponents', though the latter were quick to retort that more states had been represented in Philadelphia.

The convention opened with the selection as president of William Wilkins, sitting Jacksonian senator for Pennsylvania, a choice that one commentator attributed to the cynical calculation of certain "wiseacres" that it would "secure him to the protective policy."[29] The elevation of Wilkins was also cited as evidence that the meeting would eschew party divisions, as was the applause that greeted the appearance of John Quincy Adams in the gallery.[30] Carey's personal quarrels with several leading members continued, however, and he found himself excluded from all of the offices of the convention, as well as the committees appointed to prepare an address to the people and a memorial to Congress, an omission that he publicly denounced as "a foul deed, and highly discreditable to the parties by whose management it took place."[31] Carey did win appointment to a permanent committee, chaired by Niles, which would continue sitting after the convention adjourned to coordinate the protectionist campaign and immediately set for itself the target of raising eight thousand dollars to bankroll its activities through a subscription quota on supporters in the various states.[32] Ingersoll, meanwhile, won plaudits for his part in penning the public address and was rewarded with the mission to Washington that had escaped him at Harrisburg, despite the renewed opposition of Jonathan Roberts and others who mistrusted his motives.[33]

Reviewing recent events in the *Banner*, Raguet proudly proclaimed that "the assembling of the Free Trade Convention at Philadelphia, may be regarded as the first movement of the Free Trade *Army* upon the enemy's country." "The Tariff Convention at New York was the rally of the Northern Forces upon finding their territory invaded," he continued, "and all parties now agree, that a decisive action must be fought on the floor of Congress, during the session of that body, which will commence on the 5th of December."[34] Even the nullifiers held fire. South Carolina governor James Hamilton Jr., who we last encountered bemoaning the influence of lobbyists on the Tariff of 1824, instructed the state legislature that "by every sentiment of kindness and comity towards those Delegates, from the other Free Trade portions of the Union, who, in the recent Convention at Philadelphia, have so zealously and patriotically cooperated in the effort to obtain for our country blessings so essential to its liberty and happiness, we are bound to take no attitude, during the present session of Congress that will prevent a calm, peaceful, and satisfactory, adjustment of this great question."[35] Protectionists too looked to Washington for salvation, and friends prevailed upon Clay, who had been in political retirement since Jackson's elevation to the White House, to take a seat in the Senate in preparation to combat the "imposing proceedings, under high names, going on in Philadelphia."[36] As the Twenty-Second Congress opened its doors, the fate of the American System hung in the balance.

The Jacksonians easily controlled the House and reelected Andrew Stevenson as Speaker on the first ballot, although only by the exact number of votes required for a majority as several Northern members of the party threw their support to a rival candidate from Pennsylvania, an early indication that they would not abandon the protective policy simply to conciliate their Southern counterparts.[37] The Speaker then surprised everyone by appointing John Quincy Adams, returning to the national legislature again after a twenty-three year absence, as chair of the Committee on Manufactures. Stevenson probably intended to embarrass the ex-president by giving him responsibility for resolving rising tensions over the tariff while at the same time constraining his ability to act by packing the committee with reliable Jackson men, just as he had with Rollin C. Mallary in 1828.[38] Adams certainly did not want the assignment, considering it "of labor more burdensome than any other in the House," but the Speaker refused his request to exchange with another Massachusetts representative, and though he considered himself "no worshipper of the tariff," he would not consent to leave the manufacturing interests of his home state at the mercy of a hostile chair.[39] Whether he could do anything for those interests remained to be seen, however; one of his colleagues subsequently informed Adams that Stevenson could "not have selected seven members from the whole house so effectively suited to disagree with one another as the seven members of the committee of manufactures."[40]

Given the circumstances, Adams recognized that he could achieve nothing without the cooperation of the man who had replaced him as president. Jackson was conscious that pressure for reform was mounting in the South, and his Third Annual Message, citing "the confidence with which the extinguishment of the public debt may be anticipated," had recommended "a modification of the tariff which shall produce a reduction of our revenue to the wants of the Government and an adjustment of the duties on imports with a view to equal justice in relation to all our national interests."[41] Therefore, at the first meeting of the Committee on Manufactures on 14 December, Adams agreed "that communication might be held with the Secretary of the Treasury, to ascertain the views and wishes of the Executive, and if they had any plan in preparation upon this subject."[42] The secretary in question was Louis McLane, the factory owner who had helped send Isaac Briggs to Washington in 1816, but whose commitment to protectionism had been superseded by his loyalty to the current occupant of the White House. "Of the power of the general government on this subject I never had any doubt," he wrote to a friend prior to the commencement of the session, but "for some years past I have entertained as little of the expediency, and indeed the necessity, of confining its exercise within moderate limits. We have pushed it too far for the public peace, and must get back to reasonable ground."[43] Putting his pride aside, Adams met with McLane and informed him "that I believed the plan of reduction ought to come from the Treasury Department, and I for one should be disposed to give to such plan every aid in my power, so far as should be consistent with my duties."[44] McLane was willing but said he would need time to prepare such a plan, along with a House resolution authorizing him to do so, similar to that which had invited the intervention of his predecessor, Alexander J. Dallas, in 1816. Adams agreed to procure the latter, which he did on 19 January.[45] McLane then went to work, leaving the former president satisfied that their collaboration might be a fruitful one. "I told him I believed the reduction of the tariff must be a matter of compromise," he recorded in his diary. "I should certainly not consent to sacrifice the manufacturing interest; but something of concession would be due from that interest to appease the discontents of the South. He concurred altogether with these opinions."[46]

While the Committee on Manufactures waited on the Secretary of the Treasury, other proposals were brought forward for the consideration of Congress. In the House, George McDuffie, the South Carolina nullifier who chaired Ways and Means, presented a bill he had railroaded through that committee over the objections of several members, which would reduce all duties, currently averaging about 45 percent, to a single ad valorem rate of 12.5 percent within three years.[47] "He made a damned crazy—vile—& nonsensical speech on it—supporting the proposition that the *Cotton-planter* pays all the duty &c.," reported one Massachusetts representative. "This is foolish—& all sides except—perhaps—a half dozen of his colleagues dissent from him—but yet he left this impression on the House—that S. Car. will nullify it if something is not done."[48] Meanwhile, in the Senate, McDuffie's compatriot Robert Y. Hayne offered a similar, if slightly more moderate, scheme modeled explicitly on the memorial of the Free Trade Convention.[49] That document, produced largely by Gallatin and forwarded to Congress in January when sickness prevented the author from presenting it in person, recommended a standard rate of 20 percent.[50] Not all nullifiers approved of Gallatin's calculations; two members of the memorial committee attached an addendum that urged further reduction, while Calhoun complained that "Gallatin has betrayed the South."[51] Hayne was satisfied, however, that by equalizing the duties on manufactured articles and raw materials, this plan, like McDuffie's, would obliterate the principle of protection and confine the tariff to its true purpose of defraying the costs of government. It also proved too extreme for the majority of his colleagues, however, and was summarily shelved.[52]

On the other side of the question, the newly elected Senator Clay also recognized the necessity of reducing the public revenue now that the national debt neared extinction, but unlike Adams he was not prepared to bargain with either Jackson or the nullifiers to achieve it.[53] In caucus with political friends on 28 December, Clay put forward his own proposal for a repeal of all duties on tea, coffee, spices, and many other articles not produced in the United States, coupled with an increase in duties on several articles that were produced at home to the point that the cost of importation became prohibitory, thus serving the dual function of generating less revenue while providing even greater protection. Adams was the lone voice in opposition; while he considered the idea an ingenious one, he argued that it would satisfy neither the administration, without whose support it could not pass, nor those Southerners who accepted the constitutionality of the tariff but criticized its unequal operation, whose goodwill was needed to stifle nullification.[54] Clay brusquely replied that "he did not care who it defied. To preserve, maintain, and strengthen the American system he would defy the South, the President, and the devil." "Mr. Clay's manner, with many courtesies of personal politeness, was exceedingly peremptory and dogmatical," Adams recorded in his diary, and his audience "was as obsequious as he was super-presidential."[55] A mutual friend subsequently hinted that Clay was drunk; "he had been dining abroad" and "came to the meeting a little flustered."[56] Still, the chance for cooperation between the two men, who had worked so closely together in the past, was lost. Clay pressed ahead with a series of resolutions on the subject, which soon became bogged down in interminable debate, while Adams, excluded from subsequent caucuses, returned to his collaboration with the Secretary of the Treasury.[57]

+ + +

Having secured congressional approval, McLane embarked on an information-gathering exercise that dwarfed that carried out by Dallas sixteen years earlier. Special commissioners were appointed by the treasury at a rate of six dollars a day and charged with procuring answers to a list of forty questions from the manufacturers in their local area.[58] The process was time consuming, and not everyone possessed the patience to see it through. Mathew Carey, appointed one of the commissioners for Pennsylvania at the age of seventy-two, came out with his own proposal for a modification of the tariff in March. The Philadelphian's bitterness about his treatment in New York was evident in his condemnation of "the ultra men on both sides," and he suggested that an annual reduction of 10 percent on all rates above 25 percent until they reached that level would provide manufacturers the time they needed to adapt.[59] This plan he credited to his son, Henry, who had inherited his father's obsession with political economy and would play a prominent role in tariff debates to come. The reaction among the protectionist ranks was hostile, however. One of Clay's allies in the Senate, who Carey consulted with privately on the proposal, called it "a virtual abandonment of the whole system" and surrender to the Free Trade Convention.[60] Even his old comrade Niles believed that the scheme, though well intentioned, would serve only "to break down those institutions which he has so long, and so powerfully, labored to build up," and Carey swiftly withdrew it.[61]

Meanwhile, protectionist lobbyists descended on the national capital in unprecedented numbers. This was partly attributable to logistical advances; as Pennsylvania senator George Mifflin Dallas, son of the former Secretary of the Treasury, remarked to his wife, "the facility of coming is now such, that we are daily visited by new faces from Philadelphia."[62] More important, though, the hopes of John Harrison and Peter H. Schenck for a coordinated lobbying campaign in 1820 were finally fulfilled more than a decade later under the aegis of the New York Tariff Convention. The permanent committee appointed by that assembly was authorized "to depute, if they should deem it necessary, some person or persons to attend at Washington during the next session of congress, to support the views of this convention in regard to the cause of American industry."[63] Three agents were duly chosen to represent the major centers for manufacturing: Ingersoll, for Pennsylvania; Jonas B. Brown, a veteran of such missions, for New England; and James Lynch, a New York iron man.[64] In addition, numerous others made the pilgrimage at the behest of local organizations, or of their own volition. At one time or another, such familiar faces as Carey, E. I. du Pont, Niles, Schenck, and even Harrison Gray Otis, who had dealt the deathblow to Baldwin's bill of 1820 but now lived comfortably off income from investments in textile manufacturing, were to be glimpsed around the capitol.[65] "The manufacturers . . . are watching with lynx-eyes," Dallas informed a friend.[66] On the floor, Samuel Smith, chair of the Senate Committee on Finance, openly blamed "the lobby members, the agents of the manufacturers, . . . those interested men [who] hang on the Committee of Manufactures like an incubus," for having "put their fiat on any change [in the tariff] whatsoever."[67]

The surviving correspondence of a committee appointed by the Pennsylvania Society for the Promotion of Manufactures and the Mechanic Arts to communicate with Ingersoll and also with its own delegate in Washington, iron monger Benjamin B. Howell, provides some record of their activities.[68] The former was the first to arrive late in January, followed by Howell a few days later.[69] As Senator Smith suspected, their orders were to oppose any modification to the current rates, at least insofar as they would affect domestic industry, the admitted defects in the Tariff of 1828 notwithstanding. As the committee instructed Howell: "[O]ur plan should be to act on the defensive & maintain the protection as it exists. Such were the views of the N York convention & when we consider how many conflicting interests may be excited by a proposal of change, we cannot doubt their correctness."[70]

Introduction to the Committee on Manufactures was provided by Lewis Condict, the sole anti-Jacksonian member aside from Adams, who had served in that capacity since 1824 and who, Howell noted, "is with us thoroughly." His impression of the chair was not so favorable, however. "I ought not perhaps to have formed an opinion from our interview of an hour," he reported, "but it would be deemed a bad omen by almost any client, were he told at the outset by his own advocate, that <u>his adversary had made out a strong case</u>." The arguments of the Free Trade Convention "are quoted as authority," whereas "statements of well attested facts <u>on the other side</u>, are said to come from <u>persons who are interested</u>."[71] The protectionist agents were particularly alarmed to discover Adams's preference for abolishing the minimums system, which slaveholders blamed for the high cost of coarse textiles, but which the Pennsylvania Society committee considered "the palladium of the Woollen & Cotton manufactures."[72] At the suggestion of their men in Washington, "that it may be understood that we do not speak on our own sentiments merely," the society instigated a letter-writing campaign to convince other members of the Committee on Manufactures of the need for its retention.[73] This evidently made an impression, for Adams subsequently acknowledged "a determined opposition among the manufacturers" to his plan, though he remained convinced "that this system of minimums must ultimately be abandoned, or that there would be an insurrection in the South."[74] Meanwhile, the delegates also secured meetings with the Secretary of the Treasury and even the president himself, as well as consulting with allies in Congress and coordinating with their counterparts from other states. As Howell explained, "those who feel interest enough in the matter to take an active part need all the counsel of those qualified to instruct them."[75]

Howell stayed four weeks in Washington. "[O]ur time to this, has been, I think not unprofitably employed," he reported upon his departure. "[W]e have furnished statistics, until our stores are exhausted, and our friends are supplied," and now there was nothing left to do but wait on McLane.[76] Ingersoll, in contrast, proposed to remain indefinitely and requested an additional five hundred dollars on top of that which he had already received; the cost of a mission to Washington had evidently increased substantially since Briggs spent three months there on a two-hundred-dollar subscription in 1816.[77] This his employers refused, citing their inability to raise the necessary funds.[78] Possibly they had also begun to suspect his closeness to the administration and apparent willingness, contrary to their instructions, to advocate for a compromise involving a substantial reduction in duties.[79] Extant correspondence with their errant ambassador ends mid-March, but four months later Ingersoll wrote to the committee to deny rumors that he had "departed from the grounds of the New York Convention and of your letters to me" and "betrayed [the Society's] interests—sacrificed them to personal objects" in the pursuit of office.[80] The author's very public conversion to Jacksonism around this time surely did his cause no favors, and the committee showed little inclination to hear him out.[81] Jonathan Roberts, who had distrusted Ingersoll since the Harrisburg Convention, concluded that he had made little effort to save the tariff, and then "tax'd manufactures with a round bill of expence . . . for his pretended service."[82]

Meanwhile, having worked himself half to death, McLane finally reported his proposal to the House on 27 April, accompanied by instructions on how his friends should present it, whereupon it was immediately referred to the Committee on Manufactures.[83] Howell, who had returned to Washington after receiving notice that the report was imminent, wrote that he and other protectionist agents "have been in almost daily conference with the Secy."[84] They were cheered by McLane's willingness to adopt their suggestions on particular details, such as measures to reduce fraud, but disappointed with the significant concessions offered to their opponents, including a reduction in the average level of duties to 27 percent and abolition of the woolen minimums.[85] Partisan critics of the administration were less charitable. "The Secys plan sacrifices the American System, in some of its most important branches. It is a Southern judicious tariff," declared Clay, predicting that many Northern Jacksonians would not support it.[86] Conversely, Southern nullifiers were convinced that McLane had conceded too much to the protectionists he consulted with. The whole project, complained one, was drawn up with the "aid of Mr. Niles, the editor of the Register, of Mr. R.[edwood] Fisher, the editor of the paper set up by the manufacturers convention lately held in New York, and Mr. Brown of Boston—large woolen manufacturer."[87]

All eyes now turned to the Committee on Manufactures and its reluctant chair. Only one month previously, Adams had renewed his request to be excused, citing the labor involved in his assignment to a special committee to investigate the Second Bank of the United States. With rumors circulating of his breach with Clay and his avowed sympathies for the arguments of the Free Trade Convention, many protectionists, including Niles, were willing to see him go; as one remarked rather poetically, "the Dragon stationed at Washington to guard the golden fleece of N. England seems to have had the juices of the Lethean herbs squirted into his eyes and to have consented to its being stolen by the Southern Argonauts."[88] Instead it was the free traders, "these men one & all, who formerly were his most bitter accusers," who "covered him with eulogy, and among other things declared that he was the only individual now living, who could save the Union."[89] And so, Adams remained, presiding over daily meetings of the committee and consulting frequently with McLane over the four weeks it took to amend the latter's scheme to his satisfaction.[90]

Adams presented the committee's bill to the House on 23 May. It was, he explained, a compromise between many interests; even his colleagues reserved the right to oppose particular features of it.[91] As the accompanying report stated, the committee, "after a full and deliberate consideration of the arguments submitted to them upon this question by several of the most eminent manufacturers," nonetheless concurred with the Secretary of the Treasury in the abolition of the woolen minimums and also in seriously reducing the duty on coarse textiles, both gestures that were explicitly intended "to conciliate the interests and feelings of the South."[92] In deference to "the impression of the manufacturers," however, they proposed higher duties on many other products, including the more expensive categories of textile, than McLane had done, with a view to "reduce largely those articles which are not in competition without our own manufactures, and very little, or not at all, those that are."[93] In setting these rates, the committee were likely guided by a document prepared by Nathan Appleton, who had once traveled to Washington to lobby on the Tariff of 1824 but now sat in the national legislature himself. Appleton and his fellow Massachusetts representative John Davis had been asked by their protectionist friends in Congress to prepare a schedule of duties "making everything free which did not interfere with our own productions." A copy of this was supplied to Adams and, according to its author, "was substantially adopted in the tariff of 1832."[94] The resulting bill was therefore, according to one Treasury Department clerk, "nearly a transcript of McLane's project" in its design "but not so favourable to the South" in its detail.[95]

+ + +

Six months in construction, the bill's fate was decided within six weeks on the floor. Still, while it lasted the speechifying was as intense as ever. "You can perceive how my thoughts run, and what company I am in—the tariff, the tariff, the accursed tariff," groused one legislator three weeks after Adams's report. "From morning to night, I hear little beside. We discuss it at our boarding houses, and we discuss it in the Representative Chamber."[96] As on previous occasions, the quantity of debate should not be misread as testament to its quality. "We are doomed today to listen to another and much less animated or attractive speech on the Tariff," sighed Dallas, writing to his wife one day from his desk in the Senate. "Mr. Dickerson, of New Jersey, has the floor, and is coolly and not most elegantly going through the heavy argument—beginning before the flood. Where he will end, is unimaginable."[97] Meanwhile, a correspondent for the Philadelphia *United States Gazette*, covering the deliberations of the House, reported that "the only members who seem to be weary are they who sit in their seats, aspiring to no higher character than that of listeners." He then recounted meeting a congressman leaving the chamber who assured him that the tariff would not be considered that day, only to enter and find it had already been under discussion for an hour. "This anecdote sustains my assertion," he concluded, "that there are some who, if they listen at all, listen to very little purpose."[98]

Despite declaring himself "not over anxious for its fate," the former president took on the challenge of shepherding his measure through the House with gusto, hammering so hard on his desk during one heated exchange that he cracked a bone in his hand.[99] Opposition came from the two extremes of the tariff spectrum. Ultraprotectionists judged the level of duties inadequate "as useless as half a pair of scissors—or as to be almost a Christian" and pledged to "die in the last ditch" to preserve the existing rates; two-thirds of Adams's Massachusetts colleagues fell into this category.[100] Ultrafree traders, in contrast, considered any retention of the principle of protection, as distinct from a revenue-only tariff, to be unacceptable. But the majority of congressmen, North and South, Jacksonian and anti-, saw the opportunity for a compromise that would redress the economic grievances of the slaveholding interest and thus isolate the nullifiers without sacrificing the welfare of manufacturers. On 28 June, the bill sailed through the House by 132 votes to 65.

Arriving in the Senate the next day, the tariff bill was referred to that body's Committee on Manufactures, still chaired by Mahlon Dickerson.[101] Since New England's conversion to the protectionist cause, it was the latter, and no longer their opponents, who held the balance of power in the upper chamber, and certain members hoped to make the measure they received from the House more favorable to domestic industry, just as they had done in 1828. Chief among them was Daniel Webster, who assured one delegate to the New York Tariff Convention that "if we can make the bill what it ought to be, in regard to woolen clothes, it will do much good," and then listed several other articles that would also be "attended to."[102] Back in Boston, Abbott Lawrence had warned a public meeting that the prospect of Adams's bill passing unaltered "was worth a pilgrimage of one half of New England to Washington, to prevent it."[103] He and several other manufacturers were chosen to liaise with Webster and "explain & enforce their views on the pending measure."[104] Seizing the opportunity provided by the referral of the bill, they were able after "some labor" to persuade Dickerson's committee to accept "most" of their preferred amendments, which were reported to the Senate for its approval on 2 July.[105]

The activities of the Boston deputation did not go unnoticed. The following day, as the Senate commenced consideration of the proposed amendments, Robert Y. Hayne spotted Webster conversing from his desk with Lawrence, who was standing at the back of the chamber. The South Carolinian, who held the floor, immediately demanded to know "whether their legislation was not influenced by certain lobby members" and "those who acted as their agents within these walls." Webster acknowledged the purpose of Lawrence's visit, stating that the latter "had come here at his request, to give him information on some subjects with which he was more familiar." "But were not the citizens of this country to pay attention to their interests, whenever measures were about to be legislated of vital importance to their several interests," the Massachusetts senator enquired, citing Gallatin's defense of such practices at the Free Trade Convention, though he rejected the label "lobby members." In response, Hayne denied any intent to challenge "the right of every citizen to watch over his interests" but reiterated his opposition to "such palpable breaches of all courtesy, by a person leaning over the bar, speaking, not to one person, but to several, and interfering in the business pending."[106] This exchange testifies to both the growing presence of lobbyists in the capitol building itself and the emergence of a defense of lobbying as a right reserved to every citizen by the Constitution, contrary to Thomas Cooper's claim that it was unconstitutional because it "operates from without on the members within."[107]

Lawrence's mission was successful, for in a series of close votes the protectionists were able to increase many rates, including those on woolen textiles, with one of the Jacksonian senators from New York and both from Pennsylvania opting to please their constituents rather than embrace the administration's policy of conciliating the South.[108] "The Pressure upon your Senators from all the interior of the State, on the Tariff, cannot be conceived by those who do not witness the piles of letters, and reports of meetings, daily received," grumbled Dallas.[109] On 9 July, the bill passed by a two-thirds majority, just as it had in the other chamber, thirty-two votes to sixteen. This time, though, all but one of the nays came from Southerners who felt the modified bill was now too full of protection, despite still reducing the overall level of duties.

The House accepted some of the Senate amendments but rejected others, the most significant of which were the increased rates on woolens and cotton-bagging, both of particular importance to planters.[110] As in 1824 and 1828, a Committee of Conference was appointed to resolve the disagreements.[111] The three senators chosen were Hayne, Dickerson, and Wilkins: the first an ardent free trader, the latter two self-identified friends of domestic industry, a disposition that reflected the composition of the upper chamber. In committee, however, Wilkins, who had been elected chair of the New York Tariff Convention in order to secure him to the cause, switched sides and voted with Hayne to recede from the contested amendments. This provoked a fierce debate in the Senate where Clay, whose Kentucky constituents were the main producers of cotton-bagging, claimed that the Pennsylvanian had sacrificed the other protected interests in order to preserve the iron industry of his own state.[112] "Clay was furious," reported Dallas, "he contemplated, as a last resort, taking the attitude of pacificator as on the Missouri question:—his defeat & mortification were signal and manifest."[113] Nonetheless, the committee's report was sustained and the bill sent for the president's signature.

The Tariff of 1832 enacted the first general decrease in duties since the United States had embarked on its experiment with protectionism in 1816. Yet it also won widespread approval. "The Tariff Bill operates as a universal anodyne," Adams observed proudly soon after its passage. "All parties are claiming it exclusively as their own."[114] This outcome had seemed improbable nine months previously, when South Carolina threatened nullification and rival national Free Trade and Tariff conventions suggested a country torn down the middle. When it came to the decisive roll calls on the bill, however, taking House and Senate together, both major parties, Jacksonians and antis-, split two to one in favor.[115] The General's preference for conciliating the South no doubt influenced his supporters. "The President is exerting himself about the Tariff, and does and has done all that Man Could do," one friend of the administration remarked midway through the session.[116] Even more important, though, was the decision of Adams, as chair of the House Committee on Manufactures, to collaborate with Secretary of the Treasury McLane in designing a bill that cut out both the diehard protectionists like Clay, who wanted to increase duties to prohibitive levels, and the radical free traders like McDuffie, who demanded a tariff for revenue only. Even manufacturers who had lobbied hard against any modification came to accept the merits of Adams's scheme. "I confess my astonishment that so much noise about free trade and nullification should have aided in the production of such a Bill," wrote E. I. du Pont. "The amount of protection is not so material as the acknowledgement of the principle and that to[o] by a large majority in the house, comprehending many southern votes."[117]

The presumed deathblow to nullification struck by the new tariff was indeed the cause of much rejoicing among both parties. Jackson boasted that he had "killed the ultras, both tarifites and nullifiers," and "the south being relieved by the diminution of duties upon cotton bagging, on blankets, on course wollings [sic] and on sugar will convince the people that the whole attempt at nullification is an effort of disappointed ambition, originating with unprincipled men who would rather rule in hell, than be subordinate in heaven."[118] Webster too was convinced that "*nullification* is at an end," for "there are too many southern votes *for* [the tariff], to admit the idea of its being *nullified* by southern votes."[119] Only a minority of observers reached the opposite conclusion that, as one Virginia congressman wrote in justifying his refusal to support a reduction in rates, "its passage by southern votes" actually "diminishes our chance for future peaceable redress," by demonstrating that South Carolina could not rely on the other slave states in its crusade against the protective system and would have to act alone.[120] Crucially, however, this was also the judgment reached by the nullifier-in-chief. "The question is no longer of free trade, but liberty and despotism," Vice President Calhoun recorded. "The hope of the country now rests on our gallant little State. Let every Carolinian do his duty."[121]

+ + +

"The [Tariff] act of 1833, called a 'compromise,' was a breach of all the rules, and all the principles of legislation," recalled Missouri senator and Jacksonian stalwart Thomas H. Benton in his retirement. Benton's list of complaints was long; the bill was "kept a secret," "passed by a majority pledged to its support, and pledged against any amendments except from its managers," and sponsored by "rival politicians who had lately, and long, been in the most violent state of legislative as well as political antagonism." At the head of the list, though, was his conviction that the measure had been "concocted out of doors, managed by politicians dominated by an outside interest." Whereas most studies of the Compromise of 1833 have focused on maneuvering in the capitol, and particularly the union between Calhoun and Clay to which Benton alluded, this reference to the scheme's origins "out of doors" adds an extra dimension to an episode that many contemporaries and historians have credited with saving the country from the horrors of civil war.[122]

South Carolina's reaction to the Tariff of 1832 was swift and unequivocal. The nullifiers' well-resourced campaign ran roughshod over Unionist opposition; Carey calculated that their States Rights and Free Trade Association in a single year spent "as much as, and probably more than, the manufacturers have expended for printing in the eleven years from the middle of 1820 to the meeting of the New York Convention."[123] At the state elections in October, proponents of nullification won a sweeping victory, and within weeks the new legislature had summoned a special convention for the purpose. On 24 November, that convention adopted an Ordinance of Nullification, which declared that the Tariffs of 1828 and 1832, "purporting to be acts laying duties and imposts on foreign imports, but in reality intended for the protection of domestic manufactures," are "unauthorized by the constitution of the United States" and therefore "are null, void, and no law, nor binding upon this State, its officers or citizens."[124] This ordinance, which was drafted by William Harper, one of the authors of the radical addendum to the memorial of the Free Trade Convention, was dated to take effect on 1 February 1833, in order to provide Congress with one final chance to reduce rates to an acceptable revenue standard. According to the Nullification Convention, the Tariff of 1816, which Calhoun and many other South Carolinians had supported, was designed to arrive at such a standard, then estimated at 20 percent, after providing three years of temporary shelter for America's infant industries. Before the reduction could be effected, however, grasping manufacturers twisted that legislation into an undertaking to maintain permanent, and increasingly prohibitive, levels of protection that in time came to exceed 100 percent on some articles. South Carolina would tolerate this no longer, and with the national debt now nearing retirement, a single rate of 10 or 12 percent, making no distinction between raw materials and manufactures, would, the convention calculated, "be fully adequate to all the legitimate purposes of Government."[125]

When news of the Nullification Ordinance reached the White House, Jackson was furious. "If one drop of blood be shed there in defiance of the laws of the United States, I will hang the first man of them I can get my hands on to the first tree I can find," he reportedly vowed.[126] The General had just secured re-election with a crushing victory over Clay, particularly in the slave states, where he lost only Kentucky, which stayed true to its favorite son, and South Carolina, which signaled its disenchantment with both candidates by casting its electoral votes for John Floyd, nullifier governor of

Virginia, and Henry Lee of the Free Trade Convention. Jackson took this result as validation of his strategy of conciliating the South with tariff reform while denying the legitimacy of nullification. To this end, the president responded to the ordinance with two radically different documents. In his Fourth Annual Message, delivered on 4 December, he urged a further reduction in the level of duties "to the revenue standard" and rejected the policy of "perpetual protection."[127] This represented a clear reversal of the administration's position on the Tariff of 1832, which it had previously hailed as a resolution to the tariff question, and was received by protectionists with horror; Adams called it "a complete surrender to the nullifiers of South Carolina."[128] Just six days later, however, Jackson issued a special proclamation in which he declared the doctrine of nullification to be "*incompatible with the existence of the Union, contradicted expressly by the letter of the Constitution, unauthorized by its spirit, inconsistent with every principle on which it was founded, and destructive of the great object for which it was formed.*"[129] "You cannot conceive how the tariffites rejoiced," reported Virginia senator John Tyler, for their system "was given up by its friends almost in despair before the Proclamation," but the president's pledge gave them renewed hope; if they could block any change to the existing rates, he would enforce them, at the point of a sword, if necessary.[130]

Responsibility for averting this confrontation fell to the second session of the Twenty-Second Congress, composed of the same members who had passed the Tariff of 1832 just five months previously. There were a few critical changes in the personnel of relevant House committees, however. McDuffie was detained by his participation in the Nullification Convention, which provided a pretext for the Speaker to transfer chairmanship of Ways and Means to Gulian C. Verplanck, a Jacksonian free trader from New York.[131] Adams remained as chair of Manufactures and was ready to fight for his creation but found himself stymied by the switch of Charles Dayan, who Adams considered "a warm Jackson ... Man, but honest, able, and true to the manufacturing interest," for Michael Hoffman, a fellow New Yorker whose unswerving loyalty to the administration in pursuing savage cuts to naval funding as chair of the Committee on Naval Affairs had earned him the sardonic nickname "Admiral Hoffman."[132] "He was the most anti-manufacturing man in the house, and was purposefully put upon the Committee as a check mate upon every thing that could favour that interest," the ex-president subsequently recalled. "He baffled every proposal that I could offer in behalf of the manufactures, and by common consent, the Committee soon ceased to hold any meetings."[133]

Verplanck, whose family had made its fortune in commerce, considered the protective system to be "impolitic and unequal" but not unconstitutional, which made him a natural choice to represent the administration in the House.[134] Even before his appointment was announced, he wrote to Albert Gallatin that he would wait on "[Secretary of the Treasury] McLane's project of a tariff in detail."[135] The secretary's biographer believes that the resulting Ways and Means bill, delivered to the House on 27 December, was "largely McLane's work, or at least very close to the bill prepared under his direction in the Treasury Department."[136] Jackson too may have had a hand in it; later in life, the president would refer to "the Tariff bill prepared by McLain [sic] under my view."[137] In an accompanying report, Verplanck explained that "in adjusting the several duties, [the committee] have conformed, unless some strong reason for a different rate was perceived, to those of the tariff act of 1816."[138] Some discrimination between articles was retained, with higher duties on raw wool and iron than had been enacted in 1816, in an effort to placate key Jacksonian constituencies in New York and Pennsylvania.[139] Still, the overall package offered major concessions to the South; the remaining cotton minimums would be abolished and the average rate halved to 15 percent within just two years, which the authors considered to be the true revenue standard.[140] Unsurprisingly, Hoffman, of the Committee on Manufactures, immediately pronounced it "a Judicious Tariff."[141]

Nullifiers professed delight at the Ways and Means bill. "There is a prospect of a very considerable reduction of the duties," rejoiced McDuffie, and "the world will give South Carolina the credit of having effected it."[142] Protectionists, of course, were bitterly opposed. "Truly, Mr. *Verplanck's* bill *is* a 'bill of abominations!'" protested Niles in his *Register*, while Carey labeled it a surrender to the slave states.[143] At a meeting of anti-Jacksonian members from Massachusetts, Adams recorded that "the opinion was unanimous that its passage should be opposed."[144] Whether they could actually prevent its passage was another matter; the Jacksonians controlled the House, and Webster feared that "*party discipline*, operating on members of the Government, will lead to great sacrifices of the public interest."[145] It soon became apparent, however, that their misgivings about its provisions were shared by many across the aisle. "To coincide fully with the President, would perhaps be rather hazardous for a Pennsylvania politician," remarked a relative of Dallas's wryly, and Verplanck's bill found no support among that state's delegation, with the exception of John Gilmore, who had helped frame it on Ways and Means and was censured by his constituents for his trouble.[146] Other lawmakers questioned the timing of the measure. "All agree that the So. Ca. Ordinance is the principal obstacle," reported a South Carolina Unionist dispatched to Washington to monitor proceedings. "One member of the H. of R. from N.Y. who has ever been anti-Tariff told me that <u>his feelings</u> he was sure would accuse him of cowardice if he voted for it & he was not certain but his <u>judgement</u> would dictate that to yield at this time would establish a precedent infinitely more pernicious in future than tenfold the evils of the Tariff at present."[147]

Still, uncertain whether they could command a majority against the measure if it came to a vote, the protectionists settled on a strategy of delay. Even after South Carolina extended the deadline on the Nullification Ordinance in light of the progress made by Congress, the session was constitutionally bound to close before 4 March. "It is the policy & design of the northern men," William Hammet, House chaplain, explained to a Southern friend, "to waste time, & prevent its passage this winter, even, if there should be a majority in its favour. For this purpose amendment after amendment will be proposed," and "the opposition will have full liberty to talk, & consume time." To counter this, Hammet continued: "[T]he other side have determined not to argue on any point, farther than that the committee who reported the bill, will probably explain; nor will they allow it to be <u>amended</u>, but will take the bill, as it is, 'for better for worse.'"[148]

For weeks, the one-sided speaking went on, fortified by a stream of petitions and resolutions from protectionist meetings across the country, including one from the permanent committee of the New York Tariff Convention.[149] "A single new ray of light has not been shed by all the speeches that have been made upon the subject during the present debate," complained a correspondent of the Jacksonian *Pennsylvanian* on 15 January.[150] By the end of the month, it was reported that "even some of those who intend to vote for the bill are abandoning the expectation of its passage this session."[151] "All assent [a reduction in duties] would save the Union and the spilling of blood—but then it might break down a shoe shop, Iron foundry, cotton factory or Taylor's [*sic*] establishment—and they want a day or two to chuse [*sic*] between these difficult alternatives," groused Hoffman. The president, meanwhile, seemed entirely preoccupied with securing enactment of the Force Bill, which would authorize him to employ the army to protect customs officers in South Carolina. "I should rather think that Jackson is rather careless about the passage of the tariff bill this Session," observed Hammet. "Nullification is first to be put down—and the next session, the whole weight of the Executive influence will be thrown against the protective system and it goes down."[152] As for Clay, he too stood apart from proceedings, apparently content to let the House determine the fate of his American System. "I suspect he has not yet made up his mind what course to take on this subject," wrote Silas Wright to Martin Van Buren in mid-January, "but this town is full and filling with Eastern manufacturers and northern wool speculators who I think will incline his balance."[153]

+ + +

In fact, though Wright could not know it, Clay had been working on his own tariff proposal for some time. Jackson's rival had been sidelined during the previous session, robbed of his chance to play the "pacificator" by the combination of Adams and McLane, rendered impotent by the duplicity of William Wilkins, and then humiliated in the election that followed. He felt no obligation to sustain the Tariff of 1832, and South Carolina's ultimatum offered an opportunity to resurrect his reputation by fashioning some new, more effective compromise. Simply obstructing the Verplanck bill was insufficient, he explained, for the Twenty-Third Congress would be even more heavily Jacksonian, and once nullification was put down, "the Admon would have carried at the approaching Session a measure much more injurious to the Manufacturers." In the interim, however, Clay held an advantage, for "the Ultra Southern men were extremely unwilling that Jackson should have any credit in the adjustment of the controversy, and to prevent it were disposed to agree to much better terms for the manufacturers, if the measure originated with any other."[154] Therefore, as he subsequently recorded, he set to work with two objectives: "1st to save the Tariff and 2dly. to save the Country from Civil War."[155]

Whereas all previous tariff acts had begun life in either the offices of the Treasury Department or a congressional committee room, the bill that became the Tariff of 1833 did not even originate in Washington. Following the opening of the session, Clay retired to Philadelphia for three weeks to visit relatives. There, he later recounted: "[H]e was called upon by a committee of manufacturers, who disclosed to him their apprehensions of the imminent danger to which the tariff system was exposed, and who asked, with anxiety, what was to be done."[156] Clay did not name these manufacturers, but his friend and biographer Epes Sargent reveals that they included E. I. du Pont; at least one of the Richards brothers, Mark and Samuel, both iron founders; and J. J. Borie, merchant and cotton-mill proprietor. All were involved, at one time or another, with the Pennsylvania Society, and all were attendees at the 1831 New York Tariff Convention.[157] "It was to these individuals," Clay noted, "and not to his friends in Congress, that he first applied to know whether, in their apprehension, a long lease of the protective policy, even though on a lower scale, would not be better than the uncertain state with regard to it in which they then were. To this question not a single man (and he put it to the most intelligent individuals) hesitated for a moment to reply in the affirmative."[158]

Clay's first effort at drafting a compromise was extremely simple. The Tariff of 1832 would remain in force until 3 March 1840, and then from that date forward "all duties collected upon any article or articles whatever of foreign importation shall be equal, according to the value thereof, & solely for the purpose & with the intent of providing such revenue as may be necessary to an economical expenditure of the Govt. without regard to the protection or encouragement of any branch of domestic industry whatever."[159] "The formula traded *time*, which was of first importance to manufacturers, for *principle*, which was of first importance to the South," writes historian Merrill Peterson. "Unlike the Verplanck bill, which would preserve the principle but annihilate the manufacturers, Clay's plan would presumably save the manufacturers but abandon the principle."[160]

We do not know what the Philadelphia manufacturers made of this proposal, though Sargent claims, presumably on Clay's authority, that "they approved it."[161] Soon after the Kentuckian's return to Washington in early January, however, preliminary discussions with allies in Congress established that no such bill could pass. The most determined resistance came from Massachusetts. Webster declared his "astonishment at hearing of any intention, by Mr. Clay, to bring forward such a proposition," while Appleton later recalled that he and Davis, who had helped Adams design the Tariff of 1832, "had repeated interviews [with Clay]. The result was, *from first to last we refused to become parties to the measure*."[162] In both instances, the insuperable objection was the author's willingness to "surrender the protecting powers."[163] Consequently, the first draft was shelved, and as late as 17 January Clay informed one confidant that he had "not entirely matured any plan," and even were he to do so, he was "not satisfied that it would be expedient to offer it."[164]

These reservations notwithstanding, by the time he committed those words to paper Clay had likely already begun consulting on a second iteration of his compromise proposal. We can deduce this from a letter sent by Senator Tyler, a critic of both protection and nullification, to Governor Floyd on 10 January. Though from opposite parties, Clay and Tyler were on good personal terms; the latter admitted to having "conversed freely" with his Kentucky counterpart following Jackson's Nullification Proclamation "upon the condition of public affairs and the true glory which he had it in his power now to acquire."[165] In his letter to Floyd, Tyler echoed Clay's argument to the Philadelphia manufacturers. "The *principle* involved has appeared to me to be the main concern *with us*," meaning Southern opponents of protection, he wrote, whereas "the only ingredient worth any regard in the estimation of the manufacturer, *time*, is of little importance." "*In the strictest confidence*," Tyler then asked Floyd for his opinion on a proposition: "The duties on all unprotected articles forthwith to be abolished and on the protected a reduction of 5 or 10 pr. ct.—the duties on the protected to be abated 1/3 or 1/2 three years and a half hence and seven years hence all duties for protection to cease entirely and a general *ad valorem* to be substituted upon all importations."[166] The writer did not attribute this proposition to Clay, but a gradual reduction in duties would be a central component of the latter's final compromise package, replacing the single savage, but long-postponed, cut in his original plan. Sensitive to charges that he had abandoned the manufacturers, the Kentuckian would subsequently maintain that he never "had any interview or conference with any Southern Senator prior to its introduction" to Congress.[167] This seems unlikely, indeed Tyler's testimony elsewhere flatly contradicts it, but even if strictly true it did not, as Sargent acknowledged, prevent him from employing intermediaries who were "intimate" with various "southern gentlemen" in order to solicit their support.[168]

At the same time, Clay offered revisions designed to overcome the objections of his fellow protectionists. Sometime in late January and early February he held two private conferences with "11 or 12 Senators," at which the scheme was "fully discussed and considered." We do not know the content of that discussion, but it seems likely to have involved extending the time frame for the reduction of duties from seven to nine years and dropping the explicit renunciation of protection, following which, according to Clay, all but one of those present at the second meeting gave their assent.[169] This did not include Webster, though, who only attended the first meeting and made clear that he was "*not party to the protocols*." "What the precise plan is, or will be, I know not," he told a friend. "It is understood Mr C[lay] will agree to almost any thing, in order to settle the question, save the Nullifiers & obtain the credit of *pacification*."[170] Consultations with men of business outside of Congress also produced a mixed response. "I should be extremely unwilling upon my own convictions, however strong, to make any movement which those more immediately concerned did not approve," Clay assured one representative of the New York Tariff Convention's permanent committee, and he subsequently claimed that his faith in the measure was "fortified by frequent conferences with intelligent manufacturers, prior to its introduction."[171] But there were dissenters too, as Daniel W. Coxe, a member of the Pennsylvania Society, reported when he "canvassed with some of our most intelligent agents & manufacturers" at the request of one of Clay's allies in the Senate and found a general reluctance to make concessions while "a reduction of duties or abandonment of the Law of the last session, can only be ascribed to the threat of [South] Ca.[rolina]."[172]

If confrontation over the tariff were to be avoided, then South Carolina's assent to any compromise would also be needed. Clay later claimed that he was moved to intervene in part by compassion for Calhoun and his fellow nullifiers, recalling that his friend John M. Clayton, senator for Delaware, had gazed "upon the care-worn countenances and haggard looks of some of the delegation in Congress from South Carolina" and remarked: "Clay these are fine fellows. It won't do to let old Jackson hang them. We must save them."[173] Thomas H. Benton also alleged that Calhoun, who had re-signed the vice presidency in December 1832 in order to defend nullification in the Senate, was "evidently disturbed" by reports that the president intended to have him tried for treason, and that these reports were circulated by Clay's followers to make him more amenable to a settlement.[174] In truth, though, both men had sufficient political motive to settle the question together and prevent Jackson from marching on South Carolina, if only terms acceptable to each could be agreed upon. This seems to have been effected during an interview between the two immediately prior to the introduction of the bill; though Clay, as we have seen, denied any such meeting took place, Calhoun would subsequently acknowledge it, and several other contemporary sources do likewise, though they differ on the details.[175] Certainly rumors of a coalition were current in Washington. As early as 23 January, for example, McLane informed Van Buren that "there are obvious signs of an understanding between Clay & Calhoun, and it would not surprise me if they should ultimately agree upon some practicable scheme of readjustment."[176]

+ + +

Nonetheless, there was real astonishment when Clay presented the details of that "readjustment" to the Senate on 12 February.[177] The proposed bill took as its starting point the Tariff of 1832, which was scheduled to come into effect on 4 March 1833. Under its provisions, any duty in that act that exceeded 20 percent would be reduced by one-tenth of the excess on 1 October in 1833, 1835, 1837, and 1839, and then by three-tenths on the same date in 1841 and 1842.[178] For opponents of protection, the scheme offered an ultimate reduction in rates to the level recommended by the Free Trade Convention, along with the promise that thereafter duties shall be "laid for the purpose of raising such revenue as may be necessary to an economical administration of the Government; and, for that purpose, shall be equal upon all articles" excepting those on the "free list," which were not subject to tax.[179] For the manufacturers, it offered a smaller and more gradual reduction in rates than the Verplanck bill; eliminated the concessionary duty introduced by Adams on coarse woolens, which would hereafter be taxed the same as other textiles; and moved a number of raw materials to the free list.

Did Clay's bill abandon protection? His supporters would later claim that he never intended the final reductions to take effect, believing that either public opinion would be converted to the value of the protective policy or the needs of the treasury would provide a pretext for retaining higher rates.[180] Historians have tended to agree that it would still be practicable to encourage home industry under the terms of the scheme.[181] But what contemporaries focused on was Clay's disavowal of the argument that such encouragement, on a permanent basis, was correct in principle, a central tenet of the protectionist creed since Baldwin's bill in 1820. For Southerners, indeed, this was the primary virtue of the plan. "Bear in mind that the *principle* of protection is to be utterly abandoned," Tyler had written to Floyd back in January, contrasting it favorably to Verplanck's bill, which actually offered a greater practical reduction in duties, for that very reason.[182] And for high tariff men like Webster, it was their chief objection. The compromise "completely negatives all idea of protection," the Massachusetts senator maintained, "1. Because it expressly confines revenue to the wants of Government," and "2. Because it expressly rejects discrimination, which is the only true and practical mode of protection."[183] He would subsequently circulate copies of Clay's original draft, with its explicit renunciation of protection that had been exorcised from the Senate version, in order to prove the author's willingness to abandon the policy from the outset. In truth, though, Clay admitted as much in his speech accompanying the bill. Encouragement to industry was maintained in the decremental reduction of duties and the admission of raw materials free of tax, he contended, but after benefiting from the "nine and a half years of peace, certainty, and stability" offered by the compromise, he expected "the manufacturers, in every branch, will sustain themselves against foreign competition," and therefore "the protective principle must be said to be, in some measure, relinquished."[184] In essence, Clay was reverting to the same reasoning employed by Alexander J. Dallas to justify the initial experiment with protectionism in 1816: the progress that domestic industry would make under a temporary period of high duties would make it unnecessary for those duties to be continued permanently.

This was a far cry from the American System on which Clay had built his political career, and the reaction among protectionists who had not been privy to his plan was general dismay. "Clay has abandoned his former principles—the protective principle as it is called—& gone over considerable to Calhoun & Southern measures," reported Pennsylvania congressman Henry A. P. Muhlenberg. "The great mass of Clay's friends here at least will not go with him. Opposite extremes have met."[185] Niles, who Sargent claimed to have been part of the consultations, declared in his *Register* that "Mr. Clay's New Tariff Project will be received like a crash of thunder in the winter season, and some will hardly trust the evidence of their senses on a first examination of it—so radical and sudden is the change of policy proposed." "We render all possible respect to the motives of our honoured friend," the editor continued, "but cannot go with him in a measure, which, in our humble opinion (and *this* must be our own guide), contains the surrendry of a power which is vital to the independence of the United States."[186] Carey, whose own plan for a decremental reduction of duties had been so summarily dismissed by Clay's circle a year earlier, called it "a virtual abandonment of the protecting system, the establishment of which required the strenuous efforts of so many years."[187] In Philadelphia, a special meeting of the Pennsylvania Society was hurriedly convened; "you need not doubt, that it will be decisively condemnatory of any abandonment of the Constitution & laws by a patched up compromise," predicted Coxe to his contact in the Senate, adding: "[T]he surprise at Mr. Clay's course is almost universal."[188]

Following presentation of the bill, Calhoun spoke briefly in its favor, an intervention that provoked tumult in the galleries, not so much for anything he said on the floor as for the signal it provided that some bargain had been struck off it.[189] "The approbation given by Mr. Calhoun to the project does not recommend it. He stands too publicly pledged to a war of extermination agst. the principle of protection to acquiesce in anything which retains it," commented one Massachusetts representative.[190] The following day, over the protests of protectionist senators who wanted it sent to the Committee on Manufactures, the bill was referred to a select committee of seven with Clay at its head.[191] The other members were Calhoun, Clayton, Webster, Dallas, William C. Rives of Virginia, and Felix Grundy of Tennessee. Clay and Calhoun naturally favored the measure. Webster met it with "unrelenting hostility," as did Dallas, who considered the scheme "a mere political manoeuvre" intended to bolster its author's presidential prospects. His fellow Jacksonians Grundy and Rives, however, supported the compromise as the only viable option for securing a substantial reduction of duties and avoiding confrontation between South Carolina and the White House, which would surely demolish their party's popularity in the slave states. This gave Clay the four votes he would need to have the bill reported back safely.[192]

Matters were complicated, however, by the final member of the committee. Clayton very nearly missed out on that appointment, for on the day it was announced Jackson summoned Hugh Lawson White, serving as the temporary presiding officer of the Senate in the absence of a vice president, to request that some alternative selection be made, since the Delaware senator was "hostile to the Administration, and unfriendly to Mr. McLane." White replied that he considered the pending legislation was "a measure *above party*," and in any case it was too late to change his decision.[193] But Clayton was no blind follower of Clay; he was also committed to the protective policy and determined that if the scheme must be adopted it should at least be modified in favor of the manufacturers. "I did not rely upon my own judgment alone, nor upon that of my associates in the Senate, for the course I should adopt," he would later recall. "I sought the advice of one who was a citizen of my own State, and who stood, at the time, at the head of the manufacturing interests of the country—a man whose extensive and minute acquaintance with the whole subject of the Tariff was not exceeded by that of any other man in the nation."[194] That man was E. I. du Pont, who Clayton urged to "come among us for a few days" in order "to give me all the information in your power and your best advice in regard to the course I should pursue."[195] Fortunately, du Pont's business concerns were not pressing, his company having recently refused a sizeable gunpowder order from South Carolina on patriotic grounds, and he was able to spend some two weeks in Washington.[196] At the same time, Clayton consulted with several protectionist senators, many of whom he boarded with, and together they resolved to secure one significant amendment to the bill.[197]

The amendment that Clayton demanded would provide for all imported goods to be taxed according to their valuation at American rather than foreign ports, to take effect following the final reduction in rates scheduled for 1842. The result would be to eliminate the fraudulent undervaluation of goods by exporters, and also to increase the real level of duty because a "home valuation," as it was called, would include freight and insurance costs. This proposal was swiftly negatived by the select committee; Calhoun, Rives, and Grundy opposed it, while Webster and Dallas dissented from the entire scheme and had no interest in tinkering with its details. Clayton did, however, extract from Clay a promise to move the same amendment once the bill was returned to the Senate.[198]

The committee duly reported on 19 February, and two days later its own minor amendments were easily approved.[199] Clay then moved Clayton's amendment. This brought Calhoun to his feet, declaring that "he should be compelled to vote against the whole bill, should the amendment be adopted."[200]

Clayton replied that "he could not vote for this bill without this amendment" and threatened to table the whole scheme.[201] As debate on the floor continued, frantic negotiations were conducted behind the scenes. "We considered that a vote for the duties fixed by the act, to be assessed on this principle, was essentially to all intents and purposes a vote for *Protection*," recalled Clayton of his associates, and consequently they were determined not just to see the amendment adopted but also "to compel Mr. Calhoun and his peculiar friends in the Senate to record their votes in the most unequivocal form, on the journal in favor of that principle."[202] First Clay approached and "begged him to let them off," but he was adamant. Then Stephen Miller, the other South Carolina senator, promised to vote for the provision if Calhoun alone could be excused, but again Clayton refused. Instead, taking out his watch, he told Miller: "[A]t the end of fifteen minutes I shall move to lay the bill on the table unless within that time you inform me authoritatively that Mr. Calhoun will vote for it." Miller returned within ten, and the amendment was adopted with Calhoun voting in favor.[203]

Following this dramatic confrontation, discussion shifted to a procedural matter: whether this bill to reduce duties was still a revenue-raising one, and thus could only constitutionally originate in the House. Several senators who were otherwise sympathetic to the compromise hesitated on this point of order, and by 25 February, with only a week remaining in the session, Clay's scheme seemed destined for the same hopeless stalemate that still afflicted the other chamber. Then, without any prior notice, Kentucky representative Robert Letcher, a confidant of Clay's, rose in the House and moved to return the Verplanck Bill to committee with instructions to substitute it, word for word, with that which currently occupied the Senate. Protectionist protests that this "sudden movement" had been sprung on them as they were "collecting our papers, and putting on our outside garments to go home," were in vain; "it swept like a hurricane," Adams recorded, and within a few hours the new bill had been engrossed for a final reading, with even Verplanck voting to replace his own measure.[204] The following day, it passed the House by 119 yeas to 85 nays. The constitutional objection now removed, the only remaining obstacle to its passage by the Senate was the determination of many members that the House should first approve the Force Bill, in order, as one newspaper correspondent noted, "to present South Carolina the sword with one hand, and the olive branch with the other."[205] This was done on 1 March, and the tariff bill passed the upper chamber the same day by twenty-nine yeas to sixteen nays.

"Arguably, the tariff of 1832 was the real compromise tariff, not that of 1833," concludes Donald Ratcliffe.[206] Like many historians, Ratcliffe views the latter as a victory for protection, but in truth it offered more to critics of that doctrine than its advocates, and the divisions in Congress reflected that. Northerners had voted by a ratio of three to one for the Tariff of 1832, but they voted two to one against its replacement. The slave states, in contrast, had only split four to three in favor of Adams's bill the previous year, with much of the opposition coming from ultrafree traders in the Cotton South, but now supported Clay's scheme by an overwhelming thirteen-to-one margin, with the seven negative votes coming from isolated protectionist constituencies among the Border States. As for the major parties, the Jackson men met in caucus and resolved to support the measure in spite of its authorship; they provided 108 votes for the bill, but also 35 against, nearly half of which were cast by Pennsylvanians.[207] Conversely, Clay failed to carry a majority of the anti-administration forces with him, with thirty-four voting in favor and sixty-six against.[208] Among the latter was the entire Massachusetts delegation, including Adams, who labeled the bill "an Act for the protection of John C. Calhoun and his fellow nullifiers."[209] Analyzing the result, Webster concluded that the compromise had been passed by "all the South," "Mr C[lay]'s personal friends," and "a few good men, from the North & the Center, from various motives," over the resistance of "three fourths of the Tariff interest in both Houses."[210]

+ + +

"Our Mr. E. I. du Pont has been in Washington assisting at the treaty of peace between your friends the Nullifiers, and ours the monopolist manufacturers of the North," wrote a partner in the Du Pont gunpowder works to a mercantile company with offices in Charleston on the day after the compromise bill passed the Senate. "Peace has now been happily arranged," he added, "and we hope it will last, for both sides seem to be satisfied."[211] And so it proved. South Carolina's Nullification Convention met again on 11 March to repeal the ordinance, calling the new tariff "cause for congratulation."[212] "This is the pernicious and irreparable mischief of Clay's Bill," lamented John Quincy Adams. "It gave the show of victory to nullification at the very moment when it was at its last gasp."[213] President Andrew Jackson, in contrast, pointed to the Force Bill as evidence that it was the administration, not the nullifiers, that had triumphed, and while he privately admitted that "the [tariff] Bill which has passed is not of the exact character which I would have prefered," he nonetheless expected "that it may have a good effect in the South."[214]

As for the measure's sponsors, they prayed that its merits would be equally appreciated across the free states. Henry Clay's Compromise Tariff was not so favorable to the manufacturers as the Tariff of 1832 it replaced, but unlike the latter it did provide a final resolution to the Nullification Controversy, and the promise of stability for nine years to come. "It has brought upon Mr. Clay a tremendous storm—but it will pass away," predicted one of the Kentuckian's key allies in the Senate. "The Manufacturers are beginning to see the Compromise in its true light & it will be finally approved."[215] There was some truth to this assessment. Abbott Lawrence, for example, told Clay that while he had previously voiced "strong objections to any concessions whatever," he was "now well satisfied with the course the whole subject took in Congress" and believed that "our interests have been greatly promoted by it."[216] Many others, however, remained unconvinced. "I have never scarcely witnessed stronger dissatisfaction in any body of men, than there exists at this moment among the eastern friends (and some of the western) of the protective policy," reported one Washington correspondent as the Twenty-Second Congress drew to a close. "They consider their interests as bargained away, and sold to the south; and they express the deepest mortification that they should have them sacrificed by their own friends. They do not hesitate to tell us, that they consider the passage of the tariff bill as the knell of the American system; and they are so inveterate in their denunciations of those who have inflicted the blow, that it is impossible to expect any other result than a wide and irreconcilable division between those who have heretofore acted together, in storm as well as in sunshine."[217]

The du Pont letter also highlights the part that "outside interest," as Thomas H. Benton called it, played in the Tariff of 1833. The bill's origins were not in Washington, but in Philadelphia, where Clay was first prompted to engineer a compromise between the nullifiers and the administration by the visit of a group of factory owners well versed in campaigning for beneficial legislation. Alarmed at the prospect of the Verplanck Bill becoming law, agents of the manufacturing interest conspired with their allies in the House to stall that measure while at the same time continuing to consult with Clay and his circle as their alternative proposal took shape. The Kentuckian has won the plaudits of historians for arranging the terms of the compromise, but he allotted a significant share of the credit to his colleague John M. Clayton for insisting on the home valuation amendment, and the latter in turn emphasized the contribution of du Pont. "[H]is judgment on the subject confirmed my own opinions; and I owed while he lived a debt of gratitude for his assistance on that occasion," the Delaware senator would later record.[218] Nonetheless, despite the addition of home valuation, the passage of the compromise filled many manufacturers with dismay, particularly those who had not been party to the negotiations that preceded it. The Tariff of 1833 ensured that encouragement for domestic industry would continue, in reduced form, for the immediate future, but by ceding the argument for permanent protection it precipitated divisions among the friends of that policy that would have huge ramifications for future legislation on the subject. Furthermore, by permitting South Carolina to snatch some measure of victory from the jaws of defeat, it did nothing to discourage the sort of brinkmanship that would become more commonplace as sectional tensions continued to mount in the decades that followed.[219]

chapter five

"Trembling upon the Verge of Success and Defeat"

The Tariffs of 1842 and 1846

"IT IS MENTIONED as a remarkable coincidence," observed the *New-York Tribune* on 31 July 1846, "that one vote carried the Tariff of 1824; one vote the Tariff of 1828; one vote in each House carried the Tariff of 1842; and by one vote in the Senate the Tariff of 1846 has become a law." The *Tribune* got its figures wrong, but the pattern it identified was nonetheless significant, and certainly no coincidence; the tariff was a fiercely contested issue throughout the antebellum era, but never more so than for the two pieces of legislation covered by this chapter.[1] In part, this is attributable to the emergence of a truly competitive, and truly national, party system, which provided an effective counterweight to the pull of sectional allegiances. Indeed, it was his observation of the "progress of the tariff controversy" in the context of peak Democratic-Whig rivalry that prompted John Quincy Adams to muse that in "all great systems of policy maintained by antagonist parties and subject to deliberative decision, the opposite practical measures are modified into mutual approximation, till they come to a balance turned by a single vote."[2]

But the progress of the tariff controversy also demonstrates that the power of party, even at its height, was not determinative. In 1842, a Whig Congress's bid to reverse the Compromise of 1833 was unexpectedly stalled by the obstruction of their own man in the White House, leading to frantic negotiations that exposed regional schisms within both parties. Four years later, it was the Democrats who struggled to convert their legislative majority into the free trade reforms desired by the president and his cabinet, as a series of defections from their ranks exposed the fragility of party discipline even on this most important of measures. In both instances, the fate of the tariff would be decided by the smallest of margins, and the tactics of the

now-fragmented protectionist coalition evolved in response. Publicly continued pressure was maintained for high duties across the board through the
usual means of conventions, associations, and petitions, augmented in 1846
by the novel spectacle of a national exhibition of manufactures in the capital itself. Behind the scenes, however, following the precedent set by Henry
Clay in 1833, lobbying efforts were increasingly directed at finding a sus-
tainable accommodation between the two supposedly irreconcilable principles of protection and free trade, as members of the business community
pursued a more stable relationship with their political counterparts in Washington. The prospect of closer collaboration between lobbyists and lawmakers must have appeared all the more appealing during a period when
the tariff, as one member of Congress noted, seemed to be constantly "trembling upon the verge of success and defeat."[3]

+ + +

The passage of time under the Compromise robbed the protectionist policy
of its most celebrated and unyielding champions. Mathew Carey withdrew
from the cause in disgust at the terms of Henry Clay's scheme; though a
second financial crash, the Panic of 1837, prompted him to recant on his
promise "never again to touch the subject of political economy," he published his last work in July 1839 at the age of seventy-nine, and passed away
two months later.[4] Hezekiah Niles too slipped into retirement, leaving the
Register in the care of his son; he preceded Carey to the grave by five months.
The pervasive influence of both men's writings on the tariff was admitted
even by their detractors. "They have not only furnished the *raw materials*
of most of the speeches made in Congress and elsewhere," declared the New
York *Evening Post*, "but there is not even in the orations of Mr. Clay, as far
as we have read, a single argument which cannot be traced to the dull pages
of *Niles' Register*, or the interminable essays of Mathew Carey."[5] Less acknowledged, though, by both contemporaries and historians, was their contribution to the establishment of an effective protectionist lobby in the national capital. Carey, who once calculated that he had spent more than
$4,500 from his own purse in advocating higher duties, attended all of the
major conventions from 1819 to 1831, as well as advising his many allies in
Congress on the design of several bills, most notably through his correspondence with Eleazar Lord and Henry Baldwin in 1820.[6] Niles too played a
leading role at Harrisburg in 1827 and again in New York in 1831, where
he was chosen to coordinate the campaign to preserve the American System
from the threat of nullification in his capacity as chair of permanent committee, and was subsequently credited with a key role in drawing up the Tariff

of 1832. Both men, and also E. I. du Pont, who died suddenly of a heart attack some twenty months after his intervention with John M. Clayton to modify the design of the Compromise, provide compelling examples of the importance of lobbying to the making of United States tariff policy in the two decades following 1816. At the same time, their passing signaled the growing decentralization of organized protectionism, as the absence of acknowledged leaders outside of Congress, combined with what many saw as Clay's betrayal within it, permitted individual manufacturers more latitude to pursue their particular interests.

The political landscape was also transformed in the aftermath of the Compromise. Andrew Jackson's willingness to put down nullification by force alienated a significant portion of his Southern supporters. These states' rights men, including such anti-tariffites as Willie P. Mangum and John M. Berrien, joined with economic nationalists from the North and West, led by Clay and Daniel Webster, under the banner of the Whig Party, contesting elections nationwide against the Democratic Party headed by the president and his handpicked successor, Martin Van Buren.[7] This odd coalition was made more plausible by a shift in the terms of the tariff debate caused by Clay's retreat from the permanent and unequivocal protection promised by the American System. While free traders continued to maintain that a true revenue tariff must lay duties equally upon all articles, many protectionists now took the view that providing the rates were set with the primary object of defraying the costs of government, rather than encouraging manufactures, they might still discriminate between articles that were subject to foreign competition and those that were not. Such "incidental protection" was perfectly constitutional, Southern Whigs could argue, and many of their constituents found such arguments appealing as they contemplated economic diversification in a bid to restore their pre-Panic prosperity. "While the Free Trader doctrines are rapidly advancing in England & gaining north & west of us, I fear they are losing ground in the South," fretted one South Carolina planter to John C. Calhoun. "The whole body of Southern Whigs are tainted & will not lift a finger against the Tariff . . . while the Southern manufacturers are rising to importance & distilling poison in every neighbourhood."[8] These fears were exaggerated, but it was true that for the first time since 1816 support for higher duties could be found even in parts of the Cotton South.[9]

The depletion of the treasury as a result of the extended depression that followed the Panic made it readily apparent that new tariff legislation would be required even before the final reduction in rates under the Compromise, which was scheduled for 1 July 1842. The election of Whig presidential candidate William Henry Harrison in 1840, along with a Whig majority in both chambers of Congress, seemed certain to herald a significant increase in duties. Harrison was one of the many Americans who credited their support for protection to Carey: "since I was made a convert to the tariff system by your able arguments, I have never missed an opportunity of recommending it to my fellow citizens," he had assured the Philadelphian in 1830.[10] Unfortunately for both Harrison and the protectionists, however, the new president succumbed to pneumonia after only thirty days in office and was succeeded by his vice president, John Tyler, on 6 April 1841. Tyler was an archetypal states' rights Whig, having signaled his break with the Jackson administration by casting the lone vote against the Force Bill in the Senate, and he had also been a prominent opponent of state aid to domestic industry since he spoke out against Baldwin's bill as a junior member of the House in 1820. The Virginian entered the White House determined to preserve the Compromise inviolate, but the government's parlous financial circumstances forced him to sanction an interim measure removing some articles from the free list and raising rates on others to the 20 percent threshold established by the Tariff of 1833. This legislation was duly enacted by a special session of the Twenty-Seventh Congress in September, accompanied by a sister measure providing for the apportionment of revenue from public land sales among the states to relieve their own budget crises. To meet the objections of Tyler and other opponents of protection, a clause was inserted into this "Distribution Act" mandating that apportionment would be suspended if tariff rates were to exceed 20 percent, so that the redirecting of federal revenue under distribution could not provide a pretext for a future hike in duties.[11]

Anticipating further revision of the tariff by the regular session of the Twenty-Seventh Congress, which opened in December 1841, the president's First Annual Message allowed that "so long as the duties shall be laid with distinct reference to the wants of the Treasury," legislators would be justified in "discriminating by reference to other considerations of domestic policy connected with our manufactures," but again urged conformity to the 20 percent threshold.[12] Tyler's views on this issue, as on so many others, were not in accord with the majority of his party. Opposition inevitably coalesced around Clay, who put forth an alternative Whig program in a series of resolutions to the Senate. "He was not about to revive the contest for a protective tariff," the Kentuckian explained, but the needs of the revenue manifestly required a higher rate than 20 percent, from which manufacturers would naturally benefit, and distribution should also be continued. Having set his party on collision course with its titular head, Clay promptly resigned to begin preparing his own bid for the White House in 1844.[13]

Just as with the previous Panic in 1819, prolonged economic distress prompted mounting calls for Congress to act, and those who would benefit most directly from a general revision in rates were industrious in cultivating public opinion. Protectionist associations had disbanded or lain dormant under the Compromise, but a new generation of "Home League" societies "for the protection of domestic manufactures, the produce of American labor, and the promotion of reciprocal commerce" were established across the Northeast following the Whig victory in 1840. Their activities were loosely coordinated by a Central Committee that met under the aegis of the American Institute of the City of New York, founded in 1828 for the purpose of encouraging domestic industry in agriculture, commerce, manufacturing, and the arts. The Institute was best known for its annual fairs, where prizes were awarded for superior craftsmanship and technological innovation in a wide range of fields, but despite its professedly all-encompassing remit it was also a consistent advocate for the protection of manufactures, which made the Home League a natural extension of its mission. At its height, the latter claimed more than one hundred auxiliaries and held its own national convention in New York in April 1842.[14]

Yet while sympathetic editors trumpeted the influence that similar assemblies had exerted on past tariff legislation, press coverage of the event itself was comparatively muted. Perhaps this was because the League, in common with its host Institute, was dominated by a coterie of New York businessmen who lacked the national stature of Carey and Niles; the most notable attendee on this occasion was the Georgia Whig Berrien, who eleven years earlier had authored the address of the Philadelphia Free Trade Convention.[15] More fundamentally, it also reflected the fact that such meetings had become so much more commonplace than when the Friends of National Industry first gathered in New York more than two decades earlier. Abolitionists, temperance advocates, various religious denominations, and, of course, the major political parties all now held regular conventions, and such one-off events were now less likely to sustain the public's attention than the numbers that could be mobilized through grassroots organizing. Whether for this reason, or because this generation of protectionists lacked the cohesion of their predecessors, this would be the last general tariff convention prior to the Civil War; subsequent gatherings were industry-specific, regional in orientation, and would confine their attention to their own fields of expertise rather than calling for more wide-ranging reform.[16]

Spurred by the example set by popular crusades against Indian removal and, more recently, the congressional gag rule, pro-tariff opinion leaders also urged the enlistment of ordinary citizens to put pressure on their elected representatives. "On all hands we notice movements of the people in favor of Congressional protection," reported Philadelphia's *United States Gazette* in the spring of 1842, counseling its readers one month later to "call for it—call aloud, call again and again."[17] The abolitionists had proven the effectiveness of methods of mass campaigning with which protectionists had only experimented fitfully, from the circulation of pre-prepared printed petitions to the appointment of agents to solicit signatures, and these were now put to good use in the service of domestic industry. The ever-expanding number and reach of newspapers, combined with the proliferation of specialist publications like the American Institute's own *Journal*, which mirrored the growing antislavery press, also facilitated the dissemination and exchange of promotional materials. No longer could Carey's successors complain, as the Philadelphian had been wont to do, that the nation's editors were "either avowedly hostile, or totally indifferent."[18]

In fact, the only notable feature of the abolitionist movement that protectionists did not likewise adopt was the embrace of female participation. Women are not named as present at any of the major tariff conventions, except as confined to the spectators' gallery, and almost all protectionist associations, at least so far as surviving membership records indicate, were exclusively male. The few "Ladies" societies that are mentioned, whether real or merely a rhetorical invention of some contemporary essayist, were treated as moral exemplars, a device for the chastisement of their male counterparts who did not support the cause, rather than as a genuine voice in the public debate.[19] This finding corresponds to the argument made by several historians that women's participation in politics during this period relied in large part upon a distinction between moral issues, "objects of kindness, of benevolence, of compassion," which might include Indian removal and even slavery, and on which women, "by the law of their nature, [were] fitted above all others" to comment, and the "ordinary subjects of legislation," including no doubt the tariff, "which so profoundly agitate the men of the country; the women, so far from intermeddling with them, could scarcely be prevailed upon to bestow a thought upon them."[20]

And profoundly agitated the men of the country certainly were, as petitions pleading for tariff revision flooded the Twenty-Seventh Congress. One, from Baltimore, was fifty-six yards in length, contained 9,094 names, and took twenty-eight men to deliver.[21] Another, which had farther to travel, from Sangamon County, Illinois, was unremarkable save for the signature of a little-known Whig lawyer, Abraham Lincoln.[22] These displays of public sentiment heartened protectionist observers in the capital. "There is nothing a member of Congress can hear so quickly as the voice of the people," declared Nathan Sargent, Washington correspondent for the *Gazette* under the

pseudonym "Oliver Oldschool."[23] And friends of the tariff within the legislature pointed to the petitions as evidence of a truly nationwide demand for
a general reform of the rates. "The commercial and manufacturing interests were not alone in calling for action on this subject," declared the chair
of the Committee on Manufactures, Massachusetts representative Leverett
Saltonstall, on the floor of the House. "The agricultural interests were alike
involved in it; and they had received memorials from the South and the
West, and, no longer since than this morning from 600 or 700 persons in
Virginia, asking Congress for a tariff for the protection of domestic manufactures."[24] The result was a swiftly reached consensus on the guiding principle upon which the new tariff act should be founded, with many Northern
Democrats following the lead of their constituents by joining the Whig majority in endorsing the doctrine of incidental protection. Following a brief
"skirmish in Parliamentary tactics" in the House on the question of whether
a revenue tariff with incidental protection was the proper purview of Manufactures or Ways and Means, both committees were set to work drafting
separate bills.[25]

+ + +

The ambiguity of the doctrine of incidental protection in the abstract, however, which for many contemporary politicians was its chief virtue, also provided significant latitude for discretion in fixing the specific provisions of
legislation on the subject, which in turn opened the door for industry lobbyists. When Saltonstall was driven to lament the "want of men of business—
practical men" in Congress, it was not the first time that a chair of the Committee on Manufactures turned instead to the business community for aid.[26]
The result was a flood of correspondence, "several hundred letters" he later
estimated, a sample of which may be found in the surviving papers of a clerk
to the committee.[27] These ranged from simple answers to inquiries on prices
current, to detailed and often unsolicited instruction on appropriate rates,
such as that provided by one Philadelphia silk weaver, whose letter was
annotated by its recipient with the presumably sarcastic note: "suggesting
minutely every article & its rate of duty."[28] As they had become accustomed
to, many manufacturers also journeyed to Washington expecting an audience with the committee to plead their case for a change to the rate on this
or that article. "The City is full of tariff people, from all quarters," Saltonstall recorded in early June.[29] That same month, Sargent reported that "the
Committee of Ways and Means and the Committee on Manufactures, besides sitting seven hours a day in the House, frequently labor seven hours
more in the committee room in conjunction, in order to perfect the Tariff Bill,

and to fit it to meet the wants of every class of industry as far as it is possible to do so."[30] Lobbying on the Tariff of 1842 still resembled in form that pioneered by Isaac Briggs and Francis Cabot Lowell some three decades earlier, but the precedents established at previous sessions now encouraged a substantial expansion in its scale, with more firms willing to act independently rather than entrust the safeguarding of their interests to some central coordinating body.

It was not until 3 June, with the treasury bare, that Millard Fillmore, the chair of Ways and Means, was ready to report that committee's bill to the House.[31] Six days later, the New Yorker also reported a second bill, which would postpone for one month the reduction currently scheduled for 1 July to allow sufficient time for passage of a new schedule of duties.[32] In conformity with Clay's Senate resolutions, this "Little Tariff" would also repeal the clause in the Distribution Act that suspended its operation if duties remained above 20 percent after that date. Fillmore's second measure was taken up as a matter of urgency, for even free traders acknowledged that the revenue standard established by the Tariff of 1833 was insufficient for the present needs of government. The repeal provision was "the only stumbling-block between the parties," recorded John Quincy Adams, and after a failed attempt to strip this from the bill it passed on 15 June by a sharply partisan vote of 116 to 104, with only two Democrats willing to support continuance of the Whig-sponsored distribution policy, however desperate the country's financial state.[33] The Senate promptly removed the repeal provision and replaced it with one that merely postponed the next payment of the public land revenues until 1 August, on which date duties would be reduced to the 20 percent threshold anyway, and there would be no cause to suspend distribution. This conciliatory gesture was intended to heal the growing breach between congressional Whigs and the White House. The amended Little Tariff passed the Senate by twenty-four votes, all Whig, to nineteen on 24 June, was concurred in by the House the following day, to Adams's disgust, and was dispatched for the president's signature.[34]

Tyler vetoed the Little Tariff on 29 June. To his mind, the measure violated both the Compromise and the Distribution Act by postponing the final reduction of duties under the first and failing to suspend the operation of the second.[35] "This course [the veto] is taken, beyond all question, to satisfy the Locofocos [Democrats], who do not intend the proceeds of the Public Lands shall go to the States, because that is a Whig measure," declaimed Sargent, whose sympathies lay with the latter party.[36] But the president's decision presented protectionists with a dilemma, for it was doubtful if their favorite measure could muster sufficient support to pass without the promise of continued distribution. "We cannot carry a good bill, without the aid of our Western friends, and they will not vote for a bill, without the repealing clause," predicted Saltonstall.[37] This assessment was echoed from the other side of the equation by North Carolina's Whig senator Willie P. Mangum. "Great pains have been taken to convince [Northern & Eastern men] that their true interest is to stand by all the Measures," he informed Clay. "That Southern Whigs will go very far to gratify them in a Tariff, if they shall stand by the Land Law, & that the surrender of the Land Law, or any faltering on the subject, puts an end to all hopes for the present, of passing any Tariff Law at all."[38]

With these considerations in mind, the House continued to debate Fillmore's other bill, the "Permanent Tariff." Saltonstall, who had prepared his own bill, reluctantly came to the conclusion that the Ways and Means version would be preferred "if for no other reason, because it did come from that Committee." He was correct, for the Tariff of 1832 would be the last such act that the Committee on Manufactures would ever write, its oversight over tariff policy another casualty of the shift to incidental protection.[39] The committee's labors were not wasted, however, as the chair and his colleagues spent "10 days with the Comee of ways & means, going over their bill, to perfect it as far as possible."[40] Fillmore pledged in his capacity as floor leader to make any recommendations that would meet Salstonstall's satisfaction: "I shd have made several motions to amend, but thought it best to get what modifications I could thro' the Comee of ways and means," the Massachusetts man explained to a correspondent, adding that he considered the product of this compromise "a stout tariff bill."[41] The average rate would rise to 33 percent, significantly higher than the 20 percent mandated by the Tariff of 1833 and more comparable to its predecessor in 1832. Within that average rate there would also be considerable discrimination, with many raw materials returned to the free list, and the restoration of minimums for cotton textiles and high specific duties for iron and other manufactures.[42] This was incidental protection carried to its furthest extent, though Fillmore was adamant in his explanation to the House that "this was a revenue bill, intended to supply the wants of the Treasury; and he therefore should consider it in that point of view."[43] And crucially, like the Little Tariff before it, the Permanent Tariff also included a provision for continuing distribution.

Congressional discussion of the tariff plumbed its customary depths. Adams describes a typical day in his diary: "Cowen, of Ohio, made an earnest hour speech for a protective tariff; Andrew Kennedy, a craving, croaking, and brawling, vulgar, hour, anti-tariff, and, above all, anti-Whig speech; and Steenrod, a deep-toned, tragedy-queen declamation, on the same side.

Fornance, a drivelling changeable from Pennsylvania, drawled out, with a nasal twang, an hour of ambidexter neutrality. These men had succeeded in driving the members from their seats, till there was no quorum."[44] The lack of importance attached to debate was no surprise to Sargent. "Members come here with their minds made up," he explained to readers of the *Gazette*. "[T]hey have to vote according to the supposed interests of their constituents, and even should the information thus obtained convince them that their constituents take an erroneous view of their own interests, that they are deceived in regard to the effect of such a law upon them, such members would vote in accordance with the prejudices, and not in accordance with the true interests of their constituents." "The great misfortune of our country," the reporter added, is "that men come here to represent 'Bunkum,' and not to make laws for the *whole* nation."[45] Meanwhile, critics claimed, while legislators played out their empty rhetorical contest between the grand theories of protection and free trade on the floor, the real details were settled off it by the industry lobbyists who parleyed in private with the bill's sponsors. "One item in Mr. Fillmore's bill, now before the Senate, will serve to show the principle which actuates the ultra protectionists," complained Tyler's organ in the capital, the *Madisonian*. "The duty on *sheathing copper* was laid to protect five rolling establishments, that being the whole number in the United States, and the proprietors of them are all rich. . . . These five manufacturers have recently been in this city, and arranged every thing with Mr. Fillmore in the Committee room."[46] As far as one Democrat was concerned, the whole measure was attributable to "the logrolling & lying of the manufacturing emissaries employed to work upon the congressional committees."[47]

The Permanent Tariff passed the House on 16 July by 116 votes to 112, the Whigs having successfully resisted all efforts to strip out the distribution clause.[48] "They deserve great credit for their untiring perseverance," wrote Vermont senator Samuel C. Crafts. "They have had the whole body of Locofocos, with but one or two exceptions, and about a dozen Southern whigs, (who are <u>horizontal</u> tariff men,) to contend with; besides a threatened veto hanging over their heads."[49] Writing from his plantation, Clay urged his confederates in the Senate to follow the House's lead, sensing political advantage to be gained if the president continued to block legislation intended to bring the country out of depression: "the more Veto's [*sic*] now of right measures the better," he anticipated.[50] To that end, the Whig majority in the upper chamber banded together to reject all amendments to the bill, including those proposed by their own Finance Committee. "Upon consideration of circumstances, the exigency for money, the exigency of the times, and the delay and danger of sending the bill back to the House, we concluded, with the probability of a *veto* before our eyes, to take and pass the bill as it came to us," explained Kentucky senator John J. Crittenden, Clay's chief lieutenant.[51] The Senate duly approved the Permanent Tariff by twenty-five votes to twenty-three on 5 August. Three Southern Whigs joined the Democrats in opposition, but two more, including Berrien, deliberately absented themselves so that the bill might pass without their having to go on record in its favor.[52]

Four days later, Tyler vetoed the Permanent Tariff too, again citing the continuance of distribution as the cause.[53] He did so against the advice of Webster, whose estrangement from Clay had grown since the Compromise to the extent that he had chosen to remain when the rest of the cabinet resigned en masse over Tyler's divergence from Whig policy. The secretary of state had counseled friends in the Senate to exorcise the distribution clause from the bill, claiming that "I do not think we shall ever have a better opportunity for establishing a Tariff upon just principles & it seems to me that nothing is wanting, to render this opportunity available, but moderation & conciliation."[54] Following its passage with distribution clause intact, Webster turned his attentions to the president. "I would give almost my right hand if you could be persuaded to sign the bill," he implored, but to no avail.[55]

The veto not only cemented the congressional Whigs' breach from the president but also threatened to divide their own ranks. "Our friends of the North seem to be very seriously & sincerely apprehensive that their constituents will be disconcerted to such an extent as to be fatal in their coming elections" if they were to adjourn "without an *adequate* tariff," Crittenden warned Clay.[56] This was certainly the view of Saltonstall, who privately admitted that "as a Mass[achusetts] man I care very little for the land money."[57] Others, however, refused to surrender distribution. For many Southern and Western members, this was simply a matter of preference, but for some Whigs it was also a point of principle that Congress should not permit the executive to dictate the terms of legislation. Adams was among the latter and railed against those whose "property is chiefly in the Lowell factories" and who care "not a pepper-corn for the interest of the whole people in the public lands."[58] Several Whig caucuses were called but could not reach agreement. "Night after night have we held meetings and consultations with a view to harmonize in some course," Crittenden informed one correspondent a week after the veto was received, "but I am sorry to tell you that we have not yet reached any such conclusion, and that I look forward to the issue with some apprehension."[59]

Crittenden was right to be apprehensive, for the desperation of protectionists for some sort of tariff meant that they were effectively, as Tennessee representative Cave Johnson keenly observed, "*in market*, put up to the *highest bidder*."[60] Calhoun, whose erratic career had taken him back into the Democratic Party following Jackson's retirement, now saw an opportunity to promote his own presidential prospects. "The whigs are now devided [*sic*] into two parties; one prefering the distribution to the Tariff, & the other the Tariff to the distribution; and neither willing to join in a bill simply for revenue with us," he explained to his son-in-law.[61] But Calhoun was willing to offer more than a simple revenue bill. Rumors circulated that he was the true author of an alternative proposal, put forward by Charles J. Ingersoll, tariff lobbyist turned Democratic congressman, for "the Tariff of 1 Jany 1840 (6/10) [i.e., the Tariff of 1832 after four-tenths of the reductions mandated by the Compromise of 1833], Cash duties & home valuation." This was "a pretty fair bid" for protectionist support, in Johnson's opinion, but ultimately it proved "too low for the Tariff men & too high for Anti tariff." It did, however, prompt other Democrats to bring forward their own projects, and the prospect of the minority party fashioning a compromise with the aid of dissidents from their own ranks forced the hand of the Whig leaders. "The great champion Clay & his friends set to work & bid up at last the big [i.e., Permanent] Tariff without distribution upon condition that a separate distribution Bill should be sent to the [president] for another veto," reported Johnson. "This was of course accepted [by the Tariff Whigs], having that confidence in each other which exists among pickpockets, when their union is necessary for their own preservation or being identical in principle, having no other than to secure money on one side & political promotion on the other."[62]

These behind-the-scenes negotiations finally played out on the floor on 22 August. "We do not remember ever to have witnessed during thirty-five years [of] attendance on the House of Representatives, a more exciting scene," reported the Washington *National Intelligencer*.[63] Several tariff schemes, wildly differing in detail, were voted down one after another. Then Pennsylvania Whig Thomas McKennan moved to resurrect the bill that Tyler had vetoed, minus the distribution clause. This proposal was adopted, but a subsequent motion to engross the bill was announced as lost by a single vote, prompting "clapping of hands, and cries of 'Good.' "[64] This was silenced when a clerk informed the Speaker, Kentucky Whig John White, that the vote had been miscounted and was in fact a tie. Correction of this error threw responsibility onto White, and as a Western man he voted in the negative, once again sending the bill to defeat. Immediately, however, a motion was made to reconsider, and this time engrossment was carried by three votes. Watching from the galleries, Sargent reported that "the anxiety and intedseness [sic] of feeling was the greater, on account of several members changing their votes, which was done with extreme reluctance, and under a pressure from their colleagues, and appeals from acquaintances and friends—men of standing who were here from various parts of the country, and who were supposed to speak the sentiments of the people—not easy to resist."[65] The bill then passed the House by an even narrower margin, 104 yeas to 103 nays.[66] "The vote was taken several times & no one knew the result, untill it was declared. I never knew such an exciting moment as that when the speaker voted," Saltonstall wrote to his wife afterward, adding that "the fate of the bill is still uncertain. It will have to meet great opposition in the Senate—but I hope it will pass."[67]

In the upper chamber, attention turned to the Northern Democrats, whose support would be needed to counteract the expected defection of Southern and Western Whigs.[68] Sargent noted "the urgent appeals that every day come upon here from the Northern, Eastern, and Middle States, not to adjourn without passing a Tariff Law, and the immense solicitude manifested by various persons who have come here from different sections of the country."[69] Silas Wright, author of the Tariff of 1828 and now senator for New York, was under particular scrutiny because his mentor, Van Buren, was deemed Calhoun's main rival for the Democratic nomination in 1844. "We are now upon the third tariff of the House, a horrible bill, am miserably perplexed to know how to vote myself," he wrote on 26 August, "but as we ought to pass some bill and as this one will kill distribution, I shall vote for it, and shall do it knowing that it will make a great noise and produce great dissatisfaction both in the city of New York and at the South."[70] In fact, just as Van Buren had done on the Woollens Bill in 1827, Wright first sought to duck responsibility by failing to answer when his name was called on a motion to engross the following day. Ruel Williams, Democratic senator for Maine, then "went to the Secretary's desk, and ascertaining by counting up the yeas and nays" that the motion would fail by a single vote, he and his New York colleague requested that their names be recorded in its favor. This provided the necessary margin for passage, which was accomplished immediately thereafter without division.[71] Tyler promptly signed the new tariff into law, while once again vetoing the now separate bill continuing distribution.

An analysis of key roll calls on the Tariff of 1842 confirms the influence of the party system in shaping policymaking during this period. Taking the House and Senate together, 104 Whigs voted in favor and 46 against, while the Democrats split 79 to 24 in the opposition direction. The capacity for partisan affiliation to cut across sectional allegiances is particularly illustrated by the fact that all twenty Southerners who supported the bill were Whigs, and twenty-seven of the thirty-three Northerners who opposed it were Democrats.[72] Nonetheless, the power of party should not be overstated, for it was still the case that one in every four legislators who cast a vote did so in opposition to the majority of their fellow partisans. The number of defectors was significantly greater on this final bill, where the choice was simply to raise rates or retain the existing ones, than on its two predecessors, where the distribution clause added a different, and highly partisan, element to the mix. Not one Pennsylvania Democrat had voted for either of the first two bills, but when offered protection shorn of distribution twelve of them supported the measure and the other five abstained. Defending his course to a skeptical editor, James Buchanan, now a senator, protested: "[I]nstead of 4/5ths only of my constituents being in favor of the Tariff, I might now say that 49 out of fifty are."[73] With a single vote providing the margin of victory in each chamber, however, such excuses were not well received by the friends of free trade, who enjoyed only one month of 20 percent duties under the Compromise of 1833 before the new legislation took effect. "You will see that N[ew] York & Pennsylvania have deserted us on the Tariff & passed the bill just as they did in 1828," pronounced Calhoun. "It is a heavy blow on the South."[74]

+ + +

Just as the Tariff of 1842 was the product of Whig victory in the election of 1840, the Tariff of 1846 was presaged by Democratic triumph four years later. The return of prosperity following the revocation of the Compromise seemed to augur well for Clay, who easily secured his party's endorsement. His opponent was James K. Polk, a dark-horse selection after the convention failed to agree on several better-known candidates. When Polk's nomination was announced, he received some unsolicited advice from Robert J. Walker, senator for Mississippi but a native Pennsylvanian. "There is but one question which can by any possibility defeat your election. It is the tariff," Walker claimed. "An out & out Free trade candidate *cannot* receive the vote of Pennsylvania. This is *certain*, & without her vote we are beaten."[75] At his prompting, Polk's camp produced a public statement affirming that while their candidate was "opposed to a tariff for protection *merely*, and not for revenue," he had "heretofore sanctioned such moderate discriminating duties as would produce the amount of revenue needed, and at the same time afford reasonable incidental protection to our home industry."[76] This disingenuous testimonial was accompanied by a Democratic platform that declared that "justice and sound policy forbid the Federal Government to foster one branch of industry to the detriment of another, or to cherish the interests of one portion to the injury of another portion of our common country."[77] The Kane Letter, named for the correspondent to whom it was addressed, served its purpose. As one disappointed Clay supporter observed, Polk "was presented as the native Deity of Free trade to the South,—the Tutelar of the Manufacturing interests to Pennsylvania: Like the cameleon he was made to change his hue to that of the nearest object, & to glow through all the colors of the prism, as he made the grand tour of the Union."[78] The Democrats carried Pennsylvania, elected their man to the White House, and won majorities in both chambers of the Twenty-Ninth Congress. Walker's reward was appointment as Secretary of the Treasury in the new administration.[79]

Contrary to the many pledges made on his behalf during the campaign, Polk entered office determined to do away with the Tariff of 1842. That act, he declared in his First Annual Message of 2 December 1845, was "in violation of the cardinal principles" of a revenue tariff, citing minimums and specific duties as examples of its "heavy and unjust burdens on the farmer, the planter, the commercial man, and those of all other pursuits except the capitalist who has made his investments in manufactures."[80] Walker, who as a young man had been chosen a delegate to the Philadelphia Free Trade Convention of 1831, shared his president's ambition.[81] His treasury report, issued the following day, affirmed his belief "that no duty [should] be imposed upon any article above the lowest rate which will yield the largest amount of revenue" and recommended that to ensure equal treatment all such duties should be ad valorem. Far from protecting home industry against foreign competition, the secretary embraced Adam Smith's vision of economic growth through global free trade, with the United States enjoying a natural advantage in agriculture rather than manufacturing. "If we reduce our tariff," he predicted, "the party opposed to the corn laws of England would soon prevail and admit all our agricultural products at all times freely into her ports in exchange for her exports."[82]

Walker's reference to the Corn Laws highlights the international dimension to the passage of the Tariff of 1846, which was of greater significance than for any of its predecessors since 1816. British restrictions on the importation of grain, which particularly galled American farmers, had been introduced just one year before the United States embarked on its own experiment with protectionism, and now three decades later both were under serious threat of repeal.[83] During the 1844 campaign, Whig newspapers accused British manufacturers of raising funds to promote a Democratic victory, in the expectation that they could then sell their wares at lower rates on the American market.[84] Following Walker's report, one editor remarked that "the two Sir Roberts sing a free trade duett across the Atlantic," a nod to British prime minister Robert Peel, who was pushing for abolition of the Corn Laws, and the American Treasury secretary, whose honorary title was bestowed by a member of Congress for his supposed Anglophile sympathies.[85] In truth, there was no understanding between the two governments, which were simultaneously at odds over their joint claim to the Oregon Territory. Nonetheless, free traders in each country certainly looked eagerly for any success gained by their transatlantic counterparts. As Polk wrote to Louis McLane, his minister in London: "[I]t is by no means certain that Congress, will agree to reduce or modify our tariff as recommended in the message, without an assurance of the repeal of the corn laws, and corresponding reductions and modification of the Brittish tariff. The advocates for reduction in both countries, would be greatly strengthened, by a stipulation for a like reduction in the other."[86]

The Democratic-controlled House was happy to follow the administration's lead on the tariff. The Committee of Ways and Means, under the chairmanship of North Carolina representative James I. McKay, invited Walker to submit a bill for their consideration.[87] The secretary was determined to have legislation drawn up that met the rigorous free trade specifications set out in his report, and according to his biographer he worked on it for "several hours a day" over a period of "nearly two months."[88] He was assisted, newspaper reports claimed, by "some six or eight custom house officers" summoned to Washington with their expenses "charged per order, of the *honest* Secretary, to the expense of collecting the revenue!"[89] This executive interference in matters that were constitutionally the prerogative of the legislature attracted criticism. "A sort of special Congress—a very small Congress—a supplement of Congress, composed of subordinate custom-house officers, had been convened for the purpose of arranging the details of the bill," complained one senator. "He had gone to the room of the Committee of Ways and Means of the other House in order to attend to some business of his constituents, and there found that it had been taken possession of by these custom-house officers, who very politely told him that they would look into his business."[90] The secretary's course was a sensible one, however, for Whigs were already predicting that if the task was left to the majority in Congress, "the odds and ends of ultraism in Pa. and S. C. will not very soon agree in the policy, principles, or details in a Tariff Bill."[91] "Walker is the master spirit in all that relates to this matter, and the President I apprehend, and all the members of the Cabinet have not only given in to him but sustained and supported him," one well-informed Democrat reported. "It is therefore considered an administration measure, and party discipline is brought to bear upon it."[92]

The secretary's bill was completed in early February and sent to Ways and Means, where it remained for another two months.[93] Hearing that some Democratic members of the committee wanted to add specific duties on several articles as an inducement to key protectionist constituencies, the president summoned McKay to the White House and urged him "to preserve the ad valorem principle."[94] Polk had himself been placed on Ways and Means in 1833 to ensure the Verplanck Bill met the requirements of the Jackson administration, and he expected similar loyalty from his congressional party on this occasion.[95] The Whig minority were not even consulted: "they have no measure before them and they know nothing of the movements or of the intentions of the Chairman," one Washington correspondent reported.[96] The delay in committee was probably deliberate, to allow Britain to make progress on its repeal of the Corn Laws. Certainly, when McKay did report the bill to the House on 14 April it was virtually unchanged from the version prepared under Walker's supervision.[97]

The Walker bill contained seven categories of ad valorem rates, ranging from 75 percent, on spirits, to 5 percent. In this respect, it departed from the Compromise, which tended toward to a standard rate of 20 percent. The distribution of articles between the categories, however, was determined by calculations of maximizing revenue rather than protecting manufactures. Wool, for example, was taxed at 25 percent, only 5 percent less than woolen textiles.[98] The free list, commonly used to facilitate the importation of raw materials, was the shortest of any tariff since 1828, when partisan considerations had dictated its length. There were some deviations from this rule; most notably, iron and coal were placed in the second highest category, at 30 percent, in what critics interpreted as "a *favor* or a *bribe* to Pennsylvania."[99] Still, the measure would almost completely revoke the substantial "incidental protection" offered by its predecessor. "The new tariff seems to have been concocted with the express view of breaking down the manufacturers," was the angry verdict of one Du Pont Company director.[100]

+ + +

Barred from participation in writing the bill, protectionists out-of-doors focused their lobbying efforts on members of the legislature. Henry C. Carey, whose four-volume *Principles of Political Economy* had established him as an expert on the subject, followed his father's example by pressing upon leading politicians his own compromise scheme, which promised a middle ground between the "*ultra*" principles of permanent protection and a strict revenue tariff, but with victory in their grasp the Democratic majority were unreceptive to counterproposals.[101] For practical manufacturers, then, the priority was ensuring that Walker's measure would not weigh too heavily upon their particular industry. "The City is swarming with manufacturers who are making tremendous exertions to defeat [the tariff]," Polk recorded in his diary. "The truth is that such a struggle has rarely been witnessed in Congress, as that between the Capitalists engaged in manufactures on the one hand, and the advocates of moderate and reasonable taxes."[102] One such concerned citizen was Alfred du Pont, son of E. I., who journeyed to Washington "to say something relative to the injustice of laying a duty on Saltpetre at the very time the duty on Gunpowder is reduced."[103] Sargent, still writing for the *United States Gazette*, observed the presence of similar envoys from New England, New Jersey, New York, and Pennsylvania. Singling out one Democrat from the latter, he sarcastically suggested: "[I]f he will only turn to, and read *his own*, and the speeches of other leaders of the Polk party in Pennsylvania in 1844, his fears will all vanish; he will find that there is no cause for alarm, that he need entertain no apprehension whatever, for the fate of the Tariff of '42, *because*, as his arguments in those speeches clearly and unequivocally show that Mr. Polk is a great friend of the *protective policy*, that he is the special advocate of the tariff of '42, and the very man to preserve it."[104]

The most inventive response to Walker's bill was the organization of a huge "National Fair," allowing producers from across the Union to "give ocular demonstration of the great things which the tariff has done for us as a people."[105] Such an event had previously been mooted to coincide with deliberation on the Tariff of 1828 but rejected then as impractical, though smaller exhibitions such as those sponsored by the American Institute in New York had since become common.[106] On this occasion, it was prompted by reports that the administration had permitted an agent of British manufacturers to display their wares in a capitol committee room. "After the league between the two Sir Roberts . . . the halls of the government are yielded to England to teach, by an exhibition of her fabrics and by lectures on free trade, the American Congress their duty to Britain," groused the Philadelphia *North American*.[107] In consultation with sympathetic members of both parties, a committee was formed and invitations issued for a "National Exhibition of American Manufactures and products of Mechanical Art, at the City of Washington." The committee was largely constituted of local businessmen of no particular note, with the exception of John P. Kennedy, the Maryland novelist and politician who had composed the public address of the New York Tariff Convention of 1831.[108]

The National Fair opened on 21 May and closed two weeks later. It was housed in the largest temporary structure constructed in the United States to that date, costing some $6,000, and attracted crowds comparable to national party conventions; nearly twenty thousand visited in the first week alone.[109] Even critics acknowledged that "Washington has never been so inundated with strangers," and "viewed in the light of a great home mart, exhibiting in collective array the vast mechanical and scientific skill of the country, the '*Fair*' was certainly a spectacle of which any American might feel justly proud."[110] President Polk, who also visited on the invitation of the organizers, was less impressed, however. "The manufacturers have spent many thousands of dollars in getting up this fair, with a view no doubt to operate upon members of Congress to prevent a reduction of the present rates of duty," he recorded in his diary. "To effect this, lower prices was [*sic*] affixed to & labelled on the specimens exhibited than they are sold for in the market . . . to impress the public with the belief [in] the absurd doctrine that 'high duties make low goods.' " In his view, "the wealth exhibited at this fair & the expense attending to it prove . . . that the large capitalists owning the manufactories should rely upon their own resources not upon the bounty of the Government."[111]

The Walker Bill was not called up for consideration by McKay in the House until 15 June, two months after he first reported it.[112] That same day, the *Great Western* docked in New York carrying word that the Corn Laws had been repealed.[113] The decision to call up the tariff had been taken two weeks previously, but the timing was certainly fortuitous, and the administration's patience had been rewarded, for news of Parliament's action would surely make wavering congressmen more receptive to a reciprocal reduction in duties. Supporters of the measure also agreed in caucus that they would limit debate to three weeks, for past experience taught that the longer it went on the greater the danger their majority would dissolve.[114] Not that anything said on the floor was likely to change minds, but the Whigs could and did engage in a concerted effort to "make the bill as odious as possible" to key Democratic constituencies in order to siphon off votes. The back-and-forth reached its peak on 2 July when opponents of the measure succeeded in striking a proposed drawback on the export of preserved fish, of particular interest to Maine, and placing salt on the free list, which alarmed the New York delegation. Its friends then made a "desperate rally" and carried a motion to adjourn: "the object undoubtedly is to endeavour to train their men in better—to threaten some, coax others, and buy others with offices or the promise of offices," conjectured Sargent.[115] The following day, the decisions on drawbacks and salt were duly reversed, in the latter case by a single vote. A motion to add the Kane Letter as a statement of the scheme's guiding principles "produced some merriment" but was also rejected. The bill then passed by 114 yeas to 95 nays.[116]

The Secretary of the Treasury attended the House for the decisive vote, and upon hearing the result he seized McKay's hand, exclaiming: "we've got it through."[117] His appearance on the floor did not escape notice. "*Certain persons from the other end of the Avenue were present, and if it had been necessary to have ten more votes they could doubtless have been obtained,*" Sargent observed meaningfully.[118] There can be no doubt of the newspaperman's implication, that executive influence was employed to secure the desired outcome in the legislature. Polk's diary records his engagement of Democratic senators to coax reluctant colleagues in the other chamber.[119] Jefferson Davis, Mississippi representative and future leader of the Confederacy, was even treated to a personal audience when he expressed a wish to resign his seat in Congress to fight in the Mexican War: the president "insisted upon my remaining in the House for the few days yet required to pass the Tariff Bill," Davis recalled.[120] A striking testament to the power of party discipline is provided by the fact that in mid-May, before floor debate had even begun, McKay provided Walker with a list of 116 Democratic members whose votes he considered safe, only three more than eventually gave their support to the measure.[121]

Nevertheless, there were defections from the ranks of the majority, the most sizeable, and most predictable, of which involved Pennsylvania. "Give my respects to some of our Democratic friends in the Pennsylvania delegation, and ask them whether they *now* think that the President is a better tariff man than I am," Clay had joked to a Whig representative from that state when Walker's scheme was announced.[122] The state legislature, also in Democratic hands, instructed its delegation "to oppose all attempts to alter or modify" the Tariff of 1842, and on the final roll call eleven of Pennsylvania's twelve Democratic representatives voted against passage.[123] The lone exception was David Wilmot, of whose district it was said that "the only things people manufactured were shingles, and they stole the lumber to make them, and the only *protection* they wanted was protection from the officers of justice."[124] Wilmot would subsequently claim that if others among the delegation had been willing to join with him, they could "almost have made their own terms so far as Pennsylvania's interests were concerned," so desperate was the administration for their support.[125] His loyalty on this occasion would have momentous consequences, for historians have speculated that it won him the recognition of the Speaker one month later amid the clamor of the closing days of the session, providing the opportunity he needed to introduce the antislavery proviso for which he is famous.[126] With regard to the Walker bill, though, Pennsylvania's dissatisfaction boded ill for its fate in the Senate, where the margin between success and failure was likely to be even finer.

+ + +

The Democrats held thirty-one seats in the upper chamber to their opponents' twenty-five.[127] The tariff was read on 6 July and made the special order of business for 13 July and every day thereafter until it was disposed of, with even the chair of the Senate Finance Committee, Alabama senator Dixon H. Lewis, opposing a Whig motion to refer the bill to his own committee with a view to delaying its consideration.[128] "The passage of the tariff bill is resolved on as a party measure, and that being the case, no argument . . . will be of the least avail," reported Sargent, pointing to "the indisposition manifested by the friends of the bill to hear any thing that might be said against it, generally, to a man, leaving their seats as soon as the debate commences."[129] Indeed, the existence of such an agreement on the part of the majority was admitted by George McDuffie on the floor, when he announced that he and his associates "desired a speedy decision. And, to accomplish this, they had determined to leave the discussion to the other side of the chamber exclusively."[130]

But if debate within the Senate would not change a single vote on the bill, pressure from without still could. Pennsylvania's two Democratic senators, Simon Cameron and Daniel Sturgeon, came in for particular attention. The deluge of petitions from their constituents was such that a colleague complained that "on the meeting of the Senate every day, first they had prayers by the chaplain, then the reading of the Journal, and next an hour and [a] half consumed in the recital of a sort of funeral dirge from the pensioners of Pennsylvania."[131] Many of these pensioners also came to press their case in person; the president himself received one such delegation, who "expressed great alarm, if [the bill] passed the Senate in the form it had passed the House, that it would prostrate the iron and coal interest in Pennsylvania and reduce the Democracy of that State to a minority."[132] Within the cabinet, Secretary of State James Buchanan was rumored to be "using his secret influence to prevent a modification" of the existing rates, and to disregard the instructions of the state legislature would also surely damn either man's chance of returning for another term.[133] Cameron, who had only been elected originally with the help of Whig votes over the regular party nominee, was the first to declare his opposition. Recalling his Democratic neighbors campaigning under banners inscribed "Polk, [vice presidential candidate George M.] Dallas, and the Tariff of 1842" two years earlier, he assured his audience that "neither [Polk nor Dallas] would have got the vote of Pennsylvania without the last."[134] Sturgeon stayed silent throughout, but he too voted consistently with opponents of the bill.

The defectors were joined by John Niles of Connecticut, whose constituents, one correspondent grumbled to Walker, "have been dosed so heavily with humbug, that it is truly dangerous for a Democrat to say anything about the Tariff."[135] "The act of 1842 had never been an object of assault on the part of the Democracy of the North," Niles proclaimed, adding that "as a friend of [the] Administration, he profoundly regretted the introduction of the bill, and as a friend of the Administration he would vote against it."[136] While the bill's sponsors had been resigned to the loss of Cameron and Sturgeon, the loss of Niles too came as a shock. "The whole democratic party with very few exceptions, took it for granted that this measure was about to be carried out at the present session, when all at once the democratic senator from Connecticut intimated his determination to go against the bill," protested the Washington *Union*, mouthpiece for the administration.[137] This left the Senate seemingly heading for a tie, with twenty-eight votes on either side.

In the case of deadlock, the deciding vote would be cast by the presiding officer in the chamber: Vice President George M. Dallas. Dallas was a Democrat, a prominent member of the administration, and the uncle of Walker's wife. At the same time, he was a Pennsylvanian and thus subject to the same pressure as the Senators from his state. As he told his wife, "all sorts of ridiculous efforts are making, by letters, newspaper-paragraphs, and personal visits, to affect the Vice's casting vote, by persuasion or threat."[138] Dallas's record on the tariff was erratic, having voted in the Senate for a reduction of duties in 1832 but against the Compromise the following year, and uncertain as to what course to pursue on this occasion he sought the counsel of friends.[139] His rivals within the party, meanwhile, professed much amusement at his discomfort. "It would be fun if Dallas had to un*tie* the Tariff knot! Rare fun," joked a confidant of Buchanan.[140] The president remained sanguine, however; so much so, in fact, that when Dallas approached him with a compromise proposal "suggested by a leading manufacturer," he discouraged the vice president from pursuing it, despite the latter's warning that "if the Democrats did not agree to it he would let them know, if it came to his casting vote they might loose [*sic*] the Bill as it was."[141] "[I] am satisfied," Polk assured one anxious correspondent, "if its passage depends on his vote, that he will represent the Democracy of the nation and not the State of Pennsylvania."[142]

On the other side of the aisle, Daniel Webster was pursuing his own arrangement with a gaggle of concerned manufacturers. Following his prolonged tenure in Tyler's cabinet, and resultant spell in the political wilderness, Webster returned to the Senate in 1845 at the behest of his allies among Boston's business community. The price of his return was a $37,000 fund, the interest on which would provide him with an annual income of $1,000 for the remainder of his life. Nathan Appleton was among the fifty or so subscribers, as was Francis Cabot Lowell Jr., whose father had secured the introduction of the cotton minimum back in 1816.[143] "All Webster's political systems are interwoven with the exploration of a gold-mine for himself," sniped John Quincy Adams in his diary, but the manufacturers recognized the value of having a senator in their service.[144] After Walker's bill passed the House, Webster wrote to Appleton soliciting "the advice of our best informed and most prudent friends," and suggesting, as had now become customary, that "some intelligent Gentleman from Boston could spend the next ten days at Washington." He also asked his friend to "*book me up*" on "Tariff subjects," having neglected the topic since leaving Congress five years previously, and Appleton responded with a memorandum furnishing arguments against a reduction in duties.[145]

While he hoped to save the Tariff of 1842 intact, Webster also explored the possibility of orchestrating a compromise. "What wd. our friends say" to a reduction of 25 percent immediately and a further 8½ percent after five years, he enquired of James Kellogg Mills, another Boston entrepreneur, adding that more drastic cuts might be necessary to secure agreement.[146] Mills's circle considered and duly approved the project, but they had their own terms in mind: a one-off reduction of 25 percent in all duties currently above 30 percent, with the proviso that none be reduced below that 30 percent threshold. According to Webster, "the idea of an amendment in this form, & to this effect, originated with Mr. Edward Curtis," likely the Washington lawyer and former Whig representative of that name; and was pressed by Thomas Lamb, a Boston banker with investments in sugar; Thomas Chambers, on behalf of Pennsylvania iron and coal; and Michael Hodge Simpson, representing New England textile manufacturers.[147] This arrangement was subsequently endorsed by Appleton, Lowell, and others among Webster's wealthy benefactors, as well as agents representing paper, chemicals, linseed oil, and several other interests who had converged on Washington to preserve protection for their industries, and it was entrusted to the

Massachusetts senator for presentation in the Senate.[148] If these men could not preserve even the incidental protection offered by the Tariff of 1842, diluted as it was from the pure protection once promised under the American System, they would follow Clay's lead by seizing the initiative to salvage what practical advantage they could from the situation.

At this point however Webster, who still maintained of the Compromise of 1833 that "the principle was bad, the measure was bad, the consequences were bad," got cold feet.[149] Just as Clay had thirteen years previously, he found his political associates in Congress resistant to any hint of retreat. "I trust the compromise will not be offered," urged Sargent in the *Gazette*. "Let us have the tariff of '42, or the present British [i.e., Walker's] bill— no half and half; neither one thing nor the other, but free trade or protection."[150] Even some of those who would be most affected by the pending legislation, but who had not been consulted in drafting the substitute, disapproved of the scheme. The manufacturers "having before their eyes the unfortunate result of the last compromise on this subject, will not yield readily to another," predicted an agent of the Du Pont Company, adding: "[F]or our part we had rather bear the brunt of the new tariff than die by inches under a half way measure."[151]

Ultimately, these divisions among the protectionists were sufficient to kill the proposal. "It is a vast misfortune, that Whigs here & else where, should oppose a settlement of the Tariff question," Webster grumbled to his son. "I do not call it *a compromise*; it is no compromise; it is merely an amendment of the Bill, retaining *all* the great principles of the Act of 1842, & making reductions, which would leave all the protected interests safe, & satisfied, & yet quiet a great deal of clamor." Nonetheless, he pledged, "I shall not, of course, propose any thing, which will not have Whig support."[152] The amendment was quietly dropped, only to be revived by Simon Cameron as a last-ditch effort to avert passage of the bill and summarily rejected.[153] Still, the episode caused some lingering ill-feeling between the scheme's sponsors and their allies in Congress when letters between Webster and his collaborators were leaked to a national newspaper. "It certainly has the appearance of arrogance for these gentlemen, representing the larger and aristocratic manufacturing establishments, to undertake to *dictate* to the whigs what sort of an amendment or substitute they should offer or support, to the British tariff bill," opined Sargent. "For although they only appear in this correspondence, to approve an amendment proposed to be offered by Mr. Webster, yet the *fact* is, or at least was so understood here by every one, that this was an amendment prepared and urged upon Mr. Webster, by these gentlemen themselves."[154] It would not be the last time that one faction of manufacturers would break ranks to push their own preferred version of tariff reform.

+ + +

Meanwhile, the administration was struggling to keep the remaining Democratic senators in line. The first to cause concern was James Semple of Illinois, who Polk learned had "expressed opinions which render it doubtful how he will vote," a fact the president attributed to his disgruntlement at not being granted a military command in the Mexican War. "Several other members have similar griefs. They have either been disappointed themselves or have not obtained offices for their favourites and friends, and at this moment the great Domestic measures of the Session are endangered from these causes," he lamented in his diary, a reminder that executive influence could make enemies as easily as it could secure allies.[155] Semple was invited to the White House on 13 July and the matter seemed resolved.[156] Then, two days later, word reached the president that Semple "was packing his trunk to leave for Illinois." The Secretary of the Treasury and postmaster general were dispatched to scour the city for the disappearing senator, who was finally discovered by one of the Illinois congressional delegation at the railroad station.[157] Sargent reported that Semple had "actually got into the cars to go, when he was stopped by the friends of the Tariff bill and persuaded to remain. His vote was considered too important to be dispensed with."[158] In a hastily arranged second meeting, Semple told Polk that he was threatened by court proceedings at home, but the president "made an earnest appeal to his patriotism and for the sake of the country to remain & vote on the tariff bill," to which he finally consented.[159]

No sooner had that problem been solved than another presented itself. William Haywood, senator for North Carolina and friend of the president since college, had convinced himself that Walker's bill cut duties too far and too fast.[160] Like his Pennsylvania colleagues, Haywood was also under instruction from his state legislature, but in his case that instruction was to reform, rather than preserve, the Tariff of 1842.[161] Polk urged other Democratic members to press upon Haywood the importance of his support for the pending legislation and held personal conferences with him on 15 July and again on 23 July, during the latter of which he "begged [Haywood] for his own sake, for the sake of the country, and for the success of my administration to consider well before he voted against it." Haywood was "deeply impressed" with the president's entreaties and proposed his own compromise: if the Senate would postpone commencement of the new duties for three months, he would approve the bill. Polk was not opposed to the concession in principle, but he could not accept the practical consequence of this amendment: the bill would have to be returned to the House for concurrence, where opponents might rally their forces and defeat it. He therefore reluctantly rejected his friend's proffered olive branch.[162]

Haywood was torn. He could not amend the bill without the support of his party, had told the president that he would "rather die than vote for it" unamended, but was obliged by his state legislature to do just that.[163] And so, two days after his final meeting with Polk, the senator from North Carolina resigned. In an address to his constituents, Haywood explained that he considered it his "duty" to step down "sooner than cast my vote against my conscience for a law that I could not approve" and pointed to a clause in his instructions that required him to do just that if he was unwilling to obey.[164] Polk was "astonished" when he heard the announcement, which threw the fate of the bill into serious doubt.[165] "We have been calculating all along that it was to be carried by the casting vote of the Vice President," Democratic senator John Fairfield informed his wife, but following Haywood's resignation "the tariff is trembling upon the verge of success and defeat."[166] The *Union*, in an article titled "The Revenue Bill in Danger!" published on the evening of 25 July, labeled the North Carolinian "an apostate and a deserter, who never will be able, in the course of the longest life, to expiate one-hundredth part of the political transgression which he has this day committed.—Let this bill be lost through his dereliction, and the deepest odium will fall upon his head."[167] Opponents of Walker's scheme were surprised and delighted in equal measure. "LAUS DEO. I have just heard that MR. HAYWOOD HAS WITHIN A FEW MINUTES PAST, RESIGNED HIS SEAT IN THE SENATE!" Sargent interrupted one of his regular columns to exclaim: "[H]e has preferred this course rather than be compelled by party drill and party tyrany [sic], to vote for a bill which he considers injurious to the interests of the country."[168]

The bill now looked lost, unless one of the Whig senators could be induced to support it. The principal candidate was Spencer Jarnagin of Tennessee. Jarnagin had been instructed by the Democrat legislature of his state to seek the replacement of the specific duties in the Tariff of 1842 with ad valorem duties, just as Walker's bill proposed, and he was eager to secure his own reelection the following year.[169] The president had approached Jarnagin about his vote even before Haywood's abrupt departure and received assurance that "he conceived the tariff question settled by my election, and that moreover he was instructed to give the vote by the Tennessee Legislature."[170] Still, Polk remained doubtful, hence his desperation to have Haywood support the bill, and those doubts redoubled when word reached him on the same day that the North Carolina senator resigned that his Tennessee colleague was considering doing likewise. Hopkins Turney, Jarnagin's Democratic counterpart, was immediately summoned to the White House and charged with securing his vote.[171] Turney returned the following day with welcome news: Jarnagin "told him he would not resign his seat in the Senate, but would vote for the tariff-bill . . . & he, Turney, had no doubt he would do as he said he would."[172] Others, however, remained unconvinced. "Janngan [sic], a Whig, who has been instructed by a democratic Legislature to vote for the bill, is continually backing and filling, so that all are in doubt what he will finally do," recorded Senator Fairfield on the morning of the decisive roll call.[173]

"Every thing depended on Mr. Jarnagin's vote," Webster would later recall. The Massachusetts senator pleaded with his fellow Whig to stand with the rest of his party, and on Sunday, 26 July, the very same day that Turney was informing a relieved Polk that his vote was safe, Jarnagin sent word to Webster through two representatives that "he agreed that the Bill should not be permitted to pass." But Jarnagin first wished "to br'g the Vice President to the necessity of a cast'g vote," in the hope that Dallas would relieve him of the responsibility for defeating it. For his part, Webster "was desirous of gett'g some amendment into the Bill, so that if it should pass the Senate, there might be a chance, still, to defeat it in the House," the fear of which had caused Polk's refusal to endorse Haywood's suggested compromise. Therefore, to prevent any misunderstanding, he committed a plan to paper. First, Webster would propose a minor amendment to the bill, and Jarnagin would vote in favor, ensuring its success. Then, a motion would be made to engross the bill, the step prior to passage, but on this division Jarnagin would abstain, leaving the casting vote to Dallas. If Dallas voted "nay," the bill was dead; if he voted "yea," Jarnagin would then move to lay the bill on the table, and his vote would carry the motion. At no point would the Tennessee senator actually cast a vote against the passage of the bill, thereby allowing him to claim that he had abided by the letter, if not the spirit, of his instructions. This memorandum was carried to Jarnagin by the Tennessee representatives, and in their presence, he gave his assent.[174]

The morning of Monday, 27 July, Webster confidently informed his son that the tariff would be killed that day. On the floor, he duly moved to amend the bill, as agreed with Jarnagin. Just then, however, there came "quite an unexpected interference."[175] Webster's fellow Whig John M. Clayton, whose intervention had proved so important in 1833, proposed to commit the bill to the Committee on Finance with instructions either to restore the specific duties from the Tariff of 1842 or to at least remove the planned duties on raw materials. Clayton declared that he "was opposed to [the bill] as a whole; he felt little interest in its details, or in the fate of the pending [i.e., Webster's] amendment."[176] Under Senate rules, Clayton's twin motions to commit the bill took precedence over Webster's motion to amend it. On the first, Jarnagin voted in the negative, citing his instructions to oppose specific duties, and it was defeated. But on the second, despite an angry intervention from Turney, who reminded his Tennessee colleague "that in private conversations they had agreed that the bill as it now stood conformed to those instructions, and that they had agreed to vote for it," Jarnagin switched sides and the motion to commit carried by a single vote, with Cameron, Niles, and Sturgeon all joining the Whigs.[177]

"Everybody saw [Clayton's motion] was perfectly useless, but the Whigs could not well vote against," was Webster's retrospective verdict on what had transpired.[178] In truth, though, committal did offer an alternative means of defeating the measure. Notionally, as Jarnagin somewhat disingenuously observed in justification of his vote, "it would not hazard the safety of the bill . . . as the amendments would proceed from a committee in which there was a majority of the friends of the bill."[179] But in making amendments, the members of that committee would be bound by the instructions given to them by the Senate. If they complied with Clayton's instructions, the bill would take on a substantially more protective cast. If they refused to comply, the bill would remain trapped in committee, effectively condemning it to die a natural death with the close of the session, or, perhaps, as was rumored around Washington, buy time for the Whig governor of North Carolina to appoint a suitable replacement for Haywood.[180] The success of Clayton's motion was therefore widely viewed as tantamount to victory for opponents of tariff reform. According to Sargent, "the defeat of the bill enabled men to draw a long breath who have for weeks been so weighed down with a load of fear and anxiety as not to be able to breathe freely."[181]

But as Webster later recounted, by delaying the final confrontation Clayton's motion would have "fatal consequences."[182] Overnight, friends of the bill scrambled to find the single vote they needed to save it. Lewis, the chair of Finance, backed a proposal to bring over the Pennsylvania senators by offering further concessions on coal and iron, which was reluctantly approved by Walker.[183] Whether this would have proved sufficient to sway Cameron and Sturgeon turned out to be moot, however, for theirs were not the only votes in the market. "In the Eve'g of Monday, Mr. Jarnagin's Whig friends could not find him any where till 10 Oclock," Webster recalled. "He had been at the Presidents," and when finally located "he did not incline to talk."[184] The following morning, the Tennessee senator informed his Massachusetts colleague that while he still intended to "refuse to vote upon the engrossment of the bill, and leave its fate to be decided by Mr Dallas," his sense of "duty" required that he "cannot vote to postpone it."[185] "At the meet'g at the Presidents, on Monday Eveg, means were found to fix Mr. Jarnagin's vote for the Bill," Webster concluded, noting that the following morning "I saw Mr. Walker at the Capitol, & found him well apprised of Mr. Jarnagin's ultimate purpose."[186]

The proceedings of the Senate on Tuesday, 28 July 1846, wrote Sargent, "will be remembered by those who witnessed them, to the latest day of their lives."[187] Debate on the tariff began with a request from Lewis that his committee be discharged from their instructions. Jarnagin then rose to explain that after "mature consideration" he was convinced that no amendment could be made to the bill, and that refusing the committee's request would prevent any action on it whatsoever. Under such circumstances, he enquired, "what am I to do?," at which juncture, a watching Sargent reported, someone in the gallery muttered "resign."[188] Ignoring the interruption, the speaker declared that though he did not approve of the bill, he was instructed to support the principles on which it was designed, and he would obey those instructions. The motion to discharge the committee was then carried by twenty-eight to twenty-seven, with the Whig senator from Tennessee the only man to change his vote from the previous day. A motion to engross the bill followed, on which Jarnagin abstained as promised, leaving the vote tied at twenty-seven apiece. Called upon to break the deadlock, Dallas cast his vote in favor, declaring that as vice president he acted as "the direct agent and representative of the whole people," and was bound as such by the Democratic platform of 1844.[189] Finally, the question upon the passage of the bill was put and decided in the affirmative by twenty-eight votes to twenty-seven, Jarnagin voting with the majority.[190]

"If the manner of proceeding, which was agreed on, on Sunday Eve'g, had been permitted to be carried out, so that we could have brought on the final vote before the President & Cabinet had had an opportunity of a meet'g with Mr. Jarnagin, I have no doubt the Bill would have been defeated," was Webster's verdict.[191] Amid all the excitement, the Massachusetts senator did succeed in carrying his own amendment, which sent the bill back to the House for its concurrence, but despite efforts to revive the opposition there this was granted the following day, and the legislation was dispatched for a relieved President Polk to sign.[192] Some observers saw corruption at work; one Tennessean said of Jarnagin that he "would not hesitate to sell himself, even if it were made a condition of the bargain, to label the *price* on his front that all might read."[193] Webster, who knew a thing or two about selling himself, was more sympathetic. "I would not impute any corrupt motive to Mr. Jarnagin. There are means of influence not generally esteemed positively corrupt, which are competent to produce great effects," he explained to his son, though he added that the Tennessee senator "falsified his promises, & has thoroughly disgraced himself, forever."[194] Webster reserved his principal ire, however, for Clayton and his associates, who first blocked his efforts at compromise and then derailed his arrangement with Jarnagin. The failure of the leading Whigs to consult on a plan to kill the Walker Bill can be traced back to the falling out between Clay and Webster factions over the Compromise of 1833, which generated animosities that had festered ever since. "The Whigs have been as sheep without a shepherd," one congressman lamented, "sectional jealousies & personal rivalries have prevented all concert of action."[195]

The Tariff of 1846 produced one of the sharpest divisions between parties of any antebellum tariff legislation. Taking both chambers together, the Democrats split 140 to 21 in favor and their opponents 101 to 2 against.[196] As in 1842, partisan affiliation cut across sectional allegiance; all sixty-one Northerners who supported the bill were Democrats, and all but one of the thirty-three Southerners who opposed it were Whigs. The measure was enacted "contrary to the judgment of a majority, under the duress of a *party drill*," Haywood complained to his constituents.[197] Niles concurred, "I verily believe that there is less than one-third of this body who, in their consciences, can say they approve this bill," he proclaimed in a final effort to arrest its progress in the Senate.[198] One man to whom this surely applied was Thomas H. Benton, who reportedly remarked that "he would as soon undertake to naturalize a baboon, as to lick this tariff bill into any acceptable shape," and yet still he assisted its passage.[199] Another was Sam Houston of Texas, who admitted that "the Bill was not a very good one" but refused to do anything "which could distract the democratic party."[200] The biggest sacrifice was made by Dallas, however. The vice president was hung in effigy by his Pennsylvania constituents; such was the ferocity of their displeasure that he took out a new insurance policy on his house and urged his wife to "pack up and bring the whole brood to Washington."[201] This piece of legislation, perhaps better than any other, demonstrates the uncertainty of antebellum policymaking even at the height of the party system. Ultimately, it took a combination of Jarnagin's choice to abandon his party and Dallas's decision to remain loyal at the cost of betraying his state to pass the Tariff of 1846.

"This exercise of the taxing power, by which the great mass of consumers are made to swell the profits of a few branches of industry, was originally intended to be temporary, to be continued only so long as its continuance was necessary to the industrial independence and safety of the whole people," George M. Dallas reminded his Senate audience as he gave his decisive vote for the Tariff of 1846.[202] The vice president's statement illustrates how tariff policy had come full circle since his father's report launched the protective experiment three decades earlier. Beginning with Baldwin's bill in 1820, manufacturers and their allies had progressively expanded their original claims for state aid against foreign competition. This trend was only checked with the Tariff of 1832, and then more seriously by the Compromise of 1833, which signaled a retreat from the permanent and explicit encouragement promised by Henry Clay's "American System" in favor of the more equivocal "incidental protection." That doctrine, as ambiguous as Andrew Jackson's "judicious" tariff of the previous generation, was carried to its furthest extent in the Tariff of 1842, which manufacturers considered "a very good one" and one that "operated like magic in restoring prosperity to the whole country."[203] These gains were reversed by the Tariff of 1846, however, which proved to be the closest Congress would come to enacting a pure revenue tariff throughout the period 1816 to 1861.

Both these tariff acts attest to the small margins by which antebellum policymaking was frequently determined. The Whigs were able to carry the Tariff of 1842 over President John Tyler's obstruction, but only by sacrificing the distribution of revenue from public land sales among the states, which undermined their effort to unite Northern, Southern, and Western sections in support of a program of government-sponsored national economic development. Four years later, a bill christened for Democratic Secretary of the Treasury Robert J. Walker, sponsored by Democratic President James K. Polk, and submitted to sizeable Democratic majorities in House and Senate was saved by a single Whig vote. In circumstances such as these, with lawmakers subject to the push and pull of often conflicting partisan and sectional allegiances, the potential for a critical intervention "from without on the members within," to borrow Thomas Cooper's phrase, was significantly enhanced. And protectionists responded accordingly, embracing methods of mass campaigning that had already proved their worth for abolitionists and other antebellum reform movements, and combining them with innovations like the National Fair.

There was no single instance in which lobbying can be said to have definitively shaped either of the pieces of legislation considered here, as had been the case with Francis Cabot Lowell's advocacy of the cotton minimum in 1816, or the Harrisburg Convention's agenda-setting role for the Twentieth Congress in 1828. Yet the cumulative effect of ever-increasing numbers of manufacturers and their agents descending on the capital compelled members from protectionist constituencies to consider the cost of betraying those interests, as was demonstrated most clearly by the conduct of Pennsylvania's delegation on both occasions. And while the attempt by one clique of wealthy capitalists to fashion their own compromise proved unsuccessful in 1846, it nonetheless pointed to a growing fragmentation of the protectionist coalition, with friction over the conflicting interests of its constituent parts that had been evident as early as Lowell's undercutting of his fellow textile producers in the Tariff of 1816 now exacerbated by Clay's abandonment of the unifying principle of permanent protection in the Compromise of 1833. These tensions would only worsen during the decade that followed, as would sectional tensions over the future of slavery, brought into sharp focus by the war on Mexico that was declared by Congress just two months prior to passage of the Tariff of 1846 and David Wilmot's subsequent call for slavery to be barred from any territory acquired as a result of that conflict. All of these developments would have important consequences for congressional policymaking, especially on the tariff. For as Nathan Sargent noted during the long summer of 1842, "nothing can be predicted now with any sort of confidence, for members are not acting themselves, not as free agents, but under a high pressure of extrinsic, and out of doors influence."[204]

chapter six

"The Almighty Dollar"
The Tariffs of 1857 and 1861

O NE OF THE most unfortunate and alarming features of the politics of
the day," declared the *Pennsylvanian* in February 1857, as Congress
once again debated new tariff legislation, "is the prevalence of corruption
among those who are selected by the people as their representatives and
law-makers." "It is impossible to avoid the conclusion, that a monarch more
powerful than any European sovereign, the Almighty Dollar, is yearly gaining new strength, as the real controlling power of far too much of the legislation of the country," the editor continued. "So far has this custom pro-
gressed that our legislative halls are thronged with professional vote-sellers.
Nominally, they are lobby members, but really they sell out at so much
a head, some of the honorable members, as pigs are sold in the market."
"Nothing," he warned his readers, could be "more dangerous to a Republic
than the prevalence of such infamy."[1]

These observations suggest how far lobbying had developed from its
modest origins in the labors of Isaac Briggs and his associates following the
War of 1812. The very different circumstances that shaped the making of
tariff policy on the eve of the Civil War are illustrated by a study of the
Tariffs of 1857 and 1861. The first of these came about through another
split in the protectionist ranks; after eleven years of futile attempts to reverse Robert J. Walker's move toward the revenue standard, one faction of
manufacturers, concentrated in New England, switched tack and supported
a further reduction in duties, but one that would fall disproportionately on
raw materials and thereby enhance their own profit margins. This bill they
succeeded in carrying through an odd coalition with dedicated free traders
who favored any downward revising of the rates, but at the cost of alienating former allies who persevered in their calls for higher tariff barriers across

the board. The episode also prompted a congressional investigation into the lobbying carried out by certain textile factory owners, which heard shocking testimony of bribery and corruption within the capitol itself.

Even before the results of that investigation were known, however, the Panic of 1857 reenergized the campaign for explicit encouragement of domestic manufactures, some twenty-five years after Henry Clay had sacrificed that principle in the Compromise of 1833. Also critical was the growing power of the sectional Republican Party, which leading protectionists, most notably Henry C. Carey, strove to convert into the instrument for finally realizing Eleazar Lord's prophecy that all their success required was "union among those who ought to be united."[2] Having pushed their preferred measure through the House of Representatives, their triumph was postponed in the Senate in the summer of 1860 by a now thoroughly Southern-dominated Democratic Party, one final manifestation, it seemed, of the Slave Power stranglehold on Washington. But Abraham Lincoln's election to the White House in November of that year, and the consequent secession of seven slave states, provided the opportunity for Northern members of Congress to reaffirm the nation's commitment to the policy of protection in February 1861 and signal the commencement of a new era in American political economy.

+ + +

The Tariff of 1846 remained in force for the longest duration of any nineteenth-century schedule of duties. The economy boomed under its auspices, driven by a flood of agricultural exports across the Atlantic; as Charles I. du Pont, nephew of E. I., remarked to a relative, "not anticipating the famine in Europe all business men anticipated rough times, but Secretary Walker was really fortunate & he owes as much to Pat's potatoes for his success as a financier as to anything else."[3] With even manufacturers prospering under the revenue standard, by the mid-1850s the British ambassador to the United States was able to report that "there is very little chance of Protection being revived. Certainly not as a general principle." "The Whigs have had possession of office during a whole Presidential Term [1849–1853]," he explained, "and yet every effort that they have made, either directly or indirectly, to modify the Tariff in a Protective sense has signally failed."[4] Their inability to carve out a position sufficiently distinct from their Democratic opponents on this or any other major issue, including the future of slavery, which increasingly dominated the public's attention, contributed to the dissolution of the Whig Party soon thereafter. So too did the death of its elder statesmen Henry Clay and Daniel Webster in 1852, both men having outlived John C. Calhoun, the third of the Great Triumvirate, by two years.[5] In its place emerged the Republican Party, which in its desire to unite former Whigs and Democrats against slavery initially hesitated to take a strong stance on protection. In the party's first presidential campaign in 1856, while the Democrats boldly proclaimed their support for "progressive free trade throughout the world," the Republican platform committee, under the supervision of that rare Pennsylvania free trader David Wilmot, omitted any reference to the subject.[6]

What remained of the protectionist movement was divided and dispirited. "N. England has no influence & any effort we make is perhaps injurious rather than beneficial," lamented one Boston businessman. "Indeed I think sometimes that the best way to bring about a change & a more efficient protective system would be for N. England to declare itself the champion of free trade."[7] Pennsylvania's vote for James Buchanan in 1856, which carried the Democratic candidate into the White House, provoked further resentment: "some of our old friends say that Penna. having decided in favour of free trade democracy, must have it carried out in practice," warned a member of that state's congressional delegation.[8] And while Southern sympathy for encouraging manufactures had waxed following the Panic of 1837, it waned again in response to growing antislavery sentiment in the free states. "Just when the south was ready to receive reasonable propositions on this head, you people of the North, East, & West, raise up a bone of contention which has spoiled all, it is mere phathom [sic], an abstraction to you New England people, who I had hoped had too much hard common sense to run mad about," a South Carolina cotton mill owner chastised his Massachusetts counterpart Amos A. Lawrence, whose Uncle Abbott had advised Congress on several previous tariff bills.[9] Thus growing tensions between manufacturers with abolitionist sympathies, mainly from New England, their counterparts of a more conservative bent who predominated in the mid-Atlantic region, and the much weaker slave state wing of the protectionist coalition further reduce the likelihood of concerted action in future.

It was during this period of uncertainty that Henry C. Carey assumed his father's mantle as the nation's leading advocate of protection. Preferring weighty tomes to Mathew's rapid-fire pamphlets, though he authored his share of newspaper essays too, Henry won international acclaim for his writings on political economy. Despite never holding public office, he even received three votes for the Republican vice presidential nomination in 1856, although this honor may have been intended by the Pennsylvania delegation as a symbolic protest against the absence of a tariff plank from the platform.

A former Whig, Carey's involvement in that campaign was, he claimed, the first time that he had "engaged in the management of the machinery of politics," but his commitment to the Republican Party was conditional upon his faith that it could be made the vehicle for a resurrection of a pure protective policy.[10] Following Buchanan's victory, he actually offered to advise the incoming Democratic president on economic matters but apparently received no reply.[11] He also contemplated fashioning a new party under the banner of protectionism but was cautioned by friends that it would be "political suicide" to attempt to place that subject before the slavery issue.[12] Nonetheless, Carey continued to press upon friends in Congress the need for a general increase in rates, which he argued would benefit North and South alike by producing a "Harmony of Interests," agricultural, commercial, and manufacturing, within a self-sufficient national economy.[13] Just like his father's, Henry's vision for the country's future was a potentially unifying one, but in a context of escalating sectionalism it was uncertain how many Americans could be persuaded to subscribe to it on those terms.

Others seeking more immediate practical advantage for home industry demurred from such an ambitious scheme. They focused instead on securing repeal of the taxes that Walker had laid on raw materials in his pursuit of a genuine revenue tariff. Chief among these were textile factory owners desperate to be rid of the 30 percent ad valorem they currently paid on imported wool. This strategy was politically savvy, a correspondent of Carey's explained, "because we old Whigs can support it on the ground of protection & our Republicans who have been Democrats can support it as a free trade measure, as well as a protective one."[14] He labeled it "the Greely [sic] method," after Horace Greeley, who advocated the policy in the columns of his *New-York Tribune*.[15] Since attending the New York Tariff Convention of 1831 as an unknown spectator, Greeley had risen to become what one political collaborator called "the ablest writer on the subject of a protective tariff we have had since the time of Hezekiah Niles," with his newspaper, like Niles's *Register* before it, boasting the largest circulation of its day.[16] But Carey rejected the plan as incompatible with his "Harmony of Interests," since it sacrificed wool growers for the benefit of the manufacturers. Likely he also considered the danger such a precedent would pose to Pennsylvania's iron interests at the hands of another influential pressure group: railroad magnates seeking cheap foreign metals for their tracks. As James E. Harvey, a Carey ally, complained in his regular Washington column for the Philadelphia *North American*: "Eastern men want free wool, which certain western men oppose, who want free iron, while a class of southern men hold themselves in readiness to retaliate upon either, who shall advocate free sugar. So that in this jarring and complication of objects, each gets its share of damage, and neither is greatly helped."[17]

+ + +

The occasion for this falling out among the protectionists was the lame duck session of the Thirty-Fourth Congress that convened on 1 December 1856 to see out the final few months of Franklin Pierce's tenure in the White House. With the treasury overflowing, both Pierce and his Secretary of the Treasury James Guthrie had been urging a further reduction in rates since taking office, but the remaining friends to high duties had managed to block reform through increasingly desperate recourse to filibustering tactics. "It seems to me that the extent of our power in either House is to stave off action, by aid of the rules for impeding business. What more can a minority do & what are we but a minority?" admitted one, a week before the opening of the session.[18] This time, however, rumors circulated that representatives of various industries were willing to combine with administration support-ers to pass a bill designed in accordance with "the Greely method." "It is stated that the railroad corporations are willing to enter into, if not already committed to, an engagement to secure wool free, providing, on the other hand, that interest unites in applying the same principle to railroad iron," reported Harvey on 4 December, adding three days later that "the lobby has been largely reinforced within the last twenty four hours, and by a class of trading politicians, who care much more for gold than they do for either wool or iron."[19]

An anti-Democrat coalition, composed of Republicans and other anti-slavery factions, members of the nativist American Party, and a few Whig remnants, held a majority of seats in the House. Opposition to administra-tion policy on slavery was what united them, rather than any shared stance on the tariff. Thus the Speaker Nathaniel P. Banks was a former free trade Democrat from Massachusetts who launched his career by criticizing the influence of manufacturers in his home state, while the chair of Ways and Means, Lewis D. Campbell, was an old Ohio Whig and, by his own admis-sion, "a protectionist in principle."[20] Campbell and other like-minded members of the committee consulted with Carey on the proper course to pursue, but they too leaned toward "the Greely method." "The true remedy of increasing the rates, in order to diminish the revenue," the same solution that Henry Clay had advocated when faced with a similar surplus in 1832, "would not have the remotest chance of success," counseled Pennsylvania representative James H. Campbell. "We must look at what can be done sometimes, rather than at what we should do."[21] To this end, they sought Carey's advice on which articles could be added to the free list without harming American producers. In the case of wool, Lewis Campbell believed this might be done by removing the duty on "very fine" and "very coarse" varieties, which were not grown domestically, and retaining it for the remainder.[22] Still, his Pennsylvania namesake cautioned, "we may . . . be driven to free wool for New England, to keep the duty on our iron."[23]

At the close of the previous session, the chair of Ways and Means had reported in favor of an enlarged free list but requested that consideration be postponed until after the recess.[24] When discussion of the subject was duly resumed on 13 January 1857, Campbell announced that his committee "had received from various quarters much useful information" since his first report and offered a revised version in its place.[25] This substitute bill may have differed in detail from the original, but it was based on the same design of moving a large number of articles, some two hundred in total, to the free list while leaving the other rates set by the Tariff of 1846 unchanged. Among those to be admitted without duty was wool valued at less than 15 cents or greater than 50.[26] The purpose, Campbell explained, was in "yielding something to [the] principle of free trade," to "give incidentally protection to the various branches of American industry by taking off the duty on raw materials not produced in this country that enter into those branches of industry."[27] Five weeks of desultory debate followed, much of which, to Harvey's disgust, was "addressed to the slavery question": "no light whatever has been shed upon the real subject, and scarcely an attempt made to consider it seriously," he lamented.[28] The chief criticism came from Democrats who complained that the bill's authors had subverted the intent of the administration by departing from the revenue standard established by the Walker Tariff.[29] Still, the measure did promise to reduce the average level of duties, and after striking hemp from the proposed free list to satisfy that interest and reassuring sugar planters that their product would retain its existing rate of protection, Campbell was able to secure its passage by the House on 20 February by 110 yeas to 84 nays. Nearly seven-eighths of the Democratic votes were cast in the negative column, and more than two-thirds of the administration's opponents were in favor.[30]

The tariff bill was taken up by the Democrat-controlled Senate the same day and referred to the Committee on Finance under Robert M. T. Hunter.[31] "Solidly built, with a massive head and a determined manner," as one contemporary recalled, the Virginian "was thoroughly acquainted with parliamentary law and usages," and "his speeches on financial questions were listened to with great attention."[32] As a Southern Democrat, he was hardly sympathetic to the protectionist agenda pursued by Ways and Means in the other chamber. Even some conservative Northerners protested against New England, the heartland of abolitionism, receiving any concession at a time of rising sectional tension. The bill was "the greatest boon a federal Gov't ever gave" the textile manufacturers, wrote one, and before they have it "they ought to be made to feel, that Lawrence and Lowell [Massachusetts mill towns] are in the United States,—facts, they do not yet recognize there."[33] But Hunter also faced pressure to effect some reduction in the revenue, and quickly. David M. Stone, an editor for the free trade *Journal of Commerce*, told Hunter he would prefer to see rates cut on manufactured articles as well as raw materials but urged "that something be done with the Tariff even if it be not the best thing which wisdom could devise."[34] Similarly, J. Wiley Edmands, a financier and former congressman, warned that "the commercial community are alive to the importance of something being accomplished now, to protect them against the disaster which must follow the accumulation of so much coin in the vaults of the Treasury."[35]

On 24 February Hunter reported Campbell's bill to the Senate with amendments from his committee but also gave notice that he would propose a substitute of his own devising.[36] This he did two days later, accompanied by a speech that emphasized the need for swift action with the close of the session only one week away. Hunter's substitute proposed to reduce rates across all the categories established by the Tariff of 1846 while only slightly increasing the size of the free list, and thus it conformed much more closely to the revenue standard set by Walker than to the House version. Hemp, iron, sugar, and manufactures of wool and cotton, which the author identified as the major protectionist interests, would all be taxed at 23 percent ad valorem, down from 30 percent in the case of the first four and 25 percent for the latter. He was willing to see raw wool of all varieties reduced from 30 to 8 percent, as a boon to manufacturers, but on the intervention of Illinois senator Stephen A. Douglas his colleagues decided to adopt a modification of Campbell's formula, with wool under 20 cents admitted free and the rest at 23 percent. Following a debate that detained the Senate well past midnight, Hunter's substitute was agreed to by thirty-three votes to twelve, and then passed without division.[37]

The House refused to concur in the Senate's changes to the bill and requested a Committee of Conference.[38] Banks, as Speaker, chose the chair of Ways and Means and two other members of that committee, John Letcher of Virginia and Alexander De Witt of Massachusetts, to represent the lower chamber, while the upper chamber was represented by Hunter, Douglas, and New York senator William Seward. After a mammoth twelve-hour session, an agreement was reached: Hunter's substitute would prevail, but with the major protected articles at a marginally more generous 24 percent and the addition of a substantial portion of the larger free list from Campbell's version.[39] The conference report was duly approved by both chambers on 2 March, the penultimate day of session, by 123 votes to 72 in the House and 33 votes to 8 in the Senate. "Six men really settled the tariff," grumbled Harvey, "and Mr. Banks constituted the committee, on the part of the House, in such a manner that Pennsylvania had no voice in the decision of her great interests. Care was taken, however, that New England should be heard, and this was effectually proven, by giving her interests a degree of protection which they were not disposed to exact in the last resort."[40]

The Tariff of 1857 reduced rates to the lowest level of the nineteenth century, but this was offset for certain branches of industry by the expanded free list, meaning that protectionist opinion of the bill was less united than it had been in 1846. Taking both chambers together, Democrats voted ninety-three to six in favor of the conference report, while opponents of the administration split sixty-three to seventy-four against, a clear reversal from the parties' respective positions on Campbell's original bill, though the chair of Ways and Means was one of those who voted in the affirmative. From a sectional perspective, Southern members overwhelming endorsed the cut in duties, eighty-two to eight, while their free state counterparts divided evenly, seventy-four for and seventy-two opposed. Within the North, the most salient distinction was between wool-growing states like Ohio and Vermont, which voted twenty to five against, and wool manufacturing states like Connecticut, Maine, and Massachusetts, which voted twenty-three to zero in favor. Such was the interest the Bay State felt in this measure that Charles Sumner briefly resumed his Senate seat for the first time since his brutal beating nine months earlier at the hands of proslavery congressman Preston Brooks in order to see free wool safely through the closing days of the session.[41] The reduction on iron proved too much for Pennsylvania's delegation, though, and they split seventeen to four against, with James H. Campbell of Ways and Means among the negatives.

+ + +

"It is a little singular to reflect that a subject which, but a few years since divided and excited the whole country, should now be re-adjusted with so little feeling," mused the editor of the *Pennsylvanian* after Congress had adjourned.[42] It is true that the new tariff legislation was not prompted by any economic crisis like those that produced the Baldwin Bill of 1820 and the Tariff of 1842, nor was it marked by the kind of partisan maneuvering that yielded the Tariff of 1828, or the sectional posturing that surrounded the Tariffs of 1832 and 1833. There was no coordinated campaign for, or against, protection; no national conventions like those of 1819, 1827, and 1831; few public meetings and petitions on the issue. This does not mean, however, that there was no interest outside of the capitol, as the *Pennsylvanian's* previously cited caution against the "controlling power" of the "Almighty Dollar" testifies. What role, then, did the lobby that Harvey identified as massing at the commencement of the session play in the passage of the Tariff of 1857, and why did their activities attract public scrutiny like never before?

The answer to these questions may be found, at least in part, in an investigation into "Alleged Corruption in the Tariff of 1857" conducted by the Thirty-Fifth Congress the following year.[43] This was the first such investigation to focus on tariff legislation, though similar inquiries into all manner of subjects were becoming commonplace in the 1850s. Indeed, during the final session of the Thirty-Fourth Congress, while the tariff was still under consideration, the House had appointed a committee to look into newspaper charges relating to a bill for distributing public lands in the Minnesota Territory.[44] Harvey claimed some credit for instigating this "rumpus" in his letters to Carey, suggesting that if it uncovered evidence of wrongdoing, then "a bad odour would be given to all other schemes," including "the wool and iron operations."[45] The *North American* correspondent also warned Pennsylvania's ironmasters against sending their own agents to Washington to combat the railroad influence. "If their object be to set forth the condition of those interests & confer for a brief time with the members, there is no objection to it," he explained. "If on the other hand, the design is to station them as *videttes* [a mounted sentry posted forward of a formation's position] here, I question the policy entirely. We are just now making a concerted war on the lobby, & one class could not claim exemption more than another."[46] The Minnesota investigation resulted in expulsion proceedings against four members of Congress and served to keep the lobby influence quiet for the duration of the session.

Or so it seemed. Nine months later, however, reports emerged that an examination of the books of Lawrence, Stone & Co., recently bankrupt selling agent for several Massachusetts textile mills, had revealed an expenditure of more than $87,000 in connection to a mysterious "tariff account."[47] "The disclosure . . . excites no great surprise in well-informed circles," reported Harvey from the capital. "When the present tariff was pending, delegations representing the woolen and cotton interests, were in Washington, and understood to be well provided with the sinews of war, in order to procure such modifications as suited their interests."[48] On 15 January 1858, a committee was appointed by the House to "investigate the charges preferred against the members and officers of the last Congress, growing out of the disbursement of any sum of money by Lawrence, Stone & Co."[49] The instigator was Ohio representative Benjamin Stanton, who had labeled the Tariff of 1857 "essentially a manufacturers' bill" for its sacrifice of wool growers, and he was chosen to lead the investigation.[50]

The committee began by familiarizing themselves with the affairs of Lawrence, Stone & Co. Of the company's three senior partners, Samuel Lawrence, brother of Abbott, had fled to Europe under suspicion of embezzlement, and Jarvis Slade lay dangerously ill after attempting suicide.[51] This left William W. Stone, a familiar figure in the halls of the capitol. The committee's report noted that several of its own members were "personally cognizant" that Stone "had spent a considerable portion of his time during the last session of Congress in this city, urging the passage of the tariff of 1857."[52] So too was Harvey, who had informed Carey in December 1856 that "the movement for wool is serious. Stone is here, but not armed as the lobby directs."[53] The latter was a reference to the textile magnate's reluctance to disburse large sums of cash, a fact that recurred several times in testimony on the case. Called to testify, Stone did confess to spending some $8,000 of company money over the course of several years in the collection and publication of materials to support the case for free wool, but the committee accepted that "there is no evidence that he was personally engaged in using any corrupt means with members of Congress." Instead, his efforts in Washington "seem to have consisted mainly in endeavoring to convince members from the wool-growing States that reducing the duties on imported wool would increase the price of wool grown in the United States," the report explained, adding sardonically: "it is not strange that he should have had rather indifferent success in this enterprise."[54]

This still left $79,000 unaccounted for, however. According to Stone, his partners first "encouraged me to come to Washington and work" but subsequently became convinced "that I should not succeed, and it would be necessary to pay something."[55] To this end, and apparently without consulting him, they employed John W. Wolcott, a salesman for another Boston firm. It was to Wolcott that the bulk of the remaining money had been entrusted, and Stone disclaimed any knowledge of how it was spent, though the two men had shared lodgings in the capital: "I preferred not to know anything about it, not knowing what I might find out," he told the committee.[56] Wolcott, for his part, acknowledged that he "had intercourse with members" in relation to the tariff but denied having "possession of any funds belonging to any of the manufacturers of Massachusetts . . . for the purpose of influencing Congress upon that subject."[57] When pressed on the latter point, he refused to say whether he had received payment from Lawrence, Stone & Co. for any other purpose and was consigned to the city jail until he would consent to answer further questions. There he occupied "a cheerful apartment, with a good fire, bright sunshine coming in at the windows. He had numerous visitors, his meals were sent [to] him from a restaurant, and he certainly did not appear to suffer seriously from his martyrdom," one journalist later recalled.[58] After several weeks of confinement, friends in the House arranged his release on bail under the false pretense that his wife was sick, at which point he promptly absconded to Boston, leaving the committee bereft of its key witness.[59]

Still, sufficient testimony was collected from Stone and other parties implicated in the scheme to piece together some picture of the lobbying that surrounded the Tariff of 1857. Lawrence, Stone & Co. were hardly the only company involved; some $13,000 was contributed to their kitty by other textile firms, and many also independently dispatched their own representatives to Washington.[60] Some of these, as was usual, were the proprietors themselves, who stood to profit directly from free wool; Stone recalled the presence of manufacturers from Massachusetts, Maine, New York, Pennsylvania, and Rhode Island during his time in the capital.[61] But the investigation also uncovered the involvement of a new breed of lobbyist, at least in relation to tariff legislation: agents who were not directly interested themselves but tendered their services for hire. Thus Massachusetts lawyer George Ashmun informed the committee: "I have no sort of objection to state that I was employed and acted in behalf of gentlemen interested, and in that capacity conversed with members of Congress on the subject."[62] Ashmun had served six years in the national legislature himself, establishing a reputation as "sound, true, able, quick in his perceptions, and highly popular," before he resumed his private practice.[63] Due to his former station, he not only enjoyed friendly relations with many legislators but was also permitted by House rules to mingle with them on the floor.[64] Ashmun denied that his "professional fee" was "a proper subject of inquiry for the committee" but did acknowledge that he had received payment of $4,000 from Wolcott following passage of the bill.[65]

The free wool lobby had been cultivating opinion in favor of their pet project for years before it finally passed. Stone admitted that he had met with several newspaper editors, "conversed with them, and explained the object we had in view, and its necessity, as I thought, to the welfare of the country, and appealed to them to advocate it." He was adamant that he "never offered to pay them one farthing, and they never asked any such thing."[66] Nonetheless, wherever a suitable article did appear, large numbers of copies were bought up by the manufacturers and distributed for free, including to members of Congress, and the author often received "a bonus" for his efforts.[67] One man to receive such a reward, to the tune of $3,500, it transpired, was David M. Stone, who had pressed Hunter so earnestly for a reduction in duties while the tariff was pending.[68] Another was Thurlow Weed, New York newspaper proprietor and famed political operative, who received $5,000 in return, in his own words, "for services rendered in promoting the passage of the tariff of 1857," amounting to "argument and the presentation of what I esteemed valuable statistics in furtherance of my views."[69] Several other agents were paid smaller sums for disseminating the free wool message in lectures and pamphlets addressed to targeted constituencies, including J. N. Reynolds, a nativist politician who secured an endorsement of the measure from the New York City chapter of the American Party.[70] Thus, the committee observed, "the manufacturers sought to propitiate and conciliate leading and influential men, in all the political parties of the country, to favor their scheme." Stone's paper backed the Pierce administration, while of Weed the investigators noted: "perhaps no man in the country exerted a larger or more controlling influence over the republican party."[71] Indeed, their report continued: "[W]hen such men as Mr. Stone, of the Journal of Commerce, and Mr. Weed are employed to 'collect statistics' and write newspaper articles, everybody knows that it is not the labor which they perform, but the weight and influence of their name and character which is the main consideration for the money which is paid them."[72]

The extent to which such "influence" had been exerted on members of Congress, and what forms it took, was the main focus of the House investigation. Ashmun testified that he "did frequently, in conversations with members from my own State and other States, press the question" of free wool, and "had various documents laid before them, and urged various considerations upon them, such as could properly be addressed to the judgment of gentlemen."[73] William W. Stone was more specific, identifying ten "doubtful" legislators with whom he had "talked on the subject," including Hunter, to whom he was introduced by his editor namesake, and also Stanton, who was now chairing the inquiry. That list, he explained, excluded those firm friends of the bill that he also consulted.[74] J. Wiley Edmands, who had written to the chair of Finance on behalf of "the commercial community," was also unmasked as a free wool lobbyist, having the "management" of that interest in his hands during the first session of the Thirty-Fourth Congress and advising Ways and Means in their design of the free list that ended up a part of the Tariff of 1857.[75] So too was John D. Lang, a Maine mill owner, whose correspondence shows that he held "interviews" with both Hunter and Letcher, another member of the six-man Committee of Conference that determined the ultimate shape of the bill.[76] Weed was not asked to recount his own conversations with members while the tariff was under consideration, but Carey's spies reported that he had indeed spent time in Washington, where they suspected him of conspiring against Pennsylvania's iron interests.[77]

Whenever the committee's questioning turned from mere persuasion to the more substantial matter of bribery, however, witnesses were quick to disclaim any involvement. Typical was Ashmun's response: "I do not know of the manner in which another cent was expended; I am one of those persons who mind their own business and do not meddle with others."[78] Stone, though, was trapped into disclosing that he had paid $1,000 to a clerk on the House Committee of Claims, Abel R. Corbin. This he justified, the investigating report noted, as "a mere trifling gratuity or present, by way of acknowledgement of sundry acts of kindness and advice received from Mr. Corbin during Mr. Stone's stay in Washington."[79] The pretense was somewhat undermined not just by the scale of the sum but also by the revelation of a letter from Stone to Corbin dated March 1857, in which the former wrote: "'[T]he labourer is worthy of his hire,' and I enclose a check . . . for one thousand, in accordance with my understanding with you. You have fairly earned the money."[80] This payment, the committee deduced, was really made to the recipient "for the advantage which his official position gave him of ready access to members of the House."[81] Ironically, though, and unknown to Stone, Corbin actually used that access to lobby *against* the Tariff of 1857. He had been promoting both free wool and free iron for some time, he explained, and boasted of having been the first to suggest that the two interests combine their efforts, but he deemed Campbell's bill insufficiently free trade for his liking.[82] "Although the committee are not disposed to give Mr. Corbin all the credit which he claims for controlling the legislation of Congress on the most important measures of legislation affecting the revenue and finances of the country for the last ten years," their report dryly concluded, they were satisfied of his willingness to sell whatever influence he did possess to the highest bidder.[83]

Stone's testimony also implicated a sitting member of Congress: New York Republican Orsamus B. Matteson. The latter allegedly told him that "there were twenty-five votes in the House that could be influenced through their friends," and "some considerable sum of money must be paid" to effect it.[84] Matteson did not even vote on the passage of the tariff bill, having resigned days before the close of the Thirty-Fourth Congress to escape expulsion for his part in the Minnesota land frauds, safe in the knowledge that he had already been reelected to its successor. News of his involvement in this new scandal prompted Harvey to comment that "the inevitable Matteson had his finger in the pie, as usual."[85] He was duly called before the committee, and admitted the conversation with Stone, but claimed that "the money was not to be paid to members, but to gentlemen who influenced them." "I thought that in so important a measure he would require the assistance of those who make it a business to push claims before Congress, and who are called claim agents or lobby members," the New Yorker explained. When pressed on precisely what influence he expected such men to exert, he stated: "I think that every gentleman is influenced by his friends who call on him and show him statistics and reasons for pursuing a certain course; and these agents will not do this unless they are paid."[86] According to Stone, Matteson instructed him to place the required sum "in the hands of Mr. Greeley," but he declined the proposition, and the editor of the *Tribune* also denied any involvement, declaring that the first he knew of it was when he read about it in his own paper.[87] Once again, the money trail had run cold.

Ultimately, only two payments could be directly traced from the books of Lawrence, Stone & Co. into the pockets of legislators. The first was a "loan" of $106 that Stone made to Massachusetts representative Timothy Davis during the summer of 1856. The committee's suspicions were aroused by the charging of this transaction under the "tariff account," but the company's bookkeeper claimed this was merely a clerical error and it had since been repaid.[88] A second "loan," of $700 to Speaker Banks, was of potentially greater significance, however. This did not appear under the "tariff account," and the firm's representatives testified that it bore no relation to that legislation.[89] Still, the coincidence was sufficient to bring Banks's conduct at the previous session under fresh scrutiny. "The power of the Speaker's place was wielded against Pennsylvania then, and in a manner to justify the severest criticism as to the inspiring motives," Harvey reminded his readers. "His zeal, and that of several of the Massachusetts members, may be explained by the interest of their constituents in the object, but it was sufficiently conspicuous to attract notice, not only from that fact, but from their ready co operation with the South—which they had before denounced so fiercely."[90] Questioned whether he had sought to influence the Speaker in the conduct of his duties, Stone admitted: "I did state to Mr. Banks that I hoped he would give us a good Committee of Ways and Means" but denied anything further.[91] Though the investigating committee could not know it, Banks's correspondence from February 1857 also includes a suggestive letter from

Wolcott. "My friends are much pleased with the present position of affairs in Washington with regard to the changes in the Tariff at this session of Congress," the lobbyist wrote. "It is also becoming well understood that you are earnestly in favor of the change which manufacturers desire and that whatever is accomplished in that way will be owing to your efforts and good management alone." After hinting that Banks could expect elevation to the Senate as reward for his work on behalf of free wool, Wolcott concluded: "[I]t is the time for you to play a trump card."[92]

Based on the testimony at their disposal, however, the committee reported to the House on 27 May 1858 that "there is not a particle of evidence that any part of the sum expended by Lawrence, Stone & Co., to influence the passage of the tariff of 1857 ever went into the hands of any member of Congress." Neither Banks, Davis nor Matteson could be proven to have done anything improper, and Wolcott would not say what he had done with the money that had been entrusted to his care. In fact, after examination of the latter's business dealings the investigators reached the astonishing conclusion that "the largest portion of the $70,000, which remained in his hands after payment of $4,000 to Mr. Ashmun, has been appropriated by Walcott [sic] to his own use, and now constitutes a portion of the capital of the firm of Gardiner, Walcott [sic] & Co., bankers in Boston." The whole thing was a humbug, though whether the former wool salesman had cheated his employers or his confederates in the legislature the tribunal did not venture to determine. The only confirmed wrongdoing subject to their jurisdiction was perpetrated by Corbin, the clerk on the Committee on Claims, and he had resigned once his guilt became apparent. Two decades later, he would be caught up in another political scandal when, after marrying the sister of President Ulysses S. Grant, he colluded with speculators to corner the gold market. With Corbin gone, the committee reported: "[T]he facts disclosed by the investigation do not seem to call for any action on the part of the House," and they were duly discharged from further consideration of the subject.[93]

+ + +

While the congressional investigation into "Alleged Corruption in the Tariff of 1857" did not lead to any immediate revision of that legislation, it was heavily critical of the methods of the free wool men and indicates how far lobbying had developed since the days of Burrill, Davis & Co. "The evidence satisfies the committee that Mr. Wolcott was sent here, and authorized to pledge any amount of money, and to use any means, however corrupt, to insure the success of the measure," the authors stated. This ambitious brief was a far cry from the Wilmington factory owners' struggle to raise $200 to finance Isaac Briggs's mission to "communicate with members [of Congress] on the just & reasonable objects of the manufacturers" in 1816. The novelty of that mission was sufficient to earn it the censure of John Randolph on the floor of the House, but by the standards of four decades later it was comparatively innocuous. Stanton would subsequently describe Stone and his associates as "smooth, oily, fair spoken and to all appearance the most honest and harmless men alive," even as they worked to have representatives "seduced from their allegiance to the people" by their "subtle and unseen power."[94] Another member of the committee, serving his first term in the House, wrote to a relative while the investigation was still ongoing: "[W]hen I came on here I knew nothing of politicians. The depths of the depravity of our leading men the people never can know."[95]

Harvey was equally damning in his coverage of the investigation for the *North American*. "While professing to act in concert with our tariff interests, and affecting a community of cause, [the free wool men] were actually negotiating with th elobby [*sic*] scavengers about Washington for corrupt combinations with any party, or faction, or interest, to promote their own selfish schemes and to sacrifice the prosperity of Pennsylvania," he declared.[96] Yet his private correspondence to Carey while the bill was pending hints at a willingness to countenance similarly dubious practices to effect their shared object. "Our friends ought to be on their guard, even to the extent of fighting the devil with fire," he advised at the opening of the session. "It is said, [the combination for free wool and iron] will have the sinews of war, & we should be prepared to satisfy the hungry cravings of the camp followers."[97] And four weeks later, he berated Carey for having "wasted time & money in the elaboration of themes upon men who care not a fig for them, & who really value the issues of the mint, much more highly than political economy," adding cryptically: "if you should come here, I would like to confer with you privately on this point."[98]

Precisely what constituted "corrupt" means of lobbying was not defined by the investigation into the Tariff of 1857 or any other contemporary authority. Today, House rules prohibit members from accepting gifts of any kind from a registered lobbyist and gifts worth more than $50 from any other source. During the antebellum period, however, there was no register of lobbyists and no rule against accepting gifts.[99] The surviving correspondence of Henry Clay, for example, reveals that over his long career he received presents of numerous parcels of cloth; specimens of glass and silverware; a spade, shovel, axe, hoe, carving knife, and fork; "two pair of Indian rubber over shoes," a dozen kid gloves, countless hats, and, for the rare occasion he found himself without a hat, four combs; "a bureau travelling trunk," presumably to keep everything in; "half a dozen bottles of American Cologne water"; wallpaper; a pocket knife; a plough; a dozen scythes; and twenty-three barrels of salt.[100] These were intended, one donor explained, "as a testimonial of our respect and esteem for the great advocate of protection of domestic manufacturers," and no one seriously accused Clay of seeking to profit from these transactions, though following his apparent abandonment of the American System in the Compromise of 1833 one newspaper wit did suggest that he "get up an auction" to dispose of all the "curious articles" sent him by former supporters.[101]

Other legislators were more circumspect in their conduct. "My principle has always been to refuse all presents offered to me as a public man," recorded John Quincy Adams in his diary on receiving "several articles of the manufacture of soap" from an exhibitor at the National Fair in 1846. He initially resolved to pay for the soaps, but "my wife shamed me out of that fancy," and he reluctantly decided to accept them, reasoning that "where the value is very small, I thought it would be ridiculous to make a point upon it." Still, Adams noted, "it has not always been easy for me to draw the line of distinction."[102] Many politicians of his generation no doubt shared this uncertainty.

Then there was the matter of members socializing with lobbyists, who, as we have seen stretching right back to John Harrison and Thomas Forrest in 1820, were often their personal friends too. The current House rule defines "gift" broadly to encompass any "gratuity," "favor," "hospitality," or "entertainment." This would certainly cover Abbott Lawrence's proposal, never acted upon, in 1828 that "ten active manufacturers" come to Washington "and together give a dinner once every week to 20 Members, and give them nothing but good old honest Madeira and a plenty of the best champaine [sic] be pleasant and agreeable and there is not a doubt in my mind that every thing would be done that is required."[103] Likewise, and less speculatively, when Charles J. Ingersoll volunteered for his mission to Washington at the New York Tariff Convention of 1831, a witness later recalled that the newly appointed agent had announced: "I must have apartments in that City, I must entertain, and show to the . . ."; there the entry unfortunately ends, the following page ripped from the journal.[104] This latter example illustrates the difficulty of finding evidence of improper influence, when there was a decided disincentive for the perpetrators to preserve it. As Mathew Carey wrote to a member of the permanent committee of the convention after their delegates' stay in the capital had concluded: "[I]t is by no means the wish of my colleagues or myself to know the details of any portion of the expenditure, which prudence requires not be divulged, if any such there be."[105]

Nonetheless, there are hints in the testimony to the investigating committee, and in the newspaper discussion that surrounded it, that the treating of lawmakers had become customary by the 1850s. "I never resorted to the common trick of asking a man to go out and take a drink, or getting another to do so for me," declared one of those implicated in the free wool scheme.[106] Another denied having furnished "so much as a cocktail or plate of oysters to a member of Congress."[107] Some of the money expended on this score was defensible; members were often absent for crucial roll calls, the committee heard, "and men and carriages had to be employed to go after them and bring them up, and various expenses were incurred in that way."[108] And some was much less so, if Harvey is to be believed when he decried the employment of "female brokers" to "canvass doubtful members and subdue opposition."[109]

The current House rule also prohibits "loans" to members of the sort obtained by Davis and Banks. Such arrangements could amount to bribery if conducted on terms patently favorable to the recipient, or even in the expectation that the debt would never be collected. Certainly, Daniel Webster had lived off the credit of his benefactors, who included William W. Stone, for most of his career.[110] So far as the Massachusetts man was concerned, this was merely fair compensation for forsaking the substantially greater income he could have earned in private practice of the law for a life in public service. Even by contemporary standards, though, his conduct provoked controversy; one contributor to the "Webster fund" later speculated that it was "largely influential" in keeping the recipient from the White House, "by putting him in the position of a candidate subsidized by rich men."[111]

Other lawmakers proved more scrupulous. In 1846, while the Walker Tariff was under consideration, James K. Polk was informed by Tennessee senator Hopkins Turney of a conversation with a manufacturer in which the latter "had described the prosperity which would prevail if the pending Bill did not pass, and had said to him, Turney, that if it did not pass he could loan to him (Turney) any amount of money which he might want." "Turney was indignant at it," Polk recorded, "and considered it an attempt in this indirect way to induce him to vote against the Bill; or in other words an attempt to bribe. . . . I was shocked at the story, and said nothing but to express my astonishment."[112]

Polk's astonishment might have been less had this exchange occurred a decade later, for awareness, if not approval, of lobbying in the national capital had become widespread by the mid-1850s, through successive congressional investigations and greater coverage of the subject in the nation's press.[113] How far such lobbying was decisive in the passage of the Tariff of 1857 remains unclear, since aside from Carey and his circle there existed a general consensus on the need for some reduction in duties, and the final measure represented a compromise between free traders committed to the revenue standard and protectionists favoring an expansion of the free list. What the subsequent inquiry did disclose is the appearance of a new sort of lobbying, and a new sort of lobbyist, typified by Ashmun, prepared to hire out their skills to the highest bidder.[114] This heralded the professionalization of the practice in the post–Civil War era and the development of a justification of lobbying that moved beyond "the right of every citizen to watch over his interests," which had been the customary recourse of the "voluntary amateurs" of the past half century. As one newspaper rationalized in reporting the results of the 1858 investigation: "[T]here is no reason why a man of talent and influence who spends months in Washington collecting facts and arguments to present to members of Congress, should not be paid for his services by the parties that send him there."[115]

+ + +

"I am convinced that we shall get no economical wisdom into this government till we have a crash," predicted Charles A. Dana, managing editor of Greeley's *New-York Tribune*, to Henry C. Carey in December 1856.[116] Three months later, Congress took another step away from Carey's brand of unabashed protectionism and toward the elusive panacea of free trade. Not six months after that, the country was struck by another financial crisis like those of 1819 and 1837, bringing with it more bankruptcies, unemployment, and misery. The Panic's causes were global, but Carey was far from the only commentator to directly attribute it to passage of the Tariff of 1857.[117]

The Democratic administration was paralyzed by the Panic, with President Buchanan calling for enhanced incidental protection as part of a revenue-raising package while his Secretary of the Treasury Howell Cobb, a Georgian, denied the need for any amendment to the tariff. When questioned on the discrepancy, the latter dismissively remarked that "the President is opposing the Administration."[118] The Republicans had solidified their position as the main opposition bloc, but Carey remained frustrated by their refusal to wholeheartedly embrace protectionism. "It may be, that another party will arise, having a platform more in accordance with my views," he advised a friend late in 1857, and the following spring he was instrumental in the creation of the Home Protective Union in Philadelphia.[119] This organization, with Carey as its president, avowed that "its aim will be to make all political parties acknowledge the necessity and propriety of protecting industrial interests."[120] In this respect, the Union illustrated how protectionist strategy had evolved in response to the emergence and consolidation of a national party system. Whereas reformers of Mathew Carey's generation had proudly proclaimed their independence from parties, those of his son's would seek to work through them, recognizing their monopoly on the levers of power.[121]

The Union's pledge to cooperate with any party notwithstanding, a great rally held in June revealed that its membership was dominated by Republicans and old Whigs.[122] The Democratic press was dismissive: "[A]re we to have the representatives of that party from the Eastern States—which put forth LAWRENCE, STONE & Co. as the champions of their peculiar notions of protecting home industry and encouraging American labor, and spent $87,000 in procuring legislation to suit their purposes—to insult the intelligence and honesty of our workingmen by hypocritical harangues on the subject of a protective tariff," enquired the *Pennsylvanian*.[123] Carey was optimistic, however. "We have had a great meeting here—having for its object the reinauguration of protection as a part of the political platform," he informed one correspondent. "The ultra Republicans do not like it, & yet they will be forced to stand by it—Penn., New Jersey, Delaware & Maryland being fully determined as I think, to have nothing to do with any party that has yet to determine between free trade & protection."[124]

The Democrats' failure to tackle the economic depression contributed to their defeat in the 1858 midterms, meaning that the Republicans held a plurality in the House when the Thirty-Sixth Congress opened on 5 December 1859. But after two months of fruitless balloting, they were unable to secure the required majority for their preferred Speaker, John Sherman of Ohio, an experienced parliamentarian and firm protectionist. Carey and his allies backed Sherman's candidacy and regretted when he was eventually passed over in favor of William Pennington, who they considered "old, slow, without the first idea of parliamentary law or rules & no experience whatever."[125] At the height of the contest, a few Pennsylvania Republicans had even offered to abandon their party and support a Democrat for the post, if only one could be found who would pledge to "organize the Committee of Ways and Means in such a manner as to protect the interests of Pennsylvania," but none was forthcoming.[126] By way of compensation, Sherman was at least rewarded with chairmanship of Ways and Means. Pennington also appointed freshman Charles Francis Adams to chair of the Committee of

Manufactures, a tribute to his father, who had occupied the same position, though it was now merely a ceremonial one since the committee had not been called together within the memory of any member.[127]

Sherman delegated the preparation of new tariff legislation to Justin S. Morrill of Vermont, who he considered "eminently fitted" for the task. Morrill had been added to Ways and Means in the previous Congress and had immediately begun work on a bill even though there was little chance of its passage by the then-Democratic majority. He was friendly to the claims of manufacturers, regarding import duties "as not only a method of taxation, but as a mode of protection to existing industries in the United States with a view to encourage and increase domestic production."[128] But he also shared Carey's vision of a harmony of interests. Like the rest of the delegation from his state, he had voted against the Tariff of 1857 because it disadvantaged his wool-growing constituents. Morrill did not attend the Home Protective Union demonstration in June 1858, but Vermont senator Jacob Collamer used that occasion to decry "a mistaken notion [that] has somehow grown up of late, even among those who desire a protective tariff, that it is our business to protect only the manufacturer, and that we must do nothing that will protect the producer of the raw material."[129] Collamer's colleague shared these views, and they would guide his design of what became known as the Morrill Tariff. According to Henry Winter Davis of Maryland, who also served on Ways and Means, the appellation was deserved; "no one in the H.R. but you could have prepared it," he told the author.[130]

Though the fundamental principles of the bill were fixed in advance, there remained much scope for out-of-doors influence in deciding the details. Morrill would later claim that "the change was not asked for, and but coldly welcomed at the time by manufacturers, who always and justly fear instability," and this has led some scholars to mistakenly conclude that there was little lobbying on the subject.[131] Yet as Philip W. Magness has shown, Morrill's own correspondence reveals that this was far from the case. He and his associates were flooded with advice, offers of assistance, and pleas for protection on articles including chemicals, copper, glass, hemp, lead, oil, screws, sugar, wool, and woolens. The iron schedule alone, according to one newspaper, "required the continuous sitting for days of several leading gentleman of Pennsylvania, in and out of Congress."[132] By the time the bill was ready, Morrill professed himself "weary and worn with unending day and night labor on the Committee of Ways and Means."[133] According to Magness, who meticulously compared the rates in that original draft with the requests received by its author, "industry lobbyists directly influenced the rates of protection, categories of exemption, and even revenue collection procedures" adopted.[134]

Morrill reported his bill to the House on 19 March.[135] Its supporters claimed that the measure "merely makes specific the *ad valorem* duties under the tariff of 1846," without raising rates above a level then deemed by Robert Walker and his associates to be revenue-raising.[136] The ostensible purpose of the conversion from ad valorem to specific duties was to check the rampant undervaluation perpetrated under the existing system, but it also provided an opportunity for the committee to covertly raise the effective level of protection on many articles. The free list was also drastically scaled back, even further than under the Walker Tariff, though in this case the intent was to extend aid to as many different constituencies as possible, rather than to maximize income. In this respect, Morrill followed the same strategy that the protectionists had employed successfully in 1824. The result was a bill comprehensive in scope but complicated in operation. "A free trade tariff is easily made simple" because "they sacrifice a hundred points of solid interest in becoming so," one protectionist editor observed, whereas the proposed legislation aims "to guard every one of these interests, and to admit no leveling schedules." Still, he admitted, if the committee could "have devised less difficult paragraphs for the statement of their result, we should have been grateful."[137]

+ + +

Lobbying on the bill did not end when it left the care of Ways and Means. The case of the American Screw Company is illustrative. The country's largest producer of wood screws had already earned a reputation for using underhand methods to preserve its near-monopoly on the domestic market. It was rumored that the firm's president, William G. Angell, had paid its leading British competitor a bribe of £5,000 to refuse orders from across the Atlantic. Based in Rhode Island, the company benefited from a close relationship with Senator James F. Simmons of that state, himself a manufacturer, who intervened on its behalf during the drafting stage. Morrill was not convinced initially, however, and wrote to Angell directly to tell him that "the rates placed upon Screws now suggested by my friend Senator Simmons, upon inquiry we suppose them too much," and to ask his advice on an alternative figure "that would only fairly place you in competition with foreign trade."[138] Angell replied that he was willing to come to Washington personally to argue his case and also wrote separately to Simmons, urging him to "keep Mr. Morrill in the right track until we can see him together."[139]

In the interim, the bill had been reported to the House with a duty of 4 cents per pound on wood screws, but after meeting with its author Angell was able to report that this would be increased on the floor to 5 cents, with Morrill himself moving the necessary amendment.[140]

Another article on which the influence of lobbying was clearly felt was wool. "The new tariff bill is not likely to encounter any impediment to its passage, on the Opposition side of the House, except it should come from the Massachusetts delegation," James E. Harvey had forecast soon after it was reported. "Their manufacturing interests have been adapted to the present law [i.e., the Tariff of 1857] as far as practicable, and hence there is no particular disposition for a change," he explained, before warning any obstructionist mill owners that "the friends of a modification are strong enough to carry the bill, independent of any absence of co-operation from that quarter."[141] The woolens interest appears to have made the same calculation, for they confined their opposition to efforts to reduce the amount of wool admitted duty free. "There are some Mass. people here looking after wool: they plead vehemently agt. a change of the 20 cent limit," one Maine congressman advised Morrill while the measure was before the House.[142] Ways and Means had originally proposed reducing that limit to 16 cents to benefit wool growers, but textile producers urged the bill's creator to reconsider, among them J. Wiley Edmands, whose name had been caught up in the corruption investigation of 1858.[143] Once again, Morrill proved willing to compromise, offering an amendment that placed the limit at 18 cents: "I am for fixing the duty at such a rate as shall afford ample protection to the farmer as well as the manufacturer," he explained in its support.[144]

Carey endorsed the bill and pressed hard for its passage. His influence on the Republican ranks was acknowledged: "what ever Henry C. Carey approves will suit us," one member reportedly remarked.[145] But with protection and not antislavery as his priority, he was also willing to cross party and sectional lines. "The Southern policy [of reducing duties] is filling the pockets of those whom the South holds as enemies [i.e., New England manufacturers], while hurting all those who desire to be its friends," he warned one Virginia congressman before hinting that election to the White House would be a fitting reward for "the Virginia democrat who shall now have the courage to say that the interests of his State & those of Penna. are one & the same."[146] While the tariff was before the House, Carey spent several weeks in Washington, socializing with members of all political persuasions.[147] Harvey also lobbied for the bill, though he was not paid for this "thankless service." "Iron gentlemen stay at home, & saddle us who are toiling for bread day & night, as is my case, with the care of their interests," he grumbled to

Carey. "They make periodical excursions here & talk, but expect us to drum up votes, button-hole members, and argue their cases for patriotic considerations."[148] It was a considerable challenge to get legislation that touched so many interests safely through Congress. "Nothing less than a dictator is required for making a really good tariff," Carey observed to Morrill after yet another dispute broke out over the duty on some particular article. "Would to heaven you or I could fill the place for a week."[149]

Ultimately, it was Sherman's familiarity with the rules of the House that rescued the protectionists. "The bill became so mottled" with amendments from both friends and foes, the Ohioan recalled in his memoirs, "that Mr. Morrill, discouraged, and strongly inclined against the bill as changed, was disposed to abandon it to its fate."[150] Instead, Sherman encouraged his friend to offer a substitute that would essentially restore the bill to its original form with a few approved modifications, including those on wool and wood screws detailed earlier. The chair of Ways and Means immediately followed this with his own substitute, which was identical except in one immaterial respect. The question then being upon whether to take Sherman's substitute in place of Morrill's, the other members were precluded from altering the text of the former should they agree to adopt it; as one futilely protested, "it is now proposed, by this machinery of moving substitutes by the Committee of Ways and Means, to deprive the majority of this body of the opportunity of incorporating into the bill amendments."[151] Sherman correctly calculated that a majority of his colleagues favored some increase in rates and would therefore accept the version he had concocted with Morrill rather than risk losing everything. This maneuver was successfully executed on 10 May, and the bill passed the House the same day by 105 votes to 64, with only three Republicans going on record against it. Through Sherman's "skilful engineering," the measure was preserved "in a generally satisfactory shape, undeformed by material alterations," proclaimed the *North American*. "The Opposition majority in the House has now done its share of the work, and the responsibility must rest with the democratic majority in the Senate."[152]

The editor's wording was calculated for maximum effect on the forthcoming elections in November, for even the bill's sponsors expected it to fail in the upper chamber.[153] Carey continued to press for its passage, though, and cautioned Pennsylvania's Democratic senator William Bigler that he would be "digging the political grave of himself & his friends" if they contrived to block it.[154] Many of Bigler's neighbors evidently concurred, for he was deluged with visitors from his home state. "Democratic committees have been sent here from the iron and coal regions of Pennsylvania, under the pretence of aiding the tariff," reported Harvey, though he predicted that "if the whole party in the State should come to Washington in solid column, it would not change a vote."[155] Hunter, who as chair of the Committee on Finance took charge of the bill following its introduction on 11 May, also received warning that it was worth "20,000 votes in Pennsylvania."[156] Such pleas held no sway with the Virginian, however, who ascribed his own failure to secure the Democratic presidential nomination to opposition from the Northern wing of the party "because of my Tariff opinions."[157] On 13 June, he gave notice that, with the concordance of his committee, he would move a postponement of the subject until the following session.[158] After allowing time "for a few Buncombe speeches" from Democrats responsible to protectionist constituencies, Hunter carried out his threat, and the postponement was carried on 15 June by twenty-five votes to twenty-three, with Bigler one of only two members of his party in opposition.[159]

Even then, Carey still hoped the bill might be resurrected if the House refused to sanction additional government borrowing unless the Senate reconsider.[160] His friends rejected this plan to force a showdown with the administration as impractical, however. "It is easy for you gentlemen, to speculate in big arm chairs, & over your devilish good Hock, but we who have to sit on pine bottoms & drink no hock, must face other realities," Harvey wrote. "We have twenty or more votes for the Tariff in the House, on mere political expediency alone—men who go to oblige us, but who do not care a tittle for protection. They will not stand firm, if driven into a corner, but they will stand by us, if we do not force things."[161] Morrill concurred. "All of our men are not regulars but rather raw recruits. It would be rather a strange test at once to put them in the fire of a dead-lock," he explained to Carey. "If we can preserve our Tariff army whole until [December], we will likely win the day. I would like to win now, but at all events let us preserve our hopes."[162]

+ + +

Before Congress met again, the country would vote in the 1860 presidential election. The Democrats split irrevocably over slavery, but both camps reaffirmed their commitment to the party's 1856 free trade plank.[163] The Republican platform, in contrast both to their opponents' and to their own hesitancy four years earlier, came out explicitly for protection, proclaiming that "while providing revenue for the support of the general government by duties upon imports, sound policy requires such an adjustment of these imports as to encourage the development of the industrial interests of the whole country."[164] Gustave Koerner, one of the contributors to the drafting process, later recalled that it was Horace Greeley "who insisted upon a strong protective plank," though Koerner believed the wording adopted "amounted to no more than the establishment of a revenue tariff bill with incidental protection" and was therefore acceptable to former Democrats like himself.[165] According to Carey, it was his friend Thomas H. Dudley, representing New Jersey, who "did the work in the Committee, carrying his point against the wishes of by very far the larger portion of its members."[166] Whoever was responsible, the announcement was met with jubilation by protectionists at the convention; one witness described Pennsylvania's whole delegation "rising and swinging hats and canes."[167] They were also well satisfied with the nomination of Abraham Lincoln, a self-described "Henry Clay tariff man."[168] "Happily the Republican, or *anti-slavery party* has recently re-adopted Protection as one of the essential parts of its platform, and has nominated as its candidate for the presidency a man who has been all his life a protectionist. He *will* be elected, & we shall then have a total change in the policy of the country," Carey gleefully prophesized.[169] The slavery question dominated the campaign, of course, but following a speaking tour by Morrill and Sherman to boost the party's protectionist credentials it was the thirty-one votes that Lincoln collected from Pennsylvania and New Jersey that provided his margin of victory in the Electoral College.

But it was the lame duck session of the Thirty-Sixth Congress that convened on 3 December, the Democratic majority in the Senate still intact. On 20 December, Hunter again reported that his Finance Committee recommended the postponement of Morrill's bill, apparently killing it for another session.[170] That same day, however, South Carolina enacted its ordinance of secession, followed over the next two months by six other slave states. These movements sapped Democratic strength in the upper chamber, until 23 January, when the supporters of the bill were able to have it revived and referred to a select committee of five, consisting of Simmons, Collamer, Bigler, Hunter, and William Gwin of California.[171] Only the first two were Republicans, but with Bigler they constituted a safe majority for protection, to the extent that Hunter and Gwin did not even bother to attend meetings.[172] On 1 February, the committee reported sundry amendments, the "great bulk" of which, according to Harvey, "were suggested by Mr. Morrill and the Committee of Ways and Means."[173] "It is not changed materially and is pronounced by our friends a most excellent bill," Pennsylvania representative James H. Campbell reassured Carey.[174]

The resumption of the subject by the Senate was the signal for renewed lobbying, as many members pressed highly specific modifications to please their constituents. William Angell worried that certain importers would conspire to have the proposed duty on wood screws reduced and once again requested Simmons's intervention on his behalf; the subsequent appointment of the latter to chair the select committee must have been welcome news indeed.[175] The woolens manufacturers were less successful, however, as a handful of Republicans from wool-growing states joined with the Democrats to impose a 5 percent duty on all wool valued under 18 cents, despite Simmons's warning that it would "create a good deal of hostility in the House of Representatives."[176] The dispute over iron became so intense, Harvey reported, that "in order to have the question fairly considered, and the merits of both sides fully canvassed, Mr. Simmons had the importers and the manufacturers brought face to face, so that no misapprehension could occur. After a full discussion, the importers only differed ½ of one per cent. on the duties assessed by the bill in one particular, and the next day were willing to waive that."[177]

As he had during the previous session, Carey promoted the bill with all the resources at his disposal. He was in frequent correspondence with Morrill, Sherman, and leading Republicans in the Senate.[178] He even intervened directly with Simmons to urge the retention of the proposed duty on books, in which he had a personal interest.[179] Carey also arranged for his long-time friend William Elder to join Harvey in monitoring events in the capitol. "I have been constantly at work," Elder reported one week after the Senate began consideration of amendments to the bill, noting that his most recent contribution was to draft a speech for Bigler. If in this respect Elder's role differed little from that undertaken by the first tariff lobbyists five decades earlier, neither did his complaints. "Nobody here knows any thing," he groused to Carey. "They all preach [Robert J.] Walker & [free trade economist John Ramsay] McCulloch, and all sides believe them."[180]

The tariff bill passed the Senate on 20 February by twenty-five votes to fourteen, its triumph assured by the absence of so many Southern members. On its return to the House for concurrence, Sherman admitted that he did not approve some of the 156 amendments that had been made to it but urged his colleagues to accept them in toto or put the whole measure in peril. His advice was heeded for the most part, but even protectionists balked at imposing a revenue-raising duty on tea and coffee, two consumables that had never previously been taxed. A Committee of Conference was ordered on this clause, and under Sherman's guidance it was stricken out, to the satisfaction of both chambers.[181] The bill then went to the White House, where it awaited only the signature of a Pennsylvania Democrat to become law. "He cannot shut his eyes to the need of the protection which this bill will furnish to his own State," predicted the North American, somewhat anxiously. "Nor will he be likely to feel desirous of coming back hither with the odor of such a veto fresh upon him."[182] Buchanan duly gave his approval on 2 March, one of his final acts before Lincoln replaced him as president.

The decisive roll calls on Morrill's bill show how closely party and section were now aligned in Congress. Taking the House vote in 1860 and the Senate vote in 1861 together, the Republicans, every one of them from the free states, gave 114 ballots in favor and just 3 against.[183] Slave state Democrats split fifty-five to one in opposition to the bill, with the odd man out William Whiteley from Delaware. The much smaller number of remaining Northern Democrats also opposed it, but by a less convincing margin of sixteen to eight, with a further twenty abstaining, most likely because they did not want to offend their party by voting for protection or their constituents by voting against it. A similar division is evident among members of the American Party and other anti-administration factions from the slave states, who provided seven yeas, four nays, and fifteen abstentions. Bigler was the only senator to break party lines, though that seems to have won him little favor back home; one constituent brusquely notified him that "no Tariff sop will ever sever me from my principles nor will I ever give you credit for the passage of it—remembering as I do that your party destroyed the bill of 1842 enacted the abominable cheat of 1846 and the still worse one of 1857."[184] He was not reelected.

+ + +

On 21 February 1861, as the Morrill Bill returned to the House, its fate still undecided, Henry C. Carey once again pressed the importance of its passage on John Sherman, instructing him that "the question of the continuance or destruction of the Union is to be settled by the Committee of which you are Chairman." On an enclosed sheet, Carey sketched out two possible paths. One began with "Rejecting the Morrill Bill" and ended in "anarchy," "Union of the Border & Southern States," and "Triumph of Slavery." The other, commenced by "Passage of the Morrill Bill," concluded in "Union of the Border & Northern States" and "Triumph of freedom over Carolina & British free trader Slavery."[185] The Tariff of 1861 was perhaps not so crucial to Union victory as Carey predicted, although its revenue-raising function, further enhanced by supplementary legislation drawn up under the supervision of Justin S. Morrill, did permit the Lincoln administration to finance the war without anything like the same economic difficulties that beset its Confederate rival. Union victory, though, was certainly crucial to the continuance and consolidation of the protectionist policy through the postwar era, as the expanded capacity of central government, and the securing of that government safely in the hands of a pro-business Northern Republican Party, normalized the distribution of state aid to favored constituencies.[186]

Perhaps because the conflict had such a transformative impact upon the nation's political economy, some commentators continue to claim that the tariff, and not slavery, was the primary cause of the Civil War.[187] Morrill would later recall with amusement that shortly following the enactment of the bill that bore his name, "my picture was put forth by a rebel Virginia newspaper, with an advertisement offering a like reward for me, dead or alive ($25) that was usually offered for the recovery of runaway slaves."[188] And it is true that a consistent majority of Southerners did oppose the protective policy throughout the antebellum period, though there were also a sizeable minority for whom economic interests outweighed sectional affiliation, whether hemp producers in Kentucky, sugar planters in Louisiana, or factory owners in Maryland and Delaware. But it was secession that provided the occasion for passage of the Tariff of 1861, not vice versa. Tension between North and South over the tariff, which commenced from the moment that Alexander J. Dallas launched the protectionist experiment in 1816, reached its peak in 1832–1833 with the Nullification Crisis. Thereafter, the countervailing effect of national party competition, a political consensus in favor of the less contentious doctrine of incidental protection, and the maintenance of low rates from 1846 to 1861 effectively subordinated the tariff as a source of sectional antagonism. Morrill's bill might well have commenced a new period of escalating hostilities over the issue, but it became law three months *after* South Carolina separated from the Union.[189]

"Accept my congratulations upon the happy termination of your tariff labors. You have now connected your name with what is destined, as I think, to prove the most important measure ever adopted by Congress," Carey wrote to Morrill after passage of the bill was assured.[190] Yet the Philadelphian was also entitled to a substantial share of the credit. He had stood with the minority against the Tariff of 1857, disagreeing with "the Greely method" of encouraging manufactures by reducing duties on raw materials. But following the Panic of 1857, he had campaigned energetically to convert both policymakers and the public to his "Harmony of Interests" doctrine, which held that only a general increase in rates would benefit all constituencies and restore the country to prosperity. It was the union, on those terms, of the bulk of the manufacturing community with the antislavery Republican Party that most significantly differentiated this generation of protectionist activists from its predecessors, who had sought to navigate partisan and sectional divisions while remaining, at least outwardly, uncommitted to either side. "But for the untiring pen of Henry C. Carey, and his great personal influence, we doubt very much whether the present success would not have been postponed for several years," judged the *North American*.[191] Like his father, however, much of Carey's most effective work was done behind the scenes, through correspondence with legislators and associates in the national capital. James E. Harvey was rewarded with "a service of plate" for his "persistent & efficient efforts" both "individually & as connected with the public press" on behalf of the "protective policy," much as Eleazar Lord had been forty years earlier.[192] The Lincoln administration was even more generous, making Harvey its minister to Portugal on Carey's advice.[193] The latter was also able to arrange a place for William Elder in the Treasury Department, where he was granted full "power of attorney" to ensure the smooth operation of the new tariff.[194] Carey wanted no public appointment for himself, having followed Mathew's example in declaring himself "averse to the acceptance of any office whatsoever," but he would continue to exercise an important influence over the making of American tariff policy for decades to come.[195]

Conclusion

THE MONTH BEFORE the opening of the Thirty-Sixth Congress, as clamor for a protectionist response to the Panic of 1857 mounted, William Cullen Bryant, staunchly free trade editor of the *New York Evening Post*, sat down to answer a British friend's inquiries on the nature of American politics. Pressed for examples of "acts of tyranny exercised by the majority over the minority," Bryant could only recollect laws that had long since been repealed. "But there are examples of the tyranny of the minority," he continued. "The owners of manufacturing establishments are a minority in the United States—a minority even in Massachusetts. Include all their work people they are still a minority in every one of the states. Yet they are wealthy active and powerful—powerful through concert of action, and they have influenced even the politics of the federal government. Members of Congress and statesmen of every class have paid court to them—they have even influenced the conduct of those whose interests are not at all the same with theirs. They have tyrannized over the majority with a protective tariff."[1]

Bryant's letter points to the importance of tariff policy for many antebellum Americans, and the importance of lobbying to the making of that tariff policy. If the former is often underestimated, the latter has been virtually ignored; the complaint of James E. Harvey, as he and Henry C. Carey helped shepherd the Morrill Bill through the national legislature, that "the men who have carried the weight of much of this business, have hardly ever received the cheapest compliments of recognition," might be applied even more accurately to historians than it was to the Philadelphia newspaperman's erstwhile allies.[2] This book is intended to set the record straight and to show that party and section, the standard lenses through which the antebellum era is viewed, provide only an incomplete picture of policymaking during this formative period for the United States' political and economic development.

"What do we mean by Protection? Simply, the restriction of importations of foreign manufacturers to such an extent that their younger and less hardy American rivals may take root and flourish."[3] This was the definition offered by Horace Greeley to his readers in 1852, and it would have been just as recognizable to an earlier generation that witnessed British endeavors to stifle those infant industries brought into existence by the War of 1812. Secretary of the Treasury Alexander J. Dallas provided the blueprint for the nation's first serious experiment with protectionism: duties should be set at a level that would enable domestic producers to meet their foreign counterparts in fair competition and should cease once those producers reached sufficient maturity to free them from their dependence upon state aid. Opinion in and out of Congress was receptive, and lobbying was confined to local circles of factory owners with a direct stake in the issue. Still, the "men of talents" that these groups deputed to represent their interests in Washington, though few in number, made a noteworthy contribution to the policy-making process. The collaboration of Isaac Briggs with Thomas Newton, chair of the House Committee on Commerce and Manufactures, and his cooperation with fellow delegates in founding the capital's first lobbying outfit, heralded future efforts by protectionists to coordinate their activities, both among themselves and with sympathetic lawmakers. Francis Cabot Lowell's influence, meanwhile, was felt more immediately in the design of the Tariff of 1816 by securing the insertion of an innovative minimum valuation scheme for cotton textiles, which would become a focal point for controversy over the decades that followed.

The Panic of 1819 transformed the making of tariff policy, as activists like Mathew Carey and statesmen like Henry Clay combined to recast it as "more than a mere manufacturing question." With the Convention of the Friends of National Industry, held in New York City in 1819, advocates for increased duties pioneered a new mode of organizing on a national scale. And in the Baldwin Bill of 1820 they pressed the case for a novel brand of protectionism that promised to secure the American market exclusively for domestic producers in perpetuity, a doctrine that would become the centerpiece of Clay's famous American System. That bill was notable too for the paramount role played in its conception by Eleazar Lord, lobbyist for the American Society for the Encouragement of Domestic Manufactures, who spent several months working side by side with the chair of the Committee on Manufactures Henry Baldwin. Though their efforts were in vain on this occasion, the protectionists returned with renewed vigor four years later and were rewarded with passage of the Tariff of 1824, which offered more comprehensive, and more generous, rates than the legislation it replaced.

As the country divided over the controversial elevation of John Quincy Adams to the White House that same year, tariff policy became "an engine of *party* purposes" for ambitious politicians like Martin Van Buren. But it was the weight of public sentiment in favor of further reform, generated by a sustained protectionist campaign outside of Washington, that pushed the issue to the forefront of the congressional agenda. The Woollens Bill of 1827 originated with a deputation of textile manufacturers who urged the Committee on Manufactures to extend the minimum valuation scheme to woolen cloths. This bid foundered in the face of complaints from former associates that it was narrowly conceived from selfish motives, but it was no coincidence that the measure would mainly have benefited supporters of the administration, while those who protested loudest were already coalescing around the rival standard of Andrew Jackson. In response to this setback, leading protectionists recalibrated their strategy at the Harrisburg Convention of 1827, which dwarfed the New York meeting of eight years earlier in both scale and ambition. Now the call was for a general revision of the rates, and the efforts of the Jacksonian majority in the subsequent Congress to evade this responsibility were thwarted by a flood of petitions, public meetings, and lobbyists who testified to the need for action. It was at this point that Van Buren's intervention, in conjunction with Speaker Andrew Stevenson and Silas Wright on the Committee on Manufactures, proved crucial. The outcome surprised many and satisfied few. The lopsided "Tariff of Abominations" courted key constituencies across the mid-Atlantic and Western regions, punished New England for its loyalty to Adams, and generated futile protests from slave states that were certain to vote for his opponent regardless.

The "Little Magician" may have succeeded in electing his candidate in 1828, but his duplicity would make tariff policy a defining issue for Jackson's presidency by prompting Southerners like Thomas Cooper and John C. Calhoun to "calculate the value of the Union." As tensions between the sections escalated, protectionists and free traders held rival national conventions in 1831 to compete for popular favor. Congress responded with the Tariff of 1832, which briefly offered the prospect of genuine compromise through a substantial reduction in rates combined with a reaffirmation of the principle of protection. This measure was the product of bipartisan collaboration between Adams and Secretary of the Treasury Louis McLane, and involved extensive consultation with interests outside the capitol. But it satisfied neither Calhoun's friends in South Carolina, who responded by nullifying both this act and that of 1828, nor Clay, who resented being sidelined. Angling for another bid at the White House, the latter made a startling proposition to defuse the Nullification Crisis by replacing the Tariff of 1832 before it even came into effect. Clay's measure emerged out of a meeting with a committee of Philadelphia manufacturers, but the final version seemed to many protectionists to bear more resemblance to the terms set by the Free Trade Convention, despite the eleventh-hour intervention of E. I. du Pont with his friend, the Delaware senator John M. Clayton, securing the important "home valuation" amendment. The Compromise of 1833 preserved encouragements to industry for the immediate future, but at the cost of sacrificing the principle of protection, signaling a return to the moderate and temporary doctrines of 1816 and an effective abandonment of the American System. Thus Van Buren and Clay, in their respective efforts to build truly national parties, would leave a legacy of mistrust as sectional divisions over the tariff were papered over with nebulous slogans like "judicious tariff" and "incidental protection." The protectionist coalition, in the ascendancy since 1816, was shattered by the "Great Compromiser's" betrayal and would never regain the unity of action it had exhibited under his leadership.

The Compromise of 1833 remained in force for nine years, but the period that followed its expiration underscores the highly charged, hotly contested nature of tariff policy, as twice major legislation on the subject was left "trembling upon the verge of success and defeat." In 1842, Whig majorities in both chambers of Congress were not sufficient to overcome the veto that nominally Whig president John Tyler wielded against any attempt to raise rates without first suspending the apportionment of revenue from public land sales among the states. This issue revealed regional fissures within the party, and though the Tariff of 1842 did eventually pass many Southern and Western Whigs voted against protection once it became clear that distribution would be surrendered. Then in 1846, it was the Democratic administration of James K. Polk that struggled to push its preferred measure through a Democratic Congress. Once again, intraparty rifts were exposed as partisans from Connecticut, New Jersey, New York, and Pennsylvania revolted against Secretary of the Treasury Robert J. Walker's "revenue" bill, which only became law through the dramatic intercession of Tennessee's Whig senator Spencer Jarnagin and Pennsylvanian vice president George M. Dallas. Confronted with the same choice of following public sentiment in his state or loyally serving his party, these two men made contrasting decisions, a fact that underscores the uncertainty that so often characterized antebellum policymaking. And it was these small margins between success and failure that encouraged the continued development of lobbying, as manufacturers freed from adherence to a common agenda made the journey to Washington in ever greater numbers and experimented with new modes of exerting pressure on lawmakers, exemplified by the National Fair that attracted thousands of visitors to the capital.

By the eve of the Civil War, concerns about lobbying and the influence of the "Almighty Dollar" on federal legislation were the subject of widespread debate, while the fate of tariff policy had become entwined with the fate of the nation itself. The Tariff of 1857 was most notable at the time for the split it demarcated in the protectionist ranks between opponents of any further reduction in rates and advocates of "the Greely method" of repealing duties on raw materials to promote manufactures. A bill drafted on the latter model, which also won the support of many free traders, sailed through both chambers, but scandal erupted the following year when a congressional investigation revealed corrupt practices had been employed by certain New England textile manufacturers to procure its passage. Revelations of professional lobbyists-for-hire, the purchase of sympathetic press coverage, and suspicious payments to members of the House illustrated how much lobbying had changed since Briggs set out to represent the Wilmington manufacturers in Washington in 1816. The complexion of the country was also transformed during this period, first by the Panic of 1857, and then by the secession of seven slave states following the election of Abraham Lincoln in 1860. If the former revived public support for explicitly protectionist doctrines not popular since the days of the American System, it was the latter that afforded the opportunity for Lincoln's Republican Party to implement those doctrines in the Tariff of 1861. For Henry Carey, that act represented the completion of a project commenced by his father four decades earlier; its passage, he believed, would ensure the victory of the Union over the Confederacy, freedom over slavery, and protectionism over free trade, at least for the foreseeable future.

And so it proved, as the Civil War permanently reconfigured the political and economic landscape. The secession of the South "has released us from the bondage to cotton, which for generations has hung over us like a spell, destroying all freedom of commercial or political action, and rendering us slaves to the most absurd decisions," rejoiced one free state newspaper eleven months after Lincoln's election.[4] The demands of wartime demonstrated the potential of the industrializing Northern economy; by 1869, the number of factories in the country had doubled from the start of the conflict, and by 1873 the amount of capital invested in manufacturing had quadrupled from its conclusion.[5] Postwar reunion on the terms of the victors did little to disrupt the new status quo. "Temporary war measures," such as revenue-raising duties that exceeded even the most protective levels of the antebellum period, one commentator noted, have "brought into existence business interests largely dependent on the[ir] continuance," repeating a pattern witnessed during the War of 1812.[6] Even the New York Chamber of Commerce, a free trade stronghold for the previous half century, admitted in 1865 that "protection and encouragement which our manufactures needed and sought in vain before the war, the war has necessitated; and, henceforth, a high tariff may be regarded as the accepted policy of our country."[7]

General acceptance of a high tariff did not mean an end to lobbying on the subject, but what was at stake in congressional deliberations over post–Civil War bills was the specific distribution of benefits to constituencies competing for legislative favor, rather than the very principle of protection itself. As Marc-William Palen has recently shown, free traders were able to exert some sway among both Democrats and the Liberal Republican movement of the 1870s, but economic nationalism remained dominant in most Republican circles, and Republicans remained dominant in Washington; it was not until the second presidency of Grover Cleveland that their opponents finally gained control over the White House and both branches of Congress concurrently.[8] Thus it was the Republican Party's commitment to a policy of protectionism, as much as the North's victory over the South in the conflict that followed, that set the parameters for this new era of political economy. As John L. Hayes, prominent lobbyist and secretary of the National Association of Wool Manufacturers, wrote to Henry C. Carey in 1871, alluding to the latter's influence with the committee that wrote the party's 1860 platform, "all the thinkers of the protective school read [your books], and recognize you as their master," but "what single paragraph has done more service in our time than your resolution for protection at the convention, which nominated Lincoln and laid out the protective policy of the last decade?"[9]

Hayes's testament is fitting, for it was the energetic and creative efforts of the protectionist campaigners like Carey and their free trade counterparts that means that any study of the making of antebellum tariff policy must take account not only of congressional debates and roll calls but also what Thomas Cooper branded that "mongrel kind of *lobby* legislation attending at Washington, that operates from without on the members within."[10] Understanding their contribution requires us look beyond the final legislative outcome to the process that produced it and to give due appreciation to the rules that governed that process, the scope for individuals to shape its course, and the significance of timing and contingency. Even before Congress met, national conventions like those of 1819, 1827, and 1831, and other demonstrations of sentiment "out of doors" were orchestrated to push the tariff issue to the top of the political agenda and complement the efforts of lobbyists in the capital. The choice of a sympathetic Speaker of the House at the commencement of the session could also be decisive, and often outweighed partisan or sectional considerations for legislators with a special interest in the subject. Stevenson owed his selection in the Twentieth Congress to promises made to Northern Jacksonians that he would guarantee a protectionist majority to the Committee on Manufactures, and even on the eve of the Civil War a few Pennsylvania Republicans professed their readiness to abandon their party's candidate if a Democrat could be found willing to make the same pledge. It was during this period that skilled politicians first made effective use of the Speaker's appointing power to push through their own program. Clay showed the way by securing a congenial reception for protectionist bills in 1820 and 1824, while Van Buren relied upon Stevenson's aid to realize his "Tariff of Abominations" in 1828.

Second only to the Speaker in importance was the chair of whichever committee, or rival committees, were tasked with drafting tariff legislation. No chair was fully autonomous; Baldwin, Rollin C. Mallary, and Adams all found themselves, at one time or another, the prisoner of a hostile committee. But the discretion that the chair and his trusted colleagues enjoyed in writing bills explains the eagerness of lobbyists to cultivate their friendship, from Briggs and Newton in 1816 to Henry Carey, John Sherman, and Justin S. Morrill in 1861. A strong chair could transcend partisan or sectional constraints and seize the initiative, as Adams did when he circumvented Clay's leadership of the anti-Jacksonian forces in his collaboration with McLane on the Tariff of 1832. And in the absence of such leadership, even legislation that the political math favored might still become bogged down in endless motions to amend and interminable debate, as happened to the Verplanck Bill the following year. Even the timing of a committee's report could prove critical, as it did in 1820 when delay was at least partly to blame for the Baldwin Bill's demise, and again in 1846, when four months elapsed between Ways and Means receiving their instructions from the Treasury and their measure being called up in the House, as Democratic leaders patiently awaited news of Britain's repeal of the Corn Laws.

Once tariff legislation reached the floor, its fate was by no means assured, whatever a simple headcount of partisan affiliations or sectional allegiances might suggest. This may have been a golden age for political oratory, but far more common was the sight of congressmen "speaking for Buncombe" to rows of empty chairs. The real business of coalition-building took place behind the scenes, in private meetings like that between Clay and Calhoun in 1833, or the Whig caucuses that thrashed out a deal on protection and distribution in 1842. Mastery of parliamentary procedures could also prove invaluable, as demonstrated by Mallary when he called James Buchanan's bluff over minimums in the Tariff of 1828 and Sherman when he rescued Morrill's scheme from the mountain of amendments that threatened to suffocate it in 1860. And lobbyists continued to play their part here too; many times, commentators observed that a measure would never have passed were it not for "high pressure of extrinsic, and out of doors influence" maintained on lawmakers right up until the final ballot.[11] Any defection from party or sectional orthodoxy could prove decisive, when the margins between success and failure were so small. In 1820, 1827, 1842, and 1846, the fate of tariff legislation was determined by a single vote, and the eleventh-hour decisions of Jackson in 1824 and Van Buren in 1828 to cast their lot in with the protectionists was also pivotal in the passage of those two bills.

While revenue-raising bills were constitutionally required to originate in the House, the Senate still exercised an important, if often neglected, influence on the making of tariff policy during this period. Three times, in 1820, 1827, and 1860, the latter killed legislation that had already passed the former. The acts of 1833 and 1857 implemented formulas devised by the upper chamber, whatever the formal niceties employed to preserve the prerogative of the lower, and those of 1824 and 1828 were seriously modified there, the first to the benefit of free traders and the second to mollify protectionists. A Committee of Conference between the two chambers was required on five occasions (1824, 1828, 1832, 1857, and 1861) and on two of those (1832 and 1857) led to complaints that vital interests had been sacrificed by a few interested individuals pursuing their own agenda. And the executive branch also routinely claimed a share in the legislative power vested in Congress by the Constitution. The Tariffs of 1816, 1832, and 1846 all took shape in the Treasury Department; Jackson cast a long shadow over the Compromise of 1833, though the details were Clay's; and Tyler's vetoes set the parameters for what was politically possible in 1842. While talk of party systems implies stability, and a focus on sectional divisions suggests consistency, what really characterized policymaking during this period was confusion, conflict, and uncertainty. This was the context in which John Quincy Adams, John C. Calhoun, Henry Clay, Martin Van Buren, and Daniel Webster earned their reputations as statesmen of the highest order, and less famed politicians such as Henry Baldwin, Alexander J. Dallas, Robert M. T. Hunter, William Lowndes, Louis McLane, James I. McKay, Rollin C. Mallary, Justin S. Morrill, John Sherman, John Tod, Robert J. Walker, and Silas Wright made their own significant contributions to the making of antebellum tariff policy.

So too did those other "men of talents," that company who "have hardly ever received the cheapest compliments of recognition," the first American lobbyists. This story could not be told without mention of Nathan Appleton; Jonas B. Brown; Mathew and Henry C. Carey; Thomas Cooper; the Du Pont brothers, E. I. and Victor; Albert Gallatin; John Harrison; James E. Harvey; Charles J. Ingersoll; Abbott Lawrence; Eleazar Lord; Francis Cabot Lowell; Hezekiah Niles; Condy Raguet; William W. Stone; John W. Wolcott; and, of course, Isaac Briggs. When the latter set out for Washington in December 1815, his mission was to "communicate with members [of Congress] on the just & reasonable objects of the manufacturers."[12] Over the following half century, amateur lobbyists like Briggs would provide much-needed expertise to the preparation of tariff legislation and facilitate communication between elected representatives and their constituents. "These people [i.e., congressmen] if left alone are like a mariner without a compass," concluded Lawrence on one of his many visits to the capital. "Practical men are much wanted here."[13] And the potential value of their activities was acknowledged by contemporaries. As the Morrill Bill neared passage in the Senate, one newspaper recommended that in the future, "all large departments of business should take care to be heard, and to supply information to those who frame a Tariff bill; and, on the other hand, a committee framing a bill should solicit information on such points, and make their work complete before it gets out of committee."[14]

By the eve of the Civil War, however, the ever-increasing crowd of lobbyists that descended on Washington for each session of Congress, the signs of professionalization, and the employment of methods of persuasion that smacked of bribery and corruption were also beginning to cause palpable concern. The congressional committee appointed to investigate passage of the Tariff of 1857 concluded that the episode "shows how the legislation of the country may be influenced by large masses of capital, concentrated in the hands of a few persons having a common interest, so as to benefit that interest at the expense of the great mass of the people."[15] This verdict echoes the fears of a "tyranny of the minority" that William C. Bryant expressed to his British correspondent at the commencement of this chapter. It also suggests that five years before Abraham Lincoln famously reminded Americans of their commitment to a government "of the people, by the people, for the people," some of his fellow citizens already harbored reservations about the place of lobbying within their political system that still resonate today.

Key Congressional Roll Calls on Tariff Legislation, 1816–1861

Tariff of 1816
House vote to pass, 8 April 1816.
88 yeas, 54 nays, 37 did not vote, 3 seats vacant.
Annals of Congress, Fourteenth Congress, First Session, 1352.

TABLE A.1

Section	Yea	Nay	Did not vote	Seat vacant	Total
North	63	15	23	2	103
South	25	39	14	1	79
Total	88	54	37	3	

TABLE A.2

Party	Yea	Nay	Did not vote	Total
Federalist	24	22	17	63
Republican	64	32	20	116
Total	88	54	37	

Senate vote to engross with amendments and be read a third time,[1] 19 April 1816.
25 yeas, 7 nays, 4 did not vote, 0 seats vacant.
Annals of Congress, Fourteenth Congress, First Session, 331.

TABLE A.3

Section	Yea	Nay	Did not vote	Seat vacant	Total
North	14	2	2	0	18
South	11	5	2	0	18
Total	25	7	4	0	

TABLE A.4

Party	Yea	Nay	Did not vote	Total
Federalist	8	4	1	13
Republican	17	3	3	23
Total	25	7	4	

Baldwin Bill, 1820

House vote to pass, 29 April 1820.
91 yeas, 78 nays, 15 did not vote, 2 seats vacant.
Annals of Congress, Sixteenth Congress, First Session, 2155–2156.

TABLE A.5

Section	Yea	Nay	Did not vote	Seat vacant	Total
North	80	18	7	0	105
South	11	60	8	2	81
Total	91	78	15	2	

TABLE A.6

Party	Yea	Nay	Did not vote	Total
Federalist	13	10	3	26
Republican	78	68	12	158
Total	91	78	15	

Senate vote to postpone, 4 May 1820.
22 yeas, 21 nays, 1 did not vote, 0 seats vacant.
Annals of Congress, Sixteenth Congress, First Session, 672.

TABLE A.7

Section	Yea	Nay	Did not vote	Seat vacant	Total
North	6	16	0	0	22
South	16	5	1	0	22
Total	22	21	1	0	

Party	Yea	Nay	Did not vote	Total
Federalist	2	8	0	10
Republican	20	13	1	34
Total	22	21	1	

Tariff of 1824

House vote to pass, 16 April 1824.

107 yeas, 102 nays, 3 did not vote, 1 seat vacant.

Annals of Congress, Eighteenth Congress, First Session, 2429–2430.

TABLE A.9

Section	Yea	Nay	Did not vote	Seat vacant	Total
North	88	32	2	1	123
South	19	70	1	0	90
Total	107	102	3	1	

TABLE A.10

Party	Yea	Nay	Did not vote	Total
Adams-Clay	52	32	1	85
Crawford	10	45	0	55
Jackson	41	25	2	68
Unidentified	4	0	0	4
Total	107	102	3	

Senate vote to pass, 13 May 1824.

25 yeas, 21 nays, 1 did not vote, 1 seat vacant.

Annals of Congress, Eighteenth Congress, First Session, 743–744.

TABLE A.11

Section	Yea	Nay	Did not vote	Seat vacant	Total
North	19	4	0	1	24
South	6	17	1	0	24
Total	25	21	1	1	

Party	Yea	Nay	Did not vote	Total
Adams-Clay	8	8	0	16
Crawford	11	8	1	20
Jackson	6	5	0	11
Total	25	21	1	

Woollens Bill, 1827
House vote to pass, 10 February 1827.
106 yeas, 95 nays, 12 did not vote, 0 seats vacant.
Register of Debates, Nineteenth Congress, Second Session, 1099.

TABLE A.13

Section	Yea	Nay	Did not vote	Seat vacant	Total
North	98	21	4	0	123
South	8	74	8	0	90
Total	106	95	12	0	

TABLE A.14

Party	Yea	Nay	Did not vote	Total
Adams	83	18	9	110
Jackson	23	77	3	103
Total	106	65	12	

Senate vote to postpone, 28 February 1827.
20 yeas, 20 nays, 8 did not vote, 0 seats vacant—vice president broke tie by voting yea.
Register of Debates, Nineteenth Congress, Second Session, 496.

TABLE A.15

Section	Yea	Nay	Did not vote	Seat vacant	Total
North	1	19	4	0	24
South	19	1	4	0	24
Total	20	20	8	0	

Party	Yea	Nay	Did not vote	Total
Adams	3	15	4	22
Jackson	17	5	4	26
Total	20	20	8	

Tariff of 1828

House vote to pass, 22 April 1828.
105 yeas, 94 nays, 13 did not vote, 1 seat vacant.
Register of Debates, Twentieth Congress, First Session, 2471–2472.

TABLE A.17

Section	Yea	Nay	Did not vote	Seat vacant	Total
North	88	29	5	1	123
South	17	65	8	0	90
Total	105	94	13	1	

TABLE A.18

Party	Yea	Nay	Did not vote	Total
Adams	62	34	4	100
Jackson	43	60	9	112
Total	105	94	13	

Senate vote to pass, 13 May 1828.
26 yeas, 21 nays, 1 did not vote, 0 seats vacant.
Register of Debates, Twentieth Congress, First Session, 786.

TABLE A.19

Section	Yea	Nay	Did not vote	Seat vacant	Total
North	18	5	1	0	24
South	8	16	0	0	24
Total	26	21	1	0	

Party	Yea	Nay	Did not vote	Total
Adams	16	4	1	21
Jackson	10	17	0	27
Total	26	21	1	

Tariff of 1832

House vote to pass, 28 June 1832.
132 yeas, 65 nays, 13 did not vote, 3 seats vacant.
Register of Debates, Twenty-Second Congress, First Session, 3830.

TABLE A.21

Section	Yea	Nay	Did not vote	Seat vacant	Total
North	78	34	10	1	123
South	54	31	3	2	90
Total	132	65	13	3	

TABLE A.22

Party	Yea	Nay	Did not vote	Total
Anti-Jackson	37	24	4	65
Anti-Mason	8	7	2	17
Jackson	87	30	7	124
Nullifier	0	4	0	4
Total	132	65	13	

Senate vote to pass, 9 July 1832.
32 yeas, 16 nays, 0 did not vote, 0 seats vacant.
Register of Debates, Twenty-Second Congress, First Session, 1219.

TABLE A.23

Section	Yea	Nay	Did not vote	Seat vacant	Total
North	23	1	0	0	24
South	9	15	0	0	24
Total	32	16	0	0	

Party	Yea	Nay	Did not vote	Total
Anti-Jackson	21	1	0	22
Jackson	11	13	0	24
Nullifier	0	2	0	2
Total	32	16	0	

Tariff of 1833

House vote to pass, 26 February 1833.
119 yeas, 85 nays, 8 did not vote, 1 seat vacant.
Register of Debates, Twenty-Second Congress, Second Session, 1810–1811.

TABLE A.25

Section	Yea	Nay	Did not vote	Seat vacant	Total
North	35	81	6	1	123
South	84	4	2	0	90
Total	119	85	8	1	

TABLE A.26

Party	Yea	Nay	Did not vote	Total
Anti-Jackson	20	43	1	64
Anti-Mason	0	15	2	17
Jackson	95	27	5	127
Nullifier	4	0	0	4
Total	119	85	8	

Senate vote to pass, 1 March 1833.
29 yeas, 16 nays, 3 did not vote, 0 seats vacant.
Register of Debates, Twenty-Second Congress, Second Session, 808–809.

TABLE A.27

Section	Yea	Nay	Did not vote	Seat vacant	Total
North	10	13	1	0	24
South	19	3	2	0	24
Total	29	16	3	0	

Party	Yea	Nay	Did not vote	Total
Anti-Jackson	14	8	0	22
Jackson	13	8	3	24
Nullifier	2	0	0	2
Total	29	16	3	

Tariff of 1842
House vote to pass, 22 August 1842.
104 yeas, 103 nays, 34 did not vote, 1 seat vacant.
House Journal, Twenty-Seventh Congress, Second Session, 1385–1387.[2]

TABLE A.29

Section	Yea	Nay	Did not vote	Seat vacant	Total
North	89	28	24	1	142
South	15	75	10	0	100
Total	104	103	34	1	

TABLE A.30

Party	Yea	Nay	Did not vote	Total
Democrat	20	65	17	102
Whig	84	37	17	138
Unidentified	0	1	0	0
Total	104	103	34	

Senate vote to engross with amendments and be read a third time,[3] 27 August 1842.
24 yeas, 23 nays, 4 did not vote, 1 seat vacant.
Congressional Globe, Twenty-Seventh Congress, Second Session, 960.

TABLE A.31

Section	Yea	Nay	Did not vote	Seat vacant	Total
North	19	5	2	0	26
South	5	18	2	1	26
Total	24	23	4	1	

Party	Yea	Nay	Did not vote	Total
Democrat	4	14	3	21
Whig	20	9	1	30
Total	24	23	4	

Tariff of 1846

House vote to pass, 3 July 1846.
114 yeas, 95 nays, 15 did not vote, 2 seats vacant.
Congressional Globe, Twenty-Ninth Congress, First Session, 1053.

TABLE A.33

Section	Yea	Nay	Did not vote	Seat vacant	Total
North	51	73	9	2	135
South	63	22	6	0	91
Total	114	95	15	2	

TABLE A.34

Party	Yea	Nay	Did not vote	Total
American	0	6	0	6
Democrat	113	18	11	142
Whig	1	71	4	76
Total	114	95	15	

Senate vote to pass, 28 July 1846.
28 yeas, 27 nays, 0 did not vote, 1 seat vacant.
Congressional Globe, Twenty-Ninth Congress, First Session, 1158.

TABLE A.35

Section	Yea	Nay	Did not vote	Seat vacant	Total
North	10	16	0	0	26
South	18	11	0	1	30
Total	28	27	0	1	

TABLE A.36

Party	Yea	Nay	Did not vote	Total
Democrat	27	3	0	30
Liberty	0	1	0	1
Whig	1	23	0	24
Total	28	27	0	

Tariff of 1857

House vote to accept the report of the Committee of Conference,[4] 2 March 1857.

123 yeas, 72 nays, 38 did not vote, 1 seat vacant.

Congressional Globe, Thirty-Fourth Congress, Third Session, 971.

TABLE A.37

Section	Yea	Nay	Did not vote	Seat vacant	Total
North	60	65	19	0	144
South	63	7	19	1	90
Total	123	72	38	1	

TABLE A.38

Party	Yea	Nay	Did not vote	Total
Democrat	68	2	12	82
Anti-admn.	55	70	26	151
Total	123	72	38	

Senate vote to accept the report of the Committee of Conference, 2 March 1857.

33 yeas, 8 nays, 21 did not vote, 0 seats vacant.

Congressional Globe, Thirty-Fourth Congress, Third Session, 1062.

TABLE A.39

Section	Yea	Nay	Did not vote	Seat vacant	Total
North	14	7	11	0	32
South	19	1	10	0	30
Total	33	8	21	0	

Party	Yea	Nay	Did not vote	Total
Democrat	25	4	10	39
Anti-admn.	8	4	11	23
Total	33	8	21	

Tariff of 1861
House vote to pass, 10 May 1860.
105 yeas, 64 nays, 67 did not vote, 1 seat vacant.
Congressional Globe, Thirty-Fourth Congress, First Session, 2056.

TABLE A.41

Section	Yea	Nay	Did not vote	Seat vacant	Total
North	97	15	35	0	147
South	8	49	32	1	90
Total	105	64	67	1	

TABLE A.42

Party	Yea	Nay	Did not vote	Total
Democrat	8	57	34	99
Republican	90	3	20	113
Other anti-admn.	7	4	13	24
Total	105	64	67	

Senate vote to postpone, 15 June 1860.
25 yeas, 23 nays, 17 did not vote, 1 seat vacant.
Congressional Globe, Thirty-Fourth Congress, First Session, 3027.

TABLE A.43

Section	Yea	Nay	Did not vote	Seat vacant	Total
North	4	23	8	1	36
South	21	0	9	0	30
Total	25	23	17	1	

Party	Yea	Nay	Did not vote	Total
Democrat	25	2	11	38
Republican	0	21	4	25
Other anti-admn.	0	0	2	2
Total	25	23	17	

Senate vote to pass, 20 February 1861.
25 yeas, 14 nays, 13 did not vote, 16 seats vacant.
Congressional Globe, Thirty-Fourth Congress, Second Session, 1065.

TABLE A.45

Section	Yea	Nay	Did not vote	Seat vacant	Total
North	25	4	7	2	38
South	0	10	6	14	30
Total	25	14	13	16	

TABLE A.46

Party	Yea	Nay	Did not vote	Total
Democrat	1	14	9	24
Republican	24	0	2	26
Other anti-admn.	0	0	2	2
Total	25	14	13	

NOTES

Introduction

1. "The Tariff Convention" (from the New York *Standard*), *Banner of the Constitution* (Philadelphia), 9 November 1831. See also entry for 31 October 1831 in *Memoirs of John Quincy Adams, Comprising Portions of His Diary from 1795 to 1848*, ed. Charles Francis Adams, 12 vols. (Philadelphia, 1874–1877), 8:416–417.

2. "Republican Party Platform of 1860," 17 May 1860, *The American Presidency Project*, http://www.presidency.ucsb.edu/ws/index.php?pid=29620. For Greeley in 1831, see *The Autobiography of Horace Greeley, or Recollections of a Busy Life* (New York, 1872), 86; and in 1860, see *Memoirs of Gustave Koerner, 1809–1896*, ed. Thomas J. McCormack, 2 vols. (Cedar Rapids, IA: Torch Press, 1909), 2:87.

3. Max M. Edling, *A Hercules in the Cradle: War, Money, and the American State, 1783–1867* (Chicago: University of Chicago Press, 2014); Robin L. Einhorn, *American Taxation, American Slavery* (Chicago: University of Chicago Press, 2006).

4. Paul A. Gilje, "Review of *The Triumph of the Antebellum Free Trade Movement*. By William S. Belko," *Journal of the Early Republic* 33 (Fall 2013): 597. For similar claims, see James L. Huston, "Economic Landscapes Yet to be Discovered: The Early American Republic and Historians' Unsubtle Adoption of Political Economy," *Journal of the Early Republic* 24 (Summer 2004): 225–226; Marc-William Palen, *The "Conspiracy" of Free Trade: The Anglo-American Struggle over Empire and Economic Globalisation, 1846–1896* (Cambridge: Cambridge University Press, 2016), xxvi; Gautham Rao, *National Duties: Custom Houses and the Making of the American State* (Chicago: University of Chicago Press, 2016), 171; and Brian Schoen, *The Fragile Fabric of Union: Cotton, Federal Politics, and the Global Origins of the Civil War* (Baltimore: Johns Hopkins University Press, 2009), 8–9.

5. "The Tariff," *Illinois Gazette* (Shawneetown), 10 January 1824.

6. Stephen Mihm, in Sven Beckert et al., "Interchange: The History of Capitalism," *Journal of American History* 101 (September 2014): 525.

7. Edward Stanwood, *American Tariff Controversies in the Nineteenth Century*, 2 vols. (Boston, 1903); F. W. Taussig, *The Tariff History of the United States* (New York, 1888). Stanwood favored protection; Taussig favored free trade.

8. See Norris Watson Preyer, "Southern Support of the Tariff of 1816—A Reappraisal," *Journal of Southern History* 25 (August 1959): 306–322; Robert V. Remini, "Martin Van Buren and the Tariff of Abominations," *American Historical Review* 63 (July 1958): 903–917; John D. Macoll, "Representative John Quincy Adams's Compromise Tariff of 1832," *Capitol Studies* 1 (Fall 1972): 41–58; Merrill D. Peterson, *Olive Branch and Sword: The Compromise of 1833* (Baton Rouge: Louisiana State University Press, 1982); Phillip W. Magness, "Morrill and the Missing Industries: Strategic Lobbying Behavior and the Tariff, 1858–1861," *Journal of the Early Republic* 29 (Summer 2009): 287–329; Jonathan J. Pincus, *Pressure Groups and Politics in Antebellum Tariffs* (New York: Columbia University Press, 1977). The latter, despite its title, is largely confined to the Tariff of 1824. Judith Goldstein, *Ideas, Interests, and American Trade Policy* (Ithaca, NY: Cornell University Press, 1993), and Sidney Ratner, *The Tariff in American History* (New York: D. Van Nostrand, 1972), do adopt a broader approach, but each dispenses with the entire antebellum period in a single chapter.

Two unpublished dissertations offer only a partial corrective. William K. Bolt, "The Tariff in the Age of Jackson" (PhD diss., University of Tennessee, 2010), updates the conventional Stanwood/Taussig narrative but as the title suggests remains preoccupied with leading politicians. A revised version of this dissertation has recently been published as *Tariff Wars and the Politics of Jacksonian America* (Nashville, TN: Vanderbilt University Press, 2017). John Austin Moore, "Interests and Ideas: Industrialization and the Making of Early American Trade Policy, 1789–1860" (PhD diss., Wayne State University, 2013), demonstrates a correlation between economic developments outside of the capital and policymaking within but does not explore how the former translated into the latter.

9. John M. Belohlavek, "Economic Interest Groups and the Formation of Foreign Policy in the Early Republic," *Journal of the Early Republic* 14 (Winter 1994): 482.

10. The literature on American party politics from the 1820s to the 1850s is vast, but notable examples include Arthur M. Schlesinger Jr., *The Age of Jackson* (Boston: Little, Brown, 1945); Michael F. Holt, *The Political Crisis of the 1850s* (New York: John Wiley, 1978); Richard L. McCormick, "The Party Period and Public Policy: An Exploratory Hypothesis," *Journal of American History* 66 (September 1979): 279–298; Charles Sellers, *The Market Revolution: Jacksonian America, 1815–1846* (Oxford: Oxford University Press, 1991); Joel H. Silbey, *The American Political Nation, 1838–1893* (Stanford, CA: Stanford University Press, 1991); and Sam W. Haynes, *Unfinished Revolution: The Early American Republic in a British World* (Charlottesville: University of Virginia Press, 2010).

11. Again, the literature is vast, but recent works from this vantage point include William W. Freehling, *The Road to Disunion*, 2 vols. (Oxford: Oxford University Press, 1990–2007); Nicholas Onuf and Peter S. Onuf, *Nations, Markets, and War: Modern History and the American Civil War* (Charlottesville: University of Virginia Press, 2006); Elizabeth R. Varon, *Disunion! The Coming of the*

American Civil War, 1789–1859 (Chapel Hill: University of North Carolina Press, 2008); Schoen, *The Fragile Fabric of Union*; and Marc Egnal, *Clash of Extremes: The Economic Origins of the Civil War* (New York: Hill and Wang, 2010).

12. For that reason, this book defines the "South" as those states in which slavery was not abolished prior to the Civil War. By this definition, Delaware and Maryland, states whose economies had more in common with Pennsylvania than South Carolina, are nonetheless considered to be "Southern" states. To do otherwise would be to present an illusion that the slave South was more united on the tariff than the free North. In reality, the fact that Delaware and Maryland, along with Kentucky, Missouri, Tennessee, and even parts of Louisiana and Virginia, could be "unsound" on the tariff was precisely what worried proslavery politicians such as John Randolph and John C. Calhoun, who feared they might also be proven "unsound" on slavery in the future.

13. Entry for 29 August 1842, in Adams, *Memoirs*, 11:244–245.

14. Michael F. Holt, *The Rise and Fall of the American Whig Party: Jacksonian Politics and the Onset of the Civil War* (Oxford: Oxford University Press, 1999).

15. Rachel A. Shelden, *Washington Brotherhood: Politics, Social Life, and the Coming of the Civil War* (Chapel Hill: University of North Carolina Press, 2013).

16. Corey M. Brooks, *Antislavery Third Parties and the Transformation of American Politics* (Chicago: University of Chicago Press, 2016).

17. On the discrepancy between what the majority of delegates at the Philadelphia Convention of 1787 intended, as expressed in James Madison's claim in *Federalist* No. 63 that the new Constitution would provide for "*the total exclusion of the people in their collective capacity* from any share" (emphasis original) in governance, and what was imposed upon them subsequently by demands for a more expansive definition of popular sovereignty, as reflected in the Bill of Rights, see Christian G. Fritz, *American Sovereigns: The People and America's Constitutional Tradition before the Civil War* (Cambridge: Cambridge University Press, 2008), and Suzette Hemberger, "A Government Based on Representations," *Studies in American Political Development*, 10 (Fall 1996): 289–332. [James Madison], "The Federalist, 63," in Alexander Hamilton, John Jay, and James Madison, *The Federalist Papers*, ed. Lawrence Goldman (Oxford: Oxford University Press, 2008), 313.

18. [Gulian C. Verplanck], *The State Triumvirate, A Political Tale* (New York, 1819), 67.

19. "To C. C. Cambreleng, Esq.," *Aurora General Advertiser* (Philadelphia), 23 April 1824.

20. Robert Y. Hayne, *Register of Debates*, Twenty-Second Congress, First Session, 1178.

21. "The Prevalence of Corruption," *The Pennsylvanian* (Philadelphia), 6 February 1857.

22. There are exceptions, of course, but even those modern treatments of lobbying that begin with James Madison's *Federalist* No. 10 generally devote scant

attention to the decades that followed, picking up the story only with the post–Civil War period. See, for example, the contributors to *Dirty Deals? An Encyclopedia of Lobbying, Political Influence, and Corruption*, ed. Amy Handlin, 3 vols. (Santa Barbara, California: ABC-CLIO, 2014). Likewise, the opening chapter of William V. Luneberg, Thomas M. Susman, and Rebecca H. Gordon, *The Lobbying Manual: A Complete Guide to Federal Lobbying Law and Practice* (Chicago: ABA Publishing, 2009, 4th edition), which provides a history of federal lobbying regulation up to the mid-twentieth century, contains only a single paragraph on the period prior to the Civil War.

23. Works that highlight lobbying in the latter half of the nineteenth century include Elisabeth S. Clemens, *The People's Lobby: Organizational Innovation and the Rise of Interest Group Politics in the United States, 1890–1925* (Chicago: University of Chicago Press, 1997); Theda Skocpol, *Protecting Soldiers and Mothers: The Political Origins of Social Policy in the United States* (Cambridge, MA: Belknap Press, 1992); Margaret Susan Thompson, *The "Spider Web": Congress and Lobbying in the Age of Grant* (Ithaca, NY: Cornell University Press, 1985); and Daniel Verdier, *Democracy and International Trade: Britain, France, and the United States, 1860–1990* (Princeton, NJ: Princeton University Press, 1994).

24. Mark Summers, *The Plundering Generation: Corruption and the Crisis of the Union, 1849–1861* (Oxford: Oxford University Press, 1987) provides some useful detail on lobbying during the 1850s. For earlier isolated examples, see Corey M. Brooks, "Stoking the 'Abolition Fire in the Capitol': Liberty Party Lobbying and Antislavery in Congress," *Journal of the Early Republic* 33 (Fall 2013): 523–547; Stephen W. Campbell, "Funding the Bank War: Nicholas Biddle and the Public Relations Campaign to Recharter the Second Bank of the US, 1828–1832," *American Nineteenth Century History* 17 (September 2016): 273–299; and Jeffrey L. Pasley, "Private Access and Public Power: Gentility and Lobbying in the Early Congress," in *The House and Senate in the 1790s: Petitioning, Lobbying, and Institutional Development*, ed. Kenneth R. Bowling and Donald R. Kennon (Athens: Ohio University Press, 2002). For a rare biography of an antebellum lobbyist, see Henry Cohen, *Business and Politics in America from the Age of Jackson to the Civil War: The Career Biography of W. W. Corcoran* (Westport, CT: Greenwood Publishing, 1971). Grant D. Forsyth, "Special Interest Protectionism and the Antebellum Woolen Textile Industry: A Contemporary Issue in a Historical Context," *American Journal of Economics and Sociology* 65 (November 2006): 1025–1058; Magness, "Morrill and the Missing Industries"; and Carl E. Prince and Seth Taylor, "Daniel Webster, the Boston Associates, and the US Government's Role in the Industrializing Process, 1815–1830," *Journal of the Early Republic* 2 (Autumn 1982): 283–299 are also relevant here.

At the state level, see Douglas E. Bowers, "From Logrolling to Corruption: The Development of Lobbying in Pennsylvania, 1815–1861," *Journal of the Early Republic* 3 (Winter 1983): 439–474, and Rodney O. Davis, "Lobbying and the

Third House in the Early Illinois General Assembly," *Old Northwest* 14 (1988): 267–284.

More attention has been paid to lobbying for and against the Corn Laws in Britain during the same period, which provides a useful comparison. See Norman McCord, *The Anti-Corn Law League, 1838–1846* (London: Unwin University Press, 2nd edition, 1975); Cheryl Schonhardt-Bailey, *From the Corn Laws to Free Trade: Interests, Ideas, and Institutions in Historical Perspective* (Cambridge, MA: MIT Press, 2006); and, for a later period, Frank Trentmann, *Free Trade Nation: Commerce, Consumption, and Civil Society in Modern Britain* (Oxford: Oxford University Press, 2008).

25. David P. Currie, *The Constitution in Congress: Democrats and Whigs, 1829–1861* (Chicago: University of Chicago Press, 2005), 220–221.

26. This consideration placed a constraint on the protectionists too, for exorbitant duties would be prohibitive to commerce and therefore fail to generate sufficient revenue.

27. Robert V. Remini, *The House: The History of the House of Representatives* (New York: HarperCollins, 2007), 241. For a contrasting viewpoint, see Neil MacNeil and Richard A. Baker, *The American Senate: An Insider's History* (Oxford: Oxford University Press, 2015 pbk edition), 283: "Debates, of course, did not pass legislation. Far more than eloquent speeches was needed to persuade senators how to vote on any pending question. More vital than oratory was the backroom vote-hustling and bargaining that had marked, from its origins, the Senate's decision-making."

28. "Sayings and Doings at Washington. Number C[X]LIV," signed "Oliver Oldschool" and dated 22 June, *United States Gazette* (Philadelphia), 24 June 1842.

29. "Sayings . . . CXLII," dated 20 June, *United States Gazette*, 22 June 1842.

30. "Congressional Business," *Niles' Weekly Register* (Baltimore), 20 March 1824. This important point is also made by Shelden, *Washington Brotherhood*, 39.

31. Recent examinations of the role of ideas in the struggle over the tariff include William S. Belko, "'A Tax on the Many, to Enrich a Few': Jacksonian Democracy vs. the Protective Tariff," *Journal of the History of Economic Thought* 37 (June 2015): 277–289; Peter S. Onuf, "The Political Economy of Sectionalism: Tariff Controversies and Conflicting Conceptions of World Order," in *Congress and the Emergence of Sectionalism: From the Missouri Compromise to the Age of Jackson*, ed. Paul Finkelman and Donald R. Kennon (Athens: Ohio University Press, 2008); and Palen, *The "Conspiracy" of Free Trade*. The latter two are particularly valuable for situating those ideas in a transatlantic context.

32. Paul K. Conkin, *Prophets of Prosperity: America's First Political Economists* (Bloomington: Indiana University Press, 1980), 312–313. Similarly, James L. Huston's survey of the tariff debates of the 1820s leads him to conclude that historians "should be cautious when using political rhetoric as a basis for explaining the motivations and behaviors of individuals." James L. Huston, "Virtue Be-

sieged: Virtue, Equality, and the General Welfare in the Tariff Debates of the 1820s," *Journal of the Early Republic* 14 (Winter 1994): 544.

33. Lawrence A. Peskin, *Manufacturing Revolution: The Intellectual Origins of Early American Industry* (Baltimore: Johns Hopkins University Press, 2003).

34. See, for example, Palen, *The "Conspiracy" of Free Trade*.

35. Jeffrey Sklansky, "The Elusive Sovereign: New Intellectual and Social Histories of Capitalism," *Modern Intellectual History* 9 (April 2012): 246. Major works in this field, in addition to Palen's book cited previously, include Edward E. Baptist, *The Half Has Never Been Told: Slavery and the Making of American Capitalism* (New York: Basic Books, 2014); Sven Beckert, *Empire of Cotton: A Global History* (New York: Knopf, 2014); Joanna Cohen, *Luxurious Citizens: The Politics of Consumption in Nineteenth-Century America* (Philadelphia: University of Pennsylvania Press, 2017); and Walter Johnson, *River of Dark Dreams: Slavery and Empire in the Cotton Kingdom* (Cambridge, MA: Belknap Press, 2013). See also Rosanne Currarino, "Toward a History of Cultural Economy," *Journal of the Civil War Era* 2 (December 2012): 564–585, and Seth Rockman, "Review Essay: What Makes the History of Capitalism Newsworthy?" *Journal of the Early Republic* 34 (Fall 2014): 439–466.

36. Elizabeth Tandy Shermer, in Beckert et al., "Interchange," 535. On the same theme, see Stephen Meardon et al., Symposium on "American Political Economy from the Age of Jackson to the Civil War," *Journal of the History of Economic Thought* 37 (June 2015): 161–320, and particularly Steven G. Medema's contribution.

Chapter One: "Men of Talents": The Tariff of 1816

1. "The Manufacturing Interest," *Niles' Weekly Register* (Baltimore), 27 January 1816.

2. Minutes of Wilmington manufacturers meeting, 9 December 1815, Folder 4, Bringhurst Family Papers, Delaware Historical Society, Wilmington.

3. Isaac Briggs to Hannah Briggs, Washington, 7 January 1816, Folder "1816," Box 1, Briggs-Stabler Papers, Maryland Historical Society, Baltimore.

4. "The Manufacturing Interest," *Niles' Weekly Register*, 27 January 1816.

5. Henry Brougham, quoted in "British Distresses," *Niles' Weekly Register*, 28 December 1816.

6. "The Manufacturing Interest," *Niles' Weekly Register*, 27 January 1816. Lawrence A. Peskin, *Manufacturing Revolution: The Intellectual Origins of Early American Industry* (Baltimore: Johns Hopkins University Press, 2003) charts efforts to promote American manufacturing up to the War of 1812. On the postwar situation, see also Sam W. Haynes, *Unfinished Revolution: The Early American Republic in a British World* (Charlottesville: University of Virginia Press, 2010), 133–136.

7. Peskin, *Manufacturing Revolution*, 139–161. For an example of this redefinition in government censuses, see Michael Zakim, "Inventing Industrial Statis-

tics," *Theoretical Inquiries in Law* 11 (January 2010): 283–318. And for a useful overview of the development of the manufacturing class, see Sven Beckert, "Merchants and Manufacturers in the Antebellum North," in *Ruling America: A History of Wealth and Power in a Democracy*, ed. Steve Fraser and Gary Gerstle (Cambridge, MA: Harvard University Press, 2005).

8. Nathan Appleton, *Introduction of the Power Loom, and Origin of Lowell* (Lowell, MA, 1858).

9. "Summary Observations on the Advantages of Giving Encouragement to American Manufactures," signed "D. P. d. N." [Du Pont de Nemours], *Aurora General Advertiser* (Philadelphia), 3 April 1816.

10. "Tariff of 1789," in *Encyclopedia of Tariffs and Trade in US History*, ed. Cynthia Clark Northrup and Elaine C. Prange Turney, 3 vols. (Westport, CT: Greenwood Press, 2003), 1:1.

11. Peskin, *Manufacturing Revolution*, 89–92; Edward Stanwood, *American Tariff Controversies in the Nineteenth Century*, 2 vols. (Boston, 1903), 1:39–128.

12. James Ronaldson to Alexander James Dallas, Philadelphia, 19 December 1815, Folder 17, Box 1, George Mifflin Dallas Papers, Historical Society of Pennsylvania, Philadelphia.

13. Thomas Leiper to John Sergeant, Philadelphia, 2 January 1816, Folder 8, Box 1, John Sergeant Papers, HSP.

14. Henry Clay, *Annals of Congress*, Sixteenth Congress, First Session, 2036.

15. Thomas Jefferson to Benjamin Austin, Monticello, 9 January 1816, printed in "American Manufactures," *Niles' Weekly Register*, 24 February 1816. The formatting here is that of the *Register*. For an analysis of Jefferson's evolving position on manufactures, see Drew R. McCoy, *The Elusive Republic: Political Economy in Jeffersonian America* (New York: W. W. Norton, 1982; pbk edition), and Nicholas Onuf and Peter S. Onuf, *Nations, Markets, and War: Modern History and the American Civil War* (Charlottesville: University of Virginia Press, 2006), 240–246.

16. Max M. Edling, *A Hercules in the Cradle: War, Money, and the American State, 1783–1867* (Chicago: University of Chicago Press, 2014), 142.

17. *Annals of Congress*, Thirteenth Congress, Third Session, 1186.

18. David P. Currie, *The Constitution in Congress: The Federalist Period, 1789–1801* (Chicago: University of Chicago Press, 1997), 41–42; George B. Galloway, *History of the House of Representatives*, 2nd ed., revised by Sidney Wise (New York: Thomas Y. Crowell, 1976), 17–18.

19. On Dallas's role in the Tariff of 1816, see Raymond Walters Jr., *Alexander James Dallas: Lawyer—Politician—Financier, 1759–1817* (Philadelphia: University of Pennsylvania Press, 1943), 206–209.

20. William Montgomery to John Sergeant, Philadelphia, 12 December 1815, Folder 5, Box 1, Sergeant Papers.

21. "Tariff of Duties on Imports," *Annals of Congress*, Fourteenth Congress, First Session, appendix, 1683. On the lack of reliable information available to

policymakers in the early republic, see Martin Ohman, "The Statistical Turn in Early American Political Economy: Mathew Carey and the Authority of Numbers," *Early American Studies* 11 (Fall 2013): 486–515.

22. "Tariff of Duties on Imports," *Annals of Congress*, Fourteenth Congress, First Session, appendix, 1683.

23. "Tariff of Duties on Imports," *Annals of Congress*, Fourteenth Congress, First Session, appendix, 1685.

24. "Tariff of Duties on Imports," *Annals of Congress*, Fourteenth Congress, First Session, appendix, 1690–1693.

25. "Tariff of Duties on Imports," *Annals of Congress*, Fourteenth Congress, First Session, appendix, 1682. For a review of arguments over the constitutionality of protection in the First Congress, see Currie, *The Constitution in Congress: The Federalist Period, 1789–1801*, 53–60.

26. "Tariff of Duties on Imports," *Annals of Congress*, Fourteenth Congress, First Session, appendix, 1685.

27. "Tariff of Duties on Imports," *Annals of Congress*, Fourteenth Congress, First Session, appendix, 1686.

28. James Madison, "Seventh Annual Message," 5 December 1815, *The American Presidency Project*, http://www.presidency.ucsb.edu/ws/?pid=29457. A friend later claimed that Dallas told him the president personally suggested additional duties on several articles coming into collision with domestic manufactures. Thomas R. Gold to Mathew Carey, Whitestown, NY, 3 May 1820, Folder 3, Box 23, Edward Carey Gardiner Collection, HSP.

29. Untitled editorial, *Aurora General Advertiser*, 15 February 1816; emphasis original.

30. *Annals of Congress*, Fourteenth Congress, First Session, 960.

31. "The Tariff!" *Aurora General Advertiser*, 26 February 1816.

32. *Annals of Congress*, Fourteenth Congress, First Session, 960.

33. Galloway, *History of the House of Representatives*, 70–108; Gerald Gamm and Kenneth Shepsle, "Emergence of Legislative Institutions: Standing Committees in the House and Senate, 1810–1825," *Legislative Studies Quarterly* 14 (February 1989): 39–66; Donald R. Kennon and Rebecca M. Rogers, *The Committee on Ways and Means: A Bicentennial History, 1789–1989* (Washington, DC: US Government Printing Office, 1989).

34. Carl J. Vipperman, *William Lowndes and the Transition of Southern Politics, 1782–1822* (Chapel Hill: University of North Carolina Press, 1989), 123 (quotation) and, for Lowndes's role in the Tariff of 1816, 124–143. Also on Ways and Means were: William A. Burwell (VA, Republican), William Gaston (NC, Federalist), Samuel D. Ingham (PA, Republican), Jonathan Moseley (CT, Federalist), Thomas B. Robertson (LA, Republican), and John W. Taylor (NY, Republican). Lowndes was a Republican.

35. "National Finance—No. VIII," *Aurora General Advertiser*, 28 December 1815.

36. [James Madison], "The Federalist, 63," in Alexander Hamilton, John Jay, and James Madison, *The Federalist Papers*, ed. Lawrence Goldman (Oxford: Oxford University Press, 2008), 313; Rosemarie Zagarri, "The Family Factor: Congressmen, Turnover, and the Burden of Public Service in the Early American Republic," *Journal of the Early Republic* 33 (Summer 2013): 283–316.

37. For more on the variety of ways in which Americans communicated with their elected representatives during this period, see Daniel Peart, *Era of Experimentation: American Political Practices in the Early Republic* (Charlottesville: University of Virginia Press, 2014).

38. *Annals of Congress*, Fourteenth Congress, First Session, 1651–1656, 1656–1658.

39. Quoted in Robert V. Remini, *The House: The History of the House of Representatives* (New York: HarperCollins, 2007), 20.

40. Richard R. John and Christopher J. Young, "Rites of Passage: Postal Petitioning as a Tool of Governance in the Age of Federalism," in *The House and Senate in the 1790s: Petitioning, Lobbying, and Institutional Development*, ed. Kenneth R. Bowling and Donald R. Kennon (Athens: Ohio University Press, 2002), 136.

41. Richard S. Newman, *The Transformation of American Abolitionism: Fighting Slavery in the Early Republic* (Chapel Hill: University of North Carolina Press, 2002), 39–59.

42. John Sergeant to Robert Waln, Washington, 26 December 1815, Folder 4, Box 1, Sergeant Papers.

43. On Niles's career as a protectionist, see Norval Neil Luxon, *Niles' Weekly Register: News Magazine of the Nineteenth Century* (Baton Rouge: Louisiana State University Press, 1947), and Richard Gabriel Stone, *Hezekiah Niles as an Economist* (Baltimore: Johns Hopkins University Press, 1933).

44. Peskin, *Manufacturing Revolution*, 210.

45. Jonathan J. Pincus claims that "since 1789, manufacturers had journeyed to the capital to lobby Congress," but the earliest example he provides is from 1816. Jonathan J. Pincus, *Pressure Groups and Politics in Antebellum Tariffs* (New York: Columbia University Press, 1977), 51. Edward Stanwood agrees that 1816 "seems to have been the first instance of interested parties going in person to Washington to promote the passage of particular tariff schedules." Stanwood, *American Tariff Controversies in the Nineteenth Century*, 1:146. For earlier lobbying on other subjects, see Jeffrey L. Pasley, "Private Access and Public Power: Gentility and Lobbying in the Early Congress," in *The House and Senate in the 1790s: Petitioning, Lobbying, and Institutional Development*, ed. Kenneth R. Bowling and Donald R. Kennon (Athens: Ohio University Press, 2002), and Newman, *The Transformation of American Abolitionism*, 39–59.

46. "Isaac Briggs (1763–1825)," *Archives of Maryland (Biographical Series)*, http://msa.maryland.gov/megafile/msa/speccol/sc3500/sc3520/015800/015898 /html/15898bio.html (accessed 7 October 2015).

47. Minutes of Wilmington manufacturers meeting, 25 November 1815, Folder 4, Bringhurst Family Papers.

48. Minutes of Wilmington manufacturers meeting, 9 December 1815, Folder 4, Bringhurst Family Papers.

49. Minutes of Wilmington manufacturers meeting, 10 January 1816, Folder 4, Bringhurst Family Papers.

50. Minutes of Wilmington manufacturers meeting, 8 May 1816, and subscription list, 8 May 1816, both Folder 4, Bringhurst Family Papers.

51. Isaac Briggs to Hannah Briggs, Washington, 7 January 1816, Folder "1816," Box 1, Briggs-Stabler Papers.

52. Isaac Briggs to Hannah Briggs, Washington, 2 February 1816, Folder "1816," Box 1, Briggs-Stabler Papers.

53. Isaac Briggs to Hannah Briggs, Washington, 14 January 1816, Folder "1816," Box 1, Briggs-Stabler Papers.

54. James Burrill Jr. et al., circular letter, Providence, 20 October 1815, Folder 4, Box 1, Sergeant Papers.

55. Jeffrey L. Pasley, "Matthew Livingston Davis's Notes from the Political Underground." All other biographical details are from *Biographical Directory of the United States Congress*, http://bioguide.congress.gov/biosearch/biosearch.asp.

56. Isaac Briggs to Hannah Briggs, Washington, 7 January 1816, Folder "1816," Box 1, Briggs-Stabler Papers.

57. Isaac Briggs to Hannah Briggs, Washington, 14 January 1816, Folder "1816," Box 1, Briggs-Stabler Papers.

58. Isaac Briggs to Hannah Briggs, Washington, 20 February 1816, Folder "1816," Box 1, Briggs-Stabler Papers.

59. Isaac Briggs to Hannah Briggs, Washington, 14 January 1816, Folder "1816," Box 1, Briggs-Stabler Papers.

60. Isaac Briggs to Hannah Briggs, Washington, 30 January 1816, Folder "1816," Box 1, Briggs-Stabler Papers.

61. Armistead T. Mason to Victor du Pont, Washington, 19 January 1816, Box 16, Series A: Correspondence—Incoming, Group 3: Victor du Pont, Winterthur Manuscripts, Hagley Museum and Library, Wilmington, Delaware.

62. Isaac Briggs to Hannah Briggs, Washington, 2 February 1816, Folder "1816," Box 1, Briggs-Stabler Papers.

63. Isaac Briggs to Hannah Briggs, Washington, 7 January 1816, Folder "1816," Box 1, Briggs-Stabler Papers.

64. Isaac Briggs to Hannah Briggs, Washington, 2 February 1816, Folder "1816," Box 1, Briggs-Stabler Papers.

65. Isaac Briggs to Hannah Briggs, Washington, 2 February 1816, Folder "1816," Box 1, Briggs-Stabler Papers.

66. Young had been deputed at the same meeting as Briggs but did not actually arrive until 29 January. Isaac Briggs to Hannah Briggs, Washington, 30 January 1816, Folder "1816," Box 1, Briggs-Stabler Papers.

67. Isaac Briggs to Hannah Briggs, Washington, 2 February 1816, Folder "1816," Box 1, Briggs-Stabler Papers.

68. Charles Kinsey to Isaac Briggs, 17 March 1816, Folder "1816," Isaac Briggs Papers, Library of Congress, Washington, DC.

69. Isaac Briggs to Hannah Briggs, Washington, 7 February 1816, Folder "1816," Box 1, Briggs-Stabler Papers.

70. *Annals of Congress*, Fourteenth Congress, First Session, 960–967 (quotation 966).

71. Isaac Briggs to Hannah Briggs, Washington, 7 February 1816, Folder "1816," Box 1, Briggs-Stabler Papers.

72. "Tariff of Duties on Imports," *Annals of Congress*, Fourteenth Congress, First Session, 1690–1693. Dallas's report also proposed a schedule of articles that would be free from duty and an ad valorem rate of 15 percent for all articles neither free nor subject to any specified rate of duty. For criticism, see Mathew Carey, *Collectanea: Displaying the Rise and Progress of the Tariff System of the United States* (Philadelphia, 1833, 2nd edition), 8.

73. Douglas A. Irwin and Peter Temin, "The Antebellum Tariff on Cotton Textiles Revisited," *Journal of Economic History* 61 (September 2001): 795.

74. For calls for prohibition, see *Annals of Congress*, Fourteenth Congress, First Session, 1645–1651, 1651–1656. For Lowell's confidence that he could do without, see Stanwood, *American Tariff Controversies in the Nineteenth Century*, 1:173–174.

75. "Tariff of Duties on Imports," *Annals of Congress*, Fourteenth Congress, First Session, 1691.

76. Stanwood, *American Tariff Controversies in the Nineteenth Century*, 1:140. For repetition of this claim, see Irwin and Temin, "The Antebellum Tariff on Cotton Textiles Revisited," 779; Pincus, *Pressure Groups and Politics in Antebellum Tariffs*, 51; and Vipperman, *William Lowndes*, 141.

77. Appleton, *Introduction of the Power Loom*, 13.

78. *Annals of Congress*, Fourteenth Congress, First Session, 1201. Lowndes also defended the minimum against attacks on the floor. *Annals of Congress*, Fourteenth Congress, First Session, 1237.

79. Isaac Briggs to Hannah Briggs, Washington, 2 February 1816, Folder "1816," Box 1, Briggs-Stabler Papers.

80. *Annals of Congress*, Fourteenth Congress, First Session, 1233.

81. Victor du Pont to Henry Clay, Brandywine, 11 March 1816, in *The Papers of Henry Clay*, ed. James F. Hopkins, Robert Seagar II, Melba Porter Hay, et al., 11 vols. (Lexington: University Press of Kentucky, 1959–1992), 2:173, 174. On Clay's support for protection, and for this bill in particular, see Robert V. Remini, *Henry Clay: Statesman for the Union* (New York: W. W. Norton, 1991), 61–62, 138–139, 228.

82. *Annals of Congress*, Fourteenth Congress, First Session, 1237.

83. Isaac Briggs to William Lowndes, Washington, 12 March 1816, printed in

"Manufactures—Very Interesting," *Niles' Weekly Register*, 23 March 1816; Isaac Briggs to John W. Taylor, Washington, 18 March 1816, Folder "1816," Box 1, Briggs-Stabler Papers.

84. *Annals of Congress*, Fourteenth Congress, First Session, 1237 (quotation), 1238, 1247.

85. Webster represented New Hampshire in the Fourteenth Congress, but he would soon relocate to Massachusetts, where he spent the remainder of his career. For his views on the tariff at this time, see Robert V. Remini, *Daniel Webster: The Man and His Time* (New York: W. W. Norton, 1997), 137–140. For his relationship with wealthy capitalists, see Carl E. Prince and Seth Taylor, "Daniel Webster, the Boston Associates, and the US Government's Role in the Industrializing Process, 1815–1830," *Journal of the Early Republic* 2 (Autumn 1982): 283–299.

86. "Autobiography," in *The Papers of Daniel Webster: Correspondence*, ed. Charles Wiltse, 7 vols. (Hanover, NH: University Press of New England, 1974–1986), 1:23.

87. *Annals of Congress*, Fourteenth Congress, First Session, 1270.

88. *Annals of Congress*, Fourteenth Congress, First Session, 1271.

89. *Annals of Congress*, Fourteenth Congress, First Session, 1271.

90. *Annals of Congress*, Fourteenth Congress, First Session, 1270.

91. *Annals of Congress*, Fourteenth Congress, First Session, 1273.

92. *Annals of Congress*, Fourteenth Congress, First Session, 1325. See also Thomas R. Gold to Nathan Appleton, Washington, 5 April 1816, Folder 3, Box 3, Appleton Family Papers, Massachusetts Historical Society, Boston.

93. *Annals of Congress*, Fourteenth Congress, First Session, 1328.

94. John Randolph to James Mercer Garnett, George Town, 2 February 1816, Folder 3, Box 5, Papers of John Randolph of Roanoke, Albert and Shirley Small Special Collections Library, University of Virginia, Charlottesville. On Hamilton, see Peskin, *Manufacturing Revolution*, and Andrew Shankman, "'A New Thing on Earth': Alexander Hamilton, Pro-Manufacturing Republicans, and the Democratization of American Political Economy," *Journal of the Early Republic* 23 (Autumn 2003): 323–352.

95. John Randolph quoted in Mathew Carey, *Autobiography of Mathew Carey* (Philadelphia, 1835), 97; Remini, *Daniel Webster*, 139–140.

96. Isaac Briggs to Hannah Briggs, Washington, 2 February 1816, Folder "1816," Box 1, Briggs-Stabler Papers.

97. *Annals of Congress*, Fourteenth Congress, First Session, 1329.

98. Appleton, *Introduction of the Power Loom*, 13.

99. John C. Calhoun, "Remarks in Debate following His Speech in Reply to Henry Clay on the Subtreasury Bill" [Washington, 10 March 1838], in *The Papers of John C. Calhoun*, ed. Robert L. Meriweather, W. Edwin Hemphill, Shirley A. Book, Clyde N. Wilson, et al., 28 vols. (Columbia: University of South Carolina Press, 1959–2003), 14:193. Elsewhere Calhoun identified that friend as Sam-

uel D. Ingham, one of the protectionist members on Ways and Means. See "Memorandum (by Richard K. Cralle)" [Richmond, VA, 4 December 1831], in Calhoun, *Papers*, 11:523.

100. *Annals of Congress*, Fourteenth Congress, First Session, 1330.

101. John C. Calhoun to Bernard A. Reynolds, Washington, 5 June 1832, in Calhoun, *Papers*, 11:592.

102. *Annals of Congress*, Fourteenth Congress, First Session, 1336.

103. Rufus King to Edward King, Washington, 28 March 1816, in *Life and Correspondence of Rufus King*, ed. Charles R. King, 6 vols. (New York: G. P. Putnam's Sons, 1894–1900), 6:17.

104. *Annals of Congress*, Fourteenth Congress, First Session, 1285.

105. Vipperman, *William Lowndes*, 140–141.

106. *Annals of Congress*, Fourteenth Congress, First Session, 1313, 1314.

107. Mathew Carey, *Autobiography*, 97. In fact, the House did have a rule that no member could vote on any question in which he was "immediately and particularly interested," but this was seldom applied to general legislation. As David Currie notes, if this rule was understood to "forbid farmers to vote on measures affecting farming," then "it would be difficult to reconcile with the principle of representative government." Currie, *The Constitution in Congress: The Federalist Period, 1789–1801*, 9–10n.

108. William Milnor to John Sergeant, Washington, 23 April 1816, Folder 12, Box 1, Sergeant Papers; *Annals of Congress*, Fourteenth Congress, First Session, 1438. References for congressional roll calls on the passage of tariff legislation between 1816 and 1861 cited here and elsewhere in this book are provided in the appendix.

109. Lawrence A. Peskin, "How the Republicans Learned to Love Manufacturing: The First Parties and the 'New Economy,'" *Journal of the Early Republic* 22 (Summer 2002): 235–262.

110. Rufus King to Christopher Gore, 26 June 1816, in *Life and Correspondence of Rufus King*, 6:27.

111. Daniel Webster to Samuel Ayer Bradley, 21 April [1816], in Webster, *Papers*, 1:197; emphasis original.

112. Stanwood, *American Tariff Controversies in the Nineteenth Century*, 1:152–153. Webster was absent on the final vote.

113. William S. Belko, *Philip Pendleton Barbour in Jacksonian America: An Old Republican in King Andrew's Court* (Tuscaloosa: University of Alabama Press, 2016), 57–58; Norris Watson Preyer, "Southern Support of the Tariff of 1816—A Reappraisal," *Journal of Southern History* 25 (August 1959): 306–322; Brian Schoen, *The Fragile Fabric of Union: Cotton, Federal Politics, and the Global Origins of the Civil War* (Baltimore: Johns Hopkins University Press, 2009), 92–97; Vipperman, *William Lowndes*, 142–143. For Calhoun's subsequent characterization of the Tariff of 1816 as a "temporary" measure, with revenue "its direct and

immediate object" and protection merely "subordinate and incidental," see John C. Calhoun to Bernard A. Reynolds, Washington, 5 June 1832, in Calhoun, *Papers*, 11:591–593.

114. Minutes of Wilmington manufacturers meeting, 10 January 1816, Folder 4, Bringhurst Family Papers. Similarly, see "Meeting of Manufacturers," *Aurora General Advertiser*, 27 November 1815.

115. "Report of the Corresponding Committee of the Society for the Encouragement of Domestic Manufactures," in "Domestic Manufactures," *Niles' Weekly Register*, 12 July 1817.

116. Alexis de Tocqueville, *Democracy in America*, 2 vols. (1835–1840), vol. 2, ch. 5.

117. On these developments, see Richard D. Brown, *The Strength of a People: The Idea of an Informed Citizenry in America, 1650–1870* (Chapel Hill: University of North Carolina Press, 1996); Daniel Walker Howe, *What Hath God Wrought: The Transformation of America, 1815–1848* (Oxford: Oxford University Press, 2007); Richard R. John, "Governmental Institutions as Agents of Change: Rethinking American Political Development in the Early Republic, 1787–1835," *Studies in American Political Development* 11 (Fall 1997): 347–380; and Johann N. Neem, *Creating a Nation of Joiners: Democracy and Civil Society in Early National Massachusetts* (Cambridge, MA: Harvard University Press, 2008).

118. Peskin, *Manufacturing Revolution*, 91–118, 162–187.

119. "Domestic Manufactures," *Niles' Weekly Register*, 12 July 1817. See also *Address of the American Society for the Encouragement of Domestic Manufactures, to the People of the United States* (New York, 1817).

120. "Report of the Corresponding Committee of the Society for the Encouragement of Domestic Manufactures."

121. "Dues and Account Book—The Philadelphia Society for the Promotion of American Manufactures, 1817–1818," Volume 111 (quotation), and "Subscription Book of the Philadelphia Society for the Promotion of American Manufactures, Feb 1817-April 1819," Volume 226, both Coxe Family Papers, HSP; Mathew Carey to Victor du Pont (with enclosed prospectus), 11 March 1818, Box 16, Series A: Correspondence—Incoming, Group 3: Victor du Pont, Winterthur Manuscripts.

122. John Weidman to Jacob M. Haldeman, Union Forge, 25 October 1817, Box 13, Haldeman Family Papers, HM&L. See also John Bezis-Selfa, *Forging America: Ironworkers, Adventurers, and the Industrious Revolution* (Ithaca, NY: Cornell University Press, 2004), 211–212.

123. *Annals of Congress*, Fifteenth Congress, First Session, 2582, 2584.

Chapter Two: "More Than a Mere Manufacturing Question": The Baldwin Bill of 1820 and the Tariff of 1824

1. "Hamilton" [Mathew Carey], "New Series [Second Series], No. V. Protection of Manufactures," 3 December 1822, 8, New-York Historical Society.

2. *Annals of Congress*, Eighteenth Congress, First Session, 1963.

3. "Hamilton" [Mathew Carey], "New Series [Second Series], No. VII (Second Edition). Statistical View of the Debts of the United States. . . ," 1 January 1823, 6, Library Company of Philadelphia. On the Panic of 1819, see Daniel S. Dupre, "The Panic of 1819 and the Political Economy of Sectionalism," in *The Economy of Early America: Historical Perspectives and New Directions*, ed. Cathy Matson (University Park: Pennsylvania State University Press, 2006), and Murray N. Rothbard, *The Panic of 1819: Reactions and Policies* (New York: Columbia University Press, 1962).

4. The states represented, with number of delegates in brackets, were: Connecticut (five), Delaware (two), Maryland (two), Massachusetts (two), New Jersey (five), New York (twelve), Ohio (one), Pennsylvania (seven), and Rhode Island (one). The Anti-Masons are credited with holding the first national party convention in 1830. It was attended by delegates from ten states and one territory. James S. Chase, *Emergence of the Presidential Nominating Convention, 1789–1832* (Urbana: University of Illinois Press, 1973), 148–149.

5. *The Proceedings of a Convention of the Friends of National Industry, Assembled in the City of New-York, November 29, 1819, consisting of Delegates from the States of Massachusetts, Rhode Island, Connecticut, New-York, New-Jersey, Pennsylvania, Delaware, Maryland, and Ohio* (New York, 1819), 6 (quotation) and passim; Memorial of the Convention of the Friends of National Industry, *American State Papers, 1789–1838*, Sixteenth Congress, First Session, no. 560. For more on the auction tax measure, see Joanna Cohen, "'The Right to Purchase Is as Free as the Right to Sell': Defining Consumers as Citizens in the Auction-House Conflicts of the Early Republic," *Journal of the Early Republic* 30 (Spring 2010): 25–62.

6. Mathew Carey, *Autobiography of Mathew Carey* (Philadelphia, 1835), 92.

7. Mathew Carey, *Collectanea: Displaying the Rise and Progress of the Tariff System of the United States* (Philadelphia, 1833, 2nd edition), 18–19. For more on Carey's multifaceted career, see Cathy Matson, James N. Green, et al., "Special Issue: Ireland, America, and Mathew Carey," *Early American Studies* 11 (Fall 2013): 395–589, and Kenneth Wyer Rowe, *Mathew Carey: A Study in American Economic Development* (Baltimore: Johns Hopkins University Press, 1933).

8. Mathew Carey, *Auto Biographical Sketches: In a Series of Letters Addressed to a Friend* (Philadelphia, 1829), 4. On Carey's political economy, see also Cathy Matson, "Mathew Carey's Learning Experience: Commerce, Manufacturing, and the Panic of 1819," *Early American Studies* 11 (Fall 2013): 455–485, and Andrew Shankman, "Neither Infinite Wretchedness nor Positive Good: Mathew Carey and Henry Clay on Political Economy and Slavery during the Long 1820s," in *Contesting Slavery: The Politics of Bondage and Freedom in the New American Nation*, ed. John Craig Hammond and Matthew Mason (Charlottesville: University of Virginia Press, 2011).

9. *Annals of Congress*, Eighteenth Congress, First Session, 1962–2001 (quotations 1978, 1963).

10. "American Manufactures," 7 September 1819 (first quotation); "Public Meeting," 23 August 1819 (second quotation), both *Aurora General Advertiser* (Philadelphia). For a fuller account of the formation and activities of these societies, see Daniel Peart, "Looking Beyond Parties and Elections: The Making of United States Tariff Policy during the Early 1820s," *Journal of the Early Republic* 33 (Spring 2013): 87–108.

11. "American Manufactures," *Aurora General Advertiser*, 12 November 1819.

12. In addition to Pennsylvania, state societies were established in Connecticut, Delaware, Maryland, Massachusetts, New Jersey, New York, Ohio, and Rhode Island. *Circular and Address of the National Institution for Promoting Industry in the United States, to their Fellow-Citizens* (New York, 1820), 4. For more on the reasons why Pennsylvania became, and remained throughout the antebellum period, a protectionist stronghold, see Malcolm Rogers Eiselen, *The Rise of Pennsylvania Protectionism* (Philadelphia: Porcupine Press, 1974, reprint of 1932 edition).

13. On the evangelical societies, see Johann N. Neem, *Creating a Nation of Joiners: Democracy and Civil Society in Early National Massachusetts* (Cambridge, MA: Harvard University Press, 2008), 81–113, although Neem borrows the term "organizational repertoires" from Elisabeth S. Clemens, *The People's Lobby: Organizational Innovation and the Rise of Interest Group Politics in the United States, 1890–1925* (Chicago: University of Chicago Press, 1997).

14. *Annals of Congress*, Sixteenth Congress, First Session, 704, 708–710. What prompted Little to make this motion is unknown, but he voted in favor of every important tariff bill that came before him during a career that spanned eight Congresses, so he can certainly be counted among the friends to protection.

15. Hezekiah Niles to William Darlington, Baltimore, 11 December 1819, Folder 2, William Darlington Papers, Library of Congress, Washington, DC.

16. Although the Speaker of the House possessed the power to make all committee appointments, convention dictated that returning members from previous sessions would be reappointed unless there was good reason to do otherwise, so Clay could not simply remake Ways and Means to ensure a protectionist majority with the same ease that he could for a new committee. On Clay's skilled use of the committee system, see Robert V. Remini, *The House: The History of the House of Representatives* (New York: HarperCollins, 2007), 101–102.

17. "To the Editor," signed "Eldred Simkins," dated 2 May 1820 (from the Charleston *Southern Patriot*), *Aurora General Advertiser*, 24 May 1820.

18. The circumstances of Baldwin's election are detailed in Robert D. Ilisevich, "Henry Baldwin and Andrew Jackson: A Political Relationship in Trust?" *Pennsylvania Magazine of History and Biography* 120 (January 1996): 38–39. The other committee members were: Thomas Forrest (PA, Federalist), Peter Little (MD, Republican), Alney McLean (KY, Republican), Henry Meigs (NY, Republican), James Parker (MA, Republican), and Thomas Randolph Ross (OH, Republican).

19. William Lee to Mathew Carey, 24 February 1820, Folder 4, Box 23, Ed-

ward Carey Gardiner Collection, Historical Society of Pennsylvania, Philadelphia. Opponents of protection were less complimentary. "If Pittsburg can manufacture a sound, intelligent Statesman & correct, practical Politician out of such materials, it will not only prove her superior to Sheffield, Birmingham & Manchester; but will demonstrate irrefragably, that Domestic Manufactures require no further encouragement at the hands of your Honorable Body," wrote one to John Randolph. James Mercer Garnett to John Randolph, 9 April 1821, Reel 4, Correspondence of John Randolph to James M. Garnett, William Cabell Bruce Collection, Virginia State Library, Richmond.

20. John Harrison to Mathew Carey, 13 September 1819, Folder 3, Box 23, Gardiner Collection.

21. Peter H. Schenck to Mathew Carey, New York, 12 December 1819, Folder 1, Box 24, Gardiner Collection.

22. Condy Raguet to Mathew Carey and Samuel Jackson, Harrisburg, 17 December 1819, Folder 8, Box 22, Gardiner Collection.

23. Condy Raguet to Mathew Carey and Samuel Jackson, Washington, 30 December 1819, Folder 8, Box 22, Gardiner Collection.

24. John Harrison to Lydia Harrison, Washington, 12 January 1820, Leib-Harrison Folder, Society Large Collection, HSP.

25. John Harrison to Lydia Harrison, Washington, 12 January 1820, Leib-Harrison Folder, Society Large Collection.

26. John Harrison to Mathew Carey, Washington, 24–25 January 1820, Folder 3, Box 23, Gardiner Collection. Harrison also reported that a delegation of auctioneers from New York were in Washington on the same mission.

27. John Harrison to Lydia Harrison, Washington, 12 January 1820, Leib-Harrison Folder, Society Large Collection.

28. Peter H. Schenck to Mathew Carey, New York, 3 January 1820, Folder 1, Box 25; and John Harrison to Mathew Carey, Washington, 24–25 January 1820, Folder 3, Box 23, both Gardiner Collection. Lord had arrived around the same time as Harrison and agreed to keep up a correspondence with Philadelphia as well as New York on the latter's departure. In addition to those letters, which may be found in the Gardiner Collection, see also Eleazar Lord, "Autobiography of Eleazar Lord, LL.D" (unpublished manuscript, 1865), 142–148, Connecticut Historical Society, Hartford.

29. Eleazar Lord to Mathew Carey, n.d. [March 1820], Folder 4, Box 23, Gardiner Collection.

30. Eleazar Lord to Mathew Carey, Washington, 16 February 1820, Folder 4, Box 23; Eleazar Lord to Mathew Carey, Washington, 29 April 1820, Folder 5, Box 23; and Eleazar Lord to Mathew Carey, Washington, 18 April 1820, Folder 5, Box 23, all Gardiner Collection. For biographical details on Lord, see Lord, "Autobiography of Eleazar Lord"; Richard Perry Tison II, "Lords of Creation: American Scriptural Geology and the Lord Brothers' Assault on 'Intellectual Atheism'" (PhD diss., University of Oklahoma, 2008), 45–60; and Robert Whalen,

"Eleazar Lord and the Reformed Tradition: Christian Capitalist in the Age of Jackson," *American Presbyterians* 72 (Winter 1994): 219–228.

31. Isaac Briggs to the editors of the *National Intelligencer*, Washington, 25 March 1816, printed in "On the New Tariff" (from the Washington *National Intelligencer*), *Aurora General Advertiser*, 28 March 1816.

32. [Gulian C. Verplanck], *The State Triumvirate: A Political Tale* (New York, 1819), 68. Verplanck would subsequently be elected to Congress and tasked with authoring a tariff bill of his own; see chapter four for more on that subject.

33. Condy Raguet to Mathew Carey and Samuel Jackson, Washington, 30 December 1819, Folder 8, Box 22, Gardiner Collection. The professionalization of lobbying at the state level is examined in Douglas E. Bowers, "From Logrolling to Corruption: The Development of Lobbying in Pennsylvania, 1815–1861," *Journal of the Early Republic* 3 (Winter 1983): 439–474.

34. On the importance of "individual persuasion," and personal connections, in early American policymaking, see Catherine Allgor, *Parlor Politics: In Which the Ladies of Washington Help Build a City and a Government* (Charlottesville: University of Virginia Press, 2000); Jeffrey L. Pasley, "Private Access and Public Power: Gentility and Lobbying in the Early Congress," in *The House and Senate in the 1790s: Petitioning, Lobbying, and Institutional Development*, ed. Kenneth R. Bowling and Donald R. Kennon (Athens: Ohio University Press, 2002); and Rachel A. Shelden, *Washington Brotherhood: Politics, Social Life, and the Coming of the Civil War* (Chapel Hill: University of North Carolina Press, 2013). For housing arrangements specifically, see Shelden, *Washington Brotherhood*, 96–119, and James Sterling Young, *The Washington Community, 1800–1828* (New York: Columbia University Press, 1966), 87–109.

35. Abbott Lawrence to Amos Lawrence, Washington, 11 February 1828, Folder "1828 Feb 11–28," Box 1, Amos Lawrence Papers, Massachusetts Historical Society, Boston.

36. Eleazar Lord to Mathew Carey, Washington, 11 January 1820, Folder 4, Box 23, Gardiner Collection.

37. Henry Baldwin to Mathew Carey, Washington, 21 [January] 1820, Folder 2, Box 23, Gardiner Collection. See also Henry Baldwin to Mathew Carey, Washington, 14 January 1820, Folder 2, Box 23, Gardiner Collection.

38. Eleazar Lord to Mathew Carey, Washington, 11 January 1820, Folder 4, Box 23, Gardiner Collection.

39. Henry Baldwin to Mathew Carey, Washington, 6 February 1820, Folder 2, Box 23, Gardiner Collection.

40. Henry Baldwin to Mathew Carey, Washington, 26 February 1820, Folder 2, Box 23, Gardiner Collection. See also Lord, "Autobiography of Eleazar Lord," 143.

41. Eleazar Lord to Mathew Carey, Washington, n.d. [April 1820], Folder 5, Box 23, Gardiner Collection.

42. Memorial of the Convention of the Friends of National Industry, *American State Papers, 1789–1838,* Sixteenth Congress, First Session, no. 560.

43. *Annals of Congress,* Sixteenth Congress, First Session, 1663–1669. In the case of woolen textiles, for example, the current rate of duty was 25 percent ad valorem, the Friends of National Industry asked for 35 percent, and Baldwin's bill proposed 33 percent. Likewise, the current rate for sheet iron was a specific duty of $2.54 per hundredweight, the Friends asked for four dollars, and Baldwin proposed three dollars. He did adopt their recommendations for several other types of iron, however.

44. Henry Baldwin to Mathew Carey, Washington, 21 [January] 1820, Folder 2, Box 23, Gardiner Collection.

45. Henry Baldwin to Mathew Carey, Washington, 13 February 1820, Folder 2, Box 23, Gardiner Collection. "We are appealing to the liberality of the South to protect our manufactures," Baldwin wrote to another protectionist. "If we succeed in unnecessary legislation on the subject of Slavery it pays no debts, it will not build up our iron works. We gain nothing they lose everything." Henry Baldwin to "Gilmore" [John Gilmore?], Washington, 12 February 1820, Folder 5, Box 2, Society Small Collection, HSP.

46. Robert Pierce Forbes, *The Missouri Compromise and Its Aftermath: Slavery and the Meaning of America* (Chapel Hill: University of North Carolina Press, 2007), 97, 98–99, 124. Forbes notes that in Randolph's original formulation, the term was likely "doe face," intended to convey the timidity of a startled deer, but it became popularized as "doughface," connoting a man of no principle, easily shaped to another's will.

47. Eleazar Lord to Mathew Carey, Washington, 27 February 1820, Folder 8, Box 22, Gardiner Collection. On a similar theme, see Eleazar Lord to Mathew Carey, Washington, 1 March 1820, and Eleazar Lord to Mathew Carey, Washington, 18 March 1820, both Folder 4, Box 23, Gardiner Collection.

48. Peter H. Schenck to Mathew Carey, New York, 25 February 1820, Folder 1, Box 24, Gardiner Collection.

49. Peter Colt to Mathew Carey, Paterson, 17 April 1820, Folder 3, Box 23, Gardiner Collection. This division is reflected in the historiography. See John Ashworth, *Slavery, Capitalism, and Politics in the Antebellum Republic,* 2 vols. (Cambridge: Cambridge University Press, 1995–2007), 1:72–73, who, in contrast to Forbes, emphasizes the strength of antislavery sentiments among protectionists. And compare with Glover Moore, *The Missouri Controversy, 1819–1821* (Lexington: Kentucky University Press, 1953); and Matthew Mason, *Slavery and Politics in the Early American Republic* (Chapel Hill: University of North Carolina Press, 2006).

50. *Annals of Congress,* Sixteenth Congress, First Session, 1663–1669.

51. Eleazar Lord to Mathew Carey, Washington, 28 March 1820, Folder 4, Box 23, Gardiner Collection.

52. Eleazar Lord to Mathew Carey, Washington, 18 April 1820, Folder 5, Box 23, Gardiner Collection.

53. Henry Baldwin to Mathew Carey, Washington, 17 April 1820, Folder 2, Box 23, Gardiner Collection.

54. Mathew Carey, *Autobiography*, 83; Mathew Carey, *Sketches Towards a History of the Present Session of Congress, from December 6, 1819, to April 15, 1820* (Philadelphia, 1820), 25.

55. *Annals of Congress*, Sixteenth Congress, First Session, 1848–1849.

56. *Annals of Congress*, Sixteenth Congress, First Session, 1861. For relations between Baldwin and Lowndes, see Carl J. Vipperman, *William Lowndes and the Transition of Southern Politics, 1782–1822* (Chapel Hill: University of North Carolina Press, 1989), 204–227.

57. *Annals of Congress*, Sixteenth Congress, First Session, 1916–1946 (quotations 1921, 1921, 1917, 1943, 1917).

58. Eleazar Lord to Mathew Carey, Washington, 21 April 1820; and Eleazar Lord to Mathew Carey, Washington, n.d. [April 1820], both in Folder 5, Box 23, Gardiner Collection.

59. *Annals of Congress*, Sixteenth Congress, First Session, 2127.

60. *Annals of Congress*, Sixteenth Congress, First Session, 1933.

61. *Annals of Congress*, Sixteenth Congress, First Session, 1946.

62. Hezekiah Niles to William Darlington, Baltimore, 3 May 1820, Folder 3, Darlington Papers, LC.

63. Eleazar Lord to Mathew Carey, Washington, 11 January 1820, Folder 4, Box 23, Gardiner Collection.

64. *Annals of Congress*, Sixteenth Congress, First Session, 2002.

65. Eleazar Lord to Mathew Carey, Washington, 28 March 1820; Eleazar Lord to Mathew Carey, Washington, 31 March 1820; and William Lee to Mathew Carey, 11 February 1820, all Folder 4, Box 23, Gardiner Collection.

66. Eleazar Lord to Mathew Carey, Washington, 26 April 1820, Folder 5, Box 23, Gardiner Collection.

67. Lord, "Autobiography of Eleazar Lord," 144, 145.

68. *Annals of Congress*, Sixteenth Congress, First Session, 2100.

69. *Annals of Congress*, Sixteenth Congress, First Session, 2073.

70. Mathew Carey, *Sketches Towards a History of the Present Session of Congress*, 29.

71. Mathew Carey, *Sketches Towards a History of the Present Session of Congress*, 29; Neem, *Creating a Nation of Joiners*, 168.

72. Mathew Carey, *Sketches Towards a History of the Present Session of Congress*, 31; Edmund Ruffin, *Incidents of My Life: Edmund Ruffin's Autobiographical Essays*, ed. David F. Allmendinger Jr. (Charlottesville: University of Virginia Press, 1990), 175.

73. Eleazar Lord to Mathew Carey, Washington, 26 April 1820, Folder 5, Box 23, Gardiner Collection.

74. See, for example, Memorial of the Pennsylvania Society, *American State Papers, 1789–1838*, Sixteenth Congress, First Session, no. 590.

75. "Extract from a Member of Congress, to the Editor of the *Baltimore Patriot*, dated Washington, May 7, 1820," *Aurora General Advertiser*, 18 May 1820.

76. John Williams Walker to Thomas G. Percy, Washington, 29 April 1820, Folder 2, Box 1, John Williams Walker Papers, Alabama Department of Archives and History, Montgomery.

77. Forbes, *Missouri Compromise*, 298n10.

78. Entry for 28 April 1825, "William P. Brobson Diary, 1825–1828," ed. George H. Gibson, *Delaware History* 15 (1972–1973): 67. For more on the two-way communication between congressmen and their constituents, see Richard D. Brown, *Knowledge Is Power: The Diffusion of Information in Early America, 1700–1865* (Oxford: Oxford University Press, 1989); Noble E. Cunningham Jr., ed., *Circular Letters of Congressmen to Their Constituents, 1789–1829*, 3 vols. (Chapel Hill: University of North Carolina Press, 1978); and Richard R. John, *Spreading the News: The American Postal System from Franklin to Morse* (Cambridge, MA: Harvard University Press, 1998).

79. Eleazar Lord to Mathew Carey, Washington, 7 April 1820, Folder 4, Box 23, Gardiner Collection.

80. William Lee to Mathew Carey, Washington, 19 April 1820, Folder 4, Box 23, Gardiner Collection.

81. Harrison Gray Otis to Sally Foster Otis, "Crawfords," [Washington], 23 April 1820, Reel 7, Harrison Gray Otis Papers, MHS. See, similarly, Samuel Chandler Crafts to Eunice Todd Crafts, Washington, [16] April 1820, Crafts Family Papers, University of Vermont Libraries Center for Digital Initiatives, http://cdi.uvm.edu/collections/index.xql.

82. William Lee to Mathew Carey, Washington, 19 April 1820, Folder 4, Box 23, Gardiner Collection.

83. Eleazar Lord to Mathew Carey, Washington, 4 May 1820, Folder 5, Box 23, Gardiner Collection.

84. Hezekiah Niles to William Darlington, Baltimore, 5 May 1820, Folder 3, Darlington Papers, LC.

85. William Darlington, entry for 6 May 1820, Diary 1816–1821, William Darlington Papers, NYHS; *Annals of Congress*, Sixteenth Congress, First Session, 2171–2172, 2184–2185, 2201–2202.

86. Baldwin's opinion is reported in Eleazar Lord to Mathew Carey, Washington, 27 February 1820, Folder 8, Box 22, Gardiner Collection. For a more recent restatement of the same argument, see Forbes, *Missouri Compromise*, 122.

87. John W. Barbour to John J. Crittenden, Barboursville, VA, 31 May 1820, in *The Life of John J. Crittenden, with Selections from His Correspondence and Speeches*, ed. Ann Mary Butler Coleman, 2 vols. (Philadelphia, 1873), 1:47. On a similar theme, see "Congress" (editorial), *Richmond Enquirer*, 19 May 1820. Ironically, while Missouri was not admitted in time to vote on the tariff, the state's

newspapers were generally in favor of protection. Moore, *Missouri Controversy*, 331.

88. Eleazar Lord to Mathew Carey, Washington, 27 February 1820, Folder 8, Box 22, Gardiner Collection.

89. For accounts of the motives of Southern opponents of Baldwin's bill that do not prioritize sectional antagonism over Missouri, see William S. Belko, *Philip Pendleton Barbour in Jacksonian America: An Old Republican in King Andrew's Court* (Tuscaloosa: University of Alabama Press, 2016), 59–64, 100; Norris Watson Preyer, "Southern Support of the Tariff of 1816—A Reappraisal," *Journal of Southern History* 25 (August 1959): 315–322; and Brian Schoen, *The Fragile Fabric of Union: Cotton, Federal Politics, and the Global Origins of the Civil War* (Baltimore: Johns Hopkins University Press, 2009), 106–111. And for a contemporary perspective, see William Lowndes to Timothy Pickering, Washington, 14 April 1820, Reel 31, Timothy Pickering Papers, MHS.

It is striking that the question of whether Congress even possessed the constitutional right to lay taxes to protect domestic industry, rather than to raise revenue, an argument that would soon become the primary recourse of Southern spokesmen who feared the implications for a corresponding assumption of legislative power over slavery, was broached only once on the floor in 1820, and then by a representative from Massachusetts. See Ezekiel Whitman and reply of Henry Clay, *Annals of Congress*, Sixteenth Congress, First Session, 1998–2008, 2049. In former president James Madison's view, the tariff "divides the nation in so checkered a manner, that its issue cannot be very serious; especially as it involves no great constitutional question. . . . Instead of increasing, it might then mitigate, the alienation threatened by the Missouri controversy." James Madison to Richard Rush, 4 December 1820, in *Letters and Other Writings of James Madison*, 4 vols. (Philadelphia, 1865), 3:195.

90. "Fourth of July," *Richmond Enquirer*, 14 July 1820; emphasis original. Lord considered Newton one of few Southerners to fully understand the subject. Eleazar Lord to Mathew Carey, Washington, 26 April 1820, Folder 5, Box 23, Gardiner Collection.

91. James Burrill Jr. to Mathew Carey, Washington, 7 May 1820, Folder 2, Box 23, Gardiner Collection.

92. Rufus King to Jeremiah Mason, Washington, 4 May 1820; and Rufus King to Christopher Gore, Washington, 28 April 1820, both in *Life and Correspondence of Rufus King*, 6 vols. (New York: G. P. Putnam's Sons, 1894–1900), 6:337, 334.

93. Harrison Gray Otis to Sally Foster Otis, 5 May 1820, Reel 7, Otis Papers.

94. William Lee to Mathew Carey, 28 January 1820, Folder 4, Box 23, Gardiner Collection. Southern opponents of the tariff had hoped for this outcome too. See William Lowndes to Timothy Pickering, Washington, 14 April 1820; and 12 May 1820, both Reel 31, Pickering Papers.

95. William Lee to Mathew Carey, 22 November 1819, Folder 4, Box 23,

Gardiner Collection. See also Eleazar Lord to Mathew Carey, Washington, 21 April 1820, Folder 5, Box 23; and Peter H. Schenck to Mathew Carey, New York, 7 May 1820, Folder 1, Box 24, both Gardiner Collection.

96. Christopher Gore to Rufus King, Waltham, 29 January 1820, in *Life and Correspondence of Rufus King*, 6:261.

97. Mathew Carey, circular letter, Philadelphia, 21 November 1826, HSP.

98. Mathew Carey, circular letter, Philadelphia, 21 November 1826, HSP; Mathew Carey, *Auto Biographical Sketches*, 86.

99. Eleazar Lord to Mathew Carey, Washington, 3 May 1820; and Eleazar Lord to Mathew Carey, Washington, 4 May 1820, both in Folder 5, Box 23, Gardiner Collection.

100. Henry Shippen to John Tod, Huntingdon, 15 February 1823, Folder 8, Box 9, John Tod Papers, Pennsylvania State Archives, Harrisburg. There is some confusion over precisely what investments Baldwin held. The chairman himself would later write that at the time the bill was under consideration he was "concerned in the Rolling mill at Pittsburgh in which we manufactured iron." Henry Baldwin to John Gilmore, Philadelphia, 24 January 1833, Folder 7, Box 2, Society Small Collection.

101. Louis McLane to [John Torbert], Washington, 28 March 1820, Folder 4, Box 2, William Young Correspondence, HSP.

102. Jonathan Roberts to Mathew Roberts, Washington, 5 May 1820, Folder 12, Box 3, Jonathan Roberts Papers, HSP. For Lord's dismay at Roberts's defection, see Eleazar Lord to Mathew Carey, Washington, 1 May 1820, Folder 5, Box 23, Gardiner Collection.

103. "Review of the Speech of Harrison Gray Otis, Mayor of the City of Boston," *Banner of the Constitution* (New York City), 23 March 1831; emphasis original. Similarly, a Southern critic of the bill explained to Carey: "[W]here a great combination was formed to carry a general system into effect; where whatever examination might have taken place before the Committee it was declared on the floor of the House of Representatives that no examination of particular articles should be allowed, at least that no alteration should be admitted, but that each must be taken as a necessary part of a whole; it is not surprising that some alarm and opposition should be excited, and that many should be arrayed against a mode of Legislation certainly capable of great misapplication." Stephen Elliott to Mathew Carey, Charleston, 20 October 1820, Folder 3, Box 23, Gardiner Collection.

104. Rufus King to Jeremiah Mason, Washington, 4 May 1820, in *Life and Correspondence of Rufus King*, 6:337. See, likewise, James Burrill Jr. to Mathew Carey, Washington, 7 May 1820, Folder 2, Box 23, Gardiner Collection.

105. Eleazar Lord to Mathew Carey, Washington, 4 May 1820, Folder 5, Box 23, Gardiner Collection.

106. Jeremiah H. Pierson to Mathew Carey, Washington, 26 December 1821, Folder 1, Box 25, Gardiner Collection. Pierson was also Lord's father-in-law but

only served in the Seventeenth Congress after the latter's mission to Washington had ended.

107. Lord, "Autobiography of Eleazar Lord," 147–148. For more on the paper, see Jacob T. Walden to Mathew Carey, New York, 25 May 1820, Folder 3, Box 24, Gardiner Collection, and Lord's correspondence with Carey for the period June 1820-July 1821. For the inscription on the pitcher, see Donald L. Fennimore and Ann K. Wagner, *Silversmiths to the Nation: Thomas Fletcher and Sidney Gardiner, 1800–1842* (Winterthur, DE: Henry Francis du Pont Winterthur Museum, 2007), 155–156.

108. *Circular and Address of the National Institution for Promoting Industry in the United States*; "Proceedings of a Convention of the *Friends of National Industry*," *Patron of Industry* (New York City), 28 June 1820, emphasis original; and Carey's correspondence for the period December 1819–June 1820, Gardiner Collection.

109. Theda Skocpol, Marshall Ganz, and Ziad Munson, "A Nation of Organizers: The Institutional Origins of Civic Voluntarism in the United States," *American Political Science Review* 94 (September 2000): 527–546.

110. "Congress" (editorial), *Richmond Enquirer*, 19 May 1820.

111. One New York congressman blamed this failure once again on "the unaccountable delay of Mr. Baldwin," adding that "notwithstanding this most extraordinary conduct of the Chairman I should not be surprised to find him attributing the failure of the bill to the 'all pervading influence of the Missouri question.'" John W. Taylor to Jane Taylor, Washington, 8 February 1821, Folder 7, Box 4, John W. Taylor Papers, NYHS.

112. See, for example, Peter H. Schenck to Mathew Carey, New York, 9 December 1819, Folder 1, Box 24, Gardiner Collection. For examples of the National Institution's work, see "Address, &c.," *Patron of Industry*, 16 and 20 December 1820, and "To the Honourable the Senate and House of Representatives of the United States, in Congress Assembled," *Patron of Industry*, 13 and 17 January 1821.

113. Timothy Fuller to Lemuel Shaw, 7 March 1822, Reel 5, Lemuel Shaw Papers, MHS. Barbour, like many Southerners, had supported the Tariff of 1816, but he would vote against all subsequent efforts to raise duties. He was censured by protectionists for acting "contrary to common custom and common courtesy" in placing a majority on a committee hostile to the interest that it represented. "Hamilton" [Mathew Carey], "Third Series, No. I. To the Cotton Planters of the United States," 8 January 1823, 8, LCP. See also Belko, *Philip Pendleton Barbour*, 113–114.

114. *Annals of Congress*, Sixteenth Congress, First Session, 2140–2143 (quotation 2142), 2179.

115. Robert Selden Garnett, *Annals of Congress*, Eighteenth Congress, First Session, 1686. For Clay's response, see 1690, 1691.

116. Henry Clay to Mathew Carey, Washington, 2 January 1824, in *The Pa-*

pers of Henry Clay, ed. James F. Hopkins, Robert Seagar II, Melba Porter Hay, et al., 11 vols. (Lexington: University Press of Kentucky, 1959–1992), Supplement: 166. On Clay's role in the Tariff of 1824, see Robert V. Remini, *Henry Clay: Statesman for the Union* (New York: W. W. Norton, 1991), 228–233.

117. "Much Ado about Nothing," *Niles' Weekly Register* (Baltimore), 15 March 1823.

118. The other members were: Lewis Condict (NJ), Henry William Connor (NC), Hector Craig (NY), Walter Forward (PA), Dudley Marvin (NY), and John C. Wright (OH).

119. Compare the bill from the previous session (*Annals of Congress*, Seventeenth Congress, Second Session, 545), the letter from Richards (Mark Richards to John Tod, Philadelphia, 15 December 1823, Folder 15, Box 9, Tod Papers), and the bill reported by Tod in January 1824 (*Annals of Congress*, Eighteenth Congress, First Session, 961). See also other correspondence in Boxes 9–10 of the Tod Papers.

120. Mathew Carey to John Tod, Philadelphia, 7 December 1822, Folder 6, Box 9, Tod Papers.

121. "From the Columbia (S.C.) Telescope," *Niles' Weekly Register*, 8 September 1827.

122. *Annals of Congress*, Eighteenth Congress, First Session, 1472, 1471.

123. George McDuffie, *Annals of Congress*, Eighteenth Congress, First Session, 2407.

124. Victor du Pont to John Todd [*sic*], Brandywine, 12 December 1823, Box 6, Series A: Correspondence—Outgoing, Group 3: Victor du Pont, Winterthur Manuscripts, Hagley Museum and Library, Wilmington, DE.

125. Jonathan J. Pincus, *Pressure Groups and Politics in Antebellum Tariffs* (New York: Columbia University Press, 1977), 61 (first quotation), 64–66, 70–71 (second quotation). For the Committee of Agriculture report, see *Annals of Congress*, Eighteenth Congress, First Session, 1857–1859.

126. Jeremiah Mason to Daniel Webster, 1 February 1824, in *The Papers of Daniel Webster: Correspondence*, ed. Charles Wiltse, 7 vols. (Hanover, NH: University Press of New England, 1974–1986), 1:352. Merino sheep were an important source of the raw wool used in textile mills. For an overview of the disposition of different agricultural producers toward the tariff during this period, see Paul W. Gates, *The Farmer's Age: Agriculture, 1815–1860* (New York: Holt, Rinehart and Winston, 1960), 322–327.

127. Joel R. Poinsett to Joseph Hopkinson, Washington, [n.d.]; and Joel R. Poinsett to Joseph Hopkinson, Washington, 26 February 1824, both Volume 11, Hopkinson Family Papers, HSP.

128. Louis McLane to J. J. Milligan, Washington, 13 April 1824, Folder 3, Louis McLane Papers, Delaware Historical Society, Wilmington.

129. Charles Hammond to John C. Wright, Cincinnati, 9 April 1824, Charles Hammond Papers, Ohio History Connection, Columbus.

130. "The Tariff Bill," *Niles' Weekly Register*, 10 April 1824.

131. John Blanchard to John Tod, Bellefonte, PA, 5 April 1824, Folder 5, Box 10, Tod Papers.

132. Edward Stanwood, *American Tariff Controversies in the Nineteenth Century*, 2 vols. (Boston, 1903), 1:207.

133. Richard C. Edwards, "Economic Sophistication in Nineteenth Century Congressional Tariff Debates," *Journal of Economic History* 30 (December 1970): 838. For another recent endorsement of Stanwood's opinion and detailed coverage of the debates, see William K. Bolt, "The Tariff in the Age of Jackson" (PhD diss., University of Tennessee, 2010), 128–129, 135–153.

134. Samuel Breck, entry for 23 February 1824, Volume 2: Diary, 1823–1824, Samuel Breck Papers, HSP. For Breck's stance on the tariff, see entry for 16 February 1824.

135. Louis McLane to J. J. Milligan, Washington, 10 April 1824, Folder 3, McLane Papers.

136. Joel R. Poinsett to Joseph Hopkinson, Washington, [n.d.], Volume 11, Hopkinson Family Papers. For similar complaints, from both pro- and anti-tariff men, see John C. Wright to Charles Hammond, Washington, 9 April 1824, Hammond Papers; Andrew Jackson to Rachel Jackson, Washington, 12 April 1824, in *The Papers of Andrew Jackson*, ed. Harold D. Moser, Daniel Feller, et al., 10 vols. to date (Knoxville: University of Tennessee Press, 1980-), 5:393; and Daniel Webster to Edward Everett, 13 February 1824, in Webster, *Papers*, 1:352.

137. Rachel Shelden makes the same point in *Washington Brotherhood*, 26–27, 39.

138. "The Tariff," *Niles' Weekly Register*, 3 April 1824.

139. *Annals of Congress*, Eighteenth Congress, First Session, 1690. As early as 11 February, an opponent of the bill estimated that more than one hundred such petitions had already been received. *Annals of Congress*, Eighteenth Congress, First Session, 1481.

140. Mathew Carey, *Auto Biographical Sketches*, xi. See also Rollin C. Mallary to Mathew Carey, Washington, 5 April 1824, printed in Mathew Carey, *A Political Balance Dedicated to Those Citizens Who Would Not Sacrifice 25 Dollars in 1828 and 1832, to Preserve the Union* (Philadelphia, 1833), 6; and entry for 1 December 1829, in Mathew Carey Diaries 1828–1836, Volume 1: December 1828–30 June 1830, HSP.

141. *Annals of Congress*, Eighteenth Congress, First Session, 1685. To illustrate his point, Garnett recounted an anecdote of "a gentleman in Virginia, who last year sent a parcel of wool to the North to exchange for domestic cloth, and, when the cloth arrived, and the bale was opened, he found in it twelve copies of the Report of the Committee of Manufactures, a book of eighty or a hundred pages—no doubt throw in *gratis*, to make up for the additional cost of the cloth." "It might be questioned," Garnett added dryly, "whether the receiver regarded the present in the same light with the donor."

142. E. I. du Pont to Henry Clay, Wilmington, 13 February 1824, in Clay, *Papers*, 3:638–639.

143. Henry Clay to E. I. du Pont, Washington, 15 February 1824, in Clay, *Papers*, 3:640.

144. Henry Clay to ——, Washington, 15 February 1824, in Clay, *Papers*, 3:639–640.

145. *Annals of Congress*, Eighteenth Congress, First Session, 1578, 2206, 2218; emphasis original.

146. "To C. C. Cambreleng, Esq.," *Aurora General Advertiser*, 23 April 1824.

147. Daniel Webster, quoted in Carl E. Prince and Seth Taylor, "Daniel Webster, the Boston Associates, and the US Government's Role in the Industrializing Process, 1815–1830," *Journal of the Early Republic* 2 (Autumn 1982): 287.

148. Daniel Webster to Ezekiel Webster, Washington, 14 March 1824, in *The Writings and Speeches of Daniel Webster*, 18 vols. (Boston, 1903), 17:347; Daniel Webster to Edward Everett, 13 February 1824, in Webster, *Papers*, 1:352.

149. Thomas Handasyd Perkins to Daniel Webster, 26 January 1824, in Webster, *Papers*, 1:348.

150. Daniel Webster to Nathan Appleton, 29 March 1824, in Webster, *Papers*, 1:464; and Nathan Appleton to ——, 5 April 1861, Folder 1b, Box 9, Appleton Family Papers, MHS (quotation).

151. Nathan Appleton to Samuel Appleton, Boston, 1 May 1824, Folder 13b, Box 3, Appleton Family Papers, MHS.

152. *Annals of Congress*, Eighteenth Congress, First Session, 2026–2068 (quotation 2027).

153. Robert Y. Hayne, *Register of Debates*, Twenty-First Congress, First Session, 49.

154. William Plumer, "Reminiscences of Daniel Webster," 2 April 1853, in Webster, *Writings*, 17:550.

155. See, for examples on both sides of the debate, Nicholas Van Dyke to Victor du Pont, Washington, 26 January 1824, Box 18, Series A: Correspondence—Incoming, Group 3: Victor du Pont, Winterthur Manuscripts, and Robert Y. Hayne to Edward Everett, Washington, 13 April 1824, Reel 2, Edward Everett Papers, MHS.

156. George Featherstonhaugh to Henry Clay, 12 May 1824, in Clay, *Papers*, Supplement: 174. Similarly, Henry Clay to Mathew Carey, Washington, 2 May 1824, in Clay, *Papers*, 3:745. On Webster's role in the Tariff of 1824, see Robert V. Remini, *Daniel Webster: The Man and His Time* (New York: W. W. Norton, 1997), 219–224.

157. Martin Van Buren, "The Autobiography of Martin Van Buren," ed. John C. Fitzpatrick, *Annual Report of the American Historical Association* (Washington, 1918), 2:240. For Jackson's pronouncement, see Andrew Jackson to Littleton H. Coleman, Washington, 26 April 1824, in Jackson, *Papers*, 5:398–400. According to Pennsylvania representative Samuel D. Ingham, Clay also tried the same trick

with Adams: "Mr. Adams and Mr. Clay dined together in 1824 pending the Tariff discussions Mr. A. said he was in favor of a judicious Tariff Mr. C. replied that he preferred an injudicious Tariff, Mr. A added that he meant by judicious, a moderate tariff Mr. C said that he meant by injudicious an immoderate tariff." Samuel D. Ingham to Charles Mowry, Washington, May 1831, Box 3, Samuel D. Ingham Correspondence, Rare Book and Manuscript Library, University of Pennsylvania, Philadelphia. The occasion referred to was probably the same one recorded in the entry for 15 March 1824, in *Memoirs of John Quincy Adams: Comprising Portions of His Diary from 1795 to 1848*, ed. Charles Francis Adams, 12 vols. (Philadelphia, 1874–1877), 6:258–259. Ironically, in the past Clay had called for "a judicious tariff, carefully devised." See "Toast and Response at Public Dinner," 19 May 1821, in Clay, *Papers*, 3:81.

158. "An Inhabitant of the South," in *A Letter to the Honorable James Brown, Senator in Congress from the State of Louisiana, on the Tariff* (Washington, DC, 1823), 23–24. For more on the tariff as an issue in the 1824 election, see Daniel Peart, *Era of Experimentation: American Political Practices in the Early Republic* (Charlottesville: University of Virginia Press, 2014), and Donald Ratcliffe, *The One-Party Presidential Contest: Adams, Jackson, and 1824's Five-Horse Race* (Lawrence: University Press of Kansas, 2015).

159. Pincus, *Pressure Groups and Politics in Antebellum Tariffs*, 68–69.

160. "The Tariff Bill," *Niles' Weekly Register*, 17 April 1824.

161. Thomas Hart Benton, *Thirty Years' View; or, a History of the Working of the American Government for Thirty Years, from 1820 to 1850*, 2 vols. (New York, 1883), 1:34; "Washington, April 17" (from the Washington *National Intelligencer*), *Richmond Enquirer*, 20 April 1824.

162. Extract from undated letter from Washington, *Niles' Weekly Register*, 24 April 1824.

163. Samuel Breck to Isaac Wayne, Washington, 30 April 1824, Folder 48, Box 2, Wayne Family Papers, RBL-UP. In fact, duties on both iron and hemp were subsequently restored to the bill, though at lower levels than had passed the House. The Senate amendments are summarized in Martin Van Buren to Stephen Van Rensselaer, Washington, 6 May 1824, Folder "Van Buren, Martin," Box 15, Lee Kohns Collection, New York Public Library; and Pincus, *Pressure Groups and Politics in Antebellum Tariffs*, 69–70.

164. Elijah H. Mills to Harriette Mills, 3 April 1824, in "Letters of Hon. Elijah H. Mills," ed. Henry Cabot Lodge, *Proceedings of the Massachusetts Historical Society* 19 (1881–1882): 43.

165. The role of a Committee of Conference, which assumes greater importance in subsequent chapters, is explained in Lawrence D. Longley and Walter J. Oleszek, *Bicameral Politics: Conference Committees in Congress* (New Haven, CT: Yale University Press, 1989).

166. Untitled, *Niles' Weekly Register*, 22 May 1824. See also untitled, *Niles' Weekly Register*, 15 May 1824.

167. Thomas M. Coens, "The Formation of the Jackson Party, 1822–1825" (PhD diss., Harvard University, 2004), 54–58, 283–288.

168. Clay, as Speaker, did not vote, although his sentiments were well known.

169. John C. Wright to Charles Hammond, Washington, 22 March 1824, Hammond Papers.

170. The four-vote margin on final passage was achieved in the absence of Maryland Senator Edward Lloyd, an opponent of protection. The previous day, with Lloyd present and voting in the negative, the bill had passed to a third reading by a margin of only three votes; if Jackson and Eaton had switched sides on this roll call, the motion would have been defeated. *Annals of Congress*, Eighteenth Congress, First Session, 736.

171. Charles Hammond to John C. Wright, Cincinnati, 3 May 1824, Hammond Papers. On Jackson's role in the Tariff of 1824, see Van Buren, "The Autobiography of Martin Van Buren," 2:239–242, and Robert V. Remini, *Andrew Jackson and the Course of American Freedom, 1822–1832* (New York: Harper and Row, 1981), 67–71.

172. Henry Clay to Josiah S. Johnston, Ashland, KY, 3 September 1824, in Clay, *Papers*, 3:827.

173. See, for example, *Annals of Congress*, Eighteenth Congress, First Session, 647–649, 1918, and Thomas Cooper, *A Tract on the Proposed Alteration in the Tariff: Submitted to the Consideration of the Members from South Carolina in Congress* (New York, 1824), 4–5. For more on the constitutional objections to protection and their answers, see David P. Currie, *The Constitution in Congress: The Jeffersonians, 1801–1829* (Chicago: University of Chicago Press, 2001), 283–289.

174. John Randolph to James Mercer Garnett, 1 November 1823, Reel 4, Correspondence of John Randolph to James M. Garnett, William Cabell Bruce Collection, Virginia State Library, Richmond.

175. Missouri's three votes for the bill must have been particularly galling given how hard Randolph and other Southerners fought to have her admitted as a slave state. Louisiana's delegation also pressed for a high duty on sugar, although they ultimately voted against the bill as a whole. On regional variations within Southern political economy, see Brian Schoen, "The Burdens and Opportunities of Interdependence: The Political Economies of the Planter Class," in *The Old South's Modern Worlds: Slavery, Region, and Nation in the Age of Progress*, ed. L. Diane Barnes, Brian Schoen, and Frank Towers (Oxford: Oxford University Press, 2011), 78–80.

176. Samuel Breck to Henry C. Carey, Philadelphia, 3 April 1858, Folder 7, Box 11, Gardiner Collection.

177. Nathan Appleton to Samuel Appleton, Boston, 22 May 1824, Folder 13b, Box 3, Appleton Family Papers.

178. *Annals of Congress*, Eighteenth Congress, First Session, 2674–2675.

179. Accounts that cite the reapportionment as decisive include Judith Gold-

stein, *Ideas, Interests, and American Trade Policy* (Ithaca, NY: Cornell University Press, 1993), 51–52; and Stanwood, *American Tariff Controversies in the Nineteenth Century*, 1:200.

180. Samuel Semple to Charles I. du Pont, Steubenville, OH, 31 May 1824, Box 3, Series B: Charles Irénée du Pont, Group 5: Papers of the Children of Victor du Pont, Winterthur Manuscripts.

181. Daniel Webster to Joseph Story, 10 April 1824, in Webster, *Papers*, 1:357.

182. "From the Columbia (S.C.) Telescope," *Niles' Weekly Register*, 8 September 1827.

183. Entry for 17 December 1825, "William P. Brobson Diary," 140–141.

184. Eleazar Lord to Mathew Carey, Washington, 18 February 1820, Folder 4, Box 23, Gardiner Collection.

185. Shankman, "Neither Infinite Wretchedness nor Positive Good."

186. Eleazar Lord to Mathew Carey, Washington, 1 March 1820, Folder 4, Box 23, Gardiner Collection.

187. William Lee to Mathew Carey, 28 January 1820, Folder 4, Box 23, Gardiner Collection.

188. Jacob T. Walden to Mathew Carey, New York, 11 March 1820, Folder 3, Box 24, Gardiner Collection.

189. For two essay collections that emphasize the importance of sectionalism in this early period, see Paul Finkelman and Donald R. Kennon, eds., *Congress and the Emergence of Sectionalism: From the Missouri Compromise to the Age of Jackson* (Athens: Ohio University Press, 2008), and John Craig Hammond and Matthew Mason, eds., *Contesting Slavery: The Politics of Bondage and Freedom in the New American Nation* (Charlottesville: University of Virginia Press, 2011).

190. Willie P. Mangum to Seth Jones, Washington, 24 May 1824, in *The Papers of Willie Person Mangum*, ed. Henry Thomas Shanks, 5 vols. (Raleigh, NC: State Department of Archives and History, 1950–1956), 1:146; emphasis original. For a similar assessment, see Virginia representative George Tucker to Peachy R. Gilmer, Washington, 12 May 1824, single folder, Peachy R. Gilmer Papers, VSL.

191. Henry Clay to George Featherstonhaugh, Washington, 26 May 1824, in Clay, *Papers*, Supplement: 176.

Chapter Three: "An Engine of Party Purposes": The Woollens Bill of 1827 and the Tariff of 1828

1. *General Convention, of Agriculturalists and Manufacturers, and Others Friendly to the Encouragement and Support of the Domestic Industry of the United States* (1827).

2. "National Convention," *The Oracle of Dauphin* (Harrisburg, PA), 3 August 1827, cited in W. Kesler Jackson, "Robbers and Incendiaries: Protectionism Organizes at the Harrisburg Convention of 1827," *Libertarian Papers* 2 (2010): 13.

3. Louis McLane to the editors of the *American Watchman*, 2 July 1827, *Niles' Weekly Register* (Baltimore), 7 July 1827.

4. *Register of Debates*, Nineteenth Congress, Second Session, 861.

5. J. Leander Bishop, *A History of American Manufactures from 1608 to 1860*, 2 vols. (Philadelphia, 1861–1864), 2:313–314.

6. "Woollen Manufactures," *Niles' Weekly Register*, 6 January 1827.

7. For Webster's shares, see Carl E. Prince and Seth Taylor, "Daniel Webster, the Boston Associates, and the US Government's Role in the Industrializing Process, 1815–1830," *Journal of the Early Republic* 2 (Autumn 1982): 296. That article, along with Robert F. Dalzell, *Enterprising Elite: The Boston Associates and the World They Made* (Cambridge, MA: Harvard University Press, 1987), provides useful background on New England's conversion from commerce to manufacturing.

8. Daniel Webster to John C. Wright, Boston, 12 October 1826, in *The Papers of Daniel Webster: Correspondence*, ed. Charles Wiltse, 7 vols. (Hanover, NH: University Press of New England, 1974–1986), 2:133. On Webster's role in the Tariff of 1827, see Robert V. Remini, *Daniel Webster: The Man and His Time* (New York: W. W. Norton, 1997), 270–273.

9. Circular letter, Boston, 10 November 1826, reprinted in "Woollen Manufactures," *Niles' Weekly Register*, 25 November 1826. See also "Manufacturers Meeting," 4 November 1826, and "Woollen Manufactures," 11 November 1826, both in *Niles' Weekly Register*.

10. "Lewis Tappan, the Tariff and Slavery," *The Real Cause of the US Civil War*, http://civilwarcause.com/tappan/tappan.html, makes a persuasive case that Tappan was instrumental in securing Webster a financial stake in the Nashua Manufacturing Company, the largest textile factory in New Hampshire.

11. Joseph T. Buckingham, *Personal Memoirs and Recollections of Editorial Life*, 2 vols. (Boston, 1852), 2:8; emphasis original.

12. Mathew Carey to Daniel Webster, Philadelphia, 9 April 1833, in Webster, *Papers*, 3:239. The other two signatories were James M. Robbins and Joshua Clapp.

13. Victor du Pont to Samuel Breck, Brandywine, 11 February 1824, No. 225, Box 2, Breck Family Papers, Library Company of Philadelphia. Du Pont had urged the same point on Tod, but without success. Victor du Pont to John Todd [*sic*], Brandywine, 12 December 1823, Box 6, Series A: Correspondence—Outgoing, Group 3: Victor du Pont, Winterthur Manuscripts, Hagley Museum and Library, Wilmington, DE.

14. Callender Irvine to Christopher Vandeventer, Philadelphia, 21 April 1824, in *The Papers of John C. Calhoun*, ed. Robert L. Meriweather, W. Edwin Hemphill, Shirley A. Book, Clyde N. Wilson, et al., 28 vols. (Columbia: University of South Carolina Press, 1959–2003), 9:43–44.

15. Memorial adopted at meeting of 23 October 1826, reprinted in "Woollen Manufactures," *Niles' Weekly Register*, 18 November 1826, and remarks by Jonas B. Brown at meeting of 7 November, reported in *United States Gazette* (Philadelphia), 14 November 1826.

16. The other members were Lewis Condict (NJ, administration), Henry Connor (NC, Jackson), John Davis (MA, administration), James Stevenson (PA, Jackson), Bartow White (NY, administration), and Charles A. Wickliffe (KY, Jackson). Mallary supported the administration.

17. Aaron Tufts, quoted in "On the Subject of the Tariff, or Regulating Duties on Imports," House of Representatives Report No. 843, Twentieth Congress, First Session, 812. See also Jonas B. Brown to Victor du Pont, Washington, 14 January 1827, Box 18, Series A: Correspondence—Incoming, Group 3: Victor du Pont, Winterthur Manuscripts, and John Varnum to Leverett Saltonstall, Washington, 2 February 1827, Folder "1827–1831," Box 1, Varnum Family Papers II, Massachusetts Historical Society, Boston.

18. Under the provisions of the bill, wool products of less than 40 cents in value would be deemed to cost 40 cents, those of between 40 cents and $2.50 would be deemed to cost $2.50, and those of between $2.50 and $4.00 would be deemed to cost $4.00. *Register of Debates*, Nineteenth Congress, Second Session, 732–733.

19. Abbott Lawrence, quoted in "Manufacturers' Meeting" (from the *Boston Courier*), *United States Gazette*, 15 June 1827.

20. *Register of Debates*, Nineteenth Congress, Second Session, 745.

21. *Register of Debates*, Nineteenth Congress, Second Session, 1094.

22. *Register of Debates*, Nineteenth Congress, Second Session, 998, 1066–1067.

23. Joseph Lawrence, *Register of Debates*, Nineteenth Congress, Second Session, 1067. The crucial vote is recorded on 1098–1099. See also John Varnum to Leverett Saltonstall, Washington, 11 February 1827, Folder "1827–1831," Box 1, Varnum Family Papers II.

24. "Secret [illegible]" signed "A New Yorker" (from the Utica [illegible]), *We the People* (Washington, DC), 8 November 1828; emphasis original. My thanks to Donald Ratcliffe for providing me with a copy of this article.

25. *Register of Debates*, Nineteenth Congress, Second Session, 997.

26. Michael Hoffman, *Register of Debates*, Nineteenth Congress, Second Session, 997.

27. Jonas B. Brown, quoted in "From the Columbia (S.C.) Telescope," *Niles' Weekly Register*, 8 September 1827; emphasis original.

28. For a charge that the Woollens Bill was designed to favor large over small manufacturers, see Robert Y. Hayne to Andrew Jackson, Charleston, 5 June 1827, in *The Papers of Andrew Jackson*, ed. Harold D. Moser, Daniel Feller, et al., 10 vols. to date (Knoxville: University of Tennessee Press, 1980–), 6:332–335.

29. Jonas B. Brown to Victor du Pont, Washington, 14 January 1827, Box 18, Series A: Correspondence—Incoming, Group 3: Victor du Pont, Winterthur Manuscripts.

30. Copy of Jonas B. Brown to Victor du Pont, Washington, 18 January 1827, Box 6, Series A: Correspondence—Outgoing, Group 3: Victor du Pont, Winterthur Manuscripts.

31. Victor du Pont to Mathew Carey, 20 January 1827, Box 6, Series A: Correspondence—Outgoing, Group 3: Victor du Pont, Winterthur Manuscripts.

32. Victor du Pont to Jonas B. Brown, Brandywine, 27 January 1827, Box 6, Series A: Correspondence—Outgoing, Group 3: Victor du Pont, Winterthur Manuscripts.

33. Mathew Carey, *Auto Biographical Sketches: In a Series of Letters Addressed to a Friend* (Philadelphia, 1829), 71.

34. Mathew Carey, circular letter, Philadelphia, 14 June 1827, Historical Society of Pennsylvania, Philadelphia.

35. Mathew Carey, *Auto Biographical Sketches*, 14–15n.

36. Victor du Pont to Jonas B. Brown, Brandywine, 27 January 1827, Box 6, Series A: Correspondence—Outgoing, Group 3: Victor du Pont, Winterthur Manuscripts.

37. For Carey's publishing, see "Colbert" [Mathew Carey], Second Series, Philadelphia, 22 January–8 February 1827, LCP. For his skepticism, see Mathew Carey, circular letter, Philadelphia, 14 June 1827, HSP.

38. Henry Clay to George Featherstonhaugh, Lexington, 10 October 1824, in *The Papers of Henry Clay*, ed. James F. Hopkins, Robert Seagar II, Melba Porter Hay, et al., 11 vols. (Lexington: University Press of Kentucky, 1959–1992), Supplement: 181; emphasis original.

39. William K. Bolt, *Tariff Wars and the Politics of Jacksonian America* (Nashville, TN: Vanderbilt University Press, 2017), 63. Bolt's "The Tariff in the Age of Jackson" (PhD diss., University of Tennessee, 2010), 201n21, references two biographies of Calhoun that share this view.

40. Ephraim Bateman of New Jersey, for example, had voted for both the Tariff of 1816 and Baldwin's Bill in 1820 as a member of the House, while Calvin Willey of Connecticut and Dudley Chase of Vermont would both vote in favor of even higher duties in 1828.

41. *Senate Journal*, Nineteenth Congress, Second Session, 244, 245–246.

42. Martin Van Buren, "The Autobiography of Martin Van Buren," ed. John C. Fitzpatrick, *Annual Report of the American Historical Association* (Washington, 1918), 2:169; "Secret [illegible]" signed "A New Yorker" (from the Utica [illegible]), *We the People*, 8 November 1828.

43. James Buchanan to Thomas Elder, Washington, 13 February 1827, Folder 27, Box 52, James Buchanan Papers, HSP.

44. "Secret [illegible]" signed "A New Yorker" (from the Utica [illegible]), *We the People*, 8 November 1828.

45. Daniel Webster to William Plumer Jr., Washington, 11 February 1827, in Webster, *Papers*, 2:156; emphasis original.

46. Andrew Stewart to John Tod, Washington, 13 January 1827, Folder 1, Box 11, John Tod Papers, Pennsylvania State Archives, Harrisburg.

47. Thomas Clayton to William B. Brobson, Washington, 10 February 1827, Folder 4, Box 1, Brobson Family Papers, Delaware Historical Society, Wilmington.

48. Robert Young Hayne to Andrew Jackson, Charleston, 5 June 1827, in Jackson, *Papers*, 6:334–335; emphasis original. For a similar attempt to distinguish between Jackson-supporting and Adams-supporting protectionists, which aligns the former with the temporary and limited protectionism advocated by Alexander James Dallas's 1816 report, see William C. Rives to "Gilmer," Castle Hill, VA, 22 July 1827, Folder "July 1827," Box 44, William C. Rives Papers, Library of Congress, Washington, DC.

49. Mathew Carey, *Auto Biographical Sketches*, 126.

50. Mathew Carey, *Auto Biographical Sketches*, 123–124.

51. "At a Meeting of the Pennsylvania Society for the Promotion of Manufactures and the Mechanic Arts, Held in Philadelphia, on the 14th Day of May, 1827," *United States Gazette*, 25 May 1827.

52. See Lewis Tappan, entry for 5 June 1827, Journals and Notebooks, 1814–1869, Reel 1, Lewis Tappan Papers, LC; and Mathew Carey, circular letter, Philadelphia, 14 June 1827, HSP. This point has escaped many historians, who merely credit Carey and the Pennsylvania Society. Bolt erroneously attributes the plan to the editor of the Pennsylvania *Washington Reporter*, but the article he refers to, published on 30 April, makes no mention of a national convention; that only appears in a follow-up piece one week after the Pennsylvania Society's meeting. Bolt, *Tariff Wars*, 67; John Austin Moore, "Interests and Ideas: Industrialization and the Making of Early American Trade Policy, 1789–1860" (PhD diss., Wayne State University, 2013), 223; Lawrence A. Peskin, *Manufacturing Revolution: The Intellectual Origins of Early American Industry* (Baltimore: Johns Hopkins University Press, 2003), 216; Edward Stanwood, *American Tariff Controversies in the Nineteenth Century*, 2 vols. (Boston, 1903), 1:264.

53. Richard Rush to Charles J. Ingersoll, Washington, 5 September 1827, Folder 1, Box 4, Charles Jared Ingersoll Papers, HSP.

54. *Mercury* (Pittsburgh), 31 July 1827, cited in Malcolm Rogers Eiselen, *The Rise of Pennsylvania Protectionism* (Philadelphia: Porcupine Press, 1974, reprint of 1932 edition), 77. For the original letter, see Amos Kendall to Henry Baldwin, Frankfort, 15 July 1827, Henry Baldwin Papers, Lawrence Lee Pelletier Library, Allegheny College, Meadville, PA.

55. John C. Calhoun to James E. Colhoun, Pendleton, 26 August 1827, in Calhoun, *Papers*, 10:304.

56. Andrew Judson to Gideon Welles, Connecticut, 9 July 1827, Reel 8, Gideon Welles Papers, LC. See also "Obediah Penn" to Henry Clay, [c. 19] June 1827, in Clay, *Papers*, 6:696–698.

57. *Democratic Press* (Philadelphia), 31 May 1827, cited in Eiselen, *The Rise of Pennsylvania Protectionism*, 77–78.

58. Mathew Carey to the editors of the *National Intelligencer*, Philadelphia, 12 July 1827, reprinted in "Meetings on the Wollens [sic] Bill &c.," *Niles' Weekly Register*, 21 July 1827.

59. Untitled editorial, *Niles' Weekly Register*, 28 July 1827; emphasis original.

60. Carey had agreed to serve on Clay's electoral ticket in Pennsylvania in 1824, but only in the final weeks of the campaign after previously resisting efforts to enlist his help. Daniel Peart, *Era of Experimentation: American Political Practices in the Early Republic* (Charlottesville: University of Virginia Press, 2014), 131. Niles declined an appointment under the Adams administration because he believed it would interfere with the effectiveness of his *Weekly Register*, which was "pledged" in "support of the 'American system,'" rather than to any political favorite. Hezekiah Niles to Henry Clay, Baltimore, 2 April 1828, in Clay, 7:210.

61. Henry Clay to Benjamin W. Crowninshield, Washington, 18 March 1827, in Clay, *Papers*, 6:319–320.

62. Mathew Carey to Henry Clay, Philadelphia, 15 May 1827; and Henry Clay to Mathew Carey, Washington, 19 May 1827, both in Clay, *Papers*, 6:563, 568.

63. Richard Rush to Charles J. Ingersoll, Washington, 5 September 1827, Folder 1, Box 4, Ingersoll Papers.

64. Richard Rush to Charles J. Ingersoll, Washington, 28 May 1827 (quotation); and Richard Rush to Charles J. Ingersoll, Washington, 10 June 1827 (offer of help), both Folder 1, Box 4, Ingersoll Papers.

65. Thomas H. Baird to Henry Clay, Washington, PA, 24 May 1827, in Clay, *Papers*, 6:587.

66. Peter B. Porter to Henry Clay, Black Rock, 11 July 1827, in Clay, *Papers*, 6:760.

67. Daniel Webster to John W. Taylor, Boston, 19 June 1827; and Daniel Webster to Ezekiel Webster, 11 June, 12 July, and 20 July 1827, all in Webster, *Papers*, 2:218, 222–223, 229, 484.

68. "The Autobiography of Martin Van Buren," 2:171. For the partisan calculations that prompted Van Buren's appearance, see William L. Marcy to Martin Van Buren, Batavia, NY, 25 June 1827; and Albany, 29 January 1828, both Reel 7, Martin Van Buren Papers, LC.

69. "National Interests" (from the Albany *Argus*), *United States Gazette*, 14 July 1827.

70. E. I. du Pont to John Torbert, 21 June 1827, in *Life of Eleuthere Irénée du Pont from Contemporary Correspondence*, ed. B. G. du Pont, 11 vols. (Newark: University of Delaware Press, 1923–1927), 11:181–183; John A. Munroe, *Louis McLane: Federalist and Jacksonian* (New Brunswick, NJ: Rutgers University Press, 1973), 215–216.

71. Hezekiah Niles to E. I. du Pont, Baltimore, 26 June 1827, Box 6, Series A: Correspondence—Incoming, Group 3: Eleuthere Irénée du Pont, Longwood Manuscripts, HM&L; Eiselen, *The Rise of Pennsylvania Protectionism*, 75.

72. Reeve Huston, "Popular Movements and Party Rule: The New York Anti-Rent Wars and the Jacksonian Political Order," in *Beyond the Founders: New*

Approaches to the Political History of the Early American Republic, ed. Jeffrey L. Pasley, Andrew W. Robertson, and David Waldstreicher (Chapel Hill: University of North Carolina Press, 2004).

73. Mathew Carey, *Auto Biographical Sketches*, 131; emphasis original.

74. Mathew Carey, *Auto Biographical Sketches*, 135. This maneuver, which presumably took place in committee, is not reported in the official journal of the convention but is hinted at by the recording of a retaliatory motion on the floor by James Ronaldson, a friend of Carey's, to strike Ingersoll's name from the list of delegates, which was negatived. *Journal of a Convention of Delegates of the State of Pennsylvania, Held for the Promotion of the State Agricultural and Manufacturing Interests, at the Capitol in Harrisburg, on Wednesday, the 27th of June, A. D. 1827* (1827), 15–16.

75. "Communication," signed "M. Carey," *United States Gazette*, 16 January 1828. For more on this dispute, see Charles J. Ingersoll, J. J. Borie, Samuel Wetherill, and Redwood Fisher to Mathew Carey, Philadelphia, 3 July 1827, Folder 17, Box 22, Edward Carey Gardiner Collection, HSP, and Mathew Carey, circular letter, Philadelphia, 7 July 1827, HSP. For the proceedings of the state convention, see *Journal of a Convention of Delegates of the State of Pennsylvania*.

76. "From One of the Editors," *United States Gazette*, 1 August 1827.

77. The states represented, with number of delegates in parentheses, were: Connecticut (six), Delaware (five), Kentucky (four), Maryland (eight), Massachusetts (seven), New York (eighteen), New Hampshire (five), New Jersey (ten), Ohio (eight), Pennsylvania (sixteen), Rhode Island (four), Vermont (five), and Virginia (two). Maine also appointed five delegates, but they did not have time to attend. *General Convention, of Agriculturalists and Manufacturers*, 5.

78. The two senators did decline to sign the memorial produced by the convention, though the four representatives all signed.

79. Two of those present, Walter Forward and Thomas Ewing, would go on to serve as Secretary of the Treasury; it would have been three if Louis McLane had consented to attend.

80. Untitled editorial, *Niles' Weekly Register*, 11 August 1827.

81. "Harrisburg Convention," *United States Gazette*, 7 August 1827.

82. Friedrich List, *Outlines of American Political Economy, in a Series of Letters Addressed by Frederick List, Esq. Late Professor of Political Economy at the University of Tubingen in Germany, to Charles J. Ingersoll, Vice-President of the Pennsylvania Society for the Promotion of Manufactures and the Mechanic Arts* (Philadelphia, 1827), 6. List's writings prompted one anti-tariff congressmen to comment sarcastically, "[W]e appear to have imported a Professor from Germany, in absolute violation of the doctrines of the American System, to lecture upon its lessons." James Hamilton Jr., *Register of Debates*, Twentieth Congress, First Session, 2432. For more on List, see Margaret E. Hirst, *Life of Friedrich List and Selections from His Writings* (London, 1909).

83. Mathew Carey, quoted in "Harrisburg Convention," *United States Gazette*, 7 August 1827.

84. *General Convention, of Agriculturalists and Manufacturers*, 1–2.

85. Edward Gray to Mathew Carey, Patapsco, MD, 30 August 1827, quoted in Mathew Carey, *Auto Biographical Sketches*, 136; emphasis original.

86. "Memoirs of a Senator from Pennsylvania: Jonathan Roberts, 1771–1854," ed. Philip S. Klein, *Pennsylvania Magazine of History and Biography* 62 (October 1938): 507–508 (quotations 508); Mathew Carey, *Auto Biographical Sketches*, 135–140 (quotation 139).

87. *General Convention, of Agriculturalists and Manufacturers*, 9.

88. Mathew Carey, circular letter, Philadelphia, 14 June 1827, HSP.

89. Hezekiah Niles to Charles J. Ingersoll, Baltimore, 22 August 1827, Folder 13, Box 2, Ingersoll Papers.

90. Hezekiah Niles to William Darlington, Baltimore, 17 September 1827, Reel 1, Letters to William Darlington from J. J. Wilson and H. Niles (copy of items at the Library of Congress), Francis Harvey Green Library, West Chester University, PA.

91. Untitled editorial, *Niles' Weekly Register*, 13 October 1827; emphasis original. The address is published in the same issue, and also in *General Convention, of Agriculturalists and Manufacturers*, 11–76.

92. Untitled editorial, *Niles' Weekly Register*, 11 August 1827.

93. See, for example, [Henry Lee], *Report of a Committee of the Citizens of Boston and Vicinity, Opposed to a Further Increase of Duties on Importations* (Boston, 1828), and "A Pennsylvanian," *An Examination of the Report of a Committee of the Citizens of Boston and Its Vicinity, Opposed to a Further Increase of Duties on Importation* (Philadelphia, 1828).

94. For these meetings, see *Niles' Weekly Register*, and *United States Gazette*, September–December 1827.

95. Untitled editorial, *Niles' Weekly Register*, 11 August 1827.

96. "From the Columbia (S.C.) Telescope," *Niles' Weekly Register*, 8 September 1827.

97. David Trimble to Henry Clay, Greenupsburg, KY, 25 April 1828, in Clay, *Papers*, 7:242–243; emphasis original.

98. James Buchanan to Thomas Elder, Washington, 10 December 1827, Folder 28, Box 52, Buchanan Papers. This was also the hope of administration supporters. See Henry Clay to John J. Crittenden, Washington, 16 December 1827, in Clay, *Papers*, 6:1362–1364.

99. Merrill D. Peterson, *The Great Triumvirate: Webster, Clay, and Calhoun* (Oxford: Oxford University Press, 1987), 159.

100. Moore, "Interests and Ideas," 265; Sidney Ratner, *The Tariff in American History* (New York: D. Van Nostrand, 1972), 16; Charles Sellers, *The Market Revolution: Jacksonian America, 1815–1846* (Oxford: Oxford University Press,

1991), 296; F. W. Taussig, *The Tariff History of the United States* (New York, 1888), 88–89.

101. This interpretation was first advanced by Robert V. Remini, "Martin Van Buren and the Tariff of Abominations," *American Historical Review* 63 (July 1958): 903–917, and is endorsed by Bolt, *Tariff Wars*, 76–77; John Niven, *Martin Van Buren: The Romantic Age of American Politics* (Oxford: Oxford University Press, 1983), 199; and Peterson, *The Great Triumvirate*, 159–161.

102. *Register of Debates*, Twentieth Congress, First Session, 2472.

103. George W. Buchanan to James Buchanan, Chambersburg, PA, 20 July 1827, Folder 1, Box 2, Buchanan Papers.

104. Charles Hammond to Henry Clay, Cincinnati, 10 August 1827, in Clay, *Papers*, 6:877.

105. "The American System," *Niles' Weekly Register*, 19 January 1828.

106. Entries for 30 November 1827 and 3 December 1827, Henry R. Storrs Private Journal, Volume 4: 30 November 1827–8 December 1828, Buffalo History Museum.

107. John C. Calhoun, *Register of Debates*, Twenty-Fourth Congress, Second Session, 905.

108. William C. Rives to Judith P. Rives, Washington, 3 December 1827, Folder "1827" (2), Box 21, Rives Papers. See also Martin Van Buren to William C. Rives, Albany, 17 October 1827, and William C. Rives, "Extract of a Letter to Mr. Van Buren," 31 October 1827, both Folder "October 1827," Box 44, Rives Papers.

109. Entry for 30 November 1827, Henry R. Storrs Private Journal, Volume 4: 30 November 1827–8 December 1828. For similar reports, see entry for 5 December 1827, in *Memoirs of John Quincy Adams, Comprising Portions of His Diary from 1795 to 1848*, ed. Charles Francis Adams, 12 vols. (Philadelphia, 1874–1877), 7:369, and John C. Wright to Charles Hammond, Washington, 6 December 1827, Charles Hammond Papers, Ohio History Connection, Columbus.

110. An ill John Randolph informed a friend that "nothing but the election of Speaker could have brought me here now." John Randolph to J. R. Bryan, Washington, 5 December 1827, Section 8, Grinnan Family Papers, Virginia Historical Society, Richmond.

111. Entry for 12 December 1827, Henry R. Storrs Private Journal, Volume 4: 30 November 1827–8 December 1828.

112. Entry for 8 December 1827, Henry R. Storrs Private Journal, Volume 4: 30 November 1827–8 December 1828.

113. Entry for 11 December 1827, Henry R. Storrs Private Journal, Volume 4: 30 November 1827–8 December 1828. Very similar is Henry R. Storrs to [illegible], Washington, 11 December 1827, single folder, Henry Randolph Storrs Letters, New-York Historical Society. The other members were Lewis Condict (NJ, administration), William D. Martin (SC, Jackson), Thomas P. Moore (KY, Jackson), James S. Stevenson (PA, Jackson), William Stanbery (OH, Jackson), and Silas Wright (NY, Jackson). All but Martin represented pro-tariff constituencies, though

Moore and Stevenson had both voted against the Woollens Bill in the previous session.

114. Of Mallary, Storrs commented, "to say nothing of a particular habit of Mr. M. that unfits him half the time at least for any business, his talents were hardly above mediocrity and his personal weight in the House was nothing. He became too excessively conceited with the appointment and listened to no advice." Entry for 27 December 1827, Henry R. Storrs Private Journal, Volume 4: 30 November 1827–8 December 1828.

115. Entry for 26 March 1828, Henry R. Storrs Private Journal, Volume 4: 30 November 1827–8 December 1828. Another New York congressman, in conversation with John Quincy Adams, called Wright "a tool of Van Buren." Stephen Van Rensselaer, quoted in entry for 3 January 1828, in Adams, *Memoirs*, 7:397.

116. Silas Wright to Azariah C. Flagg, 13 December 1827, Azariah C. Flagg Papers, New York Public Library. On Wright's role in the Tariff of 1828, see John Arthur Garraty, *Silas Wright* (New York: Columbia University Press, 1949), 51–67.

117. Rollin C. Mallary, *Register of Debates*, Twentieth Congress, First Session, 862.

118. George B. Galloway, *History of the House of Representatives*, 2nd ed., revised by Sidney Wise (New York: Thomas Y. Crowell, 1976), 87. According to one member, this power had never before been delegated to a committee not tasked with a judicial matter. John C. Wright, *Register of Debates*, Twentieth Congress, First Session, 862.

119. *Register of Debates*, Twentieth Congress, First Session, 862.

120. *Register of Debates*, Twentieth Congress, First Session, 878–879, 863–864.

121. Andrew Stewart, *Register of Debates*, Twentieth Congress, First Session, 864.

122. *Register of Debates*, Twentieth Congress, First Session, 889–890.

123. E. I. du Pont to Andrew Gray, 6 January [1828], Box 3, Series A: Correspondence—Outgoing, Group 4: Eleuthere Irénée du Pont, Winterthur Manuscripts. See, likewise, [incomplete, no signature] to Jonathan Roberts, Washington, 12 January 1828, Folder 23, Box 3, Jonathan Roberts Papers, HSP, and "Sending for Persons and Papers," *United States Gazette*, 4 March 1828.

124. Elisha Whittlesey to Peter Hitchcock, Washington, 29 January 1828, Peter Hitchcock Papers, Western Reserve Historical Society, Cleveland, OH. My thanks to Donald Ratcliffe for providing me with a copy of this letter. On the Jacksonian committee members' selection of witnesses sympathetic to their plans for the tariff, see also Silas Wright to Azariah C. Flagg, Washington, 16 January 1828, Folder 10, Box 4, Flagg Papers.

125. Condict's two witnesses, Joseph Jackson and John Travers, would, respectively, participate in the New York Tariff Convention of 1831 and the Home League national convention in 1842.

126. Entry for 20 January 1828, Henry R. Storrs Private Journal, Volume 4: 30 November 1827–8 December 1828.

127. "Letter from the Senior Editor," Washington, 24 January 1828, *Niles' Weekly Register*, 26 January 1828. For the names and testimony of those examined, see "On the Subject of the Tariff," House of Representatives Report No. 843.

128. Elisha Whittlesey to Peter Hitchcock, Washington, 29 January 1828, Hitchcock Papers. For du Pont's experience with the committee, see E. I. du Pont de Nemours and Company to Francis Gurney Smith, Washington, 29 January 1828, and E. I. du Pont de Nemours and Company to Francis Gurney Smith, 31 January 1828, both in Letterbook: 30 May 1827–21 April 1829, No. 1: Letterbooks, Series A: Letters Sent, Part I: Correspondence, Records of E. I. du Pont de Nemours and Company, HM&L.

129. Entry for 20 January 1828, Henry R. Storrs Private Journal, Volume 4: 30 November 1827–8 December 1828.

130. Elisha Whittlesey to Peter Hitchcock, Washington, 29 January 1828, Hitchcock Papers.

131. Entry for 20 January 1828, Henry R. Storrs Private Journal, Volume 4: 30 November 1827–8 December 1828.

132. William L. Marcy to Martin Van Buren, Albany, 29 January 1828, Reel 7, Van Buren Papers. See, similarly, Azariah C. Flagg to Silas Wright, Albany, 10 January 1828, Folder 10, Box 4, Flagg Papers.

133. William B. Fordney to James Buchanan, Lancaster, 15 April 1828, Folder 4, Box 2, Buchanan Papers.

134. *Senate Journal*, Twentieth Congress, First Session, 385 (New York); Supplement to *Niles' Weekly Register*, 12 January 1828 (Pennsylvania).

135. Entry for 20 January 1828, Henry R. Storrs Private Journal, Volume 4: 30 November 1827–8 December 1828. And, likewise, Elisha Whittlesey to Peter Hitchcock, Washington, 29 January 1828, Hitchcock Papers.

136. *Massachusetts Journal* (Boston), quoted in Remini, "Martin Van Buren and the Tariff of Abominations," 907.

137. *National Journal* (Washington), quoted in Remini, "Martin Van Buren and the Tariff of Abominations," 908.

138. *Register of Debates*, Twentieth Congress, First Session, 1274 (bill reported), 1727–1729 (details).

139. In the case of grain farmers, the increased duty on molasses would reduce competition for their home-distilled whiskey from rum-makers. Silas Wright explained the design of the bill in a letter to Azariah C. Flagg, Washington, 7 April 1828, Folder 10, Box 4, Flagg Papers.

140. Michael Hoffman to Azariah C. Flagg, Washington, 3 February 1828, Folder 2, Box 4, Flagg Papers.

141. Entry for 6 May 1828, in Adams, *Memoirs*, 7:531.

142. Entry for 1 February 1828, Henry R. Storrs Private Journal, Volume 4: 30 November 1827–8 December 1828.

143. Henry Clay to Peter B. Porter, Washington, 1 March 1828, in Clay, *Papers*, 7:136.

144. Untitled editorial, *Niles' Weekly Register*, 15 March 1828.

145. Peter Paul Francis Degrand to Daniel Webster, Philadelphia, 7 April 1828, in Webster, *Papers*, 2:327; emphasis original.

146. Abbott Lawrence to Amos Lawrence, Washington, 2 and 3 February 1828, both Folder "1828 1–10 Feb," Box 1, Amos Lawrence Papers, MHS; Silas Wright to Azariah C. Flagg, Washington, 13 April 1828, Folder 10, Box 4, Flagg Papers.

147. Peleg Sprague, *Register of Debates*, Twentieth Congress, First Session, 2055. For Carey's resignation, see Mathew Carey, "To the Members of the Pennsylvania Society for the Promotion of Manufactures and the Mechanic Arts" (circular letter), 31 December 1827, HSP. And for the Philadelphia meeting, see "Manufacturers' Meeting," *United States Gazette*, 26 February 1828.

148. Henry Clay to George Featherstonhaugh, Washington, 18 February 1828, in Clay, *Papers*, 7:102.

149. David Barker to Daniel Hoit, Washington, 22 February 1828, Box 67, Daniel Hoit Papers, David M. Rubenstein Rare Book and Manuscript Library, Duke University, Durham, NC.

150. Henry Clay to John J. Crittenden, Washington, 14 February 1828, in Clay, *Papers*, 7:95.

151. Remini, "Martin Van Buren and the Tariff of Abominations," 910.

152. Willis Alston to Willie P. Mangum, Washington, 16 March 1828, in *The Papers of Willie Person Mangum*, ed. Henry Thomas Shanks, 5 vols. (Raleigh, NC: State Department of Archives and History, 1950–1956), 1:324.

153. *Register of Debates*, Twenty-Fourth Congress, Second Session, 921. In this speech, given a decade later, Wright actually refers to Warren R. Davis, another South Carolinian, but he must have been mistaken, for it was Martin who served on the committee.

154. James Gordon Bennett, report of a conversation with Silas Wright, in entry for 12 June 1831, Diary, June–August 1831, James Gordon Bennett Papers, NYPL.

155. For the newspaper clipping and Storrs's annotated comments, see entry for 5 June 1828, Henry R. Storrs Private Journal, Volume 4: 30 November 1827–8 December 1828.

156. *Register of Debates*, Twenty-Fourth Congress, Second Session, 905–906. Calhoun admitted: "I speak not of my own personal knowledge" but insisted that "it was generally so understood at the time; and I was informed by individuals who had a right to know, and who consulted with me what course, under the pressing difficulties of our situation, ought to be adopted, that such was the fact." Storrs believed Calhoun to be intimately involved. See his entry for 15 April 1828, Henry R. Storrs Private Journal, Volume 4: 30 November 1827–8 December 1828.

157. *Register of Debates*, Twentieth Congress, First Session, 1729–1749 (quotation 1729, amendment 1748–1749). Mallary's amendment may be compared to the recommendations of the Harrisburg Convention reported in *General Convention, of Agriculturalists and Manufacturers*, 9–10.

158. *Register of Debates*, Twentieth Congress, First Session, 1876.

159. *Register of Debates*, Twentieth Congress, First Session, 2040.

160. *Register of Debates*, Twentieth Congress, First Session, 2038. For just some of the repeated references to the Harrisburg Convention during the congressional debate on the tariff, by both supporters and opponents of the bill, see 742–743, 763, 1979, 1993, 1996, 2090–2091, 2176, 2231, 2257, 2277, 2335, 2346, 2385, 2405, 2446, 2451.

161. Samuel Finley Vinton to Ephraim Cutler, Washington, 28 March 1828, Ephraim Cutler Papers, Legacy Library, Marietta College, OH. My thanks to Donald Ratcliffe for providing me with a copy of this letter.

162. Silas Wright to Azariah C. Flagg, Washington, 7 April 1828, Folder 10, Box 4, Flagg Papers.

163. Entry for 7 April 1828, Henry R. Storrs Private Journal, Volume 4: 30 November 1827–8 December 1828.

164. Charles Miner to Letitia Miner, Washington, 21 March 1828, No. 111, Charles Miner Papers, Luzerne County Historical Society, Wilkes-Barre, PA.

165. John W. Taylor to Jane Taylor, Washington, 3 April 1828, Folder 8, Box 4, John W. Taylor Papers, NYHS.

166. "The Tariff," *Niles' Weekly Register*, 12 April 1828.

167. Samuel D. Ingham, quoted in entry for 6 March 1828, Henry R. Storrs Private Journal, Volume 4: 30 November 1827–8 December 1828.

168. *Register of Debates*, Twentieth Congress, First Session, 2252.

169. *Register of Debates*, Twentieth Congress, First Session, 2090; entry for 9 April 1828, Henry R. Storrs Private Journal, Volume 4: 30 November 1827–8 December 1828.

170. *Register of Debates*, Twentieth Congress, First Session, 2252–2253, quotation on 2253.

171. Entry for 9 April 1828, Henry R. Storrs Private Journal, Volume 4: 30 November 1827–8 December 1828. Remini mistakenly asserts that "the Mallary amendments were defeated *in toto*" and suggests the initiative to amend the bill thereafter came from Van Buren and Wright, whereas, in fact, Mallary willingly accepted Buchanan's wording as a substitute for his own, which forced the Jacksonian leaders into a hasty compromise. See Remini, "Martin Van Buren and the Tariff of Abominations," 912.

172. *House Journal*, Twentieth Congress, First Session, 518–521. In fact, every member of the Committee on Manufactures except Martin voted against this motion, which provides a neat index of protectionist sentiment on the committee.

173. *Register of Debates*, Twentieth Congress, First Session, 2289–2290. For a contemporary account of this episode, which attempts to claim the outcome as

a victory for the Jacksonians, see Michael Hoffman to Azariah C. Flagg, Washington, 27 April 1828, Folder 2, Box 4, Flagg Papers.

174. *Register of Debates*, Twentieth Congress, First Session, 2314.

175. Entry for 9 April 1828, Henry R. Storrs Private Journal, Volume 4: 30 November 1827–8 December 1828.

176. Mahlon Dickerson to Samuel J. Bayard, Suckasunny, NJ, 29 October 1831, Folder 6, Box 2, Mahlon Dickerson and Philemon Dickerson Papers, New Jersey Historical Society, Newark.

177. Henry Clay to Peter B. Porter, Washington, 2 April 1828; and Henry Clay to Peter B. Porter, Washington, 12 April 1828, both in Clay, *Papers*, 7:211–212, 225 (quotation).

178. E. I. du Pont de Nemours and Company to Kensey Johns, 13 April 1828, Letterbook: 30 May 1827–21 April 1829, No. 1: Letterbooks, Series A: Letters Sent, Part I: Correspondence, Records of E. I. du Pont de Nemours and Company.

179. Entry for 9 April 1828, Henry R. Storrs Private Journal, Volume 4: 30 November 1827–8 December 1828.

180. Augustine H. Shepperd to Bartlett Yancey, 17 April 1828, in "Letters to Bartlett Yancey," ed. J. G. De Roulhac Hamilton, *James Sprunt Historical Publications* 10 (1911): 74.

181. Entry for 15 April 1828, Henry R. Storrs Private Journal, Volume 4: 30 November 1827–8 December 1828. Storrs also believed this outcome was "to the great disappointment of their Jackson brethren from the north." Wright, however, seemed pleased by the result, writing, "[M]ay it live through the Senate, but I fear and tremble. We have made a few of the Yankees swallow," and urging his friends in New York to "recommend to the Senate the passage of the bill in its present shape." Silas Wright to Azariah C. Flagg, Washington, 22 April 1828, Flagg Papers.

182. *Register of Debates*, Twentieth Congress, First Session, 2348–2349. If nine of those sixteen New Englanders had voted the other way, the bill would have been lost.

183. Wiley Thompson, *Register of Debates*, Twentieth Congress, First Session, 2446.

184. John C. Wright to Charles Hammond, Washington, 20 April 1828, Hammond Papers. Hammond replied that "our folks did well to vote for the tariff, though they did not like it." Charles Hammond to John C. Wright, Cincinnati, 1 May 1828, Hammond Papers. My thanks to Donald Ratcliffe for providing me with copies of both letters. See also entries for 18 April 1828 and 19 April 1828, Henry R. Storrs Private Journal, Volume 4: 30 November 1827–8 December 1828.

185. *Register of Debates*, Twentieth Congress, First Session, 2471–2472.

186. John Tyler to Henry Curtis, Washington, 1 May 1828, in *The Letters and Times of the Tylers*, ed. Lyon G. Tyler, 3 vols. (Richmond, VA, 1884–1896), 1:387.

187. Entry for 6 May 1828, Henry R. Storrs Private Journal, Volume 4: 30 November 1827–8 December 1828.

188. Daniel Webster to Joseph E. Sprague, Washington, 13 April 1828, in Webster, *Papers*, 2:330; emphasis original. On Webster's role in the Tariff of 1828, see Remini, *Daniel Webster*, 295–299.

189. Entry for 15 April 1828, Henry R. Storrs Private Journal, Volume 4: 30 November 1827–8 December 1828.

190. William C. Rives to Judith P. Rives, Washington, 10 May 1828, Folder "1828" (2), Box 21, Rives Papers.

191. *Senate Journal*, Twentieth Congress, First Session, 356–358 (fourth, fifth, and sixth amendments).

192. Daniel Webster to [Joseph Story], 14 January 1828; Abbott Lawrence to Daniel Webster, Boston, 7 May 1828, both in Webster, *Papers*, 2:278, 342. For details of Lawrence's mission, see his letters to Amos Lawrence, Washington, January–February 1828, Box 1, Amos Lawrence Papers.

193. Joseph Tinker Buckingham to Daniel Webster, Boston, 7 May 1828, in Webster, *Papers*, 2:342.

194. Daniel Webster to James William Paige, 12 May 1828, in Webster, *Papers*, 2:345.

195. "Speech of Mr. Henry Williams, at the Anti-Tariff Caucus in Faneuil Hall, October 31, 1830," *Banner of the Constitution* (New York City), 26 January 1831.

196. Van Buren's remarks reported in entry for 12 May 1828, Henry R. Storrs Private Journal, Volume 4: 30 November 1827–8 December 1828. The text of Van Buren's speech is not recorded, but the New Yorker did present a copy of his instructions to the Senate on 9 May, and on the same day Webster made reference to him having "la[id] his instructions on the Table, and point[ed] to them, as his power of attorney, and as containing the directions for his vote." *Senate Journal*, Twentieth Congress, First Session, 385 (Van Buren); *Register of Debates*, Twentieth Congress, First Session, 750 (Webster). See also "The Autobiography of Martin Van Buren," 2:409.

197. John Tyler to Littleton Tazewell, Gloucester, VA, 8 May 1831, in Tyler, *Letters and Times of the Tylers*, 1:423. See also entry for 4 June 1828, Henry R. Storrs Private Journal, Volume 4: 30 November 1827–8 December 1828, and Niven, *Martin Van Buren*, 388. For more on the instruction of senators by state legislatures during this period, which would also be of importance in the passage of the Tariff of 1846, see Clement Eaton, "Southern Senators and the Right of Instruction, 1789–1860," *Journal of Southern History* 18 (August 1952): 303–319, and C. Edward Skeen, "An Uncertain 'Right': State Legislatures and the Doctrine of Instruction," *Mid-America* 73 (January 1991): 29–47.

198. Entry for 16 May 1828, Henry R. Storrs Private Journal, Volume 4: 30 November 1827–8 December 1828.

199. Untitled editorial (from the *National Journal*), *United States Gazette*, 19 May 1828.

200. Entry for 12 May 1828, Henry R. Storrs Private Journal, Volume 4: 30 November 1827–8 December 1828.

201. "The Tariff" (reprinted from the *Southern Review*, dated November 1828), *The Free Trade Advocate, and Journal of Political Economy* (Philadelphia), 28 February 1829.

202. Remini, "Martin Van Buren and the Tariff of Abominations," 911; Silas Wright to Azariah C. Flagg, Washington, 30 March 1828, Folder 10, Box 4, Flagg Papers. On the same theme, see letters of 20 March, 7 April, and 13 April in same collection.

203. Silas Wright to Azariah C. Flagg, Washington, 21 March 1828, Folder 10, Box 4, Flagg Papers.

204. John C. Calhoun, *Register of Debates*, Twenty-Fourth Congress, Second Session, 905–906. Five years before Calhoun's speech, another Southern politician wrote to Van Buren: "You are accused of inducing the southern members to make [the tariff bill] odious, in order to justify its rejection and then voting its adoption contrary to the pledge made or understood." John Forsyth to Martin Van Buren, 7 July 1832, Van Buren Papers, cited in Niven, *Martin Van Buren*, 320.

205. *Register of Debates*, Twenty-Fourth Congress, Second Session, 921.

206. *Register of Debates*, Twenty-Fourth Congress, Second Session, 906. Remini agrees that if Van Buren had voted the other way, the amendments, and consequently the bill, would have been lost. Remini, "Martin Van Buren and the Tariff of Abominations," 914–915.

207. Remini, "Martin Van Buren and the Tariff of Abominations," 916, 915.

208. *Albany Argus* (New York), 20 May 1828, cited in Remini, "Martin Van Buren and the Tariff of Abominations," 915.

209. Webster attributed the "Tariff of Abominations" label to Maryland senator Samuel Smith, and it was subsequently adopted by the Southern press. *Register of Debates*, Twentieth Congress, First Session, 756.

210. For a narrative of these political developments, see Daniel Walker Howe, *What Hath God Wrought: The Transformation of America, 1815–1848* (Oxford: Oxford University Press, 2007); Donald J. Ratcliffe, "The Crisis of Commercialization: National Political Alignments and the Market Revolution, 1819–1844," in *The Market Revolution in America: Social, Political, and Religious Expressions, 1800–1880*, ed. Melvyn Stokes and Stephen Conway (Charlottesville: University of Virginia Press, 1996); Harry L. Watson, *Liberty and Power: The Politics of Jacksonian America* (New York: Hill and Wang, 1990); and Sean Wilentz, *The Rise of American Democracy: Jefferson to Lincoln* (New York: W. W. Norton, 2005).

211. Littleton Tazewell, quoted in Tyler, *Letters and Times of the Tylers*, 3:69n1.

Chapter Four: "Calculate the Value of the Union": The Tariffs of 1832 and 1833

1. "From the Columbia (S.C.) Telescope," *Niles' Weekly Register* (Baltimore), 8 September 1827. Ironically, Cooper had begun his career as a protectionist; Hezekiah Niles even acknowledged that Cooper's early writings "did not a little

contribute" to his own faith in the policy. "President Cooper and the Tariff," *Niles' Weekly Register*, 20 March 1824. On this point, see Drew R. McCoy, *The Elusive Republic: Political Economy in Jeffersonian America* (New York: W. W. Norton, 1982, pbk edition), 246–247.

2. John C. Calhoun to [Samuel D. Ingham], Pendleton, 28 October 1827, in *The Papers of John C. Calhoun*, ed. Robert L. Meriweather, W. Edwin Hemphill, Shirley A. Book, Clyde N. Wilson, et al., 28 vols. (Columbia: University of South Carolina Press, 1959–2003), 10:312. For his part, Cooper considered Calhoun to be "the author of all the measures we condemn." Thomas Cooper to Gulian C. Verplanck, Columbia, SC, 15 May 1827, Folder 2, Box 3, Gulian C. Verplanck Papers, New-York Historical Society.

3. William Huskisson to John Backhouse, Richmond Terrace, England, 15 June 1829, in "The Papers of Sir Charles R. Vaughan," *American Historical Review* 7 (April 1902): 518.

4. John C. Calhoun to Littleton Waller Tazewell, Pendleton, 25 August 1827, in Calhoun, *Papers*, 10:300, 301.

5. See, for example, John C. Calhoun to Virgil Maxcy, 11 September 1830, in Calhoun, *Papers*, 11:226–229. Also Peter S. Onuf, "The Political Economy of Sectionalism: Tariff Controversies and Conflicting Conceptions of World Order," in *Congress and the Emergence of Sectionalism: From the Missouri Compromise to the Age of Jackson*, ed. Paul Finkelman and Donald R. Kennon (Athens: Ohio University Press, 2008), 66.

6. John C. Calhoun to Andrew Jackson, Pendleton, 10 July 1828, in *The Papers of Andrew Jackson*, ed. Harold D. Moser, Daniel Feller, et al., 10 vols. to date (Knoxville: University of Tennessee Press, 1980–), 6:481.

7. William Smith to Stephen D. Miller, 8 February 1829, William Smith Papers, SCL-UC, cited in Richard E. Ellis, *The Union at Risk: Jacksonian Democracy, States' Rights, and the Nullification Crisis* (Oxford: Oxford University Press, 1987), 44.

8. For more on the Nullification Controversy as context for the making of tariff policy during this period, see Ellis, *The Union at Risk*; William W. Freehling, *The Road to Disunion*, 2 vols. (Oxford: Oxford University Press, 1990–2007), 1:211–286; and Merrill D. Peterson, *Olive Branch and Sword: The Compromise of 1833* (Baton Rouge: Louisiana State University Press, 1982).

9. "Prospectus of the Free Trade Advocate, and Journal of Political Economy," *The Free Trade Advocate, and Journal of Political Economy* (Philadelphia), 3 January 1829. Cooper had voiced a similar concern in his speech.

10. On Raguet's career, see Stephen Meardon, "Negotiating Free Trade in Fact and Theory: The Diplomacy and Doctrine of Condy Raguet," *Journal of the History of Economic Thought* 21 (2014): 41–77.

11. "Anti-Tariff Convention" signed "A Lover of His Country" (reprinted from the New York *Evening Post*), *Banner of the Constitution* (New York City),

27 April 1831; emphasis original. For Sedgwick's authorship, see untitled editorial, *Banner of the Constitution* (Philadelphia), 4 January 1832.

12. "Appendix A: Minutes of the Meeting Referred to, at Page 366, Which Called the Free Trade Convention," in Condy Raguet, *The Principles of Free Trade, Illustrated in a Series of Short and Familiar Essays, Originally Published in the Banner of the Constitution* (Philadelphia, 1840, 2nd edition), 433–434. A narrative of the Free Trade Convention is provided by William S. Belko, *The Triumph of the Antebellum Free Trade Movement* (Gainesville: University Press of Florida, 2012).

13. Alexis de Tocqueville, *Democracy in America*, 2 vols. (1835–1840), vol. 1, ch. 12.

14. For more on the 1820 free trade convention, see Daniel Peart, *Era of Experimentation: American Political Practices in the Early Republic* (Charlottesville: University of Virginia Press, 2014), 86–88. That meeting was cited as precedent for the 1831 convention in untitled editorial, *Banner of the Constitution*, 18 May 1831.

15. Entry for 3 October 1831, in *The Diary of Philip Hone, 1828–1851*, ed. Bayard Tuckerman, 2 vols. (New York, 1889), 1:37–38. For reports of, and commentary on, the selection of delegates to the convention, see *Banner of the Constitution*, and *Niles' Weekly Register*, July–October 1831.

16. Untitled editorial, *Banner of the Constitution*, 21 September 1831.

17. For the proceedings, see *The Journal of the Free Trade Convention, Held in Philadelphia, from September 30 to October 7, 1831; and Their Address to the People of the United States: To Which is Added a Sketch of the Debates in the Convention* (Philadelphia, 1831).

18. The states represented, with number of delegates in parentheses, were: Alabama (eleven), Connecticut (three), Georgia (six), Maine (three), Maryland (four), Massachusetts (nineteen), Mississippi (one), New Jersey (ten), New York (twenty-six), North Carolina (seventeen), Pennsylvania (sixteen), Rhode Island (one), South Carolina (forty-one), Tennessee (two), and Virginia (fifty-two).

19. A contemporary view of divisions within the convention may be found in Job Johnstone to Francis Bernard Higgins, Philadelphia, 4 October 1831, Francis Bernard Higgins Papers, South Caroliniana Library, University of South Carolina, Columbia. Lee's review was *Report of a Committee of the Citizens of Boston and Vicinity, Opposed to a Further Increase of Duties on Importations* (Boston, 1828).

20. Josiah S. Johnston to Henry Clay, Philadelphia, 26 September 1831, in *The Papers of Henry Clay*, ed. James F. Hopkins, Robert Seagar II, Melba Porter Hay, et al., 11 vols. (Lexington: University Press of Kentucky, 1959–1992), 8:406.

21. John C. Calhoun to Samuel D. Ingham, Fort Hill, 31 July 1831; and John C. Calhoun to Francis W. Pickens, Fort Hill, 1 August 1831, both in Calhoun, *Papers*, 11:444, 446.

22. Job Johnstone to Francis Bernard Higgins, Philadelphia, 4 October 1831,

Higgins Papers. On Gallatin's role in the convention, see Raymond Walters Jr., *Albert Gallatin: Jeffersonian Financier and Diplomat* (New York: Macmillan, 1957), 360–362.

23. *The Journal of the Free Trade Convention*, 19–21, 31–41, 61–64; "Free Trade Convention" (from the *Columbia Telescope*), *Banner of the Constitution*, 2 November 1831; letter signed "A Member of the New York Delegation," *Niles' Weekly Register*, 22 October 1831; "Letter of Roger M. Sherman, Esq.," *Banner of the Constitution*, 23 November 1831; entry for 10 October 1831, in *Diary of Philip Hone*, 1:38–39.

24. *The Journal of the Free Trade Convention*, 26–27.

25. *The Journal of the Free Trade Convention*, 71–72.

26. "National Association, of friends of the American System" (from the *Boston Courier*), *Niles' Weekly Register*, 10 September 1831 (quotations). For the May meeting, see "Proceedings of a Convention of Delegates, Appointed by Persons Interested in the Growth and Manufacture of Wool, Held at Clinton Hall, New York," *Banner of the Constitution*, 15 June 1831. For reports of meetings to appoint delegates, see *United States Gazette* (Philadelphia), September–October 1831.

27. The states represented, with number of delegates in parentheses, were: Connecticut (60), Delaware (7), Maine (4), Maryland (34), Massachusetts (62), New Hampshire (20), New Jersey (47), New York (129), Ohio (2), Pennsylvania (100), Rhode Island (30), Vermont (8), Virginia (3), and the District of Columbia (1). For the list of delegates, see *Address of the Friends of Domestic Industry, Assembled in Convention, at New-York, October 26, 1831, to the People of the United States* (Baltimore, 1831). For the proceedings, see Hezekiah Niles, *Journal of the Proceedings of the Friends of Domestic Industry, in General Convention Met at the City of New York, October 26, 1831* (Baltimore, 1831). A subsequent attempt to hold a separate convention for the Western states was abandoned after it failed to generate much interest. See Samuel Breck, entry for 28 October 1831, Volume 4: Diary, 1827–1831, Samuel Breck Papers, Historical Society of Pennsylvania, Philadelphia; untitled editorial, *Banner of the Constitution*, 11 January 1832; "The System in Ohio," *Banner of the Constitution*, 7 March 1832.

28. Samuel Breck, entry for 25 August 1832, Volume 5: Diary, 1832–1833, Breck Papers.

29. "Memoirs of a Senator from Pennsylvania: Jonathan Roberts, 1771–1854," ed. Philip S. Klein, *Pennsylvania Magazine of History and Biography* 62 (October 1938): 510. See also Andrew M. Jones to Benjamin Jones, New York, 28 October 1831, Folder 1, Box 1, Jones and Taylor Family Papers, HSP.

30. Untitled editorial, *United States Gazette*, 3 November 1831; "The Tariff Convention" (reprinted from the New York *Standard*), *Banner of the Constitution*, 9 November 1831; and entry for 31 October 1831, in *Memoirs of John Quincy Adams, Comprising Portions of His Diary from 1795 to 1848*, ed. Charles Francis Adams, 12 vols. (Philadelphia, 1874–1877), 8:416–417.

31. Mathew Carey, *Letters to Messrs. Abbot Laurence* [sic], *Patrick Jackson, and Jonas B. Brown, Boston—Messrs. P. H. Schenck and Erastus Elsworth, New York—Messrs. Samuel Richards and Mark Richards, Philadelphia—Messrs. John M'Kim and H. W. Evans, Baltimore—and Mr. E. I. Dupont, Wilmington,* 5 nos. (Philadelphia, 1832), 5:14n.

32. Hezekiah Niles to E. I. du Pont, printed circular titled "New York Convention of the Friends of American Industry," Baltimore, [November 1831], Box 6, Series A: Correspondence—Incoming, Group 3: Eleuthere Irénée du Pont, Longwood Manuscripts, Hagley Museum and Library, Wilmington, DE.

33. Roberts, "Memoirs of a Senator from Pennsylvania," 510–511; Samuel Breck, entry for 21 August 1832, Volume 5: Diary, 1832–1833, Breck Papers. Ingersoll had prior experience of lobbying the Pennsylvania legislature, of which he was himself a member, on behalf of the Second Bank of the United States. See Stephen W. Campbell, "Funding the Bank War: Nicholas Biddle and the Public Relations Campaign to Recharter the Second Bank of the US, 1828–1832," *American Nineteenth Century History* 17 (September 2016): 281.

34. Untitled editorial, *Banner of the Constitution*, 30 November 1831; emphasis original.

35. Extracts from the message of Governor James Hamilton Jr. to the South Carolina legislature on 29 November 1831, *Banner of the Constitution*, 14 December 1831. For a subsequent claim that South Carolina would have nullified if not for the Free Trade Convention, see letter to the editor, dated Charleston, 30 April 1832, *Banner of the Constitution*, 9 May 1832.

36. Daniel Webster to Henry Clay, Boston, 5 October 1831, in *The Papers of Daniel Webster: Correspondence*, ed. Charles Wiltse, 7 vols. (Hanover, NH: University Press of New England, 1974–1986), 3:129. See, likewise, Asher Robbins to Henry Clay, Newport, RI, 25 October 1831, in Clay, *Papers*, 8:421.

37. As Donald Ratcliffe writes, "most Northern Jacksonians had to consult the sectionalist standpoint of their constituents, which frequently proved more powerful than loyalty to the new president's policies, particularly on economic issues." Ratcliffe, "The Nullification Crisis, Southern Discontents, and the American Political Process," *American Nineteenth Century History* 1 (Summer 2000): 10.

38. The other members were: John S. Barbour (VA, Jackson), Lewis Condict (NJ, anti-Jackson), Charles Dayan (NY, Jackson), James Findlay (OH, Jackson), Henry Horn (PA, Jackson), and John T. H. Worthington (MD, Jackson). All except Barbour were protectionists. See Charles J. Ingersoll to Lewis Waln, Andrew M. Jones, and William W. Young, Washington, 1 February 1832, Folder 1, Box 13, and 4 February 1832, Folder 23, Box 12, both Smith-Waln Family Papers, HSP.

39. Entries for 12 December (first quotation), 13 December (request to exchange), and 27 December 1831 (second quotation), in Adams, *Memoirs*, 8:433, 435–437, 444. See also John Quincy Adams to Charles Francis Adams, Washington, 15 December 1831, Reel 494, Adams Family Papers, American Philosophical Society, Philadelphia (originals in the Massachusetts Historical Society, Boston).

40. John Quincy Adams to Richard Rush, 3 August 1832, Adams Family Papers, MHS, cited in John D. Macoll, "Representative John Quincy Adams's Compromise Tariff of 1832," *Capitol Studies* 1 (Fall 1972): 49. See also entry for 9 January 1832, in Adams, *Memoirs*, 8:454. For Adams's appointment to the committee and subsequent role in the Tariff of 1832, see Charles Francis Adams Jr., *John Quincy Adams and Speaker Andrew Stevenson of Virginia: An Episode of the Twenty-Second Congress (1832)* (Cambridge, MA, 1906); Macoll, "Representative John Quincy Adams's Compromise Tariff of 1832"; and Leonard L. Richards, *The Life and Times of Congressman John Quincy Adams* (Oxford: Oxford University Press, 1986).

41. Andrew Jackson, "Third Annual Message," 6 December 1831, *The American Presidency Project*, http://www.presidency.ucsb.edu/ws/?pid=29473.

42. Entry for 14 December 1831, in Adams, *Memoirs*, 8:438.

43. Louis McLane to Gulian C. Verplanck, Washington, 6 November 1831, Folder 4, Box 5, Verplanck Papers. An unsympathetic observer snidely suggested that McLane would "attempt in his report to make his present & past opinions coincide as nearly as possibly." Joel R. Poinsett to Joseph Johnson, Washington, 4 February 1832, Folder "1832," Box "Correspondence, 1794–1839," Joel R. Poinsett Section, Gilpin Family Papers, HSP. For McLane's role in the Tariff of 1832, see John A. Munroe, *Louis McLane: Federalist and Jacksonian* (New Brunswick, NJ: Rutgers University Press, 1973), 339–350.

44. Entry for 25 January 1832, in Adams, *Memoirs*, 8:460.

45. *Register of Debates*, Twenty-Second Congress, First Session, 1585–1588. For collaboration between Adams and McLane, see entries for 20 December 1831, 14 January 1832, 17 January 1832, 19 January 1832, all in Adams, *Memoirs*, 8:439, 456–457, 457–458, 458–459; Louis McLane to John Quincy Adams, Washington, 24 December 1831, Reel 494; and 14 January 1832 and 16 January 1832, Reel 495, all Adams Family Papers. Clay would later complain that "the famous tariff of the Secretary of the Treasury . . . originated from a resolution in that officer's own handwriting." *Register of Debates*, Twenty-Second Congress, First Session, 1293.

46. Entry for 25 January 1832, in Adams, *Memoirs*, 8:460.

47. *Register of Debates*, Twenty-Second Congress, First Session, 1763–1765. The 45 percent figure is from Munroe, *Louis McLane*, 345–346.

48. Rufus Choate to Jonathan Shove, Washington, 3 June [1832], in "Rufus Choate Letters," *Essex Institute Historical Collections* 69 (January 1933): 81; emphasis original. See also Benjamin B. Howell to Lewis Waln, Andrew M. Jones, and William W. Young, Washington, 9 February 1832, Folder 23, Box 12, Smith-Waln Family Papers.

49. *Register of Debates*, Twenty-Second Congress, First Session, 104–105, 256–257, 623. For correspondence between Hayne and the memorial committee, see Robert Y. Hayne to Henry Lee, 5 December 1831, Lee Family Papers, MHS, cited in Belko, *The Triumph of the Antebellum Free Trade Movement*, 107, and

Albert Gallatin to Robert Y. Hayne, New York, 7 February 1832, in *The Writings of Albert Gallatin*, ed. Henry Adams, 3 vols. (Philadelphia, 1879), 2:449–450.

50. "Memorial of the Committee of the Free Trade Convention, Held at Philadelphia in September and October, 1831, Remonstrating against the Existing Tariff of Duties," in F. W. Taussig, ed., *State Papers and Speeches on the Tariff* (New York: Burt Franklin, 1968, reprint of 1895 edition).

51. John C. Calhoun to Francis W. Pickens, Washington, 2 March 1832, in Calhoun, *Papers*, 11:559. For an extended discussion of the Free Trade Convention's memorial, see Belko, *The Triumph of the Antebellum Free Trade Movement*, 71–147.

52. *Register of Debates*, Twenty-Second Congress, First Session, 591.

53. Henry Clay to Francis T. Brooke, Lexington, 4 October 1831, in Clay, *Papers*, 8:412–414. On Clay's role in the Tariff of 1832, see Robert V. Remini, *Henry Clay: Statesman for the Union* (New York: W. W. Norton, 1991), 386–392, 394–396.

54. The latter point is substantiated by the correspondence of Joel R. Poinsett, who was in Washington representing the Union, or anti-nullifier, Party of South Carolina. See Joel R. Poinsett to Joseph Johnson, Washington, 25 January 1832, and 4 February 1832, both in Folder "1832," Box "Correspondence, 1794–1839," Poinsett Section, Gilpin Family Papers.

55. Entry for 28 December 1831, in Adams, *Memoirs*, 8:444–448. For events leading up to the meeting, see the entries for 21 December, 22 December, and 26 December 1831 in the same volume, 439, 440–441, 442–443, and John W. Taylor to Jane Taylor, Washington, 24 December 1831, Folder 8, Box 4, John W. Taylor Papers, NYHS.

56. Entry for 29 December 1831, in Adams, *Memoirs*, 8:448–449.

57. Entry for 12 January 1832, in Adams, *Memoirs*, 8:455–456.

58. For a sample commission, see Louis McLane to Andrew Gray, Washington, 7 February 1832, Folder "Correspondence and Writings by Others," Box 12, Series B: Special Papers, Longwood Manuscripts.

59. Mathew Carey, *The Olive Branch No. III*, 8 nos. (Philadelphia, 1832), 3:29–30 (details of plan); 5:35 (quotation).

60. Josiah S. Johnston to Mathew Carey, Washington, 4 April 1832, Folder 5, Box 10, Josiah Stoddard Johnston Papers, HSP. See Mathew Carey to Josiah S. Johnston, Philadelphia, 14 February 1832, Folder 3, Box 10, Johnston Papers, and, for the reference to the Free Trade Convention, "Hamilton" [Mathew Carey], *The Olive Branch No. IV* (Philadelphia, 1832), 1.

61. Mathew Carey, "To the Public," dated Philadelphia, 9 April 1832, and Niles's editorial comments, *Niles' Weekly Register*, 14 April 1832.

62. George M. Dallas to Sophia Chew Nicklin Dallas, Washington, 31 May 1832, Folder 5, Box 13, George Mifflin Dallas Papers, HSP.

63. Niles, *Journal of the Proceedings of the Friends of Domestic Industry*, 12.

64. Hezekiah Niles to Mathew Carey, printed circular to the members of the

Permanent Committee of the New-York Convention from the Executive Committee, 31 December 1831, transcription of a letter sold at auction at Freeman's Auction House, Philadelphia (for Lynch and Ingersoll). My thanks to Andrew Shankman for providing me with the transcription; Patrick T. Jackson to Lewis Waln, Boston, 9 January 1832, Folder 23, Box 12, Smith-Waln Papers (for Brown); untitled report signed by Niles as chair of the permanent committee of the New York Tariff Convention, *Niles' Weekly Register*, 4 February 1832.

65. George M. Dallas to Sophia Chew Nicklin Dallas, Washington, 21 May 1832, Folder 5, Box 13, Dallas Papers (Carey); E. I. du Pont de Nemours and Company to F. G. Smith, 21 May 1832, Letterbook: 2 December 1831–20 October 1834, No. 1: Letterbooks, Series A: Letters Sent, Part I: Correspondence, Records of E. I. du Pont de Nemours and Company, HM&L (du Pont); Charles J. Ingersoll to Lewis Waln, Andrew M. Jones, and William W. Young, Washington, 12 March 1832, Folder 1, Box 13, Smith-Waln Family Papers (Niles); [Lewis Waln, Andrew M. Jones, and William W. Young] to Charles J. Ingersoll, Philadelphia, 4 February 1832, Folder 15, Box 14, Smith-Waln Family Papers (Schenck); Samuel Eliot Morison, ed., *The Life and Letters of Harrison Gray Otis, 1765–1848*, 2 vols. (Boston: Houghton Mifflin, 1913), 2:288–291 (Otis).

66. George M. Dallas to Henry D. Gilpin, [Washington], 28 January 1832, Folder 5, Box 3, Dallas Papers.

67. Samuel Smith, *Register of Debates*, Twenty-Second Congress, First Session, 186. Another Senator told Clay that his "influence over the legislation of Congress" was "more powerful and more controlling than any other man, or set of men, in the country, the manufacturers, and they alone, excepted." John Tyler, *Register of Debates*, Twenty-Second Congress, First Session, 359.

68. The committee was composed of Lewis Waln, whose interest was cotton; Andrew M. Jones, iron; and William W. Young, wool. For the appointment of the committee, see Lewis Waln, Andrew M. Jones, and William W. Young to Charles J. Ingersoll, Philadelphia, 11 January 1832, Folder 14, Box 14, Smith-Waln Family Papers.

69. Charles J. Ingersoll to Lewis Waln, Andrew M. Jones, and William W. Young, Washington, 1 February 1832, Folder 1, Box 13; and Benjamin B. Howell to Lewis Waln, Baltimore, 1 February 1832, Folder 23, Box 12, both Smith-Waln Family Papers.

70. Lewis Waln to Benjamin B. Howell, Philadelphia, 14 February 1832, Folder 14, Box 14, Smith-Waln Family Papers. For similar instructions to Ingersoll, see Lewis Waln, Andrew M. Jones, and William W. Young to Charles J. Ingersoll, Philadelphia, 11 January 1832, Folder 14, Box 14, Smith-Waln Family Papers.

71. Benjamin B. Howell to Lewis Waln, Andrew M. Jones, and William W. Young, Washington, 6 February 1832, Folder 23, Box 12, Smith-Waln Family Papers. For a similar opinion of Adams expressed to the Boston manufacturers, see Henry A. Bullard to Amos Lawrence, Washington, 29 January 1832, Folder "1832 Jan–Mar," Box 1, Amos Lawrence Papers, MHS.

72. [Lewis Waln, Andrew M. Jones, and William W. Young] to Benjamin B. Howell, Philadelphia, 26 April 1832, Folder 14, Box 14, Smith-Waln Family Papers.

73. Benjamin B. Howell to Lewis Waln, Andrew M. Jones, and William W. Young, Washington, 8 February 1832, Folder 23, Box 12, Smith-Waln Family Papers.

74. Entries for 12 February and 14 March 1832, both in Adams, *Memoirs*, 8:470, 494.

75. Benjamin B. Howell to Lewis Waln, Andrew M. Jones, and William W. Young, Washington, 16 February 1832, Folder 24, Box 12, Smith-Waln Family Papers. For more detail on these activities, see the correspondence between Howell, Ingersoll, and the Pennsylvania Society committee in Boxes 12–14, Smith-Waln Family Papers. For Ingersoll's meeting with the president, see Charles J. Ingersoll to Nicholas Biddle, Washington, 2 February 1832, in *The Correspondence of Nicholas Biddle Dealing with National Affairs, 1807–1844*, ed. Reginald C. McGrane (Boston: Houghton Mifflin, 1919), 171–172.

76. Benjamin B. Howell to Lewis Waln, Andrew M. Jones, and William W. Young, Washington, 24 February 1832, Folder 24, Box 12, Smith-Waln Family Papers.

77. Charles J. Ingersoll to Lewis Waln, Andrew M. Jones, and William W. Young, Washington, 24 February 1832, Folder 1, Box 13, Smith-Waln Family Papers.

78. Lewis Waln and William W. Young to Charles J. Ingersoll, Philadelphia, 1 March 1832, Folder 15, Box 14, Smith-Waln Family Papers.

79. See Charles J. Ingersoll to Lewis Waln, Andrew M. Jones, and William W. Young, Washington, 23 February 1832 and 25 February, both Folder 1, Box 13, and Lewis Waln and Andrew M. Jones to Charles J. Ingersoll, Philadelphia, 27 February 1832, Folder 15, Box 14, all Smith-Waln Family Papers.

80. Charles J. Ingersoll to Lewis Waln, Andrew M. Jones, and William W. Young, Philadelphia, 25 July 1832, Folder 1, Box 13, Smith-Waln Family Papers. For an example of these rumors, see untitled editorial, *United States Gazette*, 26 July 1832.

81. Lewis Waln, Andrew M. Jones, and William W. Young to Charles J. Ingersoll, Philadelphia, 30 July 1832, Folder 15, Box 14, Smith-Waln Family Papers.

82. Roberts, "Memoirs of a Senator from Pennsylvania," 512. For a fascinating commentary on Ingersoll's mission, partially cancelled out but still legible, see Samuel Breck, entry for 21 August 1832, Volume 5: Diary, 1832–1833, Breck Papers.

83. *House Journal*, Twenty-Second Congress, First Session, 666; Louis McLane to Gulian C. Verplanck, 27 April [1832] and 30 April [1832], both Folder 4, Box 5, Verplanck Papers. Many of the responses from his appointed commissioners had still not been collected by this date but were eventually published as "Documents Relative to Manufactures in the United States," which McLane pronounced "the

most useful valuable and extensive information of the manufactures of the U.S. than has ever before been presented to Congress." Louis McLane to Gulian C. Verplanck, 28 June 1832, Folder 4, Box 5, Verplanck Papers. For McLane's opinion that his tariff labors made him ill, see Louis McLane to B. C. Howard, [Washington], 26 April 1832, Folder 10, Box 45, Ferdinand J. Dreer Collection, HSP.

84. Benjamin B. Howell to Lewis Waln, Andrew M. Jones, and William W. Young, Baltimore, 16 April 1832 and 24 April 1832 (quotation), both Folder 24, Box 12, Smith-Waln Family Papers. For other reports of McLane seeking the counsel of manufacturers, see Samuel Smith to John Spear Smith, Washington, 27 April 1832 and 29 April 1832, both Section 1, Smith Family Papers, Virginia Historical Society, Richmond.

85. Benjamin B. Howell to Lewis Waln, Andrew M. Jones, and William W. Young, New York, 1 May 1832, Folder 24, Box 12, Smith-Waln Family Papers; Munroe, *Louis McLane*, 345–346.

86. Henry Clay to Peter B. Porter, Washington, 3 May 1832, in Clay, *Papers*, 8:505.

87. Duff Green to R. K. Cralle, Washington, 30 April 1832, in "John C. Calhoun as Seen by His Political Friends: Letters of Duff Green, Dixon H. Lewis, and Richard K. Cralle during the Period from 1831 to 1848," ed. Frederick W. Moore, *Publications of the Southern History Association* 7 (1903): 273–274.

88. Entry for "February, 1832," in "Diary and Letters of Charles P. Huntington," *Massachusetts Historical Society Proceedings* 57 (February 1924): 246. "It is believed that none of the best feelings exist between [Adams] & Clay," recorded one Jacksonian senator. Willie P. Mangum to James Iredell, Washington, 11 February 1832, Box 4, James Iredell Papers, David M. Rubenstein Rare Book and Manuscript Library, Duke University, Durham, NC. For Niles's views, see untitled editorial, *Niles' Weekly Register*, 31 March 1832.

89. J. J. Milligan to William P. Brobson, Washington, 21 March 1832, Folder 5, Box 1, Brobson Family Papers, Delaware Historical Society, Wilmington.

90. Macoll, "Representative John Quincy Adams's Compromise Tariff of 1832," 50; Munroe, *Louis McLane*, 347. For Adams's record of his request to be excused, see entries for 15 March, 16 March, and 19 March 1832, in Adams, *Memoirs*, 8:496–497, 497–498, 499–500. For newspaper coverage, see "Letter from Washington. No. CCXLI," dated 16 March, and "Letter from Washington. No. CCXLII," dated 19 March, both *United States Gazette*, 20 March 1832 and 22 March 1832.

91. *Register of Debates*, Twenty-Second Congress, First Session, 3090–3091. For the full report, which details the differences between the committee's bill and McLane's original, see "Report on Manufactures," *Appendix to the Register of Debates*, Twenty-Second Congress, First Session, 79–93.

92. "Report on Manufactures," *Appendix to the Register of Debates*, Twenty-Second Congress, First Session, 90, 91.

93. "Report on Manufactures," *Appendix to the Register of Debates*, Twenty-Second Congress, First Session, 91.

94. Nathan Appleton, "Sketches of Autobiography," 24, Folder 10, Box 13, Appleton Family Papers, MHS. For evidence from Adams's diary that he was influenced by Appleton's draft, see entry for 11 January 1832, in Adams, *Memoirs*, 8:455. Appleton, in turn, received extensive advice from his manufacturing friends in Boston. See Abbott Lawrence to Nathan Appleton, Boston, 3 December 1831, Folder "1831 Nov–Dec," Box 1, Amos Lawrence Papers.

95. W. T. Read to George Read, 20 June 1832, Richard S. Rodney Collection, DHS, cited in Munroe, *Louis McLane*, 347.

96. J. J. Milligan to William P. Brobson, Washington, 21 March 1832, Folder 5, Box 1, Brobson Family Papers.

97. George M. Dallas to Sophia Chew Nicklin Dallas, Washington, 23 January 1832, Folder 2, Box 13, Dallas Papers.

98. "Letter from Washington. No. CCLXXXIII," dated 23 June, *United States Gazette*, 26 June 1832.

99. John Quincy Adams to Louisa Catherine Adams, Washington, 23 May 1832, Reel 495, Adams Family Papers; Macoll, "Representative John Quincy Adams's Compromise Tariff of 1832," 55.

100. Rufus Choate to Jonathan Shove, Washington, 3 June [1832], in "Rufus Choate Letters," 81, 82. See also Louisa Catherine Adams to Mary Catherine Hellen Adams, 27 May 1832, Adams Family Papers, MHS, cited in Macoll, "Representative John Quincy Adams's Compromise Tariff of 1832," 52.

101. *Register of Debates*, Twenty-Second Congress, First Session, 1154.

102. Daniel Webster to Stephen White, Washington, 28 June 1832, in Webster, *Papers*, 3:181. For Webster's role in the Tariff of 1832, see Robert V. Remini, *Daniel Webster: The Man and His Time* (New York: W. W. Norton, 1997), 357, 359–360.

103. "The Meeting at Boston," *Niles' Weekly Register*, 16 June 1832.

104. Jeremiah Mason to Daniel Webster, Boston, 27 May 1832, in Webster, *Papers*, 3:174. See also Amos Lawrence to Mary Greene, Boston, 27 May 1832, Folder "1832 Apr–May," Box 1, Amos Lawrence Papers.

105. Abbott Lawrence to Amos Lawrence, Washington, 2 July 1832, Folder "1832," Box 1, Amos Lawrence Papers II; *Register of Debates*, Twenty-Second Congress, First Session, 1161. For Lawrence's mission, see also his letters to Amos Lawrence, Washington, 3, 6, and 9 June 1832, Folder "1832," Box 1, Amos Lawrence Papers II, and Henry A. Bullard to Amos Lawrence, Washington, 17 June 1832, Folder "1832 June," Box 1, Amos Lawrence Papers.

106. *Register of Debates*, Twenty-Second Congress, First Session, 1178–1179. For additional detail, see "Lobby Members of the Senate," *Banner of the Constitution*, 25 July 1832, and Henry Clay to Solomon Etting, Washington, 16 July 1832, in Clay, *Papers*, 8:553–554.

107. "From the Columbia (S.C.) Telescope," *Niles' Weekly Register*, 8 September 1827.

108. For details, consult *Senate Journal*, Twenty-Second Congress, First Session, covering 3–7 July 1832.

109. George M. Dallas to Henry D. Gilpin, [Washington], 3 July 1832, Folder 7, Box 3, Dallas Papers.

110. *Register of Debates*, Twenty-Second Congress, First Session, 3891–3895.

111. *Register of Debates*, Twenty-Second Congress, First Session, 1220–1221, 3908.

112. *Register of Debates*, Twenty-Second Congress, First Session, 1274–1293. Dickerson also concurred in the final report but made clear that he had tried several times to save higher duties on woolens. Wilkins had first been elected to Congress as a representative in place of James Stevenson, who had lost favor with his constituents for his part in making the Tariff of 1828.

113. George M. Dallas to Henry D. Gilpin, [Washington], 13 July 1832, Folder 7, Box 3, Dallas Papers.

114. John Quincy Adams to Louisa Catherine Adams, Philadelphia, 19 July 1832, Reel 496, Adams Family Papers.

115. Jacksonians voted ninety-eight for and forty-three against; antis- (including anti-Jacksonians and a small number of Anti-Masons) voted sixty-six for and thirty-two against.

116. Samuel Smith to John Spear Smith, Washington, 28 April 1832, Section 1, Smith Family Papers. See also John Niven, *Martin Van Buren: The Romantic Age of American Politics* (Oxford: Oxford University Press, 1983), 307.

117. E. I. du Pont de Nemours and Company to A. Naudain, 2 July 1832, Letterbook: 2 December 1831–20 October 1834, No. 1: Letterbooks, Series A: Letters Sent, Part I: Correspondence, Records of E. I. du Pont de Nemours and Company. For similar sentiments from other leading protectionists, see Carey, *Letters to Messrs. Abbot Laurence* [sic], *Patrick Jackson, and Jonas B. Brown, Boston*, 2:6, and Hezekiah Niles to John Quincy Adams, Baltimore, 14 July 1832, Reel 496, Adams Family Papers.

118. Andrew Jackson to John Coffee, Washington, 17 July 1832, in *Correspondence of Andrew Jackson*, ed. John Spencer Bassett, 7 vols. (Washington, DC: Carnegie Institution of Washington, 1926–1935), 4:462–463.

119. Daniel Webster to Stephen White, Washington, 28 June 1832, in Webster, *Papers*, 3:181; emphasis original.

120. Thomas Tyler Bouldin, notes on the tariff, [1832], Section 8, Bouldin Family Papers, VHS.

121. John C. Calhoun to Waddy Thompson Jr., Washington, 8 July 1832, in Calhoun, *Papers*, 11:604.

122. Thomas Hart Benton, *Thirty Years' View; or, a History of the Working of the American Government for Thirty Years, from 1820 to 1850*, 2 vols. (New York, 1883), 1:345.

123. Mathew Carey, *The Olive Branch No. III*, x.

124. "South Carolina Ordinance of Nullification, November 24, 1832," *The Avalon Project: Documents in Law, History and Diplomacy*, http://avalon.law .yale.edu/19th_century/ordnull.asp.

125. "Report of a Committee of the Convention, to Whom Was Referred an Act to Provide for Calling a Convention of the People of South Carolina," *State Papers on Nullification* (Boston, 1834), 2–3, 6. William Drayton, a South Carolina Unionist, noted that the Tariff of 1816 was in Congress "frequently distinguished as the South Carolina Tariff" because of the leading roles played by Lowndes and Calhoun in its enactment. William Drayton to Joel R. Poinsett, Washington, 31 December 1832, Folder 6, Box 7, Joel Roberts Poinsett Papers, HSP.

126. Jackson, quoted in Augustus C. Buell, *History of Andrew Jackson*, 2 vols. (New York, 1904), 2:245, cited in Ellis, *The Union at Risk*, 78.

127. Andrew Jackson, "Fourth Annual Message," 4 December 1832, *The American Presidency Project*, http://www.presidency.ucsb.edu/ws/?pid=29474.

128. Entry for 4 December 1832, in Adams, *Memoirs*, 8:503.

129. Andrew Jackson, "Proclamation Regarding the Nullifying Laws of South Carolina," 10 December 1832, *The American Presidency Project*, http://www .presidency.ucsb.edu/ws/index.php?pid=67078; emphasis original.

130. John Tyler to John Floyd, Washington, 13 December 1832, John Tyler Letter, VHS.

131. The other members were: Mark Alexander (VA, Jackson), Nathan Gaither (KY, Jackson), John Gilmore (PA, Jackson), Ralph I. Ingersoll (CT, anti-Jackson), James K. Polk (TN, Jackson), and Richard H. Wilde (GA, Jackson).

132. John Quincy Adams to Charles Francis Adams, Washington, 25 December 1832, Reel 496, Adams Family Papers.

133. John Quincy Adams to Charles Francis Adams, Washington, 13 March 1833, Reel 497, Adams Family Papers. For Hoffman's perspective, see Michael Hoffman to Azariah C. Flagg, Washington, 15 December 1832, Folder 2, Box 4, Azariah C. Flagg Papers, New York Public Library.

134. "A Letter to Col. William Drayton, of South Carolina, in Assertion of the Constitutional Power of Congress to Impose Protecting Duties. By Gulian C. Verplanck, One of the Representatives in Congress from the State of New York," *United States Gazette*, 7 November 1831. On Verplanck's role in the Tariff of 1833, see Robert W. July, *The Essential New Yorker: Gulian Crommelin Verplanck* (Durham, NC: Duke University Press, 1951), 156–163.

135. Gulian C. Verplanck to Albert Gallatin, 3 December 1832, Albert Gallatin Papers, NYHS, cited in Munroe, *Louis McLane*, 367.

136. Munroe, *Louis McLane*, 368. *House Journal*, Twenty-Second Congress, First Session, 105–106.

137. Andrew Jackson to Francis P. Blair, Hermitage, TN, 12 August 1841, Reel 53, Andrew Jackson Papers, Library of Congress, Washington, DC. For contemporary references to executive involvement, see Churchill C. Cambreleng to

Martin Van Buren, [Washington], 18 December 1832, in Jackson, *Correspondence*, 4:505n, and John M. Clayton, *Speech of Hon. John M. Clayton, at the Delaware Whig Mass Convention, Held at Wilmington, June 15, 1844* (New York, 1844), 5.

138. *Appendix to the Register of Debates*, Twenty-Second Congress, Second Session, 41.

139. See Edward Everett to Josiah S. Johnston, Washington, 26 December 1832, Folder 13, Box 10, Johnston Papers; W. McKnight to Harmar Denny, Pittsburgh, 4 January 1833, Harmar Denny Folder, Society Large Collection, HSP; and Louis McLane to Martin Van Buren, Washington, 23 January 1833, Reel 12, Martin Van Buren Papers, LC.

140. Munroe, *Louis McLane*, 368–369.

141. Michael Hoffman to Azariah C. Flagg, Washington, 24 December 1832, Folder 2, Box 4, Flagg Papers.

142. George McDuffie to Samuel D. Ingham, Washington, 1 January 1832 [*sic*, 1833], Folder 81, Box 1, Samuel D. Ingham Correspondence, Rare Book and Manuscript Library, University of Pennsylvania, Philadelphia.

143. "Regulation of Commerce," *Niles' Weekly Register*, 12 January 1833; "Hamilton" [Mathew Carey], *Prospects Beyond the Rubicon*, 8 nos. (Philadelphia, 1833, 3rd edition), 5:18; emphasis original.

144. Entry for 4 January 1833, in Adams, *Memoirs*, 8:517.

145. Daniel Webster to Henry Willis Kinsman, Washington, 1 January 1833, in Webster, *Papers*, 3:203; emphasis original.

146. [Illegible] Dallas to George Mifflin Dallas, Pittsburgh, 8 December 1832, Folder 2, Box 11, Dallas Papers; Malcolm Rogers Eiselen, *The Rise of Pennsylvania Protectionism* (Philadelphia: Porcupine Press, 1974, reprint of 1932 edition), 120–121.

147. [Illegible] to [no address], Washington, 23 January 1832 [*sic*, 1833], Folder 3, Box 7, Poinsett Papers. For administration complaints that the nullifiers were harming the bill's chances, see Louis McLane to Martin Van Buren, Washington, 23 January 1833, Reel 12, Van Buren Papers, and Andrew Jackson to Joel R. Poinsett, Washington, 24 January 1833, in Jackson, *Correspondence*, 5:11–12.

148. William Hammet to Thomas Willis White, Washington, 11 January 1833, William Hammet Letters, VHS. See also, on the strategy of delay, "Letter from Washington. No. CCCXXXVII," dated 11 January 1833, *United States Gazette*, 15 January 1833, and William Drayton to Joel R. Poinsett, Washington, 11 February 1833, Folder 9, Box 7, Poinsett Papers.

149. "At a Meeting of the Permanent Committee of the New York Convention . . . ," *Niles' Weekly Register*, 26 January 1833.

150. "Extract of a Letter, Dated Washington, Jan. 15, 1833," *The Pennsylvanian* (Philadelphia), 18 January 1833.

151. "Letter from Washington. No. CCCXLII," dated 22 January 1833, *United States Gazette*, 28 January 1833.

152. William Hammet to Thomas Willis White, Washington, 4 February 1833, Hammet Letters. See also Henry A. Bullard to Amos Lawrence, Washington, 31 December 1832, Folder "1832 Dec," Box 1, Amos Lawrence Papers.

153. Silas Wright Jr. to Martin Van Buren, Washington, 13 January 1833, Reel 12, Van Buren Papers.

154. Henry Clay to Thomas Speed, Lexington, 19 June 1833, in Clay, *Papers*, 8:653.

155. Henry Clay to Philip R. Fendall, Lexington, 8 August 1836, in Clay, *Papers*, 8:862. For more on Clay's motives and his role in the Tariff of 1833, see Merrill D. Peterson, *Olive Branch and Sword: The Compromise of 1833* (Baton Rouge: Louisiana State University Press, 1982), 49–84, and Robert V. Remini, *Henry Clay: Statesman for the Union* (New York: W. W. Norton, 1991), 413–435.

156. *Register of Debates*, Twenty-Fourth Congress, Second Session, 969. We are reliant upon Clay for this record of the origins of the Tariff of 1833, but it fits with the recollections of contemporaries including Webster, who opposed the compromise.

157. Epes Sargent, *The Life and Public Services of Henry Clay, Down to 1848* (Philadelphia, 1852; first edition 1848), 141. Sargent misspells "Borie" as "Bovie."

158. *Register of Debates*, Twenty-Fourth Congress, Second Session, 969.

159. "Mr. Clay's First Project," in Webster, *Papers*, 4:264. For the details of this first proposal, we are reliant upon Daniel Webster, who took a copy from an original in Clay's handwriting. See Daniel Webster to [Hiram Ketchum], Washington, 20 January 1838, in Webster, *Papers*, 3:263–264, and William Plumer, "Reminiscences of Daniel Webster," 2 April 1853, in *The Writings and Speeches of Daniel Webster*, 18 vols. (Boston, 1903), 17: 557.

160. Peterson, *Olive Branch and Sword*, 53–54; emphasis original.

161. Sargent, *The Life and Public Services of Henry Clay*, 141. In describing the meeting during a speech to the Senate in 1837, Clay does not clarify whether the other participants approved the specific details of his proposal, including the renunciation of protection, or merely the general notion of a delayed reduction in duties. *Register of Debates*, Twenty-Fourth Congress, Second Session, 969–970.

162. Daniel Webster to Hiram Ketchum, Washington, 18 January 1838, in Webster, *Writings*, 16:293, emphasis original; Nathan Appleton, speech to the House of Representatives, 5 July 1842, quoted in *Boston Courier*, 9 July 1842, cited in Peterson, *Olive Branch and Sword*, 54. For Webster's role in the Tariff of 1833, see Remini, *Daniel Webster*, 374–387.

163. Daniel Webster to [Hiram Ketchum], Washington, 20 January 1838, in Webster, *Papers*, 4:263. See also Nathan Appleton to Abbott Lawrence, Boston, 15 February 1841, Folder 3a, Box 6, and Nathan Appleton, "Sketches of Autobiography," 29, Folder 10, Box 13, both Appleton Family Papers.

164. Henry Clay to Francis T. Brooke, Washington, 17 January 1833, in Clay, *Papers*, 8:613–614.

165. The quotations here are from Tyler's letter to Floyd. Two weeks after this

letter, Clay would urge his supporters in Virginia to back Tyler's bid for reelection. See Henry Clay to Francis T. Brooke, Washington, 24 January 1833, in Clay, *Papers*, 8:615.

166. John Tyler to John Floyd, Washington, 10 January 1833, in "Original Letters," *William and Mary Quarterly* 21 (July 1912): 8–10; emphasis original.

167. *Register of Debates*, Twenty-Second Congress, Second Session, 970.

168. Lyon G. Tyler, ed., *The Letters and Times of the Tylers*, 3 vols. (Richmond, VA, 1884–1896), 1:458; Sargent, *The Life and Public Services of Henry Clay*, 141. An alternative reading would be that Tyler originated this proposition and then suggested it to Clay, but Tyler never subsequently questioned Clay's authorship of compromise.

169. Henry Clay to Nicholas Biddle, Lexington, 10 April 1833, in Clay, *Papers*, 8:637. See also Henry Clay to Daniel Webster, [Washington], 5 February 1833, in Webster, *Papers*, 3:211, which dates the second meeting to 5 February.

170. Daniel Webster to Joseph Hopkinson, 9 February 1833, in Webster, *Papers*, 3:213. For a subsequent exchange between Clay and Webster on the extent of the latter's involvement, see *Congressional Globe*, Twenty-Fifth Congress, Third Session, 172–173.

171. Henry Clay to Thomas Ellicott, Washington, 2 February 1833; and Henry Clay to James Heaton, Middletown, OH, 28 May 1833, both in Clay, *Papers*, 8:618, 642. The permanent committee had men in Washington monitoring the progress of the tariff bill, although there is little detail of their activities. See S. V. Merrick to Samuel Breck, 10 February 1833, No. 304, Box 3, Breck Family Papers, Library Company of Philadelphia.

172. D. W. Coxe to Josiah S. Johnston, Philadelphia, 8 February 1833, Folder 2, Box 11, Johnston Papers.

173. Henry Clay to John M. Clayton, Blue Licks [Nicholas County, KY], 22 August 1844, in Clay, *Papers*, 10:101–102.

174. Benton, *Thirty Years' View*, 1:343.

175. John C. Calhoun, "Remarks on Presenting a Petition against Tariff Protection," 21 July 1842, in Calhoun, *Papers*, 16:319–324. Peterson, *Olive Branch and Sword*, 69n65 identifies some of the other sources for this interview.

176. Louis McLane to Martin Van Buren, Washington, 23 January 1833, Reel 12, Van Buren Papers. Jackson had predicted "a union between Mr. Clay and Calhoun, on the Tariff" over a year earlier. Andrew Jackson to Martin Van Buren, Washington, 6 December 1831, in Jackson, *Papers*, 9:732. See also the entry for 11 February 1833, in Adams, *Memoirs*, 8:524, and Daniel Webster to Joseph Hopkinson, 9 February 1833, in Webster, *Papers*, 3:213–214.

177. *Register of Debates*, Twenty-Second Congress, Second Session, 481–482.

178. In the final act, these dates were amended, respectively, to 1 January 1834, 1836, 1838, 1840, and 1842, and 1 July 1842.

179. *Register of Debates*, Twenty-Second Congress, Second Session, 482. For reference to its similarity to the proposal of the Free Trade Convention, see, for

example, John Davis, *Register of Debates*, Twenty-Second Congress, Second Session, 1775.

180. See Sargent, *The Life and Public Services of Henry Clay*, 142–143, and Clayton, *Speech of Hon. John M. Clayton*, 3–6. But see Robert C. Winthrop to Samuel P. Gardner, Washington, 10 January 1841, Reel 23, Winthrop Family Papers, MHS, for a report that even at this late date "Mr. C thinks the principle of the Compromise Act must be adhered to, & that it will afford sufficient protection to all kinds of manufacture."

181. Maurice G. Baxter, *Henry Clay and the American System* (Lexington: University Press of Kentucky, 1995), 226n53; Remini, *Henry Clay*, 417, 424, 434; and Ratcliffe, "The Nullification Crisis," 19–20. For an alternative view, see Onuf, "The Political Economy of Sectionalism," 51, and Meardon, "Negotiating Free Trade in Fact and Theory," 70.

182. John Tyler to John Floyd, Washington, 10 January 1833, in "Original Letters," 8–10. Following the introduction of Verplanck's measure, Thomas Cooper had written to its author "the principle of protecting duties, is the basis of your bill; therefore I hope to God it may not pass." Cooper to Gulian C. Verplanck, Columbia, SC, 15 January 1833, Folder 2, Box 3, Verplanck Papers.

183. Daniel Webster to Hiram Ketchum, Washington, 18 January 1838, in Webster, *Writings*, 16:293. See also Daniel Webster, 12 February 1833, *Register of Debates*, Twenty-Second Congress, Second Session, 478–479.

184. *Register of Debates*, Twenty-Second Congress, Second Session, 461–473 (quotations 467, 467, 468). Clay also repeated this argument in letters to supporters. See Henry Clay to Thomas Speed, Lexington, 19 June 1833, in Clay, *Papers*, 8:653.

185. Henry Augustus Philip Muhlenberg to Becky Muhlenberg, Washington, 17 February 1833, Reel 4, Henry Augustus Philip Muhlenberg Papers, APS.

186. "Mr. Clay's New Tariff Project," *Niles' Weekly Register*, 16 February 1833; Sargent, *The Life and Public Services of Henry Clay*, 141.

187. Mathew Carey, *Collectanea: Displaying the Rise and Progress of the Tariff System of the United States* (Philadelphia, 1833, 2nd edition), 5.

188. D. W. Coxe to Josiah S. Johnston, 14 February 1833, Folder 2, Box 11, Johnston Papers.

189. *Register of Debates*, Twenty-Second Congress, Second Session, 477–478.

190. Edward Everett to B. F. Hallet, Washington, 17 February 1833 (draft, not sent), Reel 25, Edward Everett Papers, MHS.

191. *Register of Debates*, Twenty-Second Congress, Second Session, 484–486.

192. Daniel Webster to Nathan Appleton, 17 February 1833, in Webster, *Papers*, 3:216 (first quotation); George M. Dallas to Henry D. Gilpin, [Washington], 19 February 1833, Folder 10, Box 3, Dallas Papers (second quotation).

193. Nancy N. Scott, *A Memoir of Hugh Lawson White* (Philadelphia, 1856),

300. This marked the beginning of a breach between the two men that would result in White running against Jackson's handpicked successor, Van Buren, in the presidential election of 1836.

194. Clayton, *Speech of Hon. John M. Clayton*, 6.

195. John M. Clayton to E. I. du Pont, Washington, 13 February 1833 (photocopy), File 120, Box 8, Eleuthera Bradford du Pont Collection, HM&L. Benton states that other manufacturers were summoned too, but Clayton only mentions du Pont. Benton, *Thirty Years' View*, 1:343.

196. E. I. du Pont to Wm. Kemble, 12 January 1833, in *Life of Eleuthere Irénée du Pont from Contemporary Correspondence*, ed. B. G. du Pont, 11 vols. (Newark: University of Delaware Press, 1923–1927), 11:279; E. I. du Pont de Nemours and Company to F. G. Smith, 15 February 1833, Letterbook: 2 December 1831–20 October 1834, No. 1: Letterbooks, Series A: Letters Sent, Part I: Correspondence, Records of E. I. du Pont de Nemours and Company; E. I. du Pont to Pitray, Viel and Company, 2 March 1833, in du Pont, *Life of Eleuthere Irénée du Pont*, 11:279–280.

197. Clayton named as party to this agreement, "among others, Samuel Bed [*sic*, Bell] of New Hampshire, A.[rnold] Naudain of Delaware, Samuel Foote of Connecticut, and John Holmes of Maine." Clayton, *Speech of Hon. John M. Clayton*, 9.

198. Remini, *Henry Clay*, 427–430. Remini ends this section by stating that "Clay's gamble [on the home valuation amendment] had paid off," but he also acknowledges that "at one point Clay personally and privately entreated Clayton to free the southerners from having to accept the home valuation amendments" to no avail, so it seems a stretch to then credit Clay and not Clayton with the victory.

199. One of these was the deletion of the clause providing that from 1842 the duties laid should be "equal upon all articles," which allowed Clay to claim that the principle of protection was preserved below the 20 percent threshold established by the bill, though most manufacturers considered this as no protection at all. *Register of Debates*, Twenty-Second Congress, Second Session, 601, 690–694.

200. *Register of Debates*, Twenty-Second Congress, Second Session, 697. Calhoun and other opponents of home valuation objected that since the price of goods differed from one port to the next it could not be applied consistently and was therefore both impractical and unconstitutional.

201. *Register of Debates*, Twenty-Second Congress, Second Session, 697 (quotation), 701.

202. Clayton, *Speech of Hon. John M. Clayton*, 9.

203. This tale is recounted in Sargent, *Public Men and Events*, 1:239, the author having heard it directly from Clayton. Clay also credits Clayton and his messmates with securing the adoption of the home valuation clause. Henry Clay to John M. Clayton, Blue Licks [Nicholas County, KY], 22 August 1844, in Clay,

Papers, 10:101–102. For an account of the "curious scene" as it unfolded in the Senate, by an observer unaware of the negotiations involved, see Silas Wright to Azariah C. Flagg, Washington, 21 February 1833, Folder 12, Box 4, Flagg Papers. And for Calhoun's justification of his vote, see *Register of Debates*, Twenty-Second Congress, Second Session, 715–716.

204. *Register of Debates*, Twenty-Second Congress, Second Session, 1772–1780 (quotation 1773); entry for 5 February 1833, in Adams, *Memoirs*, 8:527. See also Benton, *Thirty Years' View*, 1:309–310, and "Extract of a Letter to the Editor of the United States Gazette, Dated Washington, Feb. 25, 1833," *United States Gazette*, 27 February 1833.

205. "From the Washington Correspondence of the N.York Journal of Commerce. Washington, Feb. 27, 1833," *United States Gazette*, 1 March 1833. For corroboration, see John Connell to Nicholas Biddle, Washington, 1 March 1833, Volume 39, Nicholas Biddle Papers, LC, and entry for 4 April 1833, in *The Life and Diary of John Floyd*, ed. Charles H. Ambler (Richmond, VA: Richmond Press, 1918), 214.

206. Ratcliffe, "The Nullification Crisis," 13.

207. On the caucus, see Nathan Appleton, "Sketches of Autobiography," 29–30, Folder 10, Box 13, Appleton Family Papers.

208. The antis- included fifteen Anti-Masons in the House, all of whom opposed the bill.

209. John Quincy Adams to Charles Francis Adams, Washington, 26 March 1833, Reel 497, Adams Family Papers.

210. Daniel Webster to [Hiram Ketchum], Washington, 20 January 1838, in Webster, *Papers*, 4:263–264.

211. E. I. du Pont [*sic*] to Pitray, Viel and Company, 2 March 1833, in du Pont, *Life of Eleuthere Irénée du Pont*, 11:279–280.

212. *State Papers on Nullification*, 346, cited in William W. Freehling, *Prelude to Civil War: The Nullification Controversy in South Carolina, 1816–1836* (New York: Harper Torchbooks, 1968), 296.

213. John Quincy Adams to Charles Francis Adams, Washington, 26 March 1833, Reel 497, Adams Family Papers.

214. Andrew Jackson to Joel R. Poinsett, Washington, 6 March 1833, in Jackson, *Correspondence*, 5:28–29.

215. Josiah S. Johnston to [no name], Washington, 1 March 1833, Folder 3, Box 11, Johnston Papers.

216. Abbott Lawrence to Henry Clay, Boston, 26 March 1833, in Clay, *Papers*, 8:635. Two months earlier, Lawrence had written to Clay protesting the surrender of protection. See entry for 17 March 1841, in Adams, *Memoirs*, 10:445.

217. "Extract of a Letter to the Editor of the United States Gazette, Dated Washington, Feb. 26, 1833," *United States Gazette*, 28 February 1833.

218. Clayton, *Speech of Hon. John M. Clayton*, 6. For Clay's views, see Henry

Clay to John M. Clayton, Blue Licks [Nicholas County, KY], 22 August 1844, in Clay, *Papers*, 10:101–102.

219. Two works that endeavor to situate the Nullification Controversy within a long-term explanation for the coming of the Civil War are Freehling, *The Road to Disunion*, and Elizabeth R. Varon, *Disunion! The Coming of the American Civil War, 1789–1859* (Chapel Hill: University of North Carolina Press, 2008).

Chapter Five: "Trembling upon the Verge of Success and Defeat": The Tariffs of 1842 and 1846

1. "Coincidences," *New-York Tribune*, 31 July 1846. Of nine major tariff bills between 1816 and 1846, the fate of four was decided by a single vote: 1820, rejected by the Senate; 1827, rejected by the Senate; 1842, passed by the House and the Senate; 1846, passed by the Senate. Of the others cited by the *Tribune*, the Tariff of 1824 passed by a margin of five in the House and four in the Senate, and the Tariff of 1828 by eleven in the House and five in the Senate, although, as noted in chapter three, the latter would likely have failed without the vote of Martin Van Buren for woolen minimums.

2. Entry for 29 August 1842, in *Memoirs of John Quincy Adams, Comprising Portions of His Diary from 1795 to 1848*, ed. Charles Francis Adams, 12 vols. (Philadelphia, 1874–1877), 11:244–245.

3. John Fairfield to Anna Fairfield, Washington, 26 July 1846, in *The Letters of John Fairfield*, ed. Arthur G. Staples (Lewiston, ME: Lewiston Journal Company, 1922), 413.

4. "An Octogenarian Citizen of Philadelphia," in [Mathew Carey], *The Querist* (Philadelphia, 1839), 10. See also Mathew Carey to Josiah S. Johnston, Philadelphia, 21 March 1833, Folder 3, Box 11, Josiah Stoddard Johnston Papers, Historical Society of Pennsylvania, Philadelphia.

5. (New York) *Evening Post*, quoted in "A Doubt Suggested!" *Niles' Weekly Register* (Baltimore), 27 March 1830; emphasis original.

6. Mathew Carey, *Collectanea: Displaying the Rise and Progress of the Tariff System of the United States* (Philadelphia, 1833, 2nd edition), 19.

7. On the Democrat-Whig party system, see Marc Egnal, *Clash of Extremes: The Economic Origins of the Civil War* (New York: Hill and Wang, 2010); Michael F. Holt, *The Rise and Fall of the American Whig Party: Jacksonian Politics and the Onset of the Civil War* (Oxford: Oxford University Press, 1999); Daniel Walker Howe, *What Hath God Wrought: The Transformation of America, 1815–1848* (Oxford: Oxford University Press, 2007); and Sean Wilentz, *The Rise of American Democracy: Jefferson to Lincoln* (New York: W. W. Norton, 2005).

8. James H. Hammond to John C. Calhoun, Silver Bluff, 26 September 1845, in *The Papers of John C. Calhoun*, ed. Robert L. Meriweather, W. Edwin Hemphill, Shirley A. Book, Clyde N. Wilson, et al., 28 vols. (Columbia: University of South Carolina Press, 1959–2003), 22:173.

9. For more detail on the changing economic landscape, see Egnal, *Clash of Extremes*, 45–72; John Austin Moore, "Interests and Ideas: Industrialization and the Making of Early American Trade Policy, 1789–1860" (PhD diss., Wayne State University, 2013), 321–350; and Brian Schoen, *The Fragile Fabric of Union: Cotton, Federal Politics, and the Global Origins of the Civil War* (Baltimore: Johns Hopkins University Press, 2009), 146–196. For a classic statement of the Southern Whig position, see William Alexander Graham to George E. Spruill, Hillsboro', NC, 18 December 1843: "I have no hesitation in saying, that whilst I think the Government should collect the least amount of money which may be necessary for an efficient public service, in laying duties to raise such sum, I would incidentally afford protection to American interests, when they were deemed of sufficient importance to deserve it, as well as counteract the effects of restrictive regulations on our trade, by foreign nations wherever it should appear expedient to do so." *The Papers of William Alexander Graham*, ed. J. G. De Roulhac Hamilton, 8 vols. (Raleigh, NC: State Department of Archives and History, 1957–1992), 2:463.

10. William Henry Harrison to Mathew Carey, Cleveland, OH, 17 November 1830, William Henry Harrison Letter, Virginia Historical Society.

11. Holt, *The Rise and Fall of the American Whig Party*, 127–136.

12. John Tyler, "First Annual Message," 7 December 1841, *The American Presidency Project*, http://www.presidency.ucsb.edu/ws/?pid=29483.

13. "Sayings and Doings at Washington. Number L," signed "Oliver Oldschool" and dated 1 March, *United States Gazette* (Philadelphia), 3 March 1842 (quotation); and *Congressional Globe*, Twenty-Seventh Congress, Second Session, 288–290. Clay presented his resolutions on 1 March, and his resignation took effect on 31 March. Ironically, Tyler had only been handed the Whig vice presidential nomination in 1840 as a sop to Clay supporters who were disappointed that their chief had been overlooked in favor of Harrison for the White House; prior to their break in 1841, the two had long been on friendly terms, as the Virginian's role in arranging the details of the Compromise of 1833 with other Southern leaders illustrates.

14. "Home League," *United States Gazette*, 15 December 1841 (quotation), and see issues October 1841–April 1842 for further details on this movement. For the one hundred auxiliaries figure, see "Protection to American Interests in Union with the Principles of True Free Trade, Illustrated by the Report of the Central Committee of the Home League, at Its Second Anniversary," *Hunt's Merchants' Magazine* (New York City), December 1843, 525.

15. "National Convention," *United States Gazette*, 23 March 1842; Moore, "Interests and Ideas," 350.

16. See, for example, *Report of the Proceedings of the National Convention of Silk Growers and Silk Manufacturers, Held in New York, Oct. 13th and 14th, 1843* (Boston, 1844, 2nd edition); *Proceedings of the Iron Convention, Held at Pittsburgh, November 21st, 22d, and 23d, 1849* (Pittsburgh, 1849).

17. "Tariff," 2 March 1842; "Sayings . . . LXXXI," dated 5 April, printed 7 April 1842, both *United States Gazette*.

18. Mathew Carey, "Prefatory Address," 1821, Library Company of Philadelphia. For the expansion and transformation of the newspaper press during this period, see Richard D. Brown, *Knowledge is Power: The Diffusion of Information in Early America, 1700–1865* (Oxford: Oxford University Press, 1989); Richard B. Kielbowicz, *News in the Mail: The Press, Post Office, and Public Information, 1700–1860s* (Westport, CT: Greenwood Press, 1989); and Thomas C. Leonard, *News for All: America's Coming-of-Age with the Press* (Oxford: Oxford University Press, 1995).

19. See, for example, "Good Example," signed "A Friend to the Fair Sex," *Patron of Industry* (New York City), 23 June 1821, on "the Ladies of the county of Courtland" who "formed a society for the encouragement of manufactures."

20. On the campaign against Indian removal, see Mary Hershberger, "Mobilizing Women, Anticipating Abolition: The Struggle against Indian Removal in the 1830s," *Journal of American History* 86 (June 1999): 15–40, and Alisse Theodore Portnoy, "'Female Petitioners Can Lawfully Be Heard': Negotiating Female Decorum, United States Politics, and Political Agency, 1829–1831," *Journal of the Early Republic* 23 (Winter 2003): 573–610. On abolitionism, see Richard S. Newman, *The Transformation of American Abolitionism: Fighting Slavery in the Early Republic* (Chapel Hill: University of North Carolina Press, 2002), and Susan Zaeske, *Signatures of Citizenship: Petitioning, Antislavery, and Women's Political Identity* (Chapel Hill: University of North Carolina Press, 2003). The quotations here are from an address on this subject by John Quincy Adams to a female audience. Entry for 4 September 1838, in Adams, *Memoirs*, 10:37.

For more on the ways in which civil society evolved during the antebellum period, see John L. Brooke, *Columbia Rising: Civil Life on the Upper Hudson from the Revolution to the Age of Jackson* (Chapel Hill: University of North Carolina Press, 2010), and Johann N. Neem, *Creating a Nation of Joiners: Democracy and Civil Society in Early National Massachusetts* (Cambridge, MA: Harvard University Press, 2008).

21. Entry for 21 April 1842, in Adams, *Memoirs*, 11:138–139.

22. Gabor S. Boritt, "Old Wine into New Bottles: Abraham Lincoln and the Tariff Reconsidered," *The Historian* 28 (February 1966): 292.

23. "Sayings . . . XL," dated 17 February, *United States Gazette*, 19 February 1842.

24. *Congressional Globe*, Twenty-Seventh Congress, Second Session, 650.

25. "Sayings . . . III," dated 3 January, *United States Gazette*, 5 January 1842; *Congressional Globe*, Twenty-Seventh Congress, Second Session, 83–87.

26. Leverett Saltonstall to Robert C. Winthrop, Washington, 1 June 1842, in *The Papers of Leverett Saltonstall, 1816–1845*, ed. Robert E. Moody, 5 vols. (Boston: Massachusetts Historical Society, 1978–1992), 4:143. See also Joshua H.

Ward to Leverett Saltonstall, 23 January 1842 and 3 February 1842, in the same volume, 17–18, 27–28.

27. Leverett Saltonstall to Henry Clay, Washington, 7 July 1842, in Saltonstall, *Papers*, 4:202.

28. William H. Horstmann to Nicholas Carroll, Philadelphia, 30 May 1842, and other letters in Nicholas Carroll Papers (II) (Collection No. 76) and Nicholas Carroll Papers (I) (Collection No. 29), both Hagley Museum and Library, Wilmington, DE.

29. Leverett Saltonstall to Robert C. Winthrop, Washington, [5 June 1842], in Saltonstall, *Papers*, 4:148.

30. "Sayings . . . CLI," dated 30 June, *United States Gazette*, 2 July 1842.

31. *Congressional Globe*, Twenty-Seventh Congress, Second Session, 574. The other members of Ways and Means were: Charles G. Atherton (NH, Democrat), John M. Botts (VA, Whig), Joseph R. Ingersoll (PA, Whig), John W. Jones (VA, Democrat), Dixon H. Lewis (AL, Democrat), Samson Mason (OH, Whig), Thomas F. Marshall (KY, Whig), Francis W. Pickens (SC, Democrat), and David Wallace (IN, Whig).

32. *Congressional Globe*, Twenty-Seventh Congress, Second Session, 604.

33. Entry for 15 June 1842, in Adams, *Memoirs*, 11:178. *House Journal*, Twenty-Seventh Congress, Second Session, 974–975.

34. *Congressional Globe*, Twenty-Seventh Congress, Second Session, 678–679, 688; entry for 25 June 1842, in Adams, *Memoirs*, 11:186–189.

35. *Congressional Globe*, Twenty-Seventh Congress, Second Session, 694–695.

36. "Sayings . . . CXLIX," dated 28 June, *United States Gazette*, 30 June 1842.

37. Leverett Saltonstall to Robert C. Winthrop, Washington, 4 July [1842], in Saltonstall, *Papers*, 4:197.

38. Willie P. Mangum to Henry Clay, Washington, 15 June 1842, in *The Papers of Henry Clay*, ed. James F. Hopkins, Robert Seagar II, Melba Porter Hay, et al., 11 vols. (Lexington: University Press of Kentucky, 1959–1992), 9:717.

39. Robert V. Remini, *The House: The History of the House of Representatives* (New York: HarperCollins, 2007), 121.

40. Leverett Saltonstall to Mary Saltonstall, Washington, 13 July [1842], in Saltonstall, *Papers*, 4:213–214. See also Leverett Saltonstall to Robert C. Winthrop, Washington, 7 July 1842, and Joseph L. Tillinghast to Leverett Saltonstall, Providence, RI, 26 October 1842, in the same volume, 207, 289–290.

41. Leverett Saltonstall to Robert C. Winthrop, Washington, 16 July [1842], in Saltonstall, *Papers*, 4:218. See also Leverett Saltonstall to Robert C. Winthrop, Washington, 12 July [1842], in the same volume, 212–213.

42. "The Tariff of 1842," in *Encyclopedia of Tariffs and Trade in US History*, ed. Cynthia Clark Northrup and Elaine C. Prange Turney, 3 vols. (Westport, CT: Greenwood Press, 2003), 1:45–61; Moore, "Interests and Ideas," 358.

43. *Congressional Globe*, Twenty-Seventh Congress, Second Session, 604.

44. Entry for 21 June 1842, in Adams, *Memoirs*, 11:182. Several similar entries may be found in the surrounding pages.

45. "Sayings . . . XXXIV," dated 10 February, *United States Gazette*, 12 February 1842.

46. "Protection with a Vengeance" (from the *Madisonian*), *The Pennsylvanian* (Philadelphia), 1 August 1842.

47. Francis P. Blair to Martin Van Buren, Washington, 4 September 1842, Reel 25, Martin Van Buren Papers, Library of Congress, Washington, DC.

48. *House Journal*, Twenty-Seventh Congress, Second Session, 1107–1109.

49. Samuel Chandler Crafts to Nathan and Mary Hill, Washington, 17 July 1842, Crafts Family Papers, *University of Vermont Libraries Center for Digital Initiatives*, http://cdi.uvm.edu/collections/index.xql.

50. Henry Clay to Willie P. Mangum, Lexington, 11 July 1842, in Clay, *Papers*, 9:731. See also Henry Clay to John Quincy Adams, Lexington, 24 July 1842, and Henry Clay to John M. Clayton, Lexington, 8 August 1842, in the same volume, 741–743, 753–754.

51. John J. Crittenden to Henry Clay, Washington, 3 August 1842, in Clay, *Papers*, 9:749.

52. *Congressional Globe*, Twenty-Seventh Congress, Second Session, 852. Samuel Chandler Crafts to Nathan and Mary Hill, Washington, 7 August 1842, Crafts Family Papers.

53. *Congressional Globe*, Twenty-Seventh Congress, Second Session, 867–868.

54. Daniel Webster to Isaac Chapman Bates, Washington, 16 July 1842, in *The Papers of Daniel Webster: Correspondence*, ed. Charles Wiltse, 7 vols. (Hanover, NH: University Press of New England, 1974–1986), 5:226.

55. Daniel Webster to John Tyler, 8 August 1842, in Webster, *Papers*, 5:236.

56. John J. Crittenden to Henry Clay, Washington, 12 August 1842, in Clay, *Papers*, 9:755; emphasis original.

57. Leverett Saltonstall to Robert C. Winthrop, Washington, 10 June 1842, in Saltonstall, *Papers*, 4:159. See also Leverett Saltonstall to Henry Clay, Washington, 7 July 1842, and Leverett Saltonstall to Mary Saltonstall, Washington, [6 August 1842], in the same volume, 202–203, 251–252.

58. Entry for 4 August 1842, in Adams, *Memoirs*, 11:228.

59. John J. Crittenden to James Harlan, [Washington], 16 August 1842, in *The Life of John J. Crittenden, with Selections from His Correspondence and Speeches*, ed. Ann Mary Butler Coleman, 2 vols. (Philadelphia, 1873), 1:193. There are several letters describing these caucuses in the correspondence of Virginia representative Alexander H. H. Stuart to his wife, Folders 13–16, Section 3, Stuart Family Papers, Virginia Historical Society, Richmond.

60. Cave Johnson to James K. Polk, Washington, 28 August 1842, in *Correspondence of James K. Polk*, ed. Wayne Cutler, 13 vols. to date (Nashville, TN: Vanderbilt University Press, 1969–), 6:102; emphasis original.

61. John C. Calhoun to Thomas G. Clemson, Washington, 22 August 1842, in Calhoun, *Papers*, 16:418.

62. Cave Johnson to James K. Polk, Washington, 28 August 1842, in Polk, *Correspondence*, 6:102–103. Ingersoll introduced his proposal in the House on 19 August. *Congressional Globe*, Twenty-Seventh Congress, Second Session, 914. "Cash duties" refers to the abolition of credit on payment of import duties, something protectionists had sought as far back as the Baldwin Bill of 1820. For corroboration of Johnson's claims, see Hopkins L. Turney to James K. Polk, Louisville, KY, 4 September 1842, in Polk, *Correspondence*, 6:106–107.

63. *National Intelligencer* (Washington) quoted in "The Revenue Bill," *United States Gazette*, 24 August 1842.

64. *Congressional Globe*, Twenty-Seventh Congress, Second Session, 925.

65. "Sayings . . . CLXCIII," dated 22 August, *United States Gazette*, 24 August 1842.

66. *House Journal*, Twenty-Seventh Congress, Second Session, 1385–1387. The *Congressional Globe* gives the vote as 105 to 103 but only lists 104 members in the yeas column; it appears that Edward Stanly, a Whig from North Carolina, voted for engrossment but then ducked the vote on the final passage when it became clear, toward the end of the alphabetical roll call, that his vote was not needed to pass the bill.

67. Leverett Saltonstall to Mary Saltonstall, 22 [*sic*, 23] August [1842], in Saltonstall, *Papers*, 4:277. The various votes are detailed in *Congressional Globe*, Twenty-Seventh Congress, Second Session, 922–926, and entry for 22 August 1842, in Adams, *Memoirs*, 11:241–243.

68. See, for example, Joseph R. Ingersoll to Henry D. Gilpin, Washington, 5 August 1842, Folder 2, Box 6, Charles Jared Ingersoll Papers, HSP.

69. "Sayings . . . CLXCV," dated 24 August, *United States Gazette*, 26 August 1842.

70. Silas Wright to Azariah C. Flagg, 26 August 1842, Azariah C. Flagg Papers, New York Public Library, cited in John Arthur Garraty, *Silas Wright* (New York: Columbia University Press, 1949), 226–227.

71. *Congressional Globe*, Twenty-Seventh Congress, Second Session, 960, simply records the vote on the motion to engross as twenty-four to twenty-three, but William Alexander Graham to Samuel S. Phelps, Raleigh, NC, in Graham, *Papers*, 3:39 (quotation), and "Sayings . . . CLXCVIII," dated 27 August, *United States Gazette*, 30 August 1842, detail the circumstances of the votes given by Williams and Wright.

72. Of the six Northern Whigs who opposed the bill, at least three, including Adams, were protesting the surrender of distribution to Tyler's vetoes rather than voting against protection. "Sayings . . . CLXCIII," dated 22 August, *United States Gazette*, 24 August 1842.

73. James Buchanan to Francis P. Blair, Lancaster, 24 September 1842, Reel

10, Blair Family Papers, LC. For letters urging Buchanan to vote for the Tariff of 1842, see Folders 6–7, Box 10, James Buchanan Papers, HSP.

74. John C. Calhoun to Andrew Pickens Calhoun, Washington, 30 August 1842, in Calhoun, *Papers*, 16:435. "Calhoon returnes to his free trade doctoring and raises the hugh and cry against Van, Wright &c. and are now labouring to rise upon their downfal, when in fact *he* is guilty of the same offence, except he displaid moore judgement in his retreat from a measure which he would doubtless have supported but for the reunion of the whigs," was the more cynical verdict of one of the South Carolinian's colleagues in the national legislature. Hopkins L. Turney to James K. Polk, Louisville, KY, 4 September 1842, in Polk, *Correspondence*, 6:106–107; emphasis original.

75. Robert J. Walker to James K. Polk, Baltimore, 30 May 1844, in Polk, *Correspondence*, 7:168.

76. James K. Polk to John K. Kane, Columbia, TN, 19 June 1844, in Polk, *Correspondence*, 7:267. This letter was then widely reprinted in the press.

77. "Democratic Party Platform of 1844," 27 May 1844, *The American Presidency Project*, http://www.presidency.ucsb.edu/ws/?pid=29573.

78. Stephen M. Chester to Henry Clay, New York, 13 November 1844, in Clay, *Papers*, 10:146.

79. For the 1844 election in Pennsylvania, see Malcolm Rogers Eiselen, *The Rise of Pennsylvania Protectionism* (Philadelphia: Porcupine Press, 1974, reprint of 1932 edition), 154–171. For Walker's role in the election, and the Tariff of 1846 more generally, see James P. Shenton, *Robert John Walker: A Politician from Jackson to Lincoln* (New York: Columbia University Press, 1961), 52–53, 74–86.

80. James K. Polk, "First Annual Message," 2 December 1845, *The American Presidency Project*, http://www.presidency.ucsb.edu/ws/?pid=29486.

81. James E. Winston, "The Mississippi Whigs and the Tariff 1834–1844," *Mississippi Valley Historical Review* 22 (March 1936): 508. Walker does not appear to have actually attended the convention.

82. Robert J. Walker, quoted in Edward Stanwood, *American Tariff Controversies in the Nineteenth Century*, 2 vols. (Boston, 1903), 2:44, 53.

83. On the growing export interests of Western grain farmers and how their shifting market orientation impacted protectionist and free trade coalitions in Congress, see Douglas A. Irwin, "Antebellum Tariff Politics: Regional Coalitions and Shifting Economic Interests," *Journal of Law and Economics* 51 (November 2008): 715–741.

84. "British Gold and the Tariff," 21 September 1844, and "British Gold," 5 October 1844, both *Niles' Weekly Register*.

85. "Pennsylvania Tariff Men," *North American and United States Gazette* (Philadelphia), 27 June 1846. For Walker's nickname, see "Sayings . . . DCXXXI," dated 21 February, *United States Gazette*, 23 February 1846. For the most comprehensive claim of some understanding between "the two Sir Roberts," see "The Tariff and the Treaty Power," *North American and United States Gazette*, 24 June 1846.

86. James K. Polk to Louis McLane, Washington, 28 January 1846, in Polk, *Correspondence*, 11:54. For more on the international dimension of the Tariff of 1846, see Sam. W. Haynes, *Unfinished Revolution: The Early American Republic in a British World* (Charlottesville: University of Virginia Press, 2010), 149–152; Scott C. James and David A. Lake, "The Second Face of Hegemony: Britain's Repeal of the Corn Laws and the American Walker Tariff of 1846," *International Organization* 43 (Winter 1989): 1–29; and Marc-William Palen, *The "Conspiracy" of Free Trade: The Anglo-American Struggle over Empire and Economic Globalisation, 1846–1896* (Cambridge: Cambridge University Press, 2016), 22–28.

87. The other members were: George Dromgoole (VA, Democrat), George Houston (AL, Democrat), Orville Hungerford (NY, Democrat), Joseph R. Ingersoll (PA, Whig), Seaborn Jones (GA, Democrat), Moses Norris Jr. (NH, Democrat), Samuel Vinton (OH, Whig), and Robert C. Winthrop (MA, Whig).

88. Shenton, *Robert John Walker*, 82.

89. "Sayings . . . DCCLXXI," dated 5 August, *United States Gazette*, 7 August 1846; emphasis original. Nine officers are named in "Sayings . . . DCXXIII," dated 11 February, *United States Gazette*, 13 February 1846. Precedents for customs officials assisting in the preparation of commercial legislation may be found in Gautham Rao, *National Duties: Custom Houses and the Making of the American State* (Chicago: University of Chicago Press, 2016).

90. John Niles, *Congressional Globe*, Twenty-Ninth Congress, First Session, 1117.

91. James Graham to William Alexander Graham, Washington, 4 January 1846, in Graham, *Papers*, 3:91.

92. Gideon Welles to Martin Van Buren, Washington, 28 July 1846, Reel 30, Van Buren Papers.

93. "Sayings . . . DCXXIII," dated 11 February, *United States Gazette*, 13 February 1846.

94. Entry for 5 March 1846, in *The Diary of James K. Polk during his Presidency, 1845 to 1849*, ed. Milo Milton Quaife, 4 vols. (Chicago: A. C. McClurg, 1910), 1:267.

95. Richard E. Ellis, *The Union at Risk: Jacksonian Democracy, States' Rights, and the Nullification Crisis* (Oxford: Oxford University Press, 1987), 80.

96. "Washington Correspondence," signed "Independent" and dated 15 March, *North American and United States Gazette*, 17 March 1846. Though see Robert C. Winthrop to Nathan Appleton, Washington, 27 February 1846, Reel 24, Winthrop Family Papers, Massachusetts Historical Society, Boston, for one protectionist member of the committee's urging of New England manufacturers to send "statements" and "agents" to "enlighten us."

97. *Congressional Globe*, Twenty-Ninth Congress, First Session, 670–671. "Washington Correspondence," dated 14 April, *North American and United States Gazette*, 16 April 1846. The bill was adopted in committee by a majority of one, with Hungerford joining the three Whigs in voting against it.

98. Worse was to come for owners of textile mills, because before the bill passed the rate on wool would be raised to 30 percent, putting it at a par with the manufactured product.

99. "Sayings ... DCXXVIII," dated 16 February, *United States Gazette*, 18 February 1846; emphasis original.

100. E. I. du Pont de Nemours and Company to William Kemble, 4 August 1846, Letterbook: 27 July 1846–28 May 1847, No. 1: Letterbooks, Series A: Letters Sent, Part I: Correspondence, Records of E. I. du Pont de Nemours and Company, HM&L.

101. Henry C. Carey to John C. Calhoun, Philadelphia, 2 March 1846 (quotation), emphasis original; Henry C. Carey to John C. Calhoun, Philadelphia, 20 July 1846; and John C. Calhoun to Henry C. Carey, Washington, 31 July 1846, all in Calhoun, *Papers*, 22:649–652; 23:341–343, 380.

102. Entry for 28 July 1846, in Polk, *Diary*, 2:52–53. See, likewise, Vice President George Mifflin Dallas's letter to his wife, Sophia Chew Nicklin Dallas, 21 May 1846, Folder 16, Box 13, George Mifflin Dallas Papers, HSP.

103. E. I. du Pont de Nemours and Company to William Kemble, 22 June 1846, Letterbook: 3 January–27 July 1846, No. 1: Letterbooks, Series A: Letters Sent, Part I: Correspondence, Records of E. I. du Pont de Nemours and Company.

104. "Sayings ... DCCLIV," dated 18 July, *United States Gazette*, 20 July 1846; emphasis original.

105. "National Fair," *North American and United States Gazette*, 15 April 1846.

106. W. P. F—— to Josiah S. Johnston, Philadelphia, 21 October 1827, Folder 8, Box 5, Johnston Papers.

107. "The National Fair," *North American and United States Gazette*, 27 March 1846. For more on activities of the British agent, a "Mr. Homer," who was "*known* to be the immediate confidant and representative of the Secretary of the Treasury," see "Washington Correspondence," dated 27 March, 15 May, and 28 May, all *North American and United States Gazette*, 30 March, 18 May, 30 May 1846, and Peter T. Homer to John C. Calhoun, Saratoga Springs, NY, 2 July 1846, in Calhoun, *Papers*, 23:264–265, which identifies Homer as a native of Massachusetts with ten years' commercial experience in London.

108. "Circular of the Committee of Superintendence of the National Exhibition of American Manufactures and Products of Mechanical Art, at the City of Washington, in May Next," *North American and United States Gazette*, 31 March 1846. There is also a likely reference to Homer, though the name was subsequently crossed through by the author, in Robert C. Winthrop to Nathan Appleton, Washington, 27 February 1846, Reel 24, Winthrop Family Papers.

109. See "The National Fair," *North American and United States Gazette*, 28 April 1846; the "Washington Correspondence" of the same paper dated 21 May–3 June; and the "National Fair" letters by Sargent, under his "Oliver Oldschool" signature, in the *United States Gazette* over the same period. The cost of the building is given in entry for 23 May 1846, in Polk, *Diary*, 1:421.

110. "From an Occasional Correspondent," *The Pennsylvanian*, 8 June 1846.

111. Entry for 23 May 1846, in Polk, *Diary*, 1:421–422.

112. *Congressional Globe*, Twenty-Ninth Congress, First Session, 976.

113. Editorial note, in Webster, *Papers*, 6:173.

114. "Sayings . . . DCCXIII," dated 30 May, *United States Gazette*, 1 June 1846.

115. "Sayings . . . DCCLXI," dated 2 July, *United States Gazette*, 4 July 1846; *Congressional Globe*, Twenty-Ninth Congress, First Session, 1047–1050. A drawback is a remittance of import duty, in this case on the material used for preserving the fish, when an article is exported.

116. "Sayings . . . DCCXLII," dated 3 July, *United States Gazette*, 6 July 1846. *Congressional Globe*, Twenty-Ninth Congress, First Session, 1050–1053.

117. "The Tariff—the Joy of the Members, and Mr. Walker and Mr. Ritchie," *New York Herald*, 5 July 1846, cited in William K. Bolt, *Tariff Wars and the Politics of Jacksonian America* (Nashville, TN: Vanderbilt University Press, 2017), 178.

118. "Sayings . . . DCCXLII," dated 3 July, *United States Gazette*, 6 July 1846; emphasis original. Also present was Thomas Ritchie, editor of the administration organ the *Union* (Washington), and Cave Johnson, the postmaster general.

119. Entry for 3 July, in Polk, *Diary*, 2:7–11.

120. "Extracts from an Autobiographical Sketch," in *The Papers of Jefferson Davis*, ed. Haskell M. Monroe Jr., et al., 12 vols. (Baton Rouge: Louisiana State University Press, 1971–2008), 2:700.

121. [P. T. Homer?] to Robert J. Walker, Washington, 13 May 1846, Container 4, Robert J. Walker Papers, LC. The signature is hard to read, but the writer of this letter, who was liaising with McKay on the tariff, may well have been the same Peter T. Homer who was exhibiting British manufactures around the capitol.

122. Henry Clay to Andrew Stewart, quoted in Eiselen, *The Rise of Pennsylvania Protectionism*, 189n90; emphasis original.

123. "Resolutions Relative to the Tariff," *United States Gazette*, 9 February 1846.

124. David R. Porter, former governor of Pennsylvania, quoted in *North American* (Philadelphia), 18 November 1846, cited in Eiselen, *The Rise of Pennsylvania Protectionism*, 206n44; emphasis original.

125. David Wilmot to B. Laporte, Montrose, 22 January 1855, reprinted in *Reporter* (Bradford), 30 April 1857, cited in Charles Buxton Going, *David Wilmot: Free-Soiler* (New York: D. Appleton and Company, 1924), 91. Wilmot's correspondence from the period suggests he was genuinely committed to a revenue tariff. David Wilmot to John Laporte, Washington, 15 December 1845, David Wilmot Folder, Society Large Collection, HSP.

126. Egnal, *Clash of Extremes*, 90.

127. New Hampshire senator Joseph Cilley had been elected by the cross-party anti-slavery "New Hampshire Alliance," but he voted consistently with the twenty-four regular Whigs in opposition to Walker's bill. See Holt, *The Rise and Fall of the American Whig Party*, 230–231.

128. *Congressional Globe*, Twenty-Ninth Congress, First Session, 1053–1057.

129. "Sayings . . . DCCLI," dated 14 July, *United States Gazette*, 16 July 1846; "Sayings . . . DCCLXI," dated 25 July, *United States Gazette*, 28 July 1846.

130. *Congressional Globe*, Twenty-Ninth Congress, First Session, 1111.

131. *Congressional Globe*, Twenty-Ninth Congress, First Session, 1132.

132. Entry for 20 July 1846, in Polk, *Diary*, 2:33.

133. Entry for 3 March 1846, in Polk, *Diary*, 1:261.

134. *Congressional Globe*, Twenty-Ninth Congress, First Session, 1112. On Cameron's election, see Eiselen, *The Rise of Pennsylvania Protectionism*, 182–183.

135. Benjamin F. Beeker to Robert J. Walker, Pomfret Landing, CT, 25 May 1846, Container 4, Walker Papers.

136. *Congressional Globe*, Twenty-Ninth Congress, First Session, 1117. Connecticut's other senator was Whig and would vote against the bill.

137. "The Revenue Bill in Danger!" *Union*, 25 July 1846, reprinted in "The Tariff," *Niles' Weekly Register*, 1 August 1846.

138. George Mifflin Dallas to Sophia Chew Nicklin Dallas, Washington, 23 July 1846, Folder 18, Box 13, Dallas Papers. For Dallas's role in the Tariff of 1846, see John M. Belohlavek, *George Mifflin Dallas: Jacksonian Patrician* (University Park: Pennsylvania State University Press, 1977), 111–118.

139. James Page to George Mifflin Dallas, 3 July 1846, and Henry M. Phillips to George Mifflin Dallas, Philadelphia, 4 July 1846, both Folder 22, Box 4, Dallas Papers.

140. J. W. Forney to Buchanan, Philadelphia, 9 July 1846, Folder 8, Box 14, Buchanan Papers.

141. Entry for 24 July 1846, in Polk, *Diary*, 2:46–47. See also George Mifflin Dallas to H. Phillips, 28 July 1846, Ferdinand J. Dreer Collection, HSP, cited in Eiselen, *The Rise of Pennsylvania Protectionism*, 194.

142. James K. Polk to Robert Armstrong, Washington, 13 July 1846, in Polk, *Correspondence*, 11:242.

143. Webster's financial dealings are detailed in "Agreement Regarding the Webster Annuity," Boston, 5 January 1846, and David Sears to Daniel Webster, Boston, 21 March 1846, both in Webster, *Papers*, 6:106–108, 130–131. Robert V. Remini, *Daniel Webster: The Man and His Time* (New York: W. W. Norton, 1997), discusses both these dealings, 600–602, and Webster's role in the Tariff of 1846, 619–624.

144. Entry for 18 September 1845, in Adams, *Memoirs*, 12:214.

145. Daniel Webster to Nathan Appleton, New York, 8 July 1846, emphasis original, and "Nathan Appleton's Memorandum on the Tariff," c. 10 July 1846, both in Webster, *Papers*, 6:175–176, 177–179.

146. Daniel Webster to James Kellogg Mills, 19 July 1846, in Webster, *Papers*, 6:184–185.

147. Daniel Webster to Fletcher Webster, Washington, 29 July 1846, in *The*

Letters of Daniel Webster, ed. C. H. Van Tyne (New York, 1902), 340–341 (quotation 340).

148. Thomas Lamb et al. to Daniel Webster, 21 July, Washington, reprinted in "From the *National Intelligencer* of Friday," *United States Gazette*, 3 August 1846. For the views of Webster's benefactors, see James Kellogg Mills to Daniel Webster, Boston, 23 July 1846, and Nathan Appleton to Daniel Webster, Boston, [23 July 1846], both in Webster, *Papers*, 6:189–190, 3:219 (misdated here but corrected 6:190n2).

149. Webster, *Writings*, 3:131, cited in Merrill D. Peterson, *Olive Branch and Sword: The Compromise of 1833* (Baton Rouge: Louisiana State University Press, 1982), 85.

150. "Sayings . . . DCCLVI," dated 20 July, *United States Gazette*, 22 July 1846. See also Daniel Webster to James Kellogg Mills, 21 July 1846, in Webster, *Papers*, 6:188.

151. E. I. du Pont de Nemours and Company to William Kemble, 24 July 1846, Letterbook: 3 January–27 July 1846, No. 1: Letterbooks, Series A: Letters Sent, Part I: Correspondence, Records of E. I. du Pont de Nemours and Company.

152. Daniel Webster to Fletcher Webster, Washington, 27 July 1846, in Webster, *Papers*, 6:194; emphasis original. See also Daniel Webster to Fletcher Webster, Washington, 29 July 1846, in Webster, *Letters*, 337–341.

153. *Congressional Globe*, Twenty-Ninth Congress, First Session, 1155.

154. "Sayings . . . DCCLXVII," dated 1 August, *United States Gazette*, 3 August 1846; emphasis original. See also "The Compromise," *United States Gazette*, 10 August 1846.

155. Entry for 11 July 1846, in Polk, *Diary*, 2:20.

156. Entry for 13 July 1846, in Polk, *Diary*, 2:24–25.

157. Entry for 15 July 1846, in Polk, *Diary*, 2:26, 27.

158. "Sayings . . . DCCLIII," dated 16 July, *United States Gazette*, 18 July 1846.

159. Entry for 15 July 1846, in Polk, *Diary*, 2:27.

160. "Address of the Hon. Wm. H. Haywood, Jr., to the People of North Carolina," *Niles' Weekly Register*, 29 August 1846.

161. Instructions reprinted in "Address of . . . Haywood," *Niles' Weekly Register*, 29 August 1846.

162. Entry for 23 July 1846, in Polk, *Diary*, 2:43–46 (quotations both 45). See also entries for 15 July 1846, 2:26, and 20 July 1846, 2:32–33.

163. Entry for 23 July 1846, in Polk, *Diary*, 2:43.

164. "Address of . . . Haywood," *Niles' Weekly Register*, 29 August 1846. For precedents for Haywood's course, see Clement Eaton, "Southern Senators and the Right of Instruction, 1789–1860," *Journal of Southern History* 18 (August 1952): 303–319, and C. Edward Skeen, "An Uncertain 'Right': State Legislatures and the Doctrine of Instruction," *Mid-America* 73 (January 1991): 29–47.

165. Entry for 25 July 1846, in Polk, *Diary*, 2:48. News of Haywood's resig-

nation circulated late on Saturday, although it was not officially communicated to the Senate until Monday morning. *Congressional Globe,* Twenty-Ninth Congress, First Session, 1141.

166. John Fairfield to Anna Fairfield, Washington, 26 July 1846, in Fairfield, *Letters,* 413.

167. "The Revenue Bill in Danger!" *Union,* 25 July 1846, reprinted in "The Tariff," *Niles' Weekly Register,* 1 August 1846. Other free traders muttered darkly that Haywood had been "bought." Charles C. Walden to John C. Calhoun, New York City, 28 July 1846, in Calhoun, *Papers,* 23:373.

168. "Sayings ... DCCLXI," dated 25 July, *United States Gazette,* 28 July 1846. Rather less generously, Massachusetts Whig representative Robert C. Winthrop described Haywood as "rather a weak-minded, undecided, sort of person, with a conscience, to be sure, (which is saying a good deal for a Statesman), but without force & firmness enough to follow its behests to the end. If he had kept his post & voted against the Bill, he would have stood better in the opinion of all parties." "Semple was ridiculous enough," he added in a second letter. "But if he tried to run away, he at least consented to run back again, & then stood fast at his post." Winthrop to Mrs. Gardner, Washington, 26 July 1846, and Winthrop to Nathan Appleton, Washington, 30 July 1846, both Reel 25, Winthrop Family Papers.

169. The instructions of the Tennessee legislature were referenced several times during debate on the bill. See, for example, *Congressional Globe,* Twenty-Ninth Congress, First Session, 1143.

170. Entry for 13 July 1846, in Polk, *Diary,* 2:25.

171. Entry for 25 July 1846, in Polk, *Diary,* 2:49.

172. Entry for 26 July 1846, in Polk, *Diary,* 2:50.

173. John Fairfield to Anna Fairfield, Washington, 28 July 1846, in Fairfield, *Letters,* 414.

174. Daniel Webster to Fletcher Webster, Washington, 29 July 1846, in Webster, *Letters,* 337–341. All quotations in this paragraph are from this letter. See also Daniel Webster, memorandum, [29 July 1846], in same volume, 341–342.

175. Daniel Webster to Fletcher Webster, Washington, 29 July 1846, in Webster, *Letters,* 338.

176. *Congressional Globe,* Twenty-Ninth Congress, First Session, 1143.

177. *Congressional Globe,* Twenty-Ninth Congress, First Session, 1144. The Senate proceedings of 27 July are described in Daniel Webster to Fletcher Webster, Washington, 29 July 1846, in Webster, *Letters,* 337–341; "Sayings ... DCCLXIII," dated 27 July, *United States Gazette,* 29 July 1846; and *Congressional Globe,* Twenty-Ninth Congress, First Session, 1141–1145.

178. Daniel Webster to Fletcher Webster, Washington, 29 July 1846, in Webster, *Letters,* 338.

179. *Congressional Globe,* Twenty-Ninth Congress, First Session, 1144.

180. Clayton admitted as much in debate the following day when he declared:

"[I]f the committee is not discharged the bill fails." *Congressional Globe*, Twenty-Ninth Congress, First Session, 1151. For rumors of a replacement for Haywood, see *Congressional Globe*, Twenty-Ninth Congress, First Session, 1144, and "The Revenue Bill in Danger!" *Union*, 25 July 1846, reprinted in "The Tariff," *Niles' Weekly Register*, 1 August 1846.

181. "Sayings . . . DCCLXIII," dated 27 July, *United States Gazette*, 29 July 1846.

182. Daniel Webster to Fletcher Webster, Washington, 29 July 1846, in Webster, *Letters*, 338.

183. Cave Johnson to James Buchanan, [Washington], 27 July 1846, Folder 10, Box 14, Buchanan Papers; Shenton, *Robert John Walker*, 84.

184. Daniel Webster to Fletcher Webster, Washington, 29 July 1846, in Webster, *Letters*, 338.

185. Spencer Jarnagin to Daniel Webster, [Washington, 28 July 1846], in Webster, *Letters*, 342.

186. Daniel Webster to Fletcher Webster, Washington, 29 July 1846, in Webster, *Letters*, 339.

187. "Sayings . . . DCCLXIV," dated 28 July, *United States Gazette*, 30 July 1846.

188. "Sayings . . . DCCLXIV," dated 28 July, *United States Gazette*, 30 July 1846.

189. *Congressional Globe*, Twenty-Ninth Congress, First Session, 1156.

190. The Senate proceedings of 28 July are described in Daniel Webster to Fletcher Webster, Washington, 29 July 1846, in Webster, *Letters*, 337–341; "Sayings . . . DCCLXIV," dated 28 July, *United States Gazette*, 30 July 1846; and *Congressional Globe*, Twenty-Ninth Congress, First Session, 1149–1158.

191. Daniel Webster to Fletcher Webster, Washington, 29 July 1846, in Webster, *Letters*, 339.

192. *Congressional Globe*, Twenty-Ninth Congress, First Session, 1165.

193. William H. Polk to James K. Polk, Naples, Italy, 6 November 1846, in Polk, *Correspondence*, 11:387; emphasis original.

194. Daniel Webster to Fletcher Webster, Washington, 29 July 1846, in Webster, *Letters*, 339.

195. Robert C. Winthrop to Mrs. Gardner, Washington, 3 March 1846, Reel 24, Winthrop Family Papers. The rivalry between Webster and Clay is documented in Holt, *The Rise and Fall of the American Whig Party*; Remini, *Daniel Webster*; and Robert V. Remini, *Henry Clay: Statesman for the Union* (New York: W. W. Norton, 1991). Webster's son circulated a report that his father would have secured the defeat of the tariff bill were it not for Clayton's intervention, until admonished by friends of the latter. "JD" [John Davis?] to John M. Clayton, Worcester, MA, 22 August [1846?], Container 1, John M. Clayton Papers, LC.

196. The Democrats' opponents included Senator Cilley and six American Party representatives, all of whom voted against the tariff. Eighty-seven percent

of the Democratic votes cast were in favor of the bill, and 98 percent of Whig votes were against. Only 1861 offers a comparable partisan division, with 89 percent of Democratic votes against the tariff bill of that year and 97 percent of Republican votes in favor.

197. "Address of ... Haywood," *Niles' Weekly Register*, 29 August 1846; emphasis original.

198. *Congressional Globe*, Twenty-Ninth Congress, First Session, 1156.

199. "Sayings ... DCCXLVIV," dated 12 July, *United States Gazette*, 14 July 1846.

200. Sam Houston to Margaret Houston, Washington, [26] July 1846, in *The Personal Correspondence of Sam Houston*, ed. Madge Thornall Roberts, 4 vols. (Denton: University of North Texas Press, 1996–2001), 2:150.

201. Belohlavek, *George Mifflin Dallas*, 114 (hung in effigy); George Mifflin Dallas to Sophia Chew Nicklin Dallas (bring the whole brood to Washington), Washington, 30 July 1846, Folder 18, Box 13, and G. —— to George Mifflin Dallas (insurance policy), Philadelphia, 4 August 1846, Folder 23, Box 4, both Dallas Papers, HSP. Barrels placed over the chimneys of factories that went out of business following passage of the tariff were derisively referred to as "Dallas night caps." Eiselen, *The Rise of Pennsylvania Protectionism*, 200.

202. *Congressional Globe*, Twenty-Ninth Congress, First Session, 1156.

203. Nathan Appleton to Henry C. Carey, Boston, 21 April 1857, Folder 4, Box 11, Edward Carey Gardiner Collection, HSP.

204. "Sayings ... CLXCVI," dated 26 August, *United States Gazette*, 27 August 1842.

Chapter Six: "The Almighty Dollar": The Tariffs of 1857 and 1861

1. "The Prevalence of Corruption," *The Pennsylvanian* (Philadelphia), 6 February 1857.

2. Eleazar Lord to Mathew Carey, Washington, 1 March 1820, Folder 4, Box 23, Edward Carey Gardiner Collection, Historical Society of Pennsylvania, Philadelphia.

3. Charles I. du Pont to Samuel Francis du Pont, Louviers, 9 May 1847, Box 3, Series B: Charles Irénée du Pont, Group 5: Papers of the Children of Victor du Pont, Winterthur Manuscripts, Hagley Museum and Library, Wilmington, DE. On a similar note, see Daniel Ullmann to Henry Clay, Philipsburg, PA, 12 July 1847, in *The Papers of Henry Clay*, ed. James F. Hopkins, Robert Seagar II, Melba Porter Hay, et al., 11 vols. (Lexington: University Press of Kentucky, 1959–1992), 10:339.

4. John F. T. Crampton to George Villiers ("Lord Clarendon"), 7 February 1853, in *Private and Confidential: Letters from British Ministers in Washington to the Foreign Secretaries in London, 1844–1867*, ed. James J. Barnes and Patience P. Barnes (Selinsgrove, PA: Susquehanna University Press, 1993), 64.

5. On the demise of the Democrat-Whig party system, see John L. Brooke,

"Party, Nation, and Cultural Rupture: The Crisis of the American Civil War," in *Practicing Democracy: Popular Politics in the United States from the Constitution to the Civil War*, ed. Daniel Peart and Adam I. P. Smith (Charlottesville: University of Virginia Press, 2015); Corey M. Brooks, *Antislavery Third Parties and the Transformation of American Politics* (Chicago: University of Chicago Press, 2016); Marc Egnal, *Clash of Extremes: The Economic Origins of the Civil War* (New York: Hill and Wang, 2010); and Michael F. Holt, *The Rise and Fall of the American Whig Party: Jacksonian Politics and the Onset of the Civil War* (Oxford: Oxford University Press, 1999). For the deaths of its leading figures, see Merrill D. Peterson, *The Great Triumvirate: Webster, Clay, and Calhoun* (Oxford: Oxford University Press, 1987).

6. "Democratic Party Platform of 1856," 2 June 1856, http://www.presidency.ucsb.edu/ws/?pid=29576, and "Republican Party Platform of 1856," 18 June 1856, http://www.presidency.ucsb.edu/ws/?pid=29619, both *The American Presidency Project*; George Winston Smith, *Henry C. Carey and American Sectional Conflict* (Albuquerque: University of New Mexico Press, 1951), 44–45. For more on how free trade and protectionist Northerners first united under the Republican antislavery banner, see Eric Foner, *Free Soil, Free Labor, Free Men: The Ideology of the Republican Party before the Civil War* (New York: Oxford University Press, 1970). For the subsequent story of how tensions between those two constituencies following the Civil War threatened to tear the party apart, see Marc-William Palen, *The "Conspiracy" of Free Trade: The Anglo-American Struggle over Empire and Economic Globalisation, 1846–1896* (Cambridge: Cambridge University Press, 2016).

7. James L. Baker to Henry C. Carey, Boston, 23 March 1856, Folder 5, Box 11, Gardiner Collection.

8. James H. Campbell to Henry C. Carey, Washington, 4 December 1856, Folder 2, Box 12, Gardiner Collection.

9. William Gregg to Amos A. Lawrence, Kalmia, SC, 2 September 1850, reprinted in Thomas P. Martin, "The Advent of William Gregg and the Graniteville Company," *Journal of Southern History* 11 (August 1945): 422. See, likewise, H. Winder to Daniel Webster, Philadelphia, 12 March 1850, in *The Papers of Daniel Webster: Correspondence*, ed. Charles Wiltse, 7 vols. (Hanover, NH: University Press of New England, 1974–1986), 7:33–34.

10. Henry C. Carey to Josiah Quincy, 28 September 1856 (draft), Gardiner Collection, cited in Smith, *Henry C. Carey and American Sectional Conflict*, 46.

11. Henry C. Carey to James Buchanan, London, 15 October 1857, Folder 22, Box 34, James Buchanan Papers, HSP.

12. See Henry C. Carey to Charles A. Dana, 10 November 1856 (draft), Folder 6, Box 19; Charles A. Dana to Henry C. Carey, New York, 16 November 1856 (quotation), Folder 5, Box 12; and E. Peshine Smith to Henry C. Carey, Albany, 28 November 1856, Folder 2, Box 18, all Gardiner Collection.

13. For Carey's best known statement of this argument, see *The Harmony of*

Interests: Agricultural, Manufacturing, and Commercial (Philadelphia, 1851). For his activities up to the 1856 election and its aftermath, see Smith, *Henry C. Carey and American Sectional Conflict*, 7–51.

14. E. Peshine Smith to Henry C. Carey, Albany, 6 November 1856, Folder 2, Box 18, Gardiner Collection.

15. E. Peshine Smith to Henry C. Carey, Albany, 28 November 1856, Folder 2, Box 18, Gardiner Collection.

16. Horace Greeley, *The Autobiography of Horace Greeley, or Recollections of a Busy Life* (New York, 1872), 86; Justin S. Morrill, "Notable Letters from My Political Friends," *The Forum* (October–December 1897): 270.

17. "From Washington," signed "Independent" and dated 5 January, *North American and United States Gazette* (Philadelphia), 7 January 1857. Carey's opposition is inferable from his incoming correspondence from E. Peshine Smith in November 1856, Folder 2, Box 18, Gardiner Collection. For more on Harvey, see Daniel W. Crofts, "James E. Harvey and the Secession Crisis," *Pennsylvania Magazine of History and Biography* 103 (April 1979): 177–195.

18. E. Peshine Smith to Henry C. Carey, Albany, 28 November 1856, Folder 2, Box 18, Gardiner Collection.

19. "From Washington," dated 4 December, and "From Washington," dated 7 December, both *North American and United States Gazette*, 6 December, 9 December 1856. See also Solomon Foot to Henry C. Carey, Washington, 6 December 1856, Folder 3, Box 13, and James H. Campbell to Henry C. Carey, Washington, 4 December 1856, Folder 2, Box 12, both Gardiner Collection.

20. *Appendix to the Congressional Globe*, Thirty-Fourth Congress, Third Session, 217. "All the Free Soil or anti-Slavery people here go in for Free Trade. Banks is a free trader . . ." complained one Boston correspondent. James L. Baker to Henry C. Carey, Boston, 15 January 1856, Folder 5, Box 11, Gardiner Collection. See also Fred Harvey Harrington, *Fighting Politician: Major General N. P. Banks* (Philadelphia: University of Pennsylvania Press, 1948), 49. The other members of the committee were: Charles Billinghurst (WI, anti-admn.), James H. Campbell (PA, anti-admn.), Howell Cobb (GA, Democrat), H. Winter Davis (MD, anti-admn.), Alexander De Witt (MA, anti-admn.), William A. Howard (MI, anti-admn.), John Letcher (VA, Democrat), John S. Phelps (MO, Democrat), and Russell Sage (NY, anti-admn.).

21. James H. Campbell to Henry C. Carey, Washington, 4 December 1856, Folder 2, Box 12, Gardiner Collection.

22. Lewis D. Campbell to Henry C. Carey, Washington, 9 July 1856, Folder 2, Box 12, Gardiner Collection. See also Henry D. Carey to Lewis D. Campbell, 29 July 1856, Folder 3, Box 1, Lewis D. Campbell Papers, Ohio History Connection, Columbus, and James H. Campbell to Henry C. Carey, Washington, 12 August 1856, Folder 2, Box 12, Gardiner Collection.

23. James H. Campbell to Henry C. Carey, Washington, 4 December 1856, Folder 2, Box 12, Gardiner Collection.

24. *Congressional Globe*, Thirty-Fourth Congress, Second Session, 2035.

25. Lewis D. Campbell, paraphrased by John Letcher, *Congressional Globe*, Thirty-Fourth Congress, Third Session, 320.

26. *Congressional Globe*, Thirty-Fourth Congress, Third Session, 315–316.

27. *Congressional Globe*, Thirty-Fourth Congress, Third Session, 320.

28. "From Washington," dated 17 January, *North American and United States Gazette*, 19 January 1857.

29. See, for example, John S. Millson, *Congressional Globe*, Thirty-Fourth Congress, Third Session, 321.

30. *Congressional Globe*, Thirty-Fourth Congress, Third Session, 742–743, 790–791.

31. *Congressional Globe*, Thirty-Fourth Congress, Third Session, 785. The other members were: Richard Brodhead (PA, Democrat), John J. Crittenden (KY, anti-admn.), James A. Pearce (MD, anti-admn.), Charles E. Stuart (MI, Democrat), and Isaac Toucey (CT, Democrat).

32. Benjamin Perley Poore, *Perley's Reminiscences of Sixty Years in the National Metropolis*, 2 vols. (Philadelphia, 1886), 1:458. On Hunter's role in the Tariff of 1857, see Henry Harrison Simms, *Life of Robert M. T. Hunter: A Study in Sectionalism and Secession* (Richmond, VA: William Byrd Press, 1935), 103–106.

33. James Brooks to R. M. T. Hunter, Office of the New York Express, New York, 24 February 1857, Folder "Br-Bu," Box 7, Hunter Family Papers, Virginia Historical Society, Richmond.

34. David M. Stone to R. M. T. Hunter, New York, 25 February 1857, Folder "S," Box 11, Hunter Family Papers.

35. J. Wiley Edmands to R. M. T. Hunter, 14 February 1857, Folder "E-F," Box 8, Hunter Family Papers.

36. *Congressional Globe*, Thirty-Fourth Congress, Third Session, 849.

37. *Appendix to the Congressional Globe*, Thirty-Fourth Congress, Third Session, 328–358, including 328 for the substitute as originally proposed, 356–357 for the amendments on wool, and 358 for the substitute as passed.

38. *Congressional Globe*, Thirty-Fourth Congress, Third Session, 959–960.

39. "From Washington," dated 1 March, *North American and United States Gazette*, 4 March 1857; *House Journal*, Thirty-Fourth Congress, Third Session, 606–609.

40. "From Washington," dated "Wednesday night" [4 March], *North American and United States Gazette*, 5 March 1857.

41. Charles Sumner to John Jay, Washington, 2 March 1857, in *The Selected Letters of Charles Sumner*, ed. Beverly Wilson Palmer, 2 vols. (Boston: Northeastern University Press, 1990), 1:473; Edward L. Pierce, ed., *Memoir and Letters of Charles Sumner*, 4 vols. (London, 1877–1893), 3:518–519.

42. "The New Tariff Bill," *The Pennsylvanian*, 6 March 1857.

43. "Alleged Corruption in the Tariff of 1857," House of Representatives Re-

port No. 414, Thirty-Fifth Congress, First Session. This episode has received barely any attention from historians. See brief mentions in Kenneth M. Stampp, *America in 1857: A Nation on the Brink* (Oxford: Oxford University Press, 1992), 26; Edward Stanwood, *American Tariff Controversies in the Nineteenth Century*, 2 vols. (Boston, 1903), 2:109–110; Mark Summers, *The Plundering Generation: Corruption and the Crisis of the Union, 1849–1861* (Oxford: Oxford University Press, 1987), 102–103; and Glyndon G. Van Deusen, *Thurlow Weed: Wizard of the Lobby* (Boston: Little, Brown, 1947), 222–223.

44. *Congressional Globe*, Thirty-Fourth Congress, Third Session, 274–277; Summers, *The Plundering Generation*, 261–263.

45. James E. Harvey to Henry C. Carey, Washington, 11 January [mislabeled "June" in catalogue] 1857, Folder 2, Box 14, Gardiner Collection. See also "From Washington," dated 13 January, *North American and United States Gazette*, 15 January 1857.

46. James E. Harvey to Henry C. Carey, Washington, 2 January [mislabeled "June" in catalogue] 1857, Folder 2, Box 14, Gardiner Collection.

47. "Great Corruption Fund," *Philadelphia Press*, 5 January 1858.

48. "From Washington," dated 31 December 1857, *North American and United States Gazette*, 2 January 1858.

49. "Alleged Corruption in the Tariff of 1857," 1; *Congressional Globe*, Thirty-Fifth Congress, First Session, 304–311. For a much earlier precedent for such an investigation, also involving allegations of lobbyists bribing members of Congress, see David P. Currie, *The Constitution in Congress: The Federalist Period, 1789–1801* (Chicago: University of Chicago Press, 1997), 232–238.

50. *Congressional Globe*, Thirty-Fourth Congress, Third Session, 589. The other members were: Sydenham Moore (AL, Democrat), Samuel Purviance (PA, Republican), William F. Russell (NY, Democrat), and Augustus R. Wright (GA, Democrat). Stanton was a Republican.

51. "Alleged Corruption in the Tariff of 1857," 17–18; entries for 28 September, 2, 9, 11 December 1857, Volume 5: 1842–1858, Amos Adams Lawrence Diaries and Account Books, Massachusetts Historical Society, Boston; and Samuel Lawrence to A. J. Hall, Boston, 3 December 1857, Amos Adams Lawrence Papers, MHS.

52. "Alleged Corruption in the Tariff of 1857," 1.

53. James E. Harvey to Henry C. Carey, Washington, 7 December 1856, Folder 2, Box 14, Gardiner Collection.

54. "Alleged Corruption in the Tariff of 1857," 3, and for Stone's testimony in full, 23–43.

55. "Alleged Corruption in the Tariff of 1857," 35.

56. "Alleged Corruption in the Tariff of 1857," 31. Four payments to Wolcott totaling $74,000 are detailed on 3–4. From his refuge in Europe, Samuel Lawrence made a similar disavowal of responsibility to his nephew, placing the blame

with Slade. Samuel Lawrence to Amos Adams Lawrence, Paris, 8 April 1858, Folder "Apr-May 1858", Box 10, Amos Adams Lawrence Papers, MHS.

57. "Alleged Corruption in the Tariff of 1857," 48.

58. Poore, *Perley's Reminiscences*, 1:531.

59. "From Washington," dated 21 May, *North American and United States Gazette*, 22 May 1858.

60. "Alleged Corruption in the Tariff of 1857," 42–33, 106–107.

61. "Alleged Corruption in the Tariff of 1857," 42.

62. "Alleged Corruption in the Tariff of 1857," 84.

63. Daniel Webster to —— Haven, [Washington], 27 September 1850, in *The Writings and Speeches of Daniel Webster*, 18 vols. (Boston, 1903), 18:391.

64. Rachel A. Shelden, *Washington Brotherhood: Politics, Social Life, and the Coming of the Civil War* (Chapel Hill: University of North Carolina Press, 2013), 27.

65. "Alleged Corruption in the Tariff of 1857," 84 (quotations), 86 (fee). Some of Ashmun's other lobbying ventures are mentioned in Henry Cohen, *Business and Politics in America from the Age of Jackson to the Civil War: The Career Biography of W. W. Corcoran* (Westport, CT: Greenwood Publishing, 1971), 177, and Summers, *The Plundering Generation*, 202. Azariah Boody, another ex-congressman, was reportedly performing a similar role for the free iron lobby at the same session. E. Peshine Smith to Henry C. Carey, Albany, 27 December 1856 and 7 February 1857, both Folder 2, Box 18, Gardiner Collection.

66. "Alleged Corruption in the Tariff of 1857," 24.

67. "Alleged Corruption in the Tariff of 1857," 13.

68. The two Stones were not related.

69. "Alleged Corruption in the Tariff of 1857," 107. For Weed's efforts to avoid testifying before the committee, see Thurlow Weed to William Seward, Albany, 5 May 1858; William Seward to Thurlow Weed, [Washington], 7 May 1858; Edwin B. Morgan to Thurlow Weed, Washington, 7 May 1858, all File Drawer 4, Thurlow Weed Papers, Rush Rhees Library, University of Rochester, NY.

70. "Alleged Corruption in the Tariff of 1857," 24–26, 86–91, 99.

71. "Alleged Corruption in the Tariff of 1857," 7, 8.

72. "Alleged Corruption in the Tariff of 1857," 8.

73. "Alleged Corruption in the Tariff of 1857," 84.

74. "Alleged Corruption in the Tariff of 1857," 33, 37. For the introduction, see David M. Stone to R. M. T. Hunter, Office of the Journal of Commerce, New York, 25 March 1856, in "Correspondence of Robert M. T. Hunter, 1826–1876," ed. Charles Henry Ambler, *Annual Report of the American Historical Association for the Year 1916* (Washington, 1918), 2:184–185.

75. "Alleged Corruption in the Tariff of 1857," 66. See also J. Wiley Edmands to Lewis D. Campbell, 22 May 1856, Folder 3, Box 1, Campbell Papers.

76. "Alleged Corruption in the Tariff of 1857," 42; John D. Lang to R. M. T.

Hunter and John Letcher, 20 February 1857, Folder "K-L," Box 10, Hunter Family Papers.

77. James E. Harvey to Henry C. Carey, Washington, 7 December 1856, Folder 2, Box 14, and E. Peshine Smith to Henry C. Carey, Albany, 27 December 1856, Folder 2, Box 18, both Gardiner Collection.

78. "Alleged Corruption in the Tariff of 1857," 86.

79. "Alleged Corruption in the Tariff of 1857," 6 (quotation), 25–26, 36–37.

80. "Alleged Corruption in the Tariff of 1857," 69.

81. "Alleged Corruption in the Tariff of 1857," 7.

82. "Alleged Corruption in the Tariff of 1857," 60–76. For an example of Corbin's work on behalf of the railroad lobby, in which he sets out a detailed plan of operations that concludes with the advice "send men who will go from room to room . . . and secure votes in detail," see A. R. Corbin to Henry Douglas Brown, Washington, 1 January 1857, Box 14, Papers of Samuel L. M. Barlow, Huntington Library, San Marino, CA.

83. "Alleged Corruption in the Tariff of 1857," 7.

84. "Alleged Corruption in the Tariff of 1857," 38, 34.

85. "From Washington," dated 24 May, *North American and United States Gazette*, 25 May 1858.

86. "Alleged Corruption in the Tariff of 1857," 82–83.

87. "Alleged Corruption in the Tariff of 1857," 38 (quotation), and for Greeley testimony, 76–78. For Matteson's involvement in various lobbying schemes, see Henry Cohen, *Business and Politics*, 111, 136, 177, 194, and Summers, *The Plundering Generation*, 87, 108, 112, 181, 211n, 262–263. For failed efforts to expel him, see David P. Currie, *The Constitution in Congress: Democrats and Whigs, 1829–1861* (Chicago: University of Chicago Press, 2005), 219–220.

88. "Alleged Corruption in the Tariff of 1857," 39–40, 99–100.

89. "Alleged Corruption in the Tariff of 1857," 39–40, 57.

90. "From Washington," dated 31 December 1857, and "From Washington," dated 16 January, both *North American and United States Gazette*, 2 January, 18 January 1858.

91. "Alleged Corruption in the Tariff of 1857," 40.

92. J. W. Wolcott to Nathaniel P. Banks, Boston, 5 February 1857, Container 12, Nathaniel Prentiss Banks Papers, Library of Congress, Washington, DC.

93. "Alleged Corruption in the Tariff of 1857," 1–9 (quotations, 5–6, 5, 8); *Congressional Globe*, Thirty-Fifth Congress, First Session, 2428.

94. Benjamin Stanton quoted in Henry Terry to O. S. Ferry, Plymouth, CT, 29 May 1860, Container 14, John Sherman Papers, LC.

95. Augustus R. Wright to Frank Wright, Washington, 19 April 1858, reproduced in an unpublished manuscript version of a biography of Augustus R. Wright by his daughter Mary Shropshire, 35, Augustus Romaldus Wright Folder, Beluah Shropshire Moseley Family Papers, LC.

96. "From Washington," dated 24 May, *North American and United States Gazette*, 25 May 1858.

97. James E. Harvey to Henry C. Carey, Washington, 7 December 1856, Folder 2, Box 14, Gardiner Collection.

98. James E. Harvey to Henry C. Carey, Washington, 2 January [mislabeled "June" in catalogue] 1857, Folder 2, Box 14, Gardiner Collection. See also James E. Harvey to Henry C. Carey, Washington, 11 January [mislabeled "June" in catalogue] 1857, Folder 2, Box 14, and S. J. Reeves to Henry C. Carey, 17 January 1857, Folder 2, Box 17, both Gardiner Collection.

99. "The House Gift Rule," *Committee on Ethics*, https://ethics.house.gov/gifts /house-gift-rule.

100. Clay, *Papers*, 8:96, 105, 254, 307, 345–346, 613, 860; 9:733, 740–741n, 763–764, 850, 851; 10:58, 111–112, 163, 185, 249, 277, 301–302, 332, 357; Supplement: 238, 239, 252.

101. H. Hays and Company to Henry Clay, Louisville, KY, 13 July 1842, in Clay, *Papers*, 9:733; untitled editorial, *The Pennsylvanian*, 18 February 1833.

102. Entry for 2 June 1846, in *Memoirs of John Quincy Adams, Comprising Portions of His Diary from 1795 to 1848*, ed. Charles Francis Adams, 12 vols. (Philadelphia, 1874–1877), 12:267.

103. Abbott Lawrence to Amos Lawrence, Washington, 11 February 1828, Folder "1828 Feb 11–28," Box 1, Amos Lawrence Papers, MHS.

104. Samuel Breck, entry for 21 August 1832, Volume 5: Diary, 1832–1833, Samuel Breck Papers, HSP.

105. Mathew Carey to Thomas Elliott, Philadelphia, 28 September 1832, Folder 7, Box 27, Gardiner Collection.

106. "Alleged Corruption in the Tariff of 1857," 75.

107. "Alleged Corruption in the Tariff of 1857," 89, and also 37 for a reference to "treating" with "suppers."

108. "Alleged Corruption in the Tariff of 1857," 75.

109. "From Washington," dated 27 December, *North American and United States Gazette*, 29 December 1856.

110. For Stone, see "Agreement Regarding the Webster Annuity," Boston, 5 January 1846, in Webster, *Papers*, 6:108.

111. Sarah Forbes Hughes, ed., *Letters and Recollections of John Murray Forbes*, 2 vols. (Boston, 1899), 1:118.

112. Entry for 25 July 1846, in *The Diary of James K. Polk during His Presidency, 1845 to 1849*, ed. Milo Milton Quaife, 4 vols. (Chicago: A. C. McClurg, 1910), 2:49. See also Andrew Johnson to unidentified Tennessean, Washington, 21 July 1846, in *The Papers of Andrew Johnson*, ed. LeRoy Graf, et al., 16 vols. (Knoxville: University of Tennessee Press, 1967–2000), 1:330–331.

113. Summers, *The Plundering Generation*.

114. Another precedent for this transformation may be found in Stephen W.

Campbell, "Funding the Bank War: Nicholas Biddle and the Public Relations Campaign to Recharter the Second Bank of the US, 1828–1832," *American Nineteenth Century History* 17 (September 2016): 273–299, which includes the enlistment of sympathetic editors, dispatching of agents to monitor legislative activity, and suspicious "loans" to elected representatives.

115. *Evening Bulletin* (Philadelphia), quoted in "Congressional Lobbying," *The Pennsylvanian*, 29 May 1858. The editor of *The Pennsylvanian* responded that the *Bulletin* "deserves a place by the side of MATTESON, WEED, GREELEY, . . . in the new catalogue of eminent diddlers."

116. Charles A. Dana to Henry C. Carey, New York, 4 December 1856, Folder 5, Box 12, Gardiner Collection.

117. Henry C. Carey, *Letters to the President, on the Foreign and Domestic Policy of the Union, and Its Effects, as Exhibited in the Condition of the People and the State* (Philadelphia, 1858).

118. Howell Cobb, quoted in James L. Huston, *The Panic of 1857 and the Coming of the Civil War* (Baton Rouge: Louisiana State University Press, 1987), 184.

119. Henry C. Carey to E. B. McDowell, 9 December 1857 (draft), Folder 7, Box 19, Gardiner Collection.

120. Circular Letter of the Home Protective Union, Philadelphia, May 1858, Reel 4, Simon Cameron Papers, LC.

121. For two different perspectives on the ways in which the development of the party system shaped even ostensibly non- or anti-partisan movements in the antebellum era, see Michael F. Holt, "The Primacy of Party Reasserted," *Journal of American History* 86 (June 1999): 151–157, and Mark Voss-Hubbard, *Beyond Party: Cultures of Antipartisanship in Northern Politics before the Civil War* (Baltimore: Johns Hopkins University Press, 2002). And for an interesting parallel, which at times overlapped with the tariff issue, see Ariel Ron's recent study of antebellum agricultural reformers, who long advocated for a "nonpartisan anti-politics" approach to their concerns but ultimately achieved their greatest successes working through the Republican Party. Ariel Ron, "Summoning the State: Northern Farmers and the Transformation of American Politics in the Mid-nineteenth Century," *Journal of American History* 103 (September 2016): 347–374.

122. Smith, *Henry C. Carey and American Sectional Conflict*, 53, 65–73.

123. "The Pretended Tariff Meeting in Our City," *The Pennsylvanian*, 17 June 1858.

124. Henry C. Carey to John McLean, 26 June 1858, John McLean Papers, LC, cited in Smith, *Henry C. Carey and American Sectional Conflict*, 73.

125. James E. Harvey to Henry C. Carey, Washington, 26 January 1860, Folder 1, Box 14, Gardiner Collection (quotation); Arthur M. Lee, "Henry C. Carey and the Republican Tariff," *Pennsylvania Magazine of History and Biography* 81 (July 1957): 297.

126. See Edward Joy Morris, *Congressional Globe*, Thirty-Sixth Congress, First Session, 636. For a discussion of the contest for the speakership that emphasizes the role of the tariff, see Richard Franklin Bensel, *Yankee Leviathan: The Origins of Central State Authority in America, 1859–1877* (Cambridge: Cambridge University Press, 1990), 47–57. An alternative explanation, that the defectors wanted to drive Sherman from the race in favor of someone from their own party more moderate on slavery, is advanced by Jeffrey A. Jenkins and Charles Stewart III, *Fighting for the Speakership: The House and the Rise of Party Government* (Princeton, NJ: Princeton University Press, 2013), 212–224.

127. Charles Francis Adams Jr., *Charles Francis Adams* (Boston, 1900), 111–112.

128. John Sherman, *Recollections of Forty Years in the House, Senate and Cabinet*, 2 vols. (Chicago, 1895), 1:149.

129. "Great Popular Rally," *North American and United States Gazette*, Supplement 16 June 1858.

130. Henry Winter Davis to Justin S. Morrill, 20 August 1859, Justin S. Morrill Papers, LC, cited in Coy F. Cross II, *Justin Smith Morrill: Father of the Land-Grant Colleges* (East Lansing: Michigan State University Press, 1999), 45. On Morrill's role in the Tariff of 1860–1861, see Cross II, *Justin Smith Morrill*, 41–54, and William Belmont Parker, *The Life and Public Services of Justin Smith Morrill* (Boston: Houghton Mifflin, 1924), 103–114. For the Republican Party's embrace of Carey's "Harmony of Interests," see Heather Cox Richardson, *The Greatest Nation of the Earth: Republican Economic Policies during the Civil War* (Cambridge, MA: Harvard University Press, 1997), 104–105. The other members of Ways and Means were: Martin J. Crawford (GA, Democrat), H. Winter Davis (MD, American Party), John S. Millson (VA, Democrat), John S. Phelps (MO, Democrat), Elbridge G. Spaulding (NY, Republican), Thaddeus Stevens (PA, Republican), and Israel Washburn Jr. (ME, Republican).

131. *Congressional Globe*, Forty-First Congress, Second Session, 3295. See, for example, Jane Flaherty, "Incidental Protection: An Examination of the Morrill Tariff," *Essays in Economic and Business History* 19 (2001): 110–111; F. W. Taussig, *The Tariff History of the United States* (New York, 1888), 150; and Daniel Verdier, *Democracy and International Trade: Britain, France, and the United States, 1860–1990* (Princeton, NJ: Princeton University Press, 1994), 70–71.

132. *New York Times*, 28 March 1860, cited in Bensel, *Yankee Leviathan*, 73.

133. Justin S. Morrill, quoted in Parker, *The Life and Public Services of Justin Smith Morrill*, 105.

134. Phillip W. Magness, "Morrill and the Missing Industries: Strategic Lobbying Behavior and the Tariff, 1858–1861," *Journal of the Early Republic* 29 (Summer 2009): 307. For the originals, see Morrill Papers.

135. *Congressional Globe*, Thirty-Sixth Congress, First Session, 1231.

136. James M. Quarles, *Congressional Globe*, Thirty-Sixth Congress, First Session, 1980.

137. "The Schedules of the New Bill," *North American and United States Gazette*, 16 March 1860.

138. Justin S. Morrill to William G. Angell, Washington, 24 February 1860, Folder 15, Box 23, James Fowler Simmons Papers, LC.

139. William G. Angell to Justin S. Morrill, Providence, RI, 2 March 1860, and William G. Angell to James F. Simmons, Providence, RI, 29 March 1860, both Folder 16, Box 23, Simmons Papers.

140. Edward Pearce to James F. Simmons, 11 May 1860, Folder 1, Box 24, Simmons Papers. For background on the American Screw Company, see George Winston Smith, "A Rising Industry's Battle for the Morrill Tariff," *Bulletin of the Business Historical Society* 16 (December 1942): 106–111.

141. "From Washington," dated 30 March, *North American and United States Gazette*, 31 March 1860.

142. Israel Washburn to Justin S. Morrill, Washington, 26 April 1860, Container 4, Morrill Papers.

143. J. Wiley Edmands to Justin S. Morrill, Boston, 15 May 1860, Container 5, Morrill Papers.

144. *Congressional Globe*, Thirty-Sixth Congress, First Session, 1975, and for his explanation of rates on wool and woolens in original version, see 1833.

145. W. H. Winder to Henry C. Carey, Philadelphia, 12 January 1859, Folder 4, Box 19, Gardiner Collection.

146. Henry C. Carey to Thomas S. Bocock, 18 April 1860 (draft), Folder 1, Box 20, Gardiner Collection. See, likewise, Henry C. Carey to [R. M. T. Hunter?], 22 March 1860 (draft), Folder 1, Box 20, Gardiner Collection.

147. Henry C. Carey to William D. Lewis, Willard's Hotel, [Washington], 4 April 1860, Folder "Henry Charles Carey Correspondence, 1860–1869," Box 6, William David Lewis Papers.

148. James E. Harvey to Henry C. Carey, "Washington, Thursday [B]" [1860], Folder 1, Box 14, Gardiner Collection.

149. Henry C. Carey to Justin S. Morrill, Philadelphia, 18 April 1860, in Morrill, "Notable Letters from My Political Friends," 147. For Carey's lobbying, see Lee, "Henry C. Carey and the Republican Tariff," 297–299, and Smith, *Henry C. Carey and American Sectional Conflict*, 56–59, 81–82, 93–94.

150. Sherman, *Recollections*, 1:152.

151. Benjamin Stanton, *Congressional Globe*, Thirty-Sixth Congress, First Session, 2052.

152. "Passage of the Tariff Bill," *North American and United States Gazette*, 11 May 1860. For the proceedings of 10 May, see *Congressional Globe*, Thirty-Sixth Congress, First Session, 2049–2056, and Sherman, *Recollections*, 1:152.

153. Sherman, *Recollections*, 1:152.

154. Henry C. Carey to ———, 4 February 1860 (draft), Folder 1, Box 20, Gardiner Collection. Another letter in Carey's correspondence suggests that the sub-

ject of the first letter, not identified there, is Bigler. George W. Scranton to Henry C. Carey, Washington, 10 April 1860, Folder 5, Box 17, Gardiner Collection.

155. "From Washington," dated 14 June, *North American and United States Gazette*, 15 June 1860.

156. Henry S. Acker to Robert M. T. Hunter, Pottsville, PA, 8 June 1860, in "Correspondence of Robert M. T. Hunter," 2:333 (quotation); *Congressional Globe*, Thirty-Sixth Congress, First Session, 2062.

157. Robert M. T. Hunter to George Booker, 14 April 1860, George Booker Papers, Duke University, cited in Huston, *The Panic of 1857 and the Coming of the Civil War*, 246.

158. *Congressional Globe*, Thirty-Sixth Congress, First Session, 2910.

159. "From Washington," dated 25 June, *North American and United States Gazette*, 26 June 1860 (quotation); *Congressional Globe*, Thirty-Sixth Congress, First Session, 3027. On Hunter's role in the Tariff of 1860–1861, see Simms, *Life of Robert M. T. Hunter*, 107–110. The other members of Hunter's committee were: Jesse D. Bright (IN, Democrat), Simon Cameron (PA, Republican), William P. Fessenden (ME, Republican), William M. Gwin (CA, Democrat), James Hammond (SC, Democrat), and James A. Pearce (MD, Democrat).

160. Henry C. Carey to John Sherman, Philadelphia, 8 June [mislabeled "January" in volume] 1860, Container 10, Sherman Papers; Muscoe Russell Hunter Garnett to his mother, Washington, 4 June 1860, Folder 16, Box 4, William Garnett Chisolm Papers, VHS.

161. James E. Harvey to Henry C. Carey, "Washington City, Thursday" [June 1860], Folder 1, Box 14, Gardiner Collection.

162. Justin S. Morrill to Henry C. Carey, Washington, 21 June 1860, Folder 4, Box 16, Gardiner Collection.

163. "Democratic Party Platform of 1860," 18 June 1860, http://www.presidency.ucsb.edu/ws/index.php?pid=29577; and "Democratic Party Platform (Breckinridge Faction)," 6 November 1860, http://www.presidency.ucsb.edu/ws/?pid =29614, both *The American Presidency Project*.

164. "Republican Party Platform of 1860," 17 May 1860, *The American Presidency Project*, http://www.presidency.ucsb.edu/ws/index.php?pid=29620.

165. *Memoirs of Gustave Koerner, 1809–1896*, ed. Thomas J. McCormack, 2 vols. (Cedar Rapids, IA: Torch Press, 1909), 2:87.

166. Henry C. Carey to E. B. Ward, 21 May 1865 (draft), Folder 2, Box 20, Gardiner Collection.

167. M. Halstead, *A History of the National Political Conventions of the Current Presidential Campaign* (Columbus, 1860), 135, cited in Malcolm Rogers Eiselen, *The Rise of Pennsylvania Protectionism* (Philadelphia: Porcupine Press, 1974, reprint of 1932 edition), 257–258. Among the "choristers" conducting this chorus of approval, the *North American* reported, was none other than David Wilmot. "Charleston, Chicago, and Protection," *North American and United States Gazette*, 21 May 1860.

168. Abraham Lincoln to Edward Wallace, 12 May 1860, quoted in Gabor S. Boritt, "Old Wine into New Bottles: Abraham Lincoln and the Tariff Reconsidered," *The Historian* 28 (February 1966): 308–309.

169. Henry C. Carey to C. N. David, 2 June 1860 (draft), Gardiner Collection, cited in Smith, *Henry C. Carey and American Sectional Conflict*, 85.

170. *Congressional Globe*, Thirty-Sixth Congress, Second Session, 154.

171. *Congressional Globe*, Thirty-Sixth Congress, Second Session, 444, 521, 536, 542.

172. "From Washington," dated 3 February, *North American and United States Gazette*, 4 February 1861.

173. "From Washington," dated 21 February, *North American and United States Gazette*, 22 February 1861 (quotation); *Congressional Globe*, Thirty-Sixth Congress, Second Session, 686–687.

174. James H. Campbell to Henry C. Carey, [early February 1861], Folder 2, Box 12, Gardiner Collection.

175. William G. Angell to James F. Simmons, Providence, RI, 17 December 1860, Folder 6, Box 24, Simmons Papers.

176. *Congressional Globe*, Thirty-Sixth Congress, Second Session, 1026–1027 (quotation 1026).

177. "From Washington," dated 18 February, *North American and United States Gazette*, 19 February 1861. For lobbying while the bill was before the Senate for a second time, see Magness, "Morrill and the Missing Industries," 321–322.

178. See, for example, Henry C. Carey to Justin S. Morrill, 18 January 1861, Folder 1, Box 20, Gardiner Collection, and Henry C. Carey to John Sherman, Philadelphia, 21 February 1861, Volume 23, Sherman Papers.

179. Henry C. Carey to James F. Simmons, Philadelphia, 13 February 1861, Folder 9, Box 24, Simmons Papers.

180. William Elder to Henry C. Carey, Washington, 15 February 1861, Folder 2, Box 13, Gardiner Collection.

181. *Congressional Globe*, Thirty-Sixth Congress, Second Session, 1196–1201, 1248, 1259; Sherman, *Recollections*, 1:153.

182. "The New Tariff," *North American and United States Gazette*, 26 February 1861.

183. For the motives of the three Republicans who voted against the bill, see "A Distinction with a Distinguished Difference," *North American and United States Gazette*, 23 May 1860.

184. James M. Hopkins to William Bigler, Lancaster, PA, 28 January 1861, Folder 13, Box 11, William Bigler Papers, HSP.

185. Henry C. Carey to John Sherman, Philadelphia, 21 February 1861, Volume 23, Sherman Papers.

186. Bensel, *Yankee Leviathan*; Richardson, *The Greatest Nation of the Earth*.

187. See, for example, David John Marotta and Megan Russell, "Protective Tariffs: The Primary Cause of the Civil War," *Marotta on Money*, http://www

.marottaonmoney.com/protective-tariffs-the-primary-cause-of-the-civil-war/, and Dennis G. Saunders, "Tariffs, Not Slavery, Precipitated the American Civil War," *The Baltimore Sun*, http://articles.baltimoresun.com/2013-07-06/news/bs-ed-get tysburg-20130706_1_slavery-constitutional-convention-secession. Historians are more circumspect, but for an argument by two economists that prioritizes tariffs, see Mark Thornton and Robert B. Eklund Jr., *Tariffs, Blockades, and Inflation: The Economics of the Civil War* (Wilmington, DE: Scholarly Resources, 2004).

188. Parker, *The Life and Public Services of Justin Smith Morrill*, 111.

189. Brian Schoen, "The Political Economies of Secession," *Journal of the History of Economic Thought* 37 (June 2015): 203–219. And for a rebuttal of the "Great Civil War Lie" that also traces the transatlantic origins of myths about the Morrill Tariff's role in provoking sectional conflict, see Marc-William Palen, "The Great Civil War Lie," *New York Times*, http://opinionator.blogs.nytimes.com /2013/06/05/the-great-civil-war-lie/, and Marc-William Palen, "The Civil War's Forgotten Transatlantic Tariff Debate and the Confederacy's Free Trade Diplomacy," *Journal of the Civil War Era* 3 (March 2013): 35–61.

190. Henry C. Carey to Justin S. Morrill, Philadelphia, 27 February 1861, in Morrill, "Notable Letters from My Political Friends," 146.

191. "A Protective Tariff," *North American and United States Gazette*, 28 February 1861.

192. Henry C. Carey to William D. Lewis, 27 February 1861 (quotation on reverse), and Henry C. Carey to William D. Lewis, 28 February 1861, both Folder "Henry Charles Carey Correspondence, 1860–1869," Box 6, Lewis Papers.

193. James E. Harvey to Henry C. Carey, Washington, 14 March 1861, and James E. Harvey to Henry C. Carey, Washington, 31 March 1861, both Folder 1, Box 14, Gardiner Collection.

194. William Elder to Henry C. Carey, Treasury Department, Washington, 21 March 1861 (quotation), and William Elder to Henry C. Carey, 20 June 1861, both Folder 2, Box 13, and Henry C. Carey to George W. Scranton, 30 March 1861 (draft), Folder 1, Box 20, all Gardiner Collection. Henry C. Carey to Samuel P. Chase, Philadelphia, 28 March 1861, Folder 4, Box 3, Samuel P. Chase Papers, HSP.

195. *Evening Transcript* (Boston), 28 November 1859, cited in Smith, *Henry C. Carey and American Sectional Conflict*, 95.

Conclusion

1. William Cullen Bryant to Alfred Field, New York, 15 November 1859, in *The Letters of William Cullen Bryant*, ed. William Cullen Bryant Jr. and Thomas G. Voss, 6 vols. (New York: Fordham University Press, 1975–1992), 4:125.

2. James E. Harvey to Henry C. Carey, "Washington, Thursday [B]" [1860], Folder 1, Box 14, Edward Carey Gardiner Collection, Historical Society of Pennsylvania, Philadelphia.

3. Horace Greeley, *Why I Am a Whig: Reply to an Inquiring Friend* (New York, [1852]), 8.

4. "Commercial Results of the War," *American Railroad Journal* (New York), 5 October 1861.

5. Sven Beckert, *The Monied Metropolis: New York City and the Consolidation of the American Bourgeoisie, 1850–1896* (Cambridge: Cambridge University Press, 2001), 145.

6. J. Laurence Laughlin, "Political Economy and the Civil War," *Atlantic Monthly* 55 (April 1885): 446, cited in Beckert, *The Monied Metropolis*, 120.

7. *Report on Emigration by a Special Committee of the Chamber of Commerce of the State of New-York, January 5, 1865* (New York, 1865), 13, cited in Beckert, *The Monied Metropolis*, 306.

8. Marc-William Palen, *The "Conspiracy" of Free Trade: The Anglo-American Struggle over Empire and Economic Globalisation, 1846–1896* (Cambridge: Cambridge University Press, 2016).

9. John L. Hayes to Henry C. Carey, Boston, 25 September 1871, Folder 3, Box 14, Gardiner Collection. For Carey's postwar influence in the Republican Party, see Palen, *The "Conspiracy" of Free Trade*, and George Winston Smith, *Henry C. Carey and American Sectional Conflict* (Albuquerque: University of New Mexico Press, 1951), 99–116.

10. "From the Columbia (S.C.) Telescope," *Niles' Weekly Register* (Baltimore), 8 September 1827.

11. "Sayings . . . CLXCVI," dated 26 August, *United States Gazette* (Philadelphia), 27 August 1842.

12. Minutes of Wilmington manufacturers meeting, 9 December 1815, Folder 4, Bringhurst Family Papers, Delaware Historical Society, Wilmington.

13. Abbott Lawrence to Amos Lawrence, Washington, 2 February 1828, Folder "1828 1–10 Feb," Box 1, Amos Lawrence Papers, Massachusetts Historical Society, Boston.

14. "The Tariff," *North American and United States Gazette* (Philadelphia), 15 February 1861.

15. "Alleged Corruption in the Tariff of 1857," House of Representatives Report No. 414, Thirty-Fifth Congress, First Session, 7.

Appendix: Key Congressional Roll Calls on Tariff Legislation, 1816–1861

1. Bill passed by the Senate on 20 April 1816 without division. *Annals of Congress*, Fourteenth Congress, First Session, 334.

2. *Congressional Globe*, Twenty-Seventh Congress, Second Session, 926, records the vote as 105 yeas to 103 nays but only lists 104 names in the yea column. The *House Journal* records the vote as 104 to 103 and also lists the same 104 names in the yea column.

3. Bill passed by the Senate on the same day without division.

4. The House and Senate originally voted to pass substantially different versions of the same bill. These votes are to accept the final version agreed on by the Committee of Conference.

Primary Sources

For the historian of lobbying in the early United States, there is no substitute for archival research in manuscript collections. Much lobbying activity simply passed unnoticed in published accounts. Thanks to the Program in Early American Economy and Society's fellowship scheme, I was able to spend an extensive period in Philadelphia-area archives, where I made particular use of the Edward Carey Gardiner Collection at the Historical Society of Pennsylvania, for Mathew and Henry Carey, as well as the former's correspondence with Eleazar Lord in 1820; the Smith-Waln Family Papers at the same repository, for the Philadelphia-coordinated lobbying campaign of 1832; and the Longwood Manuscripts, Winterthur Manuscripts, and Records of E. I. du Pont de Nemours and Company, all at the Hagley Museum and Library, Wilmington, DE, for the du Ponts. There are also sizeable collections of papers for Isaac Briggs, the original tariff lobbyist, at the Library of Congress and Maryland Historical Society, and for the Appleton Family and various Lawrences at the Massachusetts Historical Society. An unpublished autobiography of Eleazar Lord may be found at the Connecticut Historical Society, but it contains little detail on his lobbying activities. More useful, at the Historical Society of Pennsylvania (on deposit from the Library Company of Philadelphia), are several volumes of the unpublished diary of Samuel Breck, covering both his term in the House of Representatives coincident with the Tariff of 1824 and his attendance at the 1831 Tariff Convention in New York.

The efforts of lobbyists to shape the design of tariff bills may also be traced through the letters written and received by their authors. Substantial collections of correspondence exist for John Tod (1824) at the Pennsylvania State Archives in Harrisburg, Silas Wright (1828) in the Azariah C. Flagg Papers at the New York Public Library, John Quincy Adams (1832) at the Massachusetts Historical Society, Gulian C. Verplanck (the failed alternative to Clay's bill in 1833) at the New-York Historical Society, Robert M. T. Hunter (1857) at the Virginia Historical Society, and Justin S. Morrill and John Sherman (both 1861) at the Library of Congress. Smaller, but still useful, collections may be found for William Lowndes (1816) and Robert J. Walker (1846) at the same repository; Henry Baldwin (1820) at the Lawrence Lee Pelletier Library, Allegheny College, Meadville, PA; and Lewis D. Campbell (1857) at Ohio History Connection, Columbus. And for a detailed, and decidedly unsympathetic, eyewitness account of the maneuverings that resulted in the Tariff of Abominations, read the journal of New York representative Henry R. Storrs at the Buffalo History Museum, New York.

For politicians, if not for lobbyists, there is, of course, much published correspondence from this period too. For the giants whose careers spanned several of the tariff bills discussed here, see *The Papers of John C. Calhoun*, ed. Robert L. Meriweather, W. Edwin Hemphill, Shirley A. Book, Clyde N. Wilson, et al., 28 vols. (Columbia: University of South Carolina Press, 1959–2003); *The Papers of Henry Clay*, ed. James F. Hopkins, Robert Seagar II, Melba Porter Hay, et al., 11 vols. (Lexington: University Press of Kentucky, 1959–1992); *The Papers of Andrew Jackson*, ed. Harold D. Moser, Daniel Feller, et al., 10 vols. to date (Knoxville: University of Tennessee Press, 1980–); *Correspondence of James K. Polk*, ed. Wayne Cutler, 13 vols. to date (Nashville, TN: Vanderbilt University Press, 1969–); and *The Papers of Daniel Webster: Correspondence*, ed. Charles Wiltse, 7 vols. (Hanover, NH: University Press of New England, 1974–1986). Lesser figures whose writings are nonetheless of value for one or more bills include: *Life and Correspondence of Rufus King*, ed. Charles R. King, 6 vols. (New York: G. P. Putnam's Sons, 1894–1900); *The Papers of Willie Person Mangum*, ed. Henry Thomas Shanks, 5 vols. (Raleigh, NC: State Department of Archives and History, 1950–1956); *The Papers of Leverett Saltonstall, 1816–1845*, ed. Robert E. Moody, 5 vols. (Boston: Massachusetts Historical Society, 1978–1992); and *The Letters of John Fairfield*, ed. Arthur G. Staples (Lewiston, ME: Lewiston Journal Company, 1922).

Nothing beats the benefit of hindsight, and if read skeptically memoirs can also provide colorful insight into the political goings-on of the period and the motives of the participants. Most useful for this study were Mathew Carey's *Auto Biographical Sketches: In a Series of Letters Addressed to a Friend* (Philadelphia, 1829), and *Autobiography of Mathew Carey* (Philadelphia, 1835). The two overlap extensively but are not identical, and Carey makes no effort to conceal his contempt for some of his erstwhile collaborators in the protectionist cause. The "Memoirs of a Senator from Pennsylvania: Jonathan Roberts, 1771–1854," ed. Philip S. Klein, *Pennsylvania Magazine of History and Biography* 62 (October 1938): 502–551, is also useful more for Roberts's attendance at the protectionist conventions of 1827 and 1831 than for his political career. On Congress, consult Thomas Hart Benton, *Thirty Years' View; or, a History of the Working of the American Government for Thirty Years, from 1820 to 1850*, 2 vols. (New York, 1883); John Sherman, *Recollections of Forty Years in the House, Senate and Cabinet*, 2 vols. (Chicago, 1895); and Martin Van Buren, "The Autobiography of Martin Van Buren," ed. John C. Fitzpatrick, *Annual Report of the American Historical Association* (Washington, 1918), 2:5–808. Even more valuable are the diaries of two men deeply involved in tariff policymaking during this period: *Memoirs of John Quincy Adams, Comprising Portions of His Diary from 1795 to 1848*, ed. Charles Francis Adams, 12 vols. (Philadelphia, 1874–1877), and *The Diary of James K. Polk during His Presidency, 1845 to 1849*, ed. Milo Milton Quaife, 4 vols. (Chicago: A. C. McClurg, 1910).

I found newspapers helpful for identifying individuals involved in protectionist campaigns, primarily through their attendance at meetings and conventions, which then allowed me to track down manuscript collections. In this regard, specialist protectionist and free journals such as the *Banner of the Constitution* (New York City/Philadelphia), *Patron of Industry* (New York), and *The Free Trade Advocate, and Journal of Political Economy* (Philadelphia) were of particular use. For the period 1832–1861, the on-the-spot observations of congressional politicking by Washington correspondents "Oliver Oldschool" (Nathan Sargent) in the *United States Gazette* (Philadelphia) and, subsequently, "Independent" (James E. Harvey, himself a lobbying associate of Henry C. Carey) in the *North American and United States Gazette* (Philadelphia) were of immense value. For the earlier period, I turned to the more general coverage of the national legislature provided by the *Aurora General Advertiser* (Philadelphia) and *Niles' Weekly Register* (Baltimore).

Outside the capital, the proceedings of the major protectionist and free trade conventions were widely reported in the press but can also be found in the following: *The Proceedings of a Convention of the Friends of National Industry, Assembled in the City of New-York, November 29, 1819 . . .* (New York, 1819), accessible at the New-York Historical Society; *General Convention, of Agriculturalists and Manufacturers, and Others Friendly to the Encouragement and Support of the Domestic Industry of the United States* (1827), available on Internet Archive; *The Journal of the Free Trade Convention, Held in Philadelphia, from September 30 to October 7, 1831 . . .* (Philadelphia, 1831); and Hezekiah Niles, *Journal of the Proceedings of the Friends of Domestic Industry, in General Convention Met at the City of New York, October 26, 1831* (Baltimore, 1831), both held by the Library Company of Philadelphia.

For reasons explained in the introduction, I relied much less heavily on reporting of congressional debates than previous historians of tariff policymaking have done. Nonetheless, the records of the *Annals of Congress*, *Register of Debates*, and *Congressional Globe*, as well as each chamber's official *Journal*, helped me keep track of the often tortuous progress of tariff bills through the House and Senate, as well as the ways in which elected representatives reacted to out-of-doors efforts to influence the legislative agenda. Several government reports were also of especial value, namely: "Alleged Corruption in the Tariff of 1857," House of Representatives Report No. 414, Thirty-Fifth Congress, First Session; "Documents Relative to Manufactures in the United States," 2 vols., House Executive Document No. 308, Twenty-Second Congress, First Session; and "On the Subject of the Tariff, or Regulating Duties on Imports," House of Representatives Report No. 843, Twentieth Congress, First Session.

Secondary Sources

Studies of pre–Civil War lobbying are rare. Jeffrey L. Pasley, "Private Access and Public Power: Gentility and Lobbying in the Early Congress," in *The House and Senate in the 1790s: Petitioning, Lobbying, and Institutional Development*, ed. Kenneth R. Bowling and Donald R. Kennon (Athens: Ohio University Press, 2002) covers the earliest decade of the First Republic, and Mark Summers, *The Plundering Generation: Corruption and the Crisis of the Union, 1849–1861* (Oxford: Oxford University Press, 1987) covers the last. Douglas E. Bowers, "From Logrolling to Corruption: The Development of Lobbying in Pennsylvania, 1815–1861," *Journal of the Early Republic* 3 (Winter 1983): 439–474, and Rodney O. Davis, "Lobbying and the Third House in the Early Illinois General Assembly," *Old Northwest* 14 (1988): 267–284 span longer periods but focus on single states. For lobbying on specific issues, see Corey M. Brooks, "Stoking the 'Abolition Fire in the Capitol': Liberty Party Lobbying and Antislavery in Congress," *Journal of the Early Republic* 33 (Fall 2013): 523–547; Stephen W. Campbell, "Funding the Bank War: Nicholas Biddle and the Public Relations Campaign to Recharter the Second Bank of the US, 1828–1832," *American Nineteenth Century History* 17 (September 2016): 273–299; and Phillip W. Magness, "Morrill and the Missing Industries: Strategic Lobbying Behavior and the Tariff, 1858–1861," *Journal of the Early Republic* 29 (Summer 2009): 287–329. And finally, for a biography of an antebellum lobbyist, albeit one not involved with the tariff, see Henry Cohen, *Business and Politics in America from the Age of Jackson to the Civil War: The Career Biography of W. W. Corcoran* (Westport, CT: Greenwood Publishing, 1971).

The two standard texts on the making of US tariff policy remain Edward Stanwood, *American Tariff Controversies in the Nineteenth Century*, 2 vols. (Boston, 1903), and F. W. Taussig, *The Tariff History of the United States* (New York, 1888). William K. Bolt, *Tariff Wars and the Politics of Jacksonian America* (Nashville, TN: Vanderbilt University Press, 2017) updates the traditional narrative but retains its preoccupation with congressional debate. John Moore, "Interests and Ideas: Industrialization and the Making of Early American Trade Policy, 1789–1860" (PhD diss., Wayne State University, 2013) offers a different perspective on the connection between economic development and shifting regional coalitions on the tariff, an approach shared by Douglas A. Irwin in "Antebellum Tariff Politics: Regional Coalitions and Shifting Economic Interests," *Journal of Law and Economics* 51 (November 2008): 715–741. Judith Goldstein, *Ideas, Interests, and American Trade Policy* (Ithaca, NY: Cornell University Press, 1993), and Sidney Ratner, *The Tariff in American History* (New York: D. Van Nostrand, 1972) do not add anything substantive to these works, at least for the antebellum period. For specific tariff acts, see also Norris Watson Preyer, "Southern Support of the Tariff of 1816—A Reappraisal," *Journal of Southern History* 25 (August 1959): 306–322; Jonathan J. Pincus, *Pressure Groups and Politics in Antebellum Tariffs* (New York: Columbia University Press, 1977) (1824); Robert V. Remini, "Martin Van Buren and the Tariff of Abominations," *American Historical Review* 63 (July 1958): 903–917 (1828); John D. Macoll, "Representative John Quincy Adams's Compromise Tariff of 1832," *Capitol Studies* 1 (Fall 1972): 41–58; Merrill D.

Peterson, *Olive Branch and Sword: The Compromise of 1833* (Baton Rouge: Louisiana State University Press, 1982); and the Magness article cited in the previous paragraph (1861).

Lawrence A. Peskin, *Manufacturing Revolution: The Intellectual Origins of Early American Industry* (Baltimore: Johns Hopkins University Press, 2003) provides a thorough analysis of protectionist organization outside of Congress up to the conclusion of the War of 1812. For the antebellum period, the following are useful: Malcolm Rogers Eiselen, *The Rise of Pennsylvania Protectionism* (Philadelphia: Porcupine Press, 1974, reprint of 1932 edition); Grant D. Forsyth, "Special Interest Protectionism and the Antebellum Woolen Textile Industry: A Contemporary Issue in a Historical Context," *American Journal of Economics and Sociology* 65 (November 2006): 1025–1058; W. Kesler Jackson, "Robbers and Incendiaries: Protectionism Organizes at the Harrisburg Convention of 1827," *Libertarian Papers* 2 (2010): 1–22; and Carl E. Prince and Seth Taylor, "Daniel Webster, the Boston Associates, and the US Government's Role in the Industrializing Process, 1815–1830," *Journal of the Early Republic* 2 (Autumn 1982): 283–299. Of the prominent protectionists, only Mathew Carey, Henry Carey, and Hezekiah Niles have received substantial attention from scholars. For the father, see Cathy Matson, "Mathew Carey's Learning Experience: Commerce, Manufacturing, and the Panic of 1819," *Early American Studies* 11 (Fall 2013): 455–485; Kenneth Wyer Rowe, *Mathew Carey: A Study in American Economic Development* (Baltimore: Johns Hopkins University Press, 1933); and Andrew Shankman, "Neither Infinite Wretchedness nor Positive Good: Mathew Carey and Henry Clay on Political Economy and Slavery during the Long 1820s," in *Contesting Slavery: The Politics of Bondage and Freedom in the New American Nation*, ed. John Craig Hammond and Matthew Mason (Charlottesville: University of Virginia Press, 2011). For the son, see George Winston Smith, *Henry C. Carey and American Sectional Conflict* (Albuquerque: University of New Mexico Press, 1951). And for the newspaperman, see Norval Neil Luxon, *Niles' Weekly Register: News Magazine of the Nineteenth Century* (Baton Rouge: Louisiana State University Press, 1947), and Richard Gabriel Stone, *Hezekiah Niles as an Economist* (Baltimore: Johns Hopkins University Press, 1933).

The pre–Civil War free trade movement has not been comprehensively studied. Despite its title, William S. Belko, *The Triumph of the Antebellum Free Trade Movement* (Gainesville: University Press of Florida, 2012) only covers the 1831 Free Trade Convention. Stephen Meardon, "Negotiating Free Trade in Fact and Theory: The Diplomacy and Doctrine of Condy Raguet," *Journal of the History of Economic Thought* 21 (2014): 41–77, and Brian Schoen, *The Fragile Fabric of Union: Cotton, Federal Politics, and the Global Origins of the Civil War* (Baltimore: Johns Hopkins University Press, 2009) are both useful, as is Marc-William Palen, *The "Conspiracy" of Free Trade: The Anglo-American Struggle over Empire and Economic Globalisation, 1846–1896* (Cambridge: Cambridge University Press, 2016) for the latter part of the period. Daniel Peart, *Era of Experimenta-*

tion: American Political Practices in the Early Republic (Charlottesville: University of Virginia Press, 2014) also contains a brief account of the first national free trade convention in 1820.

Many politicians played their part in the making of tariff policy. Biographies of some of the most consequential include: John M. Belohlavek, *George Mifflin Dallas: Jacksonian Patrician* (University Park: Pennsylvania State University Press, 1977); John Arthur Garraty, *Silas Wright* (New York: Columbia University Press, 1949); Robert W. July, *The Essential New Yorker: Gulian Crommelin Verplanck* (Durham, NC: Duke University Press, 1951); John A. Munroe, *Louis McLane: Federalist and Jacksonian* (New Brunswick, NJ: Rutgers University Press, 1973); John Niven, *Martin Van Buren: The Romantic Age of American Politics* (Oxford: Oxford University Press, 1983); William Belmont Parker, *The Life and Public Services of Justin Smith Morrill* (Boston: Houghton Mifflin, 1924); Merrill D. Peterson, *The Great Triumvirate: Webster, Clay, and Calhoun* (Oxford: Oxford University Press, 1987); Robert V. Remini, *Andrew Jackson and the Course of American Freedom, 1822–1832* (New York: Harper and Row, 1981); Robert V. Remini, *Daniel Webster: The Man and His Time* (New York: W. W. Norton, 1997); Robert V. Remini, *Henry Clay: Statesman for the Union* (New York: W. W. Norton, 1991); Leonard L. Richards, *The Life and Times of Congressman John Quincy Adams* (Oxford: Oxford University Press, 1986); James P. Shenton, *Robert John Walker: A Politician from Jackson to Lincoln* (New York: Columbia University Press, 1961); Henry Harrison Simms, *Life of Robert M. T. Hunter: A Study in Sectionalism and Secession* (Richmond, VA: William Byrd Press, 1935); Carl J. Vipperman, *William Lowndes and the Transition of Southern Politics, 1782–1822* (Chapel Hill: University of North Carolina Press, 1989); and Raymond Walters Jr., *Alexander James Dallas: Lawyer—Politician—Financier, 1759–1817* (Philadelphia: University of Pennsylvania Press, 1943).

More work needs to be done on the international and transnational implications of tariff policymaking, but three admirable studies in this field are Sam W. Haynes, *Unfinished Revolution: The Early American Republic in a British World* (Charlottesville: University of Virginia Press, 2010); Scott C. James and David A. Lake, "The Second Face of Hegemony: Britain's Repeal of the Corn Laws and the American Walker Tariff of 1846," *International Organization* 43 (Winter 1989): 1–29; and the Palen book cited earlier. I also found it helpful to compare US agitation over tariff policy with its British counterpart, and for this I referred to Norman McCord, *The Anti-Corn Law League, 1838–1846* (London: Unwin University Press, 2nd edition, 1975); Cheryl Schonhardt-Bailey, *From the Corn Laws to Free Trade: Interests, Ideas, and Institutions in Historical Perspective* (Cambridge, MA: MIT Press, 2006); and Frank Trentmann, *Free Trade Nation: Commerce, Consumption, and Civil Society in Modern Britain* (Oxford: Oxford University Press, 2008).

Finally, the recent renewal of interest in the history of American capitalism renders the making of US tariff policy, and the role of lobbyists in antebellum policymaking more generally, a most worthy subject of attention at this moment in time. For discussions of this new historiographical departure, see Sven Beckert et al., "Interchange: The History of Capitalism," *Journal of American History* 101 (September 2014): 503–536; Rosanne Currarino, "Toward a History of Cultural Economy," *Journal of the Civil War Era* 2 (December 2012): 564–585; Stephen Meardon et al., Symposium on "American Political Economy from the Age of Jackson to the Civil War," *Journal of the History of Economic Thought* 37 (June 2015): 161–320; Seth Rockman, "Review Essay: What Makes the History of Capitalism Newsworthy?" *Journal of the Early Republic* 34 (Fall 2014): 439–466; and Jeffrey Sklansky, "The Elusive Sovereign: New Intellectual and Social Histories of Capitalism," *Modern Intellectual History* 9 (April 2012): 233–248. For the tariff specifically within these discussions, see Daniel S. Dupre, "The Panic of 1819 and the Political Economy of Sectionalism," in *The Economy of Early America: Historical Perspectives and New Directions*, ed. Cathy Matson (University Park: Pennsylvania State University Press, 2006); and Peter S. Onuf, "The Political Economy of Sectionalism: Tariff Controversies and Conflicting Conceptions of World Order," in *Congress and the Emergence of Sectionalism: From the Missouri Compromise to the Age of Jackson*, ed. Paul Finkelman and Donald R. Kennon (Athens: Ohio University Press, 2008). The works by Matson, Schoen, and Shankman cited previously are also relevant here.

Lowell, Francis Cabot, 11–12, 58, 202; and Tariff of 1816, 10, 21–22, 24, 25, 27, 29–30, 139, 154, 163, 195

Lowell, Francis Cabot, Jr., 154

Lowndes, William, 201; and Baldwin Bill (1820), 42–43; and Tariff of 1816, 15–16, 21, 22, 23–27, 29, 40–41, 225n78, 271n125

Lynch, James, 109

Madison, James, 17, 27, 28, 217n17, 236n89; and Tariff of 1816, 15, 26

Mallary, Rollin C., 200, 201, 253n114; and Harrisburg Convention (1827), 79; and Tariff of 1824, 56; and Tariff of 1828, 84, 85, 90–91, 92, 106, 201, 256n171; and Woollens Bill (1827), 69–70

Mangum, Willie P., 65, 134, 140

manufactures: concentrated in the North, 2, 11–12, 27, 49, 64–65, 99, 100, 109, 134, 192, 198–99; Alexander J. Dallas report on (1816), 13–15; defined, 11–12; Louis McLane report on (1832), 108, 267–68n83. *See also specific manufactures*

manufactures, cotton, 12, 17, 166; and Baldwin Bill (1820), 40, 49–50; and Harrisburg Convention (1827), 80; and Tariff of 1816, 16–17, 21–22, 23–26, 27, 29, 72, 195; and Tariff of 1824, 58, 72; and Tariff of 1832, 110, 266n68; and Tariff of 1833, 119, 120, 121; and Tariff of 1842, 140; and Tariff of 1857, 170, 172; and Woollens Bill (1827), 69, 70, 72

manufactures, iron, 29, 51; and Baldwin Bill (1820), 40, 49, 233n43, 233n45; and Harrisburg Convention (1827), 80; and Tariff of 1816, 14; and Tariff of 1824, 53, 57, 60, 69, 237n100, 242n163; and Tariff of 1828, 87, 90, 94, 96; and Tariff of 1832, 109, 110, 115, 266n68; and Tariff of 1833, 119, 120, 121; and Tariff of 1842, 140; and Tariff of 1846, 148, 152, 154, 159; and Tariff of 1857, 167, 168, 169, 170, 171, 172, 176, 179, 297n65;

and Tariff of 1861, 184, 186, 187, 190; and Woollens Bill (1827), 70

manufactures, woollen, 5, 199, 239n126; and Baldwin Bill (1820), 40, 49, 233n43; and Harrisburg Convention (1827), 75, 79–80; and New York Tariff Convention (1831), 104; and Tariff of 1816, 21, 29; and Tariff of 1824, 57, 62; and Tariff of 1828, 84, 85–87, 88, 90–91, 92, 93, 94, 96–97; and Tariff of 1832, 110, 111, 112, 114, 115, 116, 266n68, 270n112; and Tariff of 1833, 121, 125; and Tariff of 1846, 148, 286n98; and Tariff of 1857, 167–71, 172–78, 179, 181; and Tariff of 1861, 184, 186, 190; and Woollens Bill (1827), 67–75, 196

Martin, William D., 89–90, 255n153, 256n172

Matteson, Orsamus B., 176–77, 178, 300n115

McCulloch, John Ramsay, 190

McDuffie, George, 107, 116, 118, 119, 152

McKay, James I., 201; and Tariff of 1846, 147–48, 150–51, 287n121

McKennan, Thomas, 143

McLane, Louis, 49, 201; and Baldwin Bill (1820), 45, 51; and Harrisburg Convention (1827), 66, 78, 79, 250n79; and Tariff of 1816, 17; and Tariff of 1824, 55, 56; and Tariff of 1828, 86; and Tariff of 1832, 106–7, 108, 110, 111–12, 115, 121, 196, 200, 264n43, 264n45, 267–68n83; and Tariff of 1833, 119, 124, 127; and Tariff of 1846, 147; and Woollens Bill (1827), 74

Mexican War (1846–1848), 151, 156, 163

Miller, Stephen, 128

Mills, Elijah H., 60–61

Mills, James Kellogg, 154

minimum valuation: explained, 22; and Tariff of 1816, 22–23, 25–26, 27, 29, 30, 154, 163, 195, 225n78; and Tariff of 1824, 67; and Tariff of 1828, 88, 92, 94, 97, 278n1; and Tariff of 1832, 110, 111, 112; and Tariff of 1842,

Story, Joseph, 45
Sturgeon, Daniel, 152–53, 159
Sumner, Charles, 171

Taft, Bezaleel, Jr., 79
Tappan, Lewis, 68, 75–76, 245n10
tariff legislation, supplementary: in
  1818, 29; in 1841, 135
Tariff of 1789, 12
Tariff of 1816, 8, 10–11, 13–28, 29–30,
  32, 40, 42, 49, 54, 58, 63, 72, 117,
  163, 195, 271n125; analysis of vote
  on, 26–28, 203–4; Alexander J. Dallas
  and origins of, 13–15, 21, 22; details,
  14–15, 21, 22, 23–25; in the House,
  23–26; House Committee of Ways
  and Means and, 15–16, 21, 22, 23–24,
  40–41, 43; House Committee on
  Commerce and Manufactures and,
  19–21; in the Senate, 26
Tariff of 1820. See Baldwin Bill (1820)
Tariff of 1824, 8, 32, 52–63, 63–65, 67,
  68, 69, 72, 73, 104, 105, 112, 132,
  196; analysis of vote on, 61–63,
  205–6; Committee of Conference and,
  61; details, 54, 60–61, 67, 242n163;
  in the House, 54–60; House Committee on Agriculture and, 52–53, 54;
  House Committee on Manufactures
  and, 52, 53–54, 57–58; presidential
  election of 1824 and, 59–60, 61–62;
  in the Senate, 60–61
Tariff of 1827. See Woollens Bill (1827)
Tariff of 1828, 8, 67, 82–98, 100–101,
  110, 132, 144, 149, 172, 270n112;
  analysis of vote on, 96–97, 207–8,
  257n182; Committee of Conference
  and, 95; details, 87–88, 92, 94,
  254n139; in the House, 90–94,
  256n171, 256n172; House Committee on Manufactures and, 84–87,
  89–90, 253n118, 253n124, 256n172;
  Jacksonian party and origins of,
  82–90; presidential election of 1828
  and, 66–67, 82–83, 87–90, 95–98;
  in the Senate, 94–95, 258n196,
  259n206; Senate Committee on
  Manufactures and, 92, 94. See also
  Tariff of Abominations

Tariff of 1832, 8, 100, 106–16, 117,
  118, 121, 122, 124, 128–29, 130, 140,
  143, 162, 172, 196–97, 200; analysis
  of vote on, 113, 115, 208–9; Committee of Conference and, 115, 270n112;
  details, 111, 112, 114, 115; in the
  House, 112–13; House Committee
  of Ways and Means and, 107; House
  Committee on Manufactures and,
  106–7, 110, 111–12; in the Senate,
  113–15; Senate Committee on Manufactures and, 113–14
Tariff of 1833, 8, 100, 116–29, 129–31,
  135, 139, 140, 172; analysis of vote
  on, 128–29, 209–10, 270n115; Henry
  Clay and origins of, 121–24, 273n156,
  273n161, 274n168; details, 124–25,
  127–28, 273n159, 274n178, 276n199;
  in the House, 119–20, 128; House
  Committee of Ways and Means and,
  118–19, 148; House Committee on
  Manufactures and, 118; in the Senate,
  124–28, 276n198, 276n199, 276n200,
  276–77n203. See also Compromise of
  1833
Tariff of 1842, 8, 132, 135–45, 146,
  151, 153, 154, 155, 156, 157, 159,
  162, 171, 197; analysis of vote on,
  144–45, 210–11, 278n1; details,
  140; in the House, 139–41, 143–44;
  House Committee of Ways and
  Means and, 138–39, 140, 141; House
  Committee on Manufactures and,
  138–39, 140; in the Senate, 141–42,
  144; Senate Finance Committee and,
  141
Tariff of 1846, 8, 132, 145–61, 162–63,
  165, 169, 170, 185, 292n201; analysis
  of vote on, 161, 211–12, 278n1,
  291–92n196; details, 148, 286n98;
  in the House, 148, 150–52, 160;
  House Committee of Ways and
  Means and, 147, 148, 285n97; in the
  Senate, 152–61, 287n127, 288n136,
  289–90n165, 290n168, 290n169,
  290–91n180, 291n195; Senate Finance Committee and, 152, 158–59;
  Robert J. Walker and origins of,
  146–48

Index   323

Tariff of 1857, 8, 164–65, 168–71,
171–78, 179, 182, 184, 186, 192,
198, 202; analysis of vote on, 171,
212–13; Committee of Conference
and, 170–71; details, 169, 170, 171;
in the House, 169, 171; House Committee of Ways and Means and,
168–69, 175–76; in the Senate, 170,
171; Senate Finance Committee and,
169–70
Tariff of 1861, 8, 165, 183–91, 192,
194, 198, 202; analysis of vote on,
191, 213–14, 291–92n196; Committee of Conference and, 190; details,
185–86; in the House, 185–87, 188,
190; House Committee of Ways and
Means and, 183–85; presidential
election of 1860 and, 187–89; in
the Senate, 186–87, 189–90; Senate
Finance Committee and, 187, 189
Tariff of Abominations, 8, 67, 97,
196, 200, 259n209. *See also* Tariff
of 1828
tariff policy: historians' neglect of, 2–3,
194; historical significance of, 2–3,
6–9, 82, 194, 199–202; post–Civil
War, 8, 198–99; pre–War of 1812, 8,
12. *See also specific tariff acts*
tariff policy, constitutionality of: and
American System, 23; and incidental
protection, 134; and Nullification
Controversy, 100–101, 117; and Philadelphia Free Trade Convention (1831),
102–3; and Tariff of 1816, 14–15, 25,
26; and Tariff of 1824, 62, 236n89;
and Tariff of 1832, 106–7, 108, 116;
and Tariff of 1833, 122–23, 124–25;
and Verplanck Bill (1833), 118–19
tariff policy, for revenue, 2, 5, 8, 12,
198–99, 219n26, 236n89; and Baldwin Bill (1820), 49; and Democratic
Party, 3, 134, 166, 188; and Kane
Letter (1846), 145; and Philadelphia
Free Trade Convention (1831), 103;
and Tariff of 1816, 14, 25, 40–41,
48–49; and Tariff of 1824, 54, 61, 62,
65; and Tariff of 1832, 106, 108, 113,
116; and Tariff of 1833, 117, 118,
119, 122, 124–25; and Tariff of 1842,

135, 138, 139, 140, 143; and Tariff of
1846, 146–48, 149, 157, 162, 164,
165, 197, 287n125; and Tariff of
1857, 167, 168–70, 182; and Tariff
of 1861, 182, 185, 190, 191
tariff policy, incidental protection, 162,
192, 197, 198–99; and Democratic
Party, 138; explained, 134; and Kane
Letter (1846), 145; and Republican
Party (of Lincoln), 189; and Tariff
of 1816, 227–28n113; and Tariff of
1842, 138, 140, 148, 155; and Tariff
of 1857, 169; and Tariff of 1861, 182;
and Whig Party, 134, 138, 279n9
tariff policy, international influences on,
2, 7, 33, 165; and Nullification Controversy, 100; and Tariff of 1816,
11, 12–13, 195; and Tariff of 1846,
146–47, 148, 149, 150, 200, 286n107;
and Tariff of 1861, 191; and Woollens
Bill (1827), 67
tariff policy, "judicious," 162, 197; and
Tariff of 1824, 59, 61, 241–42n157;
and Tariff of 1832, 111; and Verplanck Bill (1833), 119
tariff policy, protective, 2, 5, 8–9, 194,
195; and Henry C. Carey, 166–67,
193; and Mathew Carey, 31, 33;
and Compromise of 1833, 124–25;
Alexander J. Dallas report on (1816),
13–15; evolution of, 8, 29–30, 63–65,
97–98, 129–31, 133–34, 162, 165–66,
191–92, 195–99; and Federalist Party,
26–27; and Andrew Jackson, 61–62;
and Nullification Controversy,
99–101, 115–16, 117; and Panic of
1819, 31, 33; and Panic of 1857, 165,
182, 194; and Republican Party (of
Jefferson), 27; and Republican Party
(of Lincoln), 1, 166, 182–83, 188–89,
191–92; and War of 1812, 11–12; and
Whig Party, 3, 134. *See also* American
System; protectionism; *and specific
tariff acts*
tariff policy, "the Greely method,":
explained, 167; and Tariff of 1857,
167, 168, 192, 198
tariff policy and antislavery, 68, 165–66,
189; and protectionism, organization

Williams, Lewis, 52
Williams, Ruel, 144
Wilmot, David, 151–52, 166, 287n125, 303n167
Wilmot Proviso, 152, 163
Winthrop, Robert C., 290n168
Wolcott, James, Jr., 57, 68, 85
Wolcott, John W., 173–74, 177–78, 202
Woodcock, David, 90
wool growers, 11, 79, 90; and Tariff of 1828, 86, 87; and Tariff of 1857, 167–68, 169, 171, 173, 184; and Tariff of 1861, 186, 190; and Woollens Bill (1827), 67, 69, 71, 73
Woollens Bill (1827), 8, 67, 69–75, 76, 77–78, 79, 80, 83, 85, 96, 144, 196,

201; analysis of vote on, 72–75, 206–7, 278n1; details, 69–70, 70–71, 246n18; in the House, 70–72; House Committee on Manufactures and, 69–70, 71; presidential election of 1828 and, 66–67, 70, 73, 74–75; in the Senate, 72
Wright, John C., 55, 61, 68, 93
Wright, Silas, 201; and Tariff of 1828, 84–86, 88, 89–90, 91, 92, 96–97, 196, 253n115, 255n153, 256n171, 257n181; and Tariff of 1833, 121; and Tariff of 1842, 144, 284n74

Young, William, 17, 20, 32, 224n66
Young, William W., 86, 266n68